ORDER AGAINST PROGRESS

ORDER AGAINST PROGRESS

Government, Foreign Investment, and Railroads in Brazil, 1854–1913

WILLIAM R. SUMMERHILL

STANFORD UNIVERSITY PRESS

Stanford, California 2003

For my parents,
Faye and William R. Summerhill, Jr.

Stanford University Press
Stanford, California

© 2003 by the Board of Trustees of the
Leland Stanford Junior University

Printed in the United States of America
on acid-free, archival-quality paper

Original Printing 2003

Last figure below indicates year of this printing:
12   11   10   09   08   07   06   05   04   03

Typeset by Tim Roberts in 10.5/13 Bembo

CONTENTS

LIST OF TABLES AND FIGURES

Tables

Figures

ACKNOWLEDGMENTS

My research in the United States, Brazil, and London was generously supported by dissertation research grants from the Joint Committee on Latin American and Caribbean Studies of the American Council of Learned Societies and the Social Science Research Council, and the U.S. Department of Education Fulbright-Hays Program; short-term field research grants funded by the Tinker and Mellon Foundations through the Centers for Latin American Studies at the University of Florida and Stanford University; a grant from International Studies and Overseas Programs at UCLA; the Harvard Business School's Alfred D. Chandler Traveling Fellowship in Business and Institutional Economic History; the Alexander Gerschenkron Prize of the Economic History Association; and a National Fellowship from the Hoover Institution at Stanford. My graduate schooling was greatly facilitated by a Foreign Language and Area Studies Fellowship at the University of Florida, a History Department Fellowship at Stanford, and the Montgomery G.I. Bill. Without the beneficence of these organizations and programs this study could not have been pursued.

The project's completion is due in large part to the assistance rendered by librarians, archivists, and collections staffs at the University of Florida; Stanford University; the Bancroft Library, UC Berkeley; the U.S. Library of Congress; Historical Collections of the Baker Library, Harvard Business School; the British Library of Political and Economic Science (LSE); Institute of Latin American Studies and Institute of Historical Research, University of London; Guildhall Library (Corporation of London); the Arquivo Público Mineiro; Universidade de São Paulo Faculdade de Direito; São Paulo Secretaria da Agricultura; Arquivo do Estado de São Paulo; Biblioteca Municipal Mário de Andrade; Ferrovias Paulistas, S.A. (Barra Funda and Jundiaí); Rede Ferroviária Federal, S.A.—Rio de Janeiro; Federação das Indústrias; Ministério da Fazenda; Biblioteca Nacional; Arquivo Nacional; Fundação Casa de Rui Barbosa; Biblioteca Estadual do Rio de Janeiro (Niterói); Arquivo Judiciário do Estado do Rio de Janeiro; Instituto Brasileiro de Geografia e Estatística; and the Instituto Histórico e Geográfico Brasileiro. The indispensable and unfailing help of Sonia Moss of Stanford's interlibrary loan department insured that scarce materials on Brazil scattered throughout the United States were available to me.

Anne Hanley, Herbert Klein, Jeffrey Lesser, Douglas Libby, Jeffrey Needell, Maria Ana Quaglino, Robert Slenes, and Gail Triner offered their knowledge of Brazilian archives and collections, as did Colin Lewis in London. Michael Pries, Maureen O'Dougherty, Jamie Jacobs, and Kelly Sabini facilitated my work by housing me on brief jaunts around Brazil. In Rio de Janeiro I am especially grateful to Roberval Oliveira Gomes of the Library of Rede Ferroviaria Federal, S.A., for providing me with microfilm; and to Roberto Menezes de Moraes, who made precious materials in his private archive accessible and who has since kindly hosted me on numerous occasions and provided countless hours of conversation about Brazilian history. I am indebted to Ken and Mary Ellen Keen for having first introduced me to Brazil, and the family of Walter and Lina Miralha Alves for hosting me in my early studies there. Numerous colleagues in graduate school patiently discussed with me the ideas in this study, and my conversations with Edward Beatty, Jenna Bednar, Eric Rauchway, and Mauricio Tenorio Trillo were especially valuable. Jamie Jacobs generously provided help in Rio on several occasions.

I appreciate the comments on specific portions of this study provided by Lee Alston, Don Brown, John Coatsworth, Lance Davis, David Denslow, Avner Greif, Gary Hawke, Maria Lúcia Lamounier, the late Nathaniel Leff, Colin Lewis, Murdo MacLeod, Jacob Metzer, José Moya, Jeffrey Needell, Douglass North, Patrick K. O'Brien, Cormac O'Gráda, Flávio Azevedo Marques de Saes, Richard Salvucci, Alan M. Taylor, Barry Weingast, and Mary Yeager; and by participants in seminars at Stanford, UCLA, Columbia, UC Berkeley, Northwestern, Illinois, Universidade de São Paulo, Universidade Estadual de Campinas, and Universidade Estadual Paulista–Araraquara, along with sessions at meetings of the American Historical Association, the All-UC Group in Economic History, the Economic History Association, and the International Economic History Association. Stanley Engerman, Stephen Haber, Herbert Klein, Naomi Lamoreaux, Jean-Laurent Rosenthal, Kenneth Sokoloff, and Gavin Wright generously read and commented on the entire book manuscript in one incarnation or another. I regret that I was not able to address every one of their suggestions. André Fonseca, Glenda Gamboa, Flávio Luíz de Souza Santos, Joseph Ryan, and Kari Zimmerman provided crucial research assistance, while Cala Dietrich, Annie Hong, Jill Lally, Yolanda McDonough, and Ji Won Shin ably aided with data entry. Norris Pope, Anna Eberhard Friedlander, Tim Roberts, and Ruth Steinberg at Stanford University Press provided invaluable editorial guidance, and proved inordinately patient when world events interrupted the progress of the manuscript on two different occasions. All errors in the study are my responsibility.

I owe a large pedagogical debt to the men who taught me Latin American history over the last two decades: the late Andrés Suarez first sparked my interest in the subject; Neill Macaulay, Jeffrey Needell, and the late John Wirth provided me with training in the history of Brazil; and the late Frederick Bowser, David Bushnell, Stephen Haber, and Murdo MacLeod taught me about Spanish America. Since my arrival at UCLA James Lockhart has continually encouraged my work. And throughout, Steve Haber proved to be an exemplary mentor and friend, and made all things possible. To him I owe an immense debt of gratitude.

My parents were especially supportive and also chased down valuable sources for me in Florida. My sister, Laura, found herself in Los Angeles while I was first assembling the pieces of this study. Over several months she cheerfully gave of her time, typing an endless series of chapter drafts for me while I was revising and teaching. She enabled me to get more done than I had imagined possible, and my debt to her for helping out in a pinch is large indeed.

A version of Chapter 7 was published as "Market Intervention in a Backward Economy: Railway Subsidy in Brazil, 1854-1913," *Economic History Review*, 1998.

NOTE ON ORTHOGRAPHY

Changes in the rules of written Portuguese make for multiple spellings of the same word (e.g., geográfico and geográphico; Brasil and Brazil) in different eras. I have attempted to maintain the original spellings in citations and, where appropriate, in the text.

NOTE ON CURRENCY UNITS

The baseline Brazilian currency unit was the milréis (sometimes written mil-réis).One milréis was expressed numerically as 1$000. One-half a milréis, or 500 réis, was written as $500. One thousand milréis was the equivalent of one conto de réis and was written as 1:000$000. In 1913, one milréis was worth US$.32.

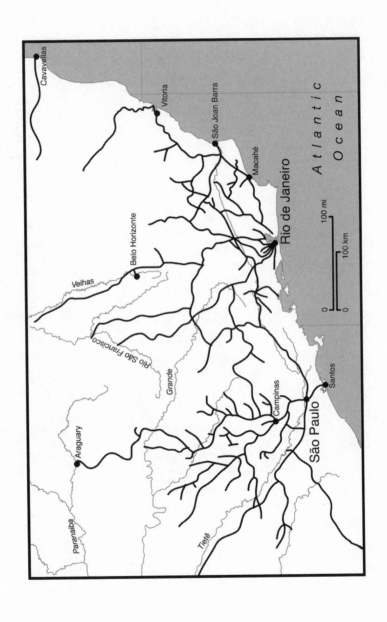

ORDER AGAINST PROGRESS

Chapter 1

Introduction

Despite its remarkable order, stability, and resources, nineteenth-century Brazil fell badly behind the industrializing countries of the North Atlantic. The proximate causes of Brazilian stagnation resided in low levels of investment and poor productivity. Allocative and technical inefficiencies hobbled Brazilian product and factor markets for much of the nineteenth century. Of all the determinants of relative economic backwardness, poor transport conditions posed the single most formidable barrier to Brazilian economic growth before 1900. Every commercialized product of farming and manufacturing had to be hauled to market, and relatively little could move by water. The prices paid for goods included a large markup, owing to the charges of carriage. Railroad expansion in the second half of the century made for continuous reductions in the costs of shipment, which integrated markets, made possible regional specialization, raised productivity, and increased Brazil's national income well above what it would have otherwise been. Railroads were not only the backbone of the export sector. They laid the groundwork for Brazil's transition to rapid economic growth after 1900. The improvement of transport conditions that railroads made possible had an enduring and important impact on Brazilian economic performance. This study is concerned with the first wave of transport improvements in modern Brazil, which began with the earliest construction of railroads in the 1850s and continued until motor vehicles began to supplant steam locomotion after the First World War.

In 1822 Brazil joined the community of independent nations with quiet ease. The heir to the Portuguese throne faced relatively little opposition from loyalists within the colony when he impetuously broke the mother country's hold over its largest and most valuable overseas possession.[1] As the new Emperor of Brazil, Dom Pedro I presided over a process that was remarkable for its exceptionality in the Americas. In that era, few of the American upstarts were able to depart the colonial fold without enduring a hard-fought war for independence, or worse still, decades of tumult and brutal internecine conflict. Brazil escaped most of these difficulties largely intact. Uncertainty nonetheless hung over Brazil's New World monarchy in the ensuing decades, during which it replaced its Emperor with a Regency, and faced serious challenges from regional separatist movements. By mid-century the Imperial government had succeeded in beating back or blandishing the forces of fragmentation, thereby securing the integrity of the new nation.

Preoccupied with state building and safeguarding the cohesion of the country, Brazil saw little in the way of economic change between Independence and mid-century.[2] Population increased steadily, through natural reproduction and (up to 1850) the importation of African slaves: the number of free persons grew from 2.8 million in 1823 to around 8.5 million in 1872, and the slave population rose from 1.1 million to 1.7 million over the same interval.[3] The economy, however, grew only little faster than Brazil's population, with growth in per capita output in the nineteenth century averaging only around one-tenth of 1 percent per year.[4] The most important change in the nation's economic organization before the 1850s was the pre-Independence opening of foreign trade, but gains from relatively more direct international commerce did not have a profound impact on growth.[5]

Material progress faltered for much of the Imperial era (1822–1889), during which numerous constraints severely curtailed economic growth. Brazil shared few of the natural, institutional, and political characteristics held to account for the success of the expanding North Atlantic economies. Except for a couple of short-lived experiments, Brazil lacked a system of free banking. Until 1882 the imperatives of political centralization permitted joint-stock companies to organize only with the approval of the Emperor's Council of State. Such extreme political "order" consigned the country's languorous stock market to a relatively unimportant role in finance until the decade preceding the advent of the Republic in 1889. In the countryside, the cost of loans was high. The institution of slavery conjoined with pervasive political patronage to insure that rural property rights remained ill-defined, rendering agricultural lending a risky and necessarily personalized activity.[6] Rural producers also labored under credit charges ranging up to 18 percent a year, and in some areas interest rates ran as high as 70 percent a year.[7] The costs of doing business in this setting were staggering, tightly fettering the economy.

With little growth in per capita product in the early decades after Independence, the initial impetus to extensive growth came from outside Brazil. Like the antebellum U.S. South, Brazil faced growing foreign demand for its agricultural produce as the century progressed. It exported a variety of goods, including sugar, hides, cotton, and jerked beef, and the climate and agronomic endowment in the center-south proved especially propitious for the production of coffee. By the 1840s coffee had emerged as Brazil's single most important export. As the major source of foreign exchange earnings, agricultural exports in general, and coffee in particular, made it possible to import productivity-raising capital goods, thus providing the fuel required for the early stage of economic transformation. Although exports increased as mid-century approached, that alone did not ensure that socially desirable, long-term investments would necessarily take root. Brazil's potential to import capital using its export earnings could only be realized if the context in which those investments would be made was altered. In a capital-poor economy, export earnings proved necessary yet insufficient to tap well-developed overseas financial markets and obtain foreign investment. Growth required a change in economic organization that would accomplish two things. First, it needed institutional arrangements capable of translating the uncertainty that investors faced into risk, which could be priced in markets. Second, it needed to reduce that risk to a level that made Brazil a desirable place to invest. The process of state building that culminated in the elimination of the last regional separatist movements in the 1840s, followed by the mid-century political *conciliação*, laid the groundwork that attracted the investments needed to overcome domestic impediments to improving the economy.

Prominent among the factors dragging on Brazil's economy was the high cost of transport. Regions that were endowed with superior agricultural fertility were hobbled by sorely inferior natural means of transporting their products to market. Except for the Amazon Basin, river transport presented innumerable natural obstacles, as most rivers south of the Amazon were non-navigable over long stretches. Good roads for wagons and wheeled vehicles were also scarce. The resulting high transport costs left product markets thin and badly fragmented. Only the wealthiest Brazilian farmers could be certain of affordable food imports in times of scarcity. At such times, poorer farmers had to place their own subsistence needs before the opportunities of the market. The margin of feasible commercial agriculture was severely restricted as a result. For much of rural society, the difficulty of securing the basic needs for survival dampened the impetus to produce high-return commercial crops. Export agriculture, then, remained confined to the littoral and its immediate hinterland. High transport charges also hit nascent manufacturers both coming and going. The cost of securing inputs over long distances, and of transporting goods to consumer markets, meant that the question of industrial location was such a tossup that few large-scale manufacturing operations even existed. Transport costs severely limited the marketing perimeters of factories. Unable to exploit potential scale economies, industry suffered from poor productivity, which often left it unable to compete with imports. In its struggle against low levels of output and relative inefficiency, Brazil epitomized economic backwardness.

Policies first pursued under Brazil's Second Reign (1840–1889) gradually eroded these major barriers to improved economic organization after 1850. The period beginning with the mid-century *conciliação* kept the political scene relatively well settled for almost four decades. Legislation enacted from the 1850s onward stripped away a number of obstacles, although others persisted.[8] The gradually shifting institutional environment facilitated, albeit with mixed success, progress toward reducing the costs of transacting. The final decade of the nineteenth century began a rather remarkable chapter in Brazil's economic history. By then, slavery had been abolished, and now, other institutional obstacles to economic growth were swept away. Foreign capital flowed to Brazil, first from Great Britain, and then by the end of the century increasingly from continental Europe and the United States. Immigrants poured into the fertile interior of the south. Brazil embarked upon modern economic growth.

After almost a century of poor economic performance, Brazil began the twentieth century rather more auspiciously. The traverse to improved growth was swift, and the nation shook off almost a century of unenviable productivity performance.[9] Over the long run, the country's institutional matrix did little to repair a poor record on distribution that was in no small part a legacy of slavery. Yet Brazil's capacity to mobilize resources and transform inputs into output ever more efficiently between 1900 and 1980 was stunning, even by First World standards. Standards of living, while slow to rise for much of the population, doubtless improved over those prevailing in the nineteenth century.[10]

One of the more obvious accomplishments in post-*conciliação* Brazil was the construction of some 24,000 kilometers of railroad in the six decades following 1850. By integrating Brazil's product markets and reducing the costs of transport, railroads played a central role in improving economic efficiency. In the colonial period authorities and entrepreneurs had done little to ameliorate the sorry state of internal transport, nor had they provided for other improvements that might have promoted long-term material progress. However, government under the Second Reign and the Republic facilitated the expansion of transport infrastructure, and each era saw its own boom decade of railroad construction. In the same way they did elsewhere around the world, railroads in Brazil reduced the costs of passenger travel and freight shipment. In the Brazilian case, however, railroads did this dramatically, reducing the real cost of overland shipment by as much as one order of magnitude between the 1860s and 1900. The impact of this improvement was profound and pervasive in an economy where commerce involved transport over considerable distances at a hefty cost.

This gradual erosion of the obstacles to growth in the second half of the nineteenth century, transport included among them, has received much attention by historians of Brazil, at least in general discussion. The broad contours and general drift of change after 1850 would seem to be well known. Indeed, the weight of the colonial heritage, the British presence, the institution of slavery, the rise of the coffee economy, and the role of the State are all addressed in a still-growing literature. While historians discuss at length the key components of Brazil's evolution, virtually no work has been done to assess the economic impact of any particular technological improvement or change in economic organization. It remains difficult to discern how important any one of these changes was to Brazil. This study begins to remedy that elision by considering in detail the consequences of railroads for Brazilian economic structure and performance before 1914.

The Questions

Modern Brazil exhibits the cumulative political, institutional, and social consequences of long-term economic underdevelopment. As a result, specialists working on Brazil could ill afford to study political and social events and processes in an economic vacuum. The literature has thus evolved around a solid core of interest in economic history, and specialists have increasingly singled out the nineteenth century for close scrutiny, given the poor record of growth before 1900. Relatively little work has focused, however, on studying strategic sectors of activity at the national level. By examining railroad development, it becomes possible to dissect a key obstacle to Brazilian economic growth. Four questions compel the course of inquiry. First, what was the direct impact of railroads on Brazil's economy? Second, what difference did it make that railroads entailed heavy involvement by government as promoter, regulator, and owner? Third, what consequences did foreign investment in the railroad sector pose for Brazil? And fourth, what role did Brazil's railroads play in determining the course of long-term change? The present volume explores the ways—and degree—to which the transport improvements embodied in the railroad made a difference to the size, structure, and pace of change of the national economy.

In pursuing these questions, much has necessarily been excluded. The study of railroads intersects with innumerable other research agendas, ranging from business histories of individual railroad companies, entrepreneurial biographies, local histories, and community studies to social history, labor relations, diplomacy, and the environment. The results presented here contain important implications for future research on these topics, but those issues are not the focus of the present work. While a more general study of the history of railroads in Brazil could incorporate this broader array of themes, it would do so only by sacrificing the rigor that is indispensable for grasping the role of railroads in long-term economic change. A rather more broad and impressionistic treatment might prove both more wide-ranging and evocative, but would also lack sufficient analytical depth, and would bring with it an unacceptably high risk of getting the fundamental features and important strands of the story wrong. In guarding against that latter possibility, the specificity and occasional formality with which the questions in the succeeding chapters are pursued is purposeful.

In examining the direct economic impact, this study draws on a monographic literature that gauges the consequences of railroads in several countries, using the tools of microeconomic benefit-cost analysis. In the past three decades there has evolved a large body of work within the new economic history devoted to defining the relative economic importance of railroads in several countries.[11] Doing the same for Brazil requires devoting a good deal of attention to the transport sector of the economy, and permits a recharacterization of the railroad's historical role in economic development.

The findings on the respective roles of foreign capital and state intervention obtain by carefully unpacking and fleshing out the chief components of the railroads' direct capital input. The second question focuses on the role of policy, and more broadly, the state, public sector, and political institutions. Extant studies of Brazilian railroad policy share two limiting characteristics. First, they tend to work at high levels of aggregation, taking an anthropomorphic "state" or "elite" as their focus. Second, they tend to be documentary or descriptive, identifying the role of the state in the economy, but stopping well short of an assessment of whether the state policies made the economy bigger or smaller, and if so, in what ways and how. In this book I relate policy to economic performance and thereby assess the state's involvement in terms of its efficiency consequences.

The third question focuses on the role of foreigners in Brazilian railroad development. Foreigners in particular, and external forces in general, have garnered a privileged position in the historiography, under the assumption that they often entailed sub-optimal outcomes for Brazil. Several chapters here specify, operationalize, and test the foreign influence in railroad development before 1914 in order to assess whether it proved costly to Brazil, and if so, to what degree.

The fourth question—the implications of railroad development for long-term change—has multiple answers, depending on the avenues of inquiry the historian chooses to pursue. Some of those answers can be informed by the tools of economic analysis. Others lie well beyond the scope of available method and theory, and answers, if posed, remain necessarily conjectural. Yet there can be little doubt that the railroad created a variety of wide-ranging effects, a number of which escape measurement, if not detection. Several of the more salient long-term consequences are addressed in the concluding chapter of this study.

Comprehensive studies of Brazilian railroads appeared as early as the 1860s, and these older treatments provide valuable description and detail. However, the modern historiography on Brazil manifests a palpable schizophrenia with respect to the impact of railroads on the economy. In the eyes of critics, railroads played a central role in intensifying Brazil's dependence on foreign product and capital markets in the second half of the nineteenth century. In that view, a railroad sector designed mainly to ship coffee and sugar, and reliant on British financing, necessarily benefited foreign investors and export agriculture at the expense of the economy as a whole. The prevailing view has been that railroads mainly "represented a privileged sector for English investments and the preeminence of a colonizing nation" over Brazil, but that analytically these studies remained lodged at the "level of folklore and sensationalism."[12] More recently, a growing monographic literature has examined the expansion of railroads, the role of government, and the ties to export agriculture, particularly in the province of São Paulo.[13] Several historians have noted that a principal impact of the railroad was to promote the expansion of coffee cultivation through the Paraíba Valley and its further extension into the São Paulo plateau.[14] Elsewhere, those same railroads are shown to have promoted the expansion of agricultural production for the internal market.[15] Other works argue that the railroad's impact was mixed, expanding both production for export and the domestic consumption, while also lowering the costs of travel.[16] The economic stimulus of the railroad in turn has been alternately characterized as beneficial and harmful. Although some specialists have viewed railroads as the key agent of productivity change in the late-nineteenth-century Brazilian economy, the claim has until now lacked an empirical basis.[17] Moreover, in the interpretation that continues to enjoy greater currency among historians, those same railroads merely affected resource savings, serving mainly to link plantations to ports and increasing dependency, satisfying planters' short-sighted thirst for short-run profits, strengthening the influence of foreigners, and promoting the expansion of Britain's informal empire, all the while failing to integrate the national territory and the national market.[18]

Confusion of this sort is clearly a renewable resource among historians, so long as there is no agreement on basic concepts, methods, and rules of evidence. The plethora of competing scenarios that characterize the railroad's impact in Brazil might be seen as a natural outcome of differing perspectives and emphases, except for two common features. First, whether favorable, unfavorable, or dispassionate in their assessments of the railroad, all assert its importance by identifying one or more linkages between railroads and the level and structure of economic activity. Second, few of these various perspectives document the strength of the linkages they invoke, and fewer still assess empirically the railroad's consequences. The literature neither evaluates the efficacy of policy, nor assesses the costs of foreign investment, nor gauges the impact of railroads on Brazil's economy. Indeed, most studies fail to define even a single yardstick by which those outcomes might even be measured.[19] Two problems of interpretation result. The first is a substantial gap in our understanding of how, where, and when the railroad made a difference, whether that difference might be important, and in what ways. The second is the resulting underdevelopment of Brazilian economic historiography, a field into which the new economic history is at last making substantial inroads.

The present study, based on extensive research in archives and libraries in Brazil, the United States, and Britain, provides results that are sharply at odds with standing conclusions about the impact of nineteenth-century transport improvements in Brazil. Although railroads indeed held profound consequences for Brazil, they were not those frequently imputed in the historiography. By relying heavily on subsidies, foreign capital, and government regulation, Brazil both obtained the railroad projects that it sought and succeeded in capturing substantial gains from them. Thanks in large part to the resource savings generated by these railroads, Brazil emerged around 1900 as one of the fastest-growing economies in the Western world.[20]

The Approach

The approach to Brazilian railroads derives first from advances made in the new economic history, which offer a useful way of assessing and understanding important economic outcomes in the past. The defining attributes of such an approach are the use of economic theory to model explicitly important features and relationships, a reliance on quantitative evidence from the past to illustrate those relationships, and the use of basic statistical techniques to organize those facts in a way that creates, as best as possible, a single, internally consistent story.[21] The new economic history weds theory to fact in order to distill interpretations that possess both logical consistency and verisimilitude, a goal commonly shared by historians of various methodological bents. Some comment is warranted regarding the main elements of the new economic history: theory-derived economic models, explicit counterfactuals, quantitative evidence, and statistical analysis. How people allocate resources under conditions of scarcity occupies most economic inquiry, along with the collective implications of those decisions for regions and entire nations. In its most elementary form, it invokes a fairly simple assumption, namely that individuals do the best they can for themselves under the circumstances, and then focuses on how outcomes change when those circumstances are altered. Models that examine the collective outcomes of human choices are metaphors, and nothing more. They abstract heavily from reality and necessarily leave out much in order to focus on what is believed to be important. Because there is risk that the excluded elements may well be of greater importance in the end than what has been included, model-building necessarily requires sensitivity tests, in order to determine whether the model possesses the desired degree of realism. Just as all historical inquiry proceeds from assumptions, so does economic history. However, by making models both explicit, and falsifiable, cliometrics not only clarifies the terms of the inquiry but also renders the enterprise of scholarly research open and accessible, and its results replicable.[22]

In much of this study the railroad's role is examined through a comparison juxtaposing what is known about the Brazilian economy with a hypothetical Brazil that has been deprived of its railroads. Counterfactual explorations of this sort, though controversial, especially among historians, have much to recommend them and remain indispensable in causal analysis.[23] In particular, the approach recognizes that, by laying bare the central assumptions of inquiry, explicit counterfactual reasoning promises and delivers more insight than the covert counterfactuals that lurk in narrative histories. The approach here blends the general relationships established by the covering laws of economic theory with the historically specific conditions that characterized Brazil. The counterfactual conditions that it exploits are thus both nomothetic and ideographic in nature.

Relationships between the constituent parts of basic economic models involve elements whose relative magnitudes can be measured and represented by a number. Company profits, the value of agricultural output in a particular region, the trend in the terms of trade for a country, and the level of gross national product are elementary examples. No numeric value associated with any of these is inherently more reliable than any other kind of fact. Indeed, quantitative analysis is potentially riddled with bogus precision. It nonetheless offers the singular advantage of gauging orders of magnitude, and it allows arguments to be refined within margins of error that are tighter—and more meaningful—than those implicit in qualitative assessments of "big," "small," "prominent," and "insignificant."[24] Many key features of the human condition in the past, along with their proximate and distal determinants, are readily quantifiable, and such quantification sheds considerable light on old and new questions alike.

Finally, the techniques of statistics provide not only a means of organizing a large volume of quantifiable evidence, but also the most powerful approach to the the the analysis of causation. While much quantitative history unfortunately uses statistical analysis as a substitute for theory rather than its complement, when properly applied in the setting of testable implications derived from theoretically informed models, statistics possess two valuable attributes. First is the ability to measure the relative strength of a particular cause, factor, or effect. The second is falsifiability. If an argument is set up in such a way that the historian making it can step off the curb with the testable implications of a theory in hand only to be flattened in mid-street by contrary empirical results, then there is in place a powerful check on the researcher's analysis and a useful safeguard against unreliable findings. Few approaches to the past offer such a clear-cut way of assessing the reliability of the history being told. Falsifiability is indispensable to crafting an enduring story, and statistical techniques are a means by which arguments about both simple and complex economic relationships in the past may be falsified.

Themes, Issues, and the Course of the Study

The principal finding in the chapters that follow is that by hauling products and transporting passengers at a lower cost than the technologically inferior modes of transport they supplanted, railroads in Brazil reduced the prices that consumers paid for merchandise, increased the prices that producers received, improved the mobility of labor, boosted output and income, and laid the groundwork for pivotal structural shifts that came about in the first half of the twentieth century. The emphasis of this study is on four areas of inquiry. The main questions it addresses lie at the intersection of the major themes of Latin American economic history: poor productivity performance, relative economic backwardness, the foreign presence, and the role of politics and institutions in promoting or hindering economic growth. These four areas are all illuminated by the railroad's role in increasing Brazil's level of economic activity, best measured in terms of increase in output. It is a fair question as to whether or not such an emphasis is the best way to proceed. Many specialists on Latin America would maintain that a focus on allocative efficiency is the wrong tack. Economic "miracles" abound in post-1945 Latin America. Each successive miracle is recognized ever more widely as not bringing about equally miraculous gains for the bulk of the population. The emphasis, it might be argued, should instead be on development, a process of growth that distributes its fruits more broadly and in a sustainable fashion.

Three proximate issues motivate this study's focus on the railroad's implications for the level of output. The first of these is the spurious tension between "growth" (defined as an increase in the level of GDP per capita) and "underdevelopment" that prevails in many studies of Latin America. Gross domestic product is the value of final goods and services produced in an economy, and equals national income, irrespective of the distribution of that income. By contrast, development comprises, in its simplest definition, an enduring economic process that benefits all of the population substantially, and not just a small portion of it.[25] For decades it has been a commonplace that economic growth in Latin America grows awry and metastasizes into underdevelopment, leaving people worse off.[26] Curiously, in that view, more becomes less, less becomes more, and having less and spreading it around is normatively better. Such a perspective frankly runs against logic and the long-term historical record. Development still proves to be dismal when total income is low, no matter how evenly it is distributed. While separating the level of income from the degree of development may well be a useful schematic or rhetorical device, it analytically poses a false dichotomy.[27] Brazil's GDP, for example, was historically and comparatively low, and especially so through the nineteenth century when the industrializing nations forged ahead. If all of Brazil's income in 1900 had been redistributed equally across its denizens, by international standards, GDP per capita still would have been very small. A more even distribution of the economy's output would certainly be more fair by normative standards. But if the level of output was very low—as was Brazil's—little about that picture would resemble "development." In short, development requires not just a distribution of the social surplus that benefits all of society, but also the creation of a surplus large enough to do some good.

The second reason to focus on the level of economic activity is the central role played by economic growth in raising standards of living over the long haul. Growth—an increase in the size of the economy—often does not translate immediately into widespread welfare gains. While neither a higher level of GDP nor its more even distribution is in and of itself sufficient to generate development, in a long-term perspective growth proves to be indispensable. Indeed, historically the main source of development has not been short-run miracles, nor has it been wide-scale redistributions. It has, instead, been a steady, sustained rise in per capita output over the very long run.[28] While it is granted that national income, adjusted by population, is an imperfect indicator of human welfare, it nonetheless remains the best global measure available to researchers in economic history. Persistently low levels of GDP cripple development, and raising income improves prospects over the long haul.

Considerable debate during the last several decades focuses on whether sustained increases in GDP result from "leading sectors," or instead unfold across a broad front of changes. Most generalizations about the process of modern economic growth remain embedded in the insights gleaned from the experience of the advanced, industrializing North Atlantic economies. There are still few results rooted in an understanding of the long-term experience of relatively poor economies to see how this process unfolded outside the industrializing nations. In the industrialized economies, no single advance in technology or change in economic organization placed them on a path of long-term sustained growth and rising standards of living. Rather, a wide range of factors impelled progress. In relatively backward economies, there is similarly little prospect of a cure-all. Nonetheless, in different settings than those found in the North Atlantic economies, the effects of some changes might be magnified or diminished. Such was the case in Brazil, where the railroad's impact on income and growth proved to be profound. This study is explicitly designed to identify one of the key factors underpinning not an early "miracle," but rather the transition to long-term sustained growth in a relatively backward economy.

The third reason for the emphasis on growth is a practical one. There is a dearth of information with which to assess more broadly the consequences of railroads for the distribution of income, and hence the breadth of material progress. Social historiography, so often the central font of results on income distribution for other societies, has yet to provide conventional indicators of distribution and standards of living for nineteenth-century Brazil.[29] In the absence of these indicators, additional results must await additional research. Nonetheless, the railroad's consequences for human well-being may be inferred by reference to some simple indicators of factor payments, as is done in the concluding chapter.

The narrative in the following chapters is analytical rather than chronological, organized around the four broad questions specified above. Overland transport in Brazil was in a sorry state at the end of the colonial era. The character of transport before the railroads, the policies designed to attract investment in the new technology, and the early challenges faced by the Brazilian government in ameliorating poor transport conditions occupy Chapter 2. Pre-rail transport was costly because topography, climate, and in-

stitutions conjoined to make the common mule the optimal mode of overland shipment for much of Brazil. Even where improved roads existed, overland transport remained relatively expensive. Because of the inefficiencies
inherent to this technology, it remained a costly means of conveyance.[30] This
condition improved only with the construction of the railroad. Chapter 3
introduces railroad development into the story. It examines how Brazil fostered railroad expansion, providing an overview of the salient characteristics
of early railroad finance, promotion policy, and government ownership.

Chapters 4 and 5 take up the book's first main question and assess the direct impact of the railroad by examining the resources saved through its provision of two main classes of transport services. In one strand of the historical literature, foreign-financed railroads purportedly brought little gain to
Latin American countries.[31] Chapter 4 examines the economic impact of
railroads in Brazil through an analysis of freight services, while Chapter 5
turns to the railroad provision of passenger transport. Both chapters use a
simple, albeit formal, model to do so, although the intuition behind that
model does not require a firm grasp of the formalization. In brief, Chapters
4 and 5 gauge the importance of the railroad by considering a historically
relevant counterfactual scenario: How much was Brazilian GDP increased by
the reductions in the cost of transport made possible by the railroads? That
question is unanswerable using presently available theory and method. This
study thus poses and answers a closely related yet different question: How
much would Brazilian GDP have been reduced in 1913 had the economy
been deprived of railroads? The answer to this second question is by no
means an answer to the first. But the second question has the distinct advantage of being answerable. That answer informs, in a very reasonable fashion,
one's beliefs about what the answer to the first question is likely to be. Chapters 4 and 5 assess the contribution of railroad transport services to the level
and pace of economic activity by comparing the actual economy in 1913 to
a counterfactual economy that is forced to adjust to the higher cost of transport without railroads.

Chapter 6 analyzes the principal structural changes that railroad market
integration made possible in Brazilian manufacturing and agriculture. Its
findings cut across two broad themes. The first of these is the issue of "tropical development," a question that addressed the limits and possibilities of export-led economic growth and diversification among the world's tropical regions during the late nineteenth and early twentieth centuries.[32] The focus is
important because it takes geography, climate, and resources as important factors bearing on the course of material progress and structural change in regions and nations considered to be on the periphery of the world economy.

Those factors jointly constrain crop choices and the economy's output mix, and thus pose profound implications for the pace of progress in the agricultural sector of the economy. As such, there may exist limits to the degree of structural change that transport improvements created, given the agronomic endowment and setting. Railroads were in no way tailor-made to promote one path of economic change over another. The setting and prevailing conditions mattered. Structural consequences are an empirical question, the answer to which cannot be easily deduced from stylized impressions.

Economic dependency is one such stylized fact, one that enjoyed great currency in discussions of Brazilian development, and one that serves as a second theme of Chapter 6. Dependency "theory" was a hodgepodge of loosely related concepts that, as an interpretive framework, focused on the role of external factors in poor economic performance, skewed income distribution, and political authoritarianism. While no single version of the dependency approach ever emerged as preeminent, the vast bulk of dependency-inspired analyses falls into one of two categories. The first of these was the "development of underdevelopment." In that version, foreign investment, foreign trade, and the structure of the world economy conjoined to drain off the dependent economy's resources. That perspective focused directly on the ties binding the national economy to that of the world market, focusing on the leakage of profits to foreign investors and the export of surplus value.[33] It is closely related to the concept of an "informal empire of free trade and investment" established by Great Britain and presumably so inimical to material progress in Brazil.[34] The second variant stressed "dependent development," in which a peripheral economy's position in the world economy created an array of class coalitions and a national state that fostered economic growth, but growth that heavily favored a cabal of influential foreigners and privileged domestic elites.[35] Though dependency's prominence as an interpretive framework has faded in recent years, that decline came about more as a result of dependency perspectives simply falling out of fashion rather than as a result of new, theoretically informed empirical insights. Few studies rigorously assessed the benefits and costs of the foreign presence in the economy, opting instead to turn away from it.

Chapter 6 employs a wide range of evidence to demonstrate the structural consequences of Brazilian railroad development. Conclusions derived from both variants of dependency fare equally poorly when tested against this evidence. Internal features, and not external constraints, proved to be key determinants of both the railroad's gains and structural consequences in Brazil. The historiography has stressed the lost opportunities for industrialization imposed by railroad development in Latin American economies. There is little doubt that latecomers to the industrial revolution have economic and social structures that look very different from those of the industrializing North Atlantic nations.[36] In the early twentieth century the share of manufacturing in total output was still relatively low in Brazil and few Brazilians yet worked in factories. What is at issue is the origin of this industrial "lag" in Brazil. Railroads in Brazil putatively forged new ties, and strengthened old ones, to the advanced, industrializing nations of the North Atlantic. Those relations are presumed either to have precluded "development" as a possibility, or at the very least to have twisted its results.[37] Chapter 6 carefully explores the basic features of the connection between Brazilian railroads, the demand for foreign inputs, manufacturing, and export agriculture. It is not the case that Brazilian railroads created large outflows of profits, draining the economy of capital. Nor did railroads favor "export-led" growth in Brazil. The rapid extension of railroads in Brazil after the 1870s brought with it a pronounced response on the part of the internal sector of the economy to the opportunities created by cheap transport. The fact that railroads provided little special stimulus to Brazilian manufacturing must be interpreted in light of the fact that they did not do very much for industry in the relatively advanced economies either.

Chapter 7 examines the business of railroading in Brazil in light of public-transport policy—the nexus of "state" and "economy." Those policies on the part of the Brazilian state involved incentives to investment, the regulation of foreign- and domestically owned railroads, and outright government ownership. These issues also relate to the concerns of dependency interpretations insofar as they deal with the profits, and the distribution of social benefits, from railroad companies. However, they directly intersect the concerns of the literature on business imperialism as well. There, the focus is on the degree of control, bargaining power, and thus capacity to extract a share of the social surplus that British firms held in Latin America.[38] The chapter explores the consequences of those policies through a comparison of company profits (both subsidized and unsubsidized) and the social rates of return on railroad capital. The results reveal that British railroads did not enjoy high profits compared to Brazilian-owned lines. Importantly, Brazil's formal political institutions were critical to determining the distributive consequences of subsidies and regulation. British-owned railroads had profit records that were, at best, no better than those of privately owned Brazilian railroads. Government-owned railroads had the lowest profits, thanks to their vulnerability to political pressure for low freight rates. This led to distortions, as one might expect. Nonetheless, the average social rates of return on the largest railroads were high, and regulation by the government worked to ensure that a large share of this surplus remained in Brazil.

Chapter 8 concludes by discussing effects arising from railroad development that, while escaping the measures of the preceding chapters, may
nonetheless be quite important to the course of long-term change. Five areas garner particular attention. The first is the railroad's effects on Brazil's social and political map. Second is the potential for the railroad to exacerbate
inequalities in income and wealth in a relatively backward economy under-
going modernization. The third is the railroad's interaction with Brazilian
political organization, which ironically reinforced some long-standing internal barriers to trade. Fourth is the role of the railroad in fostering domestic entrepreneurship and financial institutions. Finally, there is the railroad's role in promoting market interventions by the state, interventions that
were doubtless salutary in the short term yet costly over the long haul.

Economic historians attribute various effects to railroad construction,
ranging from accelerated frontier settlement in the United States to the
usurpation of land owned by indigenous populations in Mexico. In Brazil,
two analogous processes may be identified. First, during the early decades of
railroad development, the uneven pattern of subsidy and construction aided
in concentrating the slave population in the center-south. The resulting sec-
tionalism likely helped undercut the status quo supporting slavery in Brazil's
Parliament.[39]

Second, because railroads were typically first built in economies that were
largely agricultural, they created new opportunities for the accumulation of
wealth through land holding. A large share of the increase in income attributable to the reduced cost of transport accrued directly to those who owned
land. The historiography points to two conflicting tendencies arising from
this process in Brazil. One is that income and wealth may have become more
concentrated, either because landowners became wealthier or because of
usurpation by the powerful against the poor. Given that the aggregate patterns of the distribution of land, income, and wealth for Brazil are not yet
well established, that hypothesis cannot be thoroughly explored, although
evidence suggests that concentration did occur in places such as the *contestado* region as a result of the railroad's interaction with the political environment. The second result of the railroad's impetus to rising land values was the
new opportunities for ownership on the expanding agricultural frontier. The
case of São Paulo, where large numbers of immigrant laborers settled and became farm owners, illustrates the railroad's potential in this regard. In the
context of rising land values, any tendencies toward worsening income distribution that the railroad might have exacerbated were compounded by two
additional features. The first was Brazil's long-standing failure to define and
adequately enforce property rights in land. The second was the legacy of slavery, which skewed income distribution dramatically by depriving a large

share of the population of the opportunity to earn the full return from their labor. As such, the question of distribution extends well beyond the consequences of the railroad and awaits archival-based investigation into the patterns of wealth holding. Preliminary indications, discussed in the conclusion, suggest that distributional changes during railroad expansion were modest.

More in evidence was the institutional response that railroads induced with respect to fiscal practices. Because railroads brought new markets into close competition, within the overall gains they created there were relatively inefficient agricultural producers who would be put out of business. Brazil's formal institutions proved responsive to the needs of those parties, and interstate taxation of commerce steadily increased through the turn of the century. A partially offsetting loss, in part attributable to the railroad's gains, obtained. The persistence of such obstacles to efficiency after 1900 again reveals the importance of institutional and political factors in determining the course of growth and distribution that Brazil followed in the ensuing century. The railroad's consequences in Brazil were embedded not in Brazil's dependent position in the world economy, but deeply so in the political institutions of the Empire and Republic. If the railroad was America's first big business, then it was even more so in Brazil, and in this regard had the expected effects. Stock markets were so thin that they barely existed on the eve of the railroad age. Although railroads did not lead to a stock market boom, they did over time lead to a substantial expansion of the scope and size of the domestic equity markets. If railroads had not sparked a good share of the growth in Brazil's formal capital markets, then some other activity likely would have. Nonetheless, it was railroad companies that accounted for the single largest capitalized sector of activity in domestic equity and debt markets by the 1880s.

Finally, railroads were not only Brazil's first big business, they were also Brazil's first big market intervention in the context of relative economic backwardness. Regulation and subsidy proceeded with little regard for their efficiency consequences. But by demonstrating new ways for government to create large private benefits for the politically enfranchised, the railroads paved the way for a burgeoning state sector whose long-run beneficial impact is very much in doubt. Increasingly frequent interventions in finance, commodity markets, and trade protectionism in the Old Republic gave way to inward-looking development under Vargas.[40] If the direct economic impact of the railroads in 1913 was strong, then they may be credited with a good portion of Brazil's economic gains in its first stage of modern economic growth. But if railroads paved the way for a ponderous state pursuing distortionary and costly policies later in the century, then they may be culpable in equal degree.

Chapter 2

Transport in Nineteenth-Century Brazil

The extent to which the introduction of railroads made a difference to Brazil depended heavily on the state of the pre-rail transport system. Irrespective of locale, pre-rail transport was backward, slow, and costly. At the mid–nineteenth century Brazil remained saddled with a transport technology little different from that found in the Old Testament. At the root of Brazil's poor transport conditions lay a single major cause: topography proved exceedingly unfavorable to the movement of people and merchandise. For those regions of Brazil that were not served by unimpeded river navigation, all freight and passengers moved overland before 1854 using human and animal power, just as they had for centuries.

Transport in this manner was made exceptionally difficult by coastal hills and mountains that extend from the northeast to the far south. Brazil's severe topography ensured that movement overland proceeded at a plodding pace, perpetually subject to the risks posed by both the terrain and the vagaries of tropical and subtropical conditions. Freight shipment and passenger travel by the traditional modes of transport occurred over relatively unimproved routes, some of which had been in use since the earliest decades of colonial settlement. One foreign consul aptly summed up the enduring impediments posed by the Brazilian terrain when he noted: "The mountains are too high to scale, the rivers too wide to bridge. It is thus that the energies of nature have hampered the spirit of man."[1]

If the exigencies of overland movement in Brazil were universally oner-ous, rivers could be more forgiving. Rivers in the north, deep in the upper interior, and in the far southwest were capable of providing effective alter-natives to overland movement. Watercraft, ranging from dugout canoes to small sailing vessels, plied the navigable portions of all of Brazil's interior wa-terways. Those water routes were of the utmost importance to commercial activities in their respective regions. However, as it would turn out, the very areas that possessed the greatest agricultural fertility, those with the brightest prospects for the accumulation of wealth, and the ones that ultimately expe-rienced the most settlement, were not well served by natural waterways. Brazil's agricultural hinterland did not enjoy access to cheap waterborne shipment to anywhere near the degree to which nature privileged farmers in the United States.

In Brazil, colonial administrators, and later the Imperial and provincial governments, undertook modest efforts to improve transport conditions. The same severe terrain and weather that impeded movement also worked every-where in Brazil to make road building and maintenance, canal construction, and the de-obstruction of rivers prohibitively costly. In that context, the lim-ited public resources of the newly independent Brazil brought relatively little relief in the first half of the nineteenth century to a population burdened by virtually impassable and treacherous trade routes. It was only with the con-struction of railroads in the 1850s and 1860s, and their relatively more rapid expansion in the 1880s, that Brazil became significantly less fettered by its own topography.

Overland Transport

Up through the mid–nineteenth century, and even afterwards in areas not served by rail, overland movement in Brazil proceeded by various relatively archaic means. Predominant among these was the ubiquitous pack mule—the *besta*, *muar*, or *cargueiro*—usually organized in a train, or *tropa*. These groups of mules, typically ranging in size from six animals to as many as forty and sometimes even more, were owned and operated by muleteers, known alternately as *arrieros*, *tropeiros*, and *almocreves*. Also employed in carrying, where conditions either permitted or dictated it, were horses, wagons, ox-drawn carts, and even human porters in regions where animals were in short supply and labor-market conditions sufficiently poor.[2] Both animals and travelers moved overland sharing the same crude trails and roads. The estab-lishment of these relatively simple roads in colonial Brazil had accompanied the gradual occupation of the coast and the extension of settlement inland in the sixteenth and seventeenth centuries. Often mere ruts and trails, they linked port towns to areas beyond the steep coastal escarpment, just as the railroads that would come later did. Limited access to the interior—a direct result of the poor conditions encountered on these routes—constrained westward expansion. The array of roads carved out by Brazilians up and down the coast reflected the prevailing patterns of occupation. Except for a few areas of relatively heavy interior settlement, such as the gold- and diamond-mining regions in Minas Gerais and farther west, Brazil's population was concentrated on the littoral.

The earliest "roads" of the colonial era were extraordinarily primitive, often indigenous in origin, and used largely by missionaries and slave-raiding parties to penetrate the interior.[3] To contemporaries, "road" was taken to mean any path that was open to pack animal traffic, and a number of them ran from the coast across the *serra* in the colony's center-south. The discovery of gold at the end of the seventeenth century in the interior regions of São Paulo and what would later become Minas Gerais naturally sparked great interest in locating or creating new land routes from the coast.[4] During the eighteenth century additional roads for mule convoys were either adapted from extant indigenous paths or carved out anew. By the early nineteenth century the pattern of trade routes that would endure until the expansion of the railroad was well in place. Ports such as Recife, Salvador, Rio de Janeiro, Porto de Estrella, Angra dos Reis, Paraty, Santos, and Porto Alegre were by 1800 already active centers of colonial commerce that linked themselves to their immediate hinterlands via rudimentary road networks. In Brazil's center-south the Caminho Novo, Caminho do Secretário, the Rio–São Paulo Road, and the Estrada do Commércio were major colonial roads in heavy use at the beginning of the nineteenth century.[5] Late-colonial roads in São Paulo ran hundreds of kilometers into the interior, to entrepôts from which canoes carried the trade to Mato Grosso.[6] When the nascent coffee boom in the 1830s created "new" port towns, such as Ubatuba, it also brought with it new roads for moving goods.[7]

From north to south the excruciatingly poor conditions encountered on Brazilian roads hobbled the rural economy. At the heart of the pre-rail transport bottleneck in nineteenth-century Brazil was the woeful inadequacy of the means of communication inherited from the colonial era. The primary difficulties those conditions presented were compounded by both the torpor and brigandage pervading overland trade routes. The alarming incidence of highway robbery around Rio de Janeiro at the time of Independence caused one contemporary to complain that "soon the roads will become impassable."[8] Unfortunately, there are no comprehensive surveys of transport conditions in Brazil that would permit a systematic evaluation of all of the problems then plaguing the industry. Nonetheless, travelers to the country,

Brazilian officials, and foreign consuls all paid careful attention to transport conditions and left behind a wealth of commentary from which the general state of affairs may be gleaned. Quantitative sources, employed in subsequent chapters, yield more exact measures of the costs resulting from the pre-railroad transport technology. Contemporary observers, however, who regularly offered up scathing attacks on the country's backward state of transport, placed this concern squarely among the most important obstacles to economic growth in Brazil. Indeed, it was argued that the lack of good roads alone was worse than all of the other problems confronting the economy of the new nation.[9]

Even after mid-century, Brazil claimed only a few "highways" that could be considered to be in an improved state. Tropical conditions necessitated the surfacing of those routes with macadam to maintain a minimum semblance of passability. The Minister of Agriculture's report to the legislature in 1869 described lucidly the immediate problem this posed for Brazil's rural economy:

> Roads that give access to the interior of the country are rare. As a rule they offer passage so difficult that to make it a few leagues is a sacrifice for travelers, even more so for the movement of cargo. The consequence is that cultivation is reduced to a narrow zone, from which farmers obtain profits after transporting their goods that are barely sufficient to remunerate them for their labor and capital. Further inland, planting is limited to what is strictly necessary for local consumption. Any surplus goes unused because the costs of getting it out [to market] exceed its value.[10]

Much of rural Brazil remained deprived of transport improvements. Only exceptional conditions made it feasible to produce a marketable surplus since the normal margins of cultivation were so restricted.[11] For example, in Pernambuco in 1864, at the height of the cotton boom created by the U.S. Civil War, it was anticipated that if a fall in cotton prices came about "production will again be checked by the high cost of transport in a country of vast area almost destitute of roads."[12] The total length of road in the province at that time that was considered passable on a year-round basis was only 200 kilometers.[13] As late as the early 1870s just four routes radiated outward from the port of Recife, providing only 316 kilometers of maintained roads.[14] "Otherwise," one observer averred, "the means of communication consist of trails rendering the transit from one point to another very slow, costly, and fatiguing."[15]

Even after early railroads were constructed in Brazil's long-settled northeast, the continuing absence of a well-developed wagon road network capable of providing feeder routes was a brake on regional development. Pernambuco's sugar producers foundered in part because "the progress of the traffic was checked by a want of roads. . . . Produce was usually carried on the backs of horses, as there were no roads [that] wheeled carriages could travel on to the railway."[16] The president of the province went on record in 1866, saying that the roads were limited "to such a restricted zone that they were far from satisfying the needs of agriculture, which demands as an indispensable condition of development the expansion of these and other means of communication."[17] Further north, at the provincial capital of Maranhão, "the only road on the island was practicable for carts for the distance of about ten miles."[18] In Pará in the late 1850s there was "not a single road in the province properly so called."[19] In Paraiba the "routes up the country are seldom better than mere mule tracks, and, in many instances it is impossible to traverse them without guides."[20]

Mid-nineteenth-century road conditions did not improve as one headed south. Agriculture in Bahia languished "owing to the horrible state of the intransitable roads, or rather paths, which exist in the interior."[21] In Espírito Santo the provincial president wrote in the 1850s that outside of a few trails maintained for colonists, "this province does not have a single road that merits the name."[22] In the large interior province of Minas Gerais, shoddy or nonexistent roads continued to limit access to fertile land and mineral ore deposits well after the initial penetration of the region by rail. One of the area's most astute observers, concerned precisely about getting the province's iron goods to market in the 1880s, asserted that "outside of the south of the province, where coffee is cultivated on a large scale, and which is less poorly served in terms of communications, the state of transportation is deplorable. One finds nary a single good road." He went on to note that from the terminus of the Dom Pedro II Railway, half of the route to the town of Diamantina was open only to oxcarts, which struggled to make steep ascents and descents. Beyond Itabira, the "road" became a mere trail for the final 100 kilometers. Over that stretch, "mules are necessary to move goods, at times only with difficulty. The situation is the same throughout the interior of the province: where roads are inadequate for the passage of carts, transport is effected on the backs of beasts."[23] The region's leading mining engineer similarly lamented the obstacles to marketing imposed by the lack of effective "means of communication" in the province.[24]

Looking back on the state of affairs in São Paulo during the 1830s and 1840s, the roads over the Serra do Mar that were trafficked by mules were recalled as "frightful precipices that often devour the loaded animals."[25] By the 1860s the province of São Paulo possessed numerous routes that were open to carts and stagecoaches, at least during the dry season. Nonetheless, the provincial president sympathized with those who shipped freight along the main artery from the highland plateau to the port of Santos in 1865, commenting that "the poor quality of its construction, and the traffic of thousands of animals and carts that daily use the Santos road, are sufficient to explain the bad state of passage that it offers."[26] In the far south of the country, contemporaries mocked the very appellation employed in Brazil: "The so-called roads are undeserving of the name, except in the immediate neighborhood of towns, so shortly afterwards they diverge into mere tracks or horse-paths."[27] Road improvements, such as paving and ditching, were far from common in nineteenth-century Brazil. The provinces of Rio de Janeiro, São Paulo, and Paraná provide examples of the best available road technology of the era. In Rio de Janeiro, the Estrada da Serra da Estrela was an early paved public road, whereas the União e Indústria road and the Mangaratiba were paved roadways that operated on a commercial toll basis. Both toll roads languished in precarious financial circumstances, with the Mangaratiba proving to be an early failure and the União e Indústria unable to compete with the railroad in the long term.[28] São Paulo's main road to Santos eventually underwent paving in some sections, but only in the decade before it was obviated by railroad competition. Paraná's Caminho da Graciosa similarly provided improvements to shippers, but it too effectively succumbed to the advance of railroads.[29] As promising as these internal improvements were, they came late, and were all too rare in Brazil.

In short, on the eve of the railway age, the palpable scarcity of roads, and the poor conditions encountered where roads were available, had consigned the transportable goods-producing sectors of the Brazilian economy to a grim existence. While the evidence proffered by contemporaries, both native and foreign, is largely anecdotal in nature, it serves well to delineate the dismal state of pre-rail overland transport in Brazil. Additional quantitative evidence, presented in subsequent chapters, will reveal that the costs of pre-rail transport were right in line with contemporary opinion. One writer summed up the sentiments of the time quite well by alleging that Brazil at mid-century was in fact virtually devoid of anything resembling a true transport sector, since "carrying cargo on the backs of beasts . . . does not warrant the label 'transportation industry.' "[30]

But a transportation industry it was. In the more populous provinces, tens of thousands of mules plied rural paths and roads, each making several journeys each year. Brazil's poor roads comprised only part of the overland-transport problem, because they were but one component of the transport technology. Also important was the challenge of obtaining a sufficient supply of the additional inputs required to produce transport services. For Brazil's muleteers and farmers, provisioning the primitive transport sector with mules proved to be an additional source of difficulty. Given the topography and prevailing conditions, mules represented the optimal choice of pack animal throughout much of the country. Purveyors of overland freight services relied on them more than any other species as beasts of burden. They were surer of foot than horses, relatively cheap to feed, and possessed an unmatched reputation for endurance and survivability. For the most part it was mules that traversed the sinuous routes over steep terrain to make the trip from Brazil's interior to the coast.[31]

Because of the strong demand for transport services and the derived demand for essential inputs, mule breeding came to be an important activity in Brazil. In the first half of the nineteenth century it became clear that securing an adequate flow of pack animals would prove to be an enduring problem. Concern over the issue created quasi-official interest in arrangements to procure them.[32] In the end, most mules appear to have been supplied by private entrepreneurs dedicated to provisioning the market.[33] While mules were bred throughout Brazil, large-scale mule supply was concentrated in the far south. At mid-century Brazilians raised and drove to market tremendous herds of these animals, which were then sold to middlemen and muleteers in major hinterland entrepôts such as Sorocaba, São Paulo.[34] From there, the new owners dispersed the great herds through marketing networks, effectively scattering mules throughout the major agricultural regions, where they were employed in providing the transportation services so sorely needed throughout Brazil.

The combination of poor roads and the slow speed of travel conjoined to make for high transport costs. For rural producers, urban consumers, and merchants, poor overland-transport conditions were reflected in shipping charges and fees that often proved prohibitively expensive. For travelers, those same conditions created high travel costs due to extensive travel time, danger, and discomfort. The fact that the overland-transport sector at mid-century was technologically inefficient and costly in comparison with alternatives, such as water shipment or railroads, did not mean that no goods or people moved at all. It did mean that the costs arising from overland shipment and travel severely restricted the marketing perimeters of Brazilian farmers and nascent manufacturers.

By the early nineteenth century the trails and roads in Pernambuco, Bahia, Rio de Janeiro, and São Paulo were heavily trafficked, even in the wet season. But freight loads, particularly on long hauls, were limited largely to goods that had relatively high value-to-weight ratios, such as coffee, cotton, and sugar. Commercial passenger travel confined itself to those roads open to *diligências*, or stagecoaches. The torpor of shipment overland meant that the goods that were shipped moved to market "morosely, in trains of mules, by roads almost always rudimentary and malconserved."[35] Needless to say, the conditions and technology of overland transport in Brazil weighed heavily on the scarce resources of the rural economy.

Additional evidence on the high direct costs of shipping merchandise over Brazilian roads, presented in Chapter 4, bears out the complaints of contemporaries who decried the lost opportunities arising from the burden of pre-rail transport charges. Worse still, beyond those direct costs to shippers were additional, indirect costs. The sluggish pace of movement, and the seasonal impediments posed by tropical conditions, created inventory and storage requirements. High transport charges and the uncertainty of the availability of transport services in the rainier months meant that producers had to hold larger inventories of goods, and that goods spent longer times in transit on average. Even with good weather, speeds of mule trains were as slow as 10 kilometers a day.[36] The resulting inventory costs would have been vastly reduced by a more rapid mode of shipment. Because the value of holding inventories was priced in terms of opportunity, the high interest rates arising from Brazil's severely underdeveloped capital markets meant that those inventory costs were proportionally greater in Brazil than in countries where credit was more readily available.

While the burden of these direct and indirect costs to shippers was readily apparent to contemporaries, its magnitude is difficult to express. It can only be measured in terms of the output obviated by those severe conditions. There was little doubt among men who lived at the time that the total cost to the economy from overland shipment was large. In Rio Grande do Sul, "transport overland is much more difficult than that by water, and in fact in this respect the province is very backward."[37] The British consul to Bahia, eager to stake out new opportunities for trade with the United Kingdom, opined that "one cannot but regret that so much wealth, mineral and agricultural, lies useless from the want of roads and facilities of transport to and from the interior."[38]

The natural marketing barriers thrown up by overland-transport conditions were overcome only in periods when the prices for agricultural products were not swamped by transport costs. By the end of the Brazilian cotton boom, a commercial representative in Bahia was able to observe that "a few years ago no cotton, the produce of this province, was exported, because the difficulties of transport from the interior could only be compensated by the extraordinary high prices which have been obtained of late for the product."[39] After 1865, cotton prices declined with the recovery of production in the U.S. South. Absent a compensating reduction in transport costs in Brazil, the fall in the world price of cotton vastly reduced the margin of feasible cultivation for Brazilian cotton growers. The weight of transport costs soon again heavily circumscribed the reach of the market for Brazilian cotton, just as it always had for most Brazilian farm goods.

These burdens of transport were not confined to agriculture. Affordable transport was a key precondition for industrialization. Nowhere were the limited marketing perimeters arising from poor transport more clear than in the case of the crude farmer's iron widely produced in Minas Gerais. The observations of nineteenth-century iron experts illustrate precisely the way in which pre-rail transport worked against the extension of markets. Indeed, the implications of their analyses conforms with the empirical results obtained in later chapters of this volume. In Minas, the cost of carrying iron overland in the 1880s was between 800 réis ($800) and 860 réis per ton-kilometer.[40] Dr. Henrique Gorceix, the leading mining engineer in the province, noted that carrying one ton of iron a distance of 186 kilometers effectively doubled the delivered price of iron over its price at the foundry in 1880. Costly overland transport imposed severe limits on the market that could be served by an iron foundry.

The extent to which backward transport conditions bounded product markets is illustrated by substituting the freight rail charges encountered elsewhere in Brazil for the *mineiro* pack animal rates. Had that very same region of Minas Gerais been served by the Dom Pedro II railroad in 1888, the per-kilometer freight rate for iron would have been, at most, less than one-fourth the charge by mule.[41] By rail, the cost of hauling iron 200 kilometers would have added only 25 percent to its delivered price, instead of the 100 percent increase incurred when shipment was made by pack animal. That same ton of iron, shipped at the railroad freight rates, could have been carried almost 900 kilometers before the delivered price would have doubled the "factory-gate" price.

The pre-rail freight charges cited for Minas are apparently among the lowest at that time in the regions studied by contemporaries. As one traveled to the north, "where the means of communication are even worse," the unit charge to carry iron was higher still. There, the price of delivered iron goods was so high that common iron implements were rare. Iron "became almost a luxury good, and it is a sign of great abundance to have one's animals branded."[42] To carry a ton of iron ingots on mule back to Diamantina, a 340-kilometer journey from Ouro Preto, would have cost some 1$365 per kilometer in 1880, and the 170-kilometer trip to Conceição would have cost 1$553 per kilometer—almost twice the per-kilometer charge around Ouro Preto. For this same distance, the railroad freight charges would have been but one-eighth of the mule rate.[43]

The efficiency consequences of this problem are clear in the context of high overland-transport costs. Product markets were badly fragmented and autarchic. Freight charges drove a large wedge between the producers and consumers of transportable products and limited profoundly the degree of market integration and the resultant gains from trade and regional specialization. Output and income across the economy were low as a result. The highly restricted margins of cultivation resulting from that wedge meant, for example, that wheat grown in the interior of Rio Grande do Sul could not even compete in coastal Brazilian ports with imported grains from North America, so costly was transport to market.[44]

Brazilians complained about the sorry state of travel on public roads in the early nineteenth century, regularly seeking government aid.[45] The very conditions that made road building so difficult in the first place compounded the impediments to internal improvements. One consul observed that "the floods of winter render the maintenance of any roads in the interior beyond the mule paths almost impossible."[46] Given the difficulties of movement, there were frequent demands for government assistance in effecting road improvements. More surprising is the fact that, in spite of the attention the problem attracted, those improvements garnered only limited investment from Brazil's central government. Institutional arrangements explain in part the relative lack of involvement on the part of central authorities. The Additional Act of 1834 to the Brazilian Constitution of 1824 vested provincial administrations with authority over public works, highways, and navigation within their borders.[47] Those provisions did not preclude central-government involvement in improvements. Officials of the ministries of interior and agriculture did keep tabs on transport conditions, and the government occasionally became directly involved with projects designed to attract colonists, or those that were otherwise in the service of important interests.[48] However, with a few exceptions, the Imperial administration simply transferred a modicum of fiscal resources to the provinces, leaving the provision of the additional resources needed for road construction and maintenance up to provincial authorities. With respect to roads, as late as 1878 Brazil's agriculture minister noted: "Lamentably, the municipalities have no income, provincial income is insufficient, and in the present financial and economic circumstances the State has to attend to multiple duties, and cannot undertake what a vast plan of communications would require."[49] The road projects that were underwritten by provincial governments had to be carefully selected to insure the best use of the limited revenues available to them; even then, construction and maintenance works might well be abandoned when financial difficulties arose.[50]

Where government failed to command and allocate resources for roads, private firms seemed to fare little better. At mid-century a number of wagon road companies were created in Brazil, devoted to establishing improved highways in regions where their organizers anticipated that agricultural conditions would enable them to tap future production for export. Wagon roads, particularly when paved with crushed stone and possessing good bridges, certainly improved the conditions of overland transport. They did so, however, only with the additional costs stemming from higher investment and maintenance requirements. While the upgraded routes made for less wear and tear on animals, travelers, and merchandise, they did not fundamentally alter the technology of transport. Stone paving was expensive, as were repairs and upkeep. Initial clearing and construction was costly as well, requiring heavy outlays on the part of organizers. Charges to ship freight in 1870 on the busiest of the improved roads in the far south, the Estrada da Graciosa, actually exceeded the costs of shipment by mule elsewhere.[51] On the much-vaunted União e Indústria road, which linked Petrópolis to Juíz de Fora, the maximum freight rates were set by contract with the province of Rio de Janeiro in 1859. Even there, those charges were high, rivaling mule freight rates on the less-improved roads of São Paulo.[52] High as those rates were, they were insufficient to cover the capital costs of the road company, even before it countenanced railroad competition.[53] There were clearly limits to the efficiency gains in transport that could be generated by road improvements in the nineteenth century, and Brazil would await the construction and expansion of railroads before the costs arising from the overland movement of freight and passengers would be reduced.

Waterways

That transport conditions might be seen as a drag on economic progress in Brazil comes as a bit of a surprise when considering the country's natural endowment of waterways. A glance at the map reveals an extensive array of rivers running through Brazil's interior. Among these the most prominent were the Amazon, Tocantins, Parnaiba, São Francisco, Jequitinonha, Rio Doce, Paraíba do Sul, and the Paraná.[54] Indeed, with one of the largest river systems in the world, one would expect that Brazil's internal waterways might present ample opportunities for cheap inland navigation, much akin to the Mississippi and its tributaries in the United States. Moreover, coastal transport was widely available along Brazil's Atlantic seaboard. Coastwise shipment, or *cabotagem*, was much less costly than overland transport, and proved to be important both before and after the construction of railroads.[55] Similarly, freely navigable rivers (or major portions thereof), where available, provided perfectly effective substitutes for overland shipment. In the regions served by such waterways freight shipment and passenger travel by boat predominated in the nineteenth century.

Yet rivers in much of Brazil were useless for long-haul freight service.[56] Except for the Amazon and its tributaries, Brazilians did not rely upon internal waterways for a large share of the economy's long-haul transport service. The railroads that were constructed after mid-century served precisely those areas that lacked navigable waterways. Over the long term, it was in those very regions that agronomic endowments proved most favorable to commercial farming. Indeed, because of its insalubrious tropical environment and the absence of readily marketable commodities, little settlement ever occurred in the Amazon basin. Ironically, despite the river's ready navigability, the rates charged for shipment by boat in the nineteenth century were held by contemporaries to be quite high.[57] Still, while the Amazon's relatively cheap transport potential was tremendously useful for shipping rubber, few other opportunities developed in the region. As for the remainder of Brazil's settled far north and part of the northeast, the first major survey of river transport conditions, conducted in 1907, summed it up rather abruptly, reporting that "like Ceará, Rio Grande do Norte, and Parahyba, Pernambuco has no river navigation."[58]

Major rivers located in other relatively important regions of settlement typically proved only partly navigable. The Rio São Francisco, Brazil's most important interior waterway after the Amazon, first opened to steam navigation in 1867, but its upper portion was "much impeded by rapids and falls."[59] Those seeking to travel into the interior from the coast found the river viable from Pirapora to Petrolina-Joazeiro, but beyond that navigation was interrupted by various obstacles. Movement on the river was blocked entirely by the steep Paulo Affonso falls. Through passage, along with the prospects of the region itself, depended ultimately on connecting the São Francisco Valley to the coast by rail.[60] By contrast, Alagôas benefited from the navigable lower stretch of the São Francisco, and by the twentieth century numerous small boats, *barcaças*, along with a steam navigation company, plied the river in the state.[61] Of Brazil's littoral states south of the Amazon, Bahia was the most navigable. Although it was served at various points along the São Francisco by a major shipping firm, the Empreza de Navegação Bahiana Steam Navigation Company, almost all of the state's river traffic was concentrated close to ports near the capital.

Rivers in what would become the more economically dynamic region of the center-south were even less useful for carrying freight. The Paraíba do Sul, in the heart of the nineteenth-century coffee-growing region, presented a poor means of transport, "the river being so broken by rocks in many places, requiring a skillful navigation."[62] At mid-century coffee was sent to market over intermittent stretches, such as that from Resende to Barra do Piraí. By 1863 there were forty boats with capacities ranging from 300 arrobas

(4.5 metric tons) to as many as 1,000 arrobas (15 metric tons) moving on this stretch of the river.[63] These were put out of business soon after the extension of the railroad through the valley and provide one of the few localized cases where rivers and rails were substitutes in an economically important region. Just like the Rio São Francisco, the Paraíba do Sul could not be navigated all the way to the coast, and two of Brazil's earliest railroads were constructed precisely to connect the Paraíba Valley with the port city of Rio de Janeiro. Once the wave of coffee had passed through the Valley in the 1890s, the river garnered little notice except as another obstacle to traverse. By the turn of the century the limited viability of the river no longer attracted attention. Its natural limitations and its diminished stature as a trade route were characterized by the observation that "the rivers that bathe the state of Rio de Janeiro do not serve well for navigation."[64]

São Paulo possessed a number of potentially important waterways. Yet, to the extent that the rivers in the western part of the province were navigable, they flowed toward the Rio Paraná, rather than toward the Brazilian coast, which was of little immediate help in moving goods and people in and out of settled areas. Moreover, the waterways survey reported that "the Tietê, Paranapanema, Rio Grande and its great tributaries, among them the Mogy-Guassu, Piracicaba and others, do not permit navigation except in small stretches, thanks to the large number of rapids that obstruct the bed."[65] Brazil's far south would prove to possess a fertile agricultural hinterland, but in Paraná the rivers were "of no importance."[66] Like São Paulo, Paraná was "cut by large and voluminous rivers; however, these serve more to fertilize the lands through which they pass than for navigation, such are the obstacles they pose to boats, even those of small dimensions."[67] Rio Grande do Sul had slightly better river access to its interior, but movement across the state could only be effected overland, and that required crossing the *serra* with pack animals.

Especially striking was the dearth of opportunities for uninterrupted long-haul river transport deep in Brazil's western provinces, in spite of the fact that rivers penetrated far into the region, joining it to the Amazon Basin. Mato Grosso possessed numerous such waterways, but they were so impeded that by the twentieth century the province depended on the Madeira-Mamoré railroad to connect the navigable portions of its rivers. Various rivers crossed Goiás, the most important of which was the Araguaya. It proved to be sufficiently obstructed that most freight moved overland to and from Rio de Janeiro, even through the turn of the century.[68] In 1864 the cost of transporting goods to the region from the coast by pack animal increased the final delivered prices of relatively high-value merchandise in the far west by as much as a factor of five.[69]

As in the case of overland communications, Brazil's central government undertook only modest efforts to improve the access to, and navigability of, inland waterways. Internal improvements of this variety rarely bore fruit in the nineteenth century. Sundry schemes to open up obstructed rivers, and even connect them via a series of canals, were pondered and studied after mid-century.[70] The Brazilian agriculture ministry, charged with improving internal communications, intermittently commissioned explorations and project assessments for various waterways.[71] Although contemporary cost-benefit analyses frequently presented a rather rosy picture of the expected results of river improvements, it seems that few, if any, of the projects were undertaken. While all may have been technically feasible, the anticipated expenses of dredging, channeling, and canal building proved prohibitive. As the century progressed the cost effectiveness of such measures diminished greatly in the presence of new technologies like the railroad.

The single most important way in which the Brazilian government promoted river transport before 1914 was by paying subsidies to shipping companies operating on the navigable sections of major waterways. Subsidies were not limited to riverboats. Coastwise shipping firms also benefited from various incentive arrangements effected with the government. By 1882 the central government subsidized the operations of nine different coastal and riverine steamship lines, each of which provided small to modest levels of transport services.[72] In 1908 some thirteen different major shipping lines carried freight and passengers along Brazil's major waterways and coastline. Eight of these collected government subsidies for the transport services they produced.[73]

The coastwise carrying trade was another important form of water transport in Brazil. For the most part, it complemented, rather than substituted for, overland shipment. The coastwise movement of goods and people had been important to the commerce of the country since the arrival of Europeans. Constrained only by the accessibility of ports and the limits to the shipping technology itself, coastal shipment, or *cabotagem*, provided an inexpensive, reasonably secure, and timely mode of transport. Early railroads in Brazil almost always began at a port and quickly headed inland, precisely to avoid the prospects of competing with coastal steamers and smaller cargo boats. Rail lines ran parallel with the coast over long distances only when they were so far in the interior that water competition was a remote concern. So relatively superior was coastal movement that neither roads, nor the railroads that followed them, could hope to compete, much less prevail, over the ships that regularly plied coastal ports.

In Brazil there was a potentially important exception to the purely complementary character of coastal shipping and overland transport by railroad.

In cases where railroads replaced the joint overland–coastwise provision of transport service, some substitution between rails and water was clearly present. This possibility is of particular interest, because the analysis in the following chapters takes non-rail shipment by land, rather than by water, as the relevant substitute mode for railroads. However, should it be the case that an appreciable portion of railroad transport services could have been supplied by coastwise shipping, then the assumption of pure complementarity between water shipment and overland transport is unwarranted. In terms of the argument about the substitutability of various modes of carrying in Brazil, the larger the share of the "coastal" portion of joint coastal-overland shipment during the pre-rail era, the less realistic is the use of mules alone as the relevant substitute for railroads.

Some evidence for the presence of joint overland–coastal shipment may be gleaned from the economic geography of the littoral before 1850. Before the extension of the nation's railroads, the Brazilian coast was marked by numerous small ports. These ports typically located their economic origins in a purely local product, such as sugar and rum in the case of Paratí. Later on, some of those ports came to link interior producers of other goods to larger port cities up and down the coast. Many of these smaller ports declined when inland railroads drew off their commerce with the interior. Such cases make it possible to argue that, in the absence of railroads, freight would not have been carried solely by pack animals, but would have instead been carried by some combination of land and water modes of conveyance. To the extent that water is a substitute for rails, the importance ascribed to the railroad in Chapter 4 in relieving transport bottlenecks would be exaggerated. Indeed, the degree of that overstatement would be proportional to the share of transport services accounted for by the joint water-overland shipment in the pre-rail era. However, the fact that so few of Brazil's rail lines paralleled the coast indicates that railroads held no competitive advantage in this market. Railroads and the coastwise trade were complements, not substitutes.

Conclusion

The physical inaccessibility and relative economic isolation of Brazil's fertile interior regions resulted mainly from the limited possibilities for shipment by river. That this feature made a big difference to the economy can best be illustrated through the example provided by transport on the Amazon River. The charge to shippers for 1 ton-kilometer of freight service on the Amazon was around $o96 in 1913. Charging all of the government subsidy to the Amazon River Steam Navigation Company in that year against the firm's freight services would raise the unit cost of shipment to around $127.[74] Neither charge is very far from the average charge for the same service on Brazil's railroads that year. The availability of transport services that were so inexpensive in Brazil's far north stands in sharp contrast to the dearth of affordable interior transport elsewhere in the country. The implication of this is striking. If those interior regions of Brazil whose opening to intensive trade and production awaited the construction of railroads had instead been served by rivers that were as readily navigable as the Amazon, the transport cost burden of overland shipment would have been virtually irrelevant. In that case, the impact of the railroad as a relatively more efficient transport technology would have been vastly reduced. Or, in other words, had the Tocantins and Araguaya in Brazil's far west been as navigable as the Cumberland River in the United States, had the Paraíba Valley been served by the St. Johns River, the highlands of São Paulo by the Ohio River, the *agreste* and *sertão* of Brazil's northeast by the Tennessee River, and Santa Catarina by the Chattahoochee, then Brazil's natural endowment of waterways would have permitted transport with an efficiency equal to that of the eastern United States. The real resource costs from transport would have been vastly reduced. The point is that Brazil south of the Amazon did not possess such an endowment of readily navigable waterways, and the fact that shipment by river in 1913 was as cheap as by rail was meaningless for those regions that historically relied on beasts of burden for transport services.

In short, before the construction of railroads a large share of all but the most localized freight services in Brazil was overland, and for most of Brazil, river transport was complementary to overland conveyance. Railroads, when constructed, put muleteers out of business, but typically had little bearing on the coastwise or riverine shipment of goods and passengers. The enduring dearth of a large, interconnected grid of railroads after the turn of the century, linking north to south and the coast to the deep interior, is often taken as evidence that the transport improvements undertaken somehow failed to integrate the national market. That view treats railroad lines mechanically, holding that they connected sections of Brazil more closely to overseas markets than to Brazil itself. It misses entirely the complementary character of railroads and waterways. The coast of Brazil was almost perfectly integrated by relatively cheap transport. As one observer put it, "The great means of communication in Brazil has been, is, and probably always will be the sea."[75] What mattered to the prospects for development in Brazil's interior was the absence of ready substitutes for shipment by pack animal. That lacuna meant that any amelioration of the poor internal-transport conditions that prevailed at mid-century would have to await the arrival of the railroad.

Chapter 3

Railroad Policy, Finance, and Expansion

Despite Brazil's need to alleviate its horrendous transport bottleneck, the country entered the railroad age only after the middle of the nineteenth century. The sheer expense inherent to large investment projects with high fixed costs complicated railroad development. That railroads appeared in Brazil several decades after the technology first migrated across the Atlantic indicates the extent to which railroad expansion was delayed by both capital market conditions and ineffective public intervention. Railroad development depended critically on financial conditions, at home and abroad, and on public promotion. Public promotion took two main forms: government subsidy to private investment and outright government ownership.

The principal barrier to improving overland transport in Imperial Brazil was the difficulty in obtaining financing. Railroads were costly and lumpy investments, requiring previously unimaginable amounts of capital in Brazil. Moreover, as investment projects their prospects were uncertain. There was clearly demand for transport services in Brazil, but it was unclear if that demand was large enough to remunerate transport projects with large capital requirements, and hence high fixed costs. If the depth of Brazil's market for transport services was unknown, and the railroad's prospects uncertain, how were the nation's producers and consumers to obtain the railroads they sought? Government subsidy proved to be the mechanism that attracted investment both at home and from abroad, sparking Brazil's first wave of railroad development.

This chapter proceeds in four sections. The first part examines how the government eventually succeeded in attracting railroad investment to Brazil. The chapter then turns to the sources of private railroad financing, both foreign and domestic. The third section charts the role of the state as an increasingly important owner and operator of railroads. The chapter concludes by tracing the general contours of Brazilian railroad expansion through 1913.

Government Promotion of Railroads

Three fundamental features of government involvement in railroad development emerged under the Empire. First, efforts to create investment incentives, in the form of guaranteeing minimum dividends to shareholders in many railroad companies, were critical to mobilizing savings, both domestically and abroad, and converting those savings into railroad-specific capital in Brazil. Second, direct government ownership and operation of railroads (including the country's largest and most heavily trafficked line) characterized a large portion of the railroad sector by 1913. Third, the rates that railroads charged for their services were regulated by the Brazilian government from the very outset. These three areas of government involvement ensured that railroad concessions, investment, and regulation emerged as heavily politicized activities.

The granting of concession—a common government function everywhere—assigned to an individual the right to construct a particular railroad. Concession alone was insufficient to promote railroad development, as the challenges confronting these projects were formidable in Brazil. Indeed, the railroad came to Brazil relatively late. As a transport technology, steam locomotion first arrived in the Americas in the 1820s. Railroads began to diffuse to Latin America not long after the early expansion of the railroad system in the United States. By 1837, Cuba, still a colony of Spain, possessed the first operating steam railroad in the western hemisphere outside of the United States. The creation of railroads elsewhere in Latin America faltered soon thereafter. Loan default in the early post-independence years cut off much of the region from long-term foreign investment until after mid-century.[1] Notably, the relative scarcity of financial capital throughout Latin America lamentably did not induce institutional responses that made for more vibrant domestic capital markets. In most of Spanish America fund-raising for military purposes diverted resources from internal improvements. While Brazil was more orderly than Spanish America through the 1830s and 1840s, the political uncertainty of the First Reign and the Regency was sufficient to forestall attempts to construct the country's first railroads. Before 1852, the

Brazilian government displayed a familiar reluctance to involve itself heavily in railroad projects. In the same fashion in which it eschewed expensive commitments to large-scale road and waterway improvements, it avoided railroad policies that might lead to heavy fiscal demands on the new state.

The Imperial government made its first railroad concession in 1835, soliciting a line to link the Côrte (Rio de Janeiro) to one of the adjoining provinces. In spite of great interest, a pressing need for cheap transport, and the ready expenditure of energy and resources on the part of entrepreneurs, no road was ever constructed under the concession's original terms because no concessionaire ever raised sufficient funds. In an attempt to ensure that Brazilian shippers would reap immediate benefits from the new technology, that first concession dictated the maximum rates that could be charged for freight and passenger services.[2] Given the rate structure imposed as a provision of the concession, it is likely that potential investors expected low to negative profits. Early uncertainty over the prospects of turning a profit on lines for which the potential traffic levels were unknown and for which rates were regulated made investors particularly wary. Only after attaching a minimum guaranteed dividend to the concession did the Brazilian government find that financiers were forthcoming with funds.

Various groups in pre-1850 Brazil, landowners prominent among them, had long clamored for government aid to improve communication and reduce the high costs of overland transport. Brazil's post-1850 transport policies were a direct response to their demands. In spite of the existence of an open concessions policy and piecemeal incentives to attract railroad investment, the expansion of the system lagged badly through the 1860s and 1870s. Brazilian railroad concessions merely ceded permission to organize a company and build a railroad on a particular route. They were not especially difficult to garner, since they were by and large without cost to the government. By 1890, Brazil's central and state governments had granted some 255 concessions for privately organized railroad trunk lines and extensions.[3] While each case differed in its details, concessions shared in common several basic elements.[4] The essential one was the right to construct a line across properties along the approved route. A feature many concessions shared was the right to exploit woodlands near the planned route of the railroad for fuel and construction materials. Yet another common feature was an exemption from import duties for construction materials and rolling stock purchased abroad. Importantly, concessions often came with a "privileged" zone of operation of various sizes, for a fixed period of time. This gave the proposed railroad protection from competition from any other lines that might later be constructed nearby, often for as long as the term of the concession. However, given the government's intent to regulate the freight and passenger rates of railroad companies, protection from potential competition proved to be a wholly inadequate incentive for investment.

Investment depended on savings. Transforming savings into investment— mobilizing capital—was neither an easy nor frictionless process. In particular, institutional arrangements were of paramount importance in obtaining investment financing. This was especially true for the large, lumpy investments that railroads entailed. Railroads required tremendous amounts of capital at the time, much more than any other kind of project. Some simple comparisons reveal just how much. By the mid-1880s, the stock of physical capital of a relatively modest railroad, such as the Recife-to-Caruarú line, while valued at less than 12 million milréis, was still more than that of Brazil's *entire* cotton textile industry.[5] A typically massive coffee *fazenda* in the Paraiba Valley in the mid-1880s, with almost 900,000 fruit-bearing coffee trees planted on more than 700 hectares and worked by almost three hundred slaves, would be assessed at a little more than half a million milréis, less than the tiniest of Brazilian railroads at the time.[6] The wealth represented by the stock of Brazilian slaves in 1887—more than 750,000 people—exceeded 338 million milréis at prevailing prices.[7] Yet the value of the reproducible physical capital in Brazilian railroads outstripped this figure by more than 40 percent. Compared to other investment projects in nineteenth-century Brazil, railroads were easily the most expensive. If mobilizing capital for industrialization was challenging, then doing so for railroads proved difficult in the extreme. In 1852 the Brazilian Parliament modified the early concessions through new legislation that guaranteed a minimum dividend on specific railroad projects as a way of assuaging investor concerns over the riskiness of these projects. Thereafter, government increasingly assumed the role of railroad promoter, and eventually owner and operator.[8] Brazil's railroad sector, however, arose in the absence of any master plan. Early intentions on the part of many officials involved constructing lines from the coast to the São Francisco River, creating what it was hoped would be a vast interior system of communications. While a number of national railroad plans appeared on paper, the lines that were ultimately subsidized and constructed were less the result of a larger vision than the government's response to countless local demands for improved transport.[9]

The burst of new concessions in the late 1860s and early 1870s was leveraged by the growth of investment guarantees following the passage of the Imperial Railroad Law of 1873.[10] While not all of those concessions bore fruit, that legislation conjoined with two external factors to speed up the pace of railroad construction in Brazil. The first of these was the falling prices of railroad inputs, namely steel rails, which reduced the cost of construction from the 1880s onward.[11] The second was a large capital outflow from Britain that made railroad financing increasingly more affordable for Brazil.[12] Gradually, government at both the central and provincial levels grew more directly involved in the construction and operation of the country's railroad sector, further fueling railroad expansion.

There were two main periods of central government legislative activity in granting railroad subsidies. The first, beginning in 1852, saw project-specific legislation that offered guaranteed dividends to investors in particular railroads. The second period, beginning in 1873, was marked by legislation that provided dividend guarantees on the first line to be constructed in each province thereafter.[13] *Fazendeiros* needing cheap transport, and potential railroad promoters, had lobbied for precisely such a measure.[14] The 1873 law was clearly designed to accelerate the construction of rail lines across the Empire, especially in regions where the prospects of such projects turning a profit for their owners were relatively less promising. The measure was also intended to circumvent obstacles erected by Brazil's 1860 Company Law, which made it particularly difficult to organize joint-stock companies in Brazil.

While many contemporaries welcomed the 1873 law, and far-flung regional interests were pleased that the Imperial government had weighed in to support railroad construction, early reaction was not universally sanguine. Rio de Janeiro's leading commercial newspaper contended that the law was too complicated to suit the tastes of British shareholders and investors, editorializing in favor of a more aggressive stance toward attracting investment. It stressed that "Brazil needs a complete railroad system; on it depends the welfare of the country and the development of its industry and commerce."[15] With some delay, the early project-specific guarantees, along with the guarantee provisions of the Law of 1873, gave rise to a loose array of regional networks that linked the coast to the interior and traversed the relatively more populated regions of the country.

Under the Empire public policy toward railroad concession and promotion involved various arms of government. At the base were the two houses of Parliament, the Chamber of Deputies and the Senate, which, subject to Imperial sanction, were empowered to pass authorizing legislation like the laws of 1852 and 1873. Enactment of that legislation fell under the purview of administrative law, as practiced by the Minister of Empire at first (later the Minister of Agriculture), in conjunction with the Emperor's hand-picked Council of State. Legislation reconstituting the Council in 1842 charged its Section of Empire with the study and review of all proposed public works and approval of any acts of organization or statutes, along with the approval of all foreign companies, irrespective of the nature of their business. The passage of Brazil's first Commercial Code in 1850, and its parliamentary modifications in 1860 and 1882, left this feature of railroad concession untouched, and Brazil's Council of State screened requests for railroad concession and subsidy until the demise of the Empire in 1889. In 1861 the government established a Ministry of Agriculture in order to administer policies bearing on agriculture, manufacturing, communications, and public works. While the new Ministry took over from the Ministry of Empire the day-to-day work of the government in railroad concessions, it continued to refer all proposals for concession and subsidy to the Section of Empire for approval.[16]

Because Brazil's guarantee policy implied payments to railroad companies from the Treasury when a guaranteed railroad's net revenues proved insufficient to pay dividends, the Ministry of Treasury also played a role in railroad policy, as did the Section of Finance of the Council of State. In particular, requests to increase the amount of capital enjoying a dividend guarantee, operations of guaranteed railroads that potentially impinged on government finance, and the expenditure on government-owned railroads, all required the study and approval of the Section of Finance, along with approval from the full Council of State.[17] The interplay between Parliament, on the one hand, and the administrative apparatus on the other, was both subtle and complex. Though the Cabinet had considerable leeway to assign subsidies after they had been authorized, it could not step far beyond the bounds imposed by the Chamber. If it did so, it potentially confronted a withdrawal of confidence and political crisis.

With its guaranteed dividends, Brazil subsidized railroads in a very different fashion from the United States. There, most of the early assistance to railroads was local.[18] Later on, federal government aid came in the form of land grants. In Brazil, by contrast, the bulk of aid to railroads came from the central government. Provinces could provide guarantees as well, but given their lack of fiscal resources, such guarantees ultimately implied the backing of the central treasury.[19] Virtually none of the aid to railroads came in the form of land grants. Some of the aid was granted as construction subsidies, in lieu of guaranteed dividends to investors.[20] But most of Brazil's railroad subsidies were in dividend guarantees. This policy reflected features of Brazilian political economy that differed greatly from the United States. First of all, given its severely underdeveloped capital markets, only Brazil's central government, with its reputation for having never defaulted on a foreign loan, commanded the credibility needed to guarantee investor returns. This was especially true in the mid–nineteenth century, when various countries competitively pursued similar railroad subsidy programs.[21] Second of all, to provide land grants

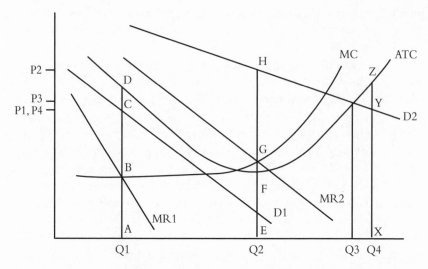

Figure 3.1. Three scenarios showing the relationship between railroad revenue and cost for different levels of demand.

NOTE: ATC is the average total cost of producing a unit of transport services. MC represents the marginal cost. D1 and D2 are demand curves, whereas MR1 and MR2 represent the corresponding marginal revenue curves that tie the quantity of transport services (Q) to its price (P) in the market. Q1, Q2, and Q3 represent the three different scenarios for the quantity of services produced, which are elaborated in the text.

Brazil would have had to establish clearly defined property rights in land and sort out which lands were truly publicly owned and which were not. For both practical and political reasons such an approach to subsidy proved unfeasible.

Subsidies to railroads in Brazil were required because private financiers feared that their profits would prove insufficient. Investor concerns stemmed from three distinct sources. First, the level of demand for a railroad's services was truly unknown before the railroad was built. Second, railroad construction and operation were capital-intensive activities that required large amounts of capital relative to outlays on labor and fuel, which meant that high financing costs had to be met even before the railroad entered operation. Moreover, railroads were "lumpy." They had to operate at a sufficient scale to make business sense. Lumpiness meant that the initial project could not be too small. This was quite different from many industries, such as textile mills, where single looms could be added to the firm's capital stock as needed. The third reason investors required subsidies was that railroads were especially expensive in Brazil, where the same terrain and climate that made roads so difficult to construct and maintain also raised the costs of railroad construction and operation over what it would otherwise be.

Since a railroad involved hefty financial charges and possibly years of no dividends, while at the same time potentially confronting limited demand in the market for its services, potential investors had plenty of reason to be wary. But railroad investors, especially foreign investors, had yet a fourth concern. Their investment would be at risk of expropriation, if not through outright seizure, by the government reneging on its guarantees. Individual investors would be left with little recourse under such circumstances. Once the railroad was built, it could not be easily dug up and hauled away. As a result, the roadbed, and even rolling stock, were potentially sunk costs by the time the railroad was in operation. Should the Brazilian government choose not to pay the guaranteed dividends once a railroad was in place, all the while setting the prices of railroad services very low, then investor profits would suffer greatly. The effect would be a drawn-out expropriation, an outcome investors naturally sought to avoid at all costs.

Figure 3.1 illustrates these obstacles to railroad investment in Brazil. In the figure, the cost of producing a unit of transport services is given by the average total cost (ATC) curve, which includes both fixed and operating costs. MC represents the marginal cost curve, the cost the railroad would pay to produce an additional unit of transport services. The first obstacle to creating the railroad was insufficient demand for its services, or more correctly, the fear on the part of potential investors that demand would prove insufficient when the railroad was built. In the first scenario, let demand for transport in the region served by the railroad be given by D_1, the schedule that relates the quantity of transport services (Q) and their price (P) in the market. To maximize its profits, the railroad will produce a quantity (Q_1, in this scenario) where the additional revenue it receives just equals the cost of supplying the last unit of output, given by the intersection of MC and MR_1 (marginal revenue) at point B. This is level Q_1, and the price, read off the demand curve, is P_1. Here, the unit revenue is represented by the line AC, which is greater than line AB. As such, revenues are more than sufficient to cover the marginal costs, which are largely the operating costs of the railroad. However, the unit cost, represented by line AD, clearly exceeds unit revenues (line AC). As such, the railroad cannot recover its total costs, and thus cannot produce investor profits that are sufficient to justify the investment. Note that, even if the railroad could discriminate perfectly among its customers, extracting from them the entire consumer's surplus, it still could not turn a profit if the demand schedule lay below the average cost curve. Confronted with this possibility, investors would go elsewhere. Note here as well that, should the government intervene by setting a high price for the railroad's services, it would provide no help at all. If the government were to dictate a higher price, say P2 or greater, shippers would simply vanish from this market.

The second obstacle to investment was the risk of expropriation-by-regulation. Given the same technology, and hence the same cost curves, suppose the railroad now confronts sufficient demand, represented by schedule D2. If the railroad could set its own price, then it would maximize its profits again by producing a level of transport services where the marginal revenue (represented by MR2) just equals marginal cost, at point G. There the railroad produces Q2 units of transport services, and sets its price at P2. In this case, the profits would be handsome. Unit revenue (EH) is not only sufficient to cover the marginal costs of service (EG), but is greater than average cost (EF). The unit profit here is HF, which is clearly positive. Investors would be eager to construct and operate a railroad under these circumstances.

Government, serving its shipping constituents, would unlikely brook this situation. As the government has regulatory powers, it, and not the railroad, selects the price the railroad charges. One solution that would keep the railroad running, yet eliminate the "gouging" of shippers, would be to set price to equal the average cost, at P_3. In that case, the railroad could earn the market rate of profit, while shippers would get a price less than P_4. In fact, this would be a welfare-improving step that would make the economy bigger than if there were no intervention at all. But there would be nothing to stop the government from pushing price even lower. Indeed, it could set price at P_3. At that price, shippers would consume Q_4 units of the railroad's services. For the railroad, unit revenues would come to XY, less than cost, which would be XZ, and profit would be negative. The railroad could choose to shut down, but it would be costly indeed to close up shop, dig up track, sell off rolling stock, and the like. Irrespective of whatever price it might set early on, in this stylized exposition the government has no way to commit credibly to not set price even lower. Confronted with the risk of expropriation in this manner, investors would shy away from the project.

A variant of these two obstacles is further suggested by the diagram. Let the initial demand confronting the railroad be D1. Once in place, however, cheap transport services would encourage the expansion of activities that use transport intensively. Over time, then, demand in this scenario would grow, shifting to D2. If railroad investors were confident of this, and sufficiently patient, they could hope to recoup early losses in later periods. Nonetheless, so long as government could adjust price, the railroad would find itself back in the second situation, with the same implications for its investors.

For Brazil these mechanisms conjoined to create a problem that markets alone could not surmount. Investors required some assurance that they would not be hit with permanent losses when they chose to apply their funds to railroads. While there were several possible ways of doing this, the option Brazilian officials selected was to promise a transfer of income to investors in the case that unit revenue fell below unit cost. This took the form of dividend guarantees, set as a percentage of the pre–agreed upon value of the railroad's capital. In the first instance, this meant that investors would receive from the government a unit subsidy equal to CD, the amount required to bring revenues up to a normal rate of profit. In the second instance, it meant that if price was set too low, the government would compensate investors with YZ. In the third instance, the government subsidy further smoothed out the time profile of investor earnings, compensating them until demand for the railroad's services grew to a sufficient level, thus overcoming investor impatience.

These examples, set in logical rather than historical time, lead to a further question. Could not the Brazilian government renege on its promise to transfer subsidy income to railroad investors? Indeed it could, and there were several ways it might do so. At any moment of any day, the Brazilian state could have ceased to pay the promised subsidies. Or, instead, it could set fares so low that, even with the income transfer, railroads would have to use the subsidies to cover their variable costs, leaving them with no profit. In cases such as these, the beneficiaries of reneging would be the state and consumers of transport services. That the Brazilian government did not systematically pursue these measures requires an explanation rooted in the long term. Expropriation could easily have brought very high gains in the short run. But it would also have burned Brazil's bridge to the capital market. Short-term gains of this sort would have brought very high long-term costs. Once-bitten, twice-shy investors (whether Brazilian or foreign) would not have returned to invest again. Anticipating a continuing need for capital, the Brazilian state could not afford to alienate investors permanently. The net present value of doing so was no doubt large and negative.

Given that railroad development in Brazil derived its greatest political support from an important domestic constituency, foreign investors were all too aware of the risks involved. Indeed, only when the government guaranteed them a minimum return on their capital were funds forthcoming. Guarantees assuaged the two main concerns of investors. With respect to insufficient demand, a guaranteed minimum return would provide investors with the opportunity cost of their funds until sufficient demand in the region had developed. Moreover, the guarantee mechanism put the Brazilian government on record. That record was part and parcel of the reputational mechanism that smoothed lending in the international capital markets. Should Brazil default, or expropriate, then it would find it costly in the extreme to get new loans when needed. Investors knew that, and understood that with the guarantees came the government's credibility in financial markets. It could expropriate anytime it wanted, but to do so would mean severe costs to Brazil.

The policy of subsidizing railroads using dividend guarantees was well received both within Brazil and abroad. Favorable publicity both confirmed and bolstered investor interest and confidence in Brazilian railroads.[22] Guarantees to pay dividends were extended to an ever-increasing number of new railroad projects through the end of the Empire. However, from 1890 onward the Republican government granted relatively few new dividend guarantees. The more prominent feature of government involvement in railroads became direct ownership on the part of the state.

Railroad Finance

Foreign and domestic investors responded to the dividend guarantees established by Brazil's central and provincial governments by channeling funds into new railroads. While an important portion of early railroad investment was domestic, much of it was foreign in origin. More generally, the second half of the nineteenth century witnessed a tremendous export of capital from the advanced, industrializing countries of the North Atlantic "center" to the countries of the relatively laggard "periphery."[23] In Brazil a large share of this capital inflow took the form of investments in railroads. Numerous railroad companies, including early major lines such as the Recife and San Francisco, the Bahia and San Francisco, and the San Paulo Railway, were constructed and operated by British companies, funded directly by shareholders in the City of London.[24] Such lines were archetypes of the "free-standing" companies that typified British overseas investment, matching British capital to projects with the prospect of profit.[25] In the context of the relatively thin and segmented Brazilian capital market, access to both debt and equity finance in Britain proved in the long term to be indispensable to the expansion of Brazil's railroad sector.

At the time, Brazil was simply one among numerous overseas outlets for British capital. Indeed, early on, the capital flows from Britain targeted the expanding North American republic as one of the major recipients of funds.[26] In the southern hemisphere Brazil was the single largest Latin American recipient of British capital through the late 1880s (Argentina held that distinction thereafter).[27] Outside of government debt, the largest sector of British investment in Brazil was railroads.[28] Through 1930, somewhere between one-third and one-half of all foreign investment in Brazil stemming from securities issued in overseas markets went to finance railroad development.[29] Considering that an appreciable share of the public debt was issued in London for government-built lines, direct and indirect railroad investment was easily the single most important category of British capital flows to Brazil.

Brazilian domestic savings further provided an important source of railroad investment, although they were wholly inadequate for the total requirements of the railroad sector, for two reasons. First, only those Brazilians wealthy enough to accumulate savings were in a position to invest in any activity, and for the rural upper class, slaves (before the 1880s), and to a lesser extent land, were attractive investments with solid profits. Second, Brazil lacked an efficient capital market by the standards of the advanced economies, and this made it difficult to mobilize large amounts of capital for any kind of project. Informal credit was costly, and banks were, for much of this period, limited to commercial operations. Investment banking did not exist, although banks did buy shares of companies to hold in their own asset portfolios.[30] The Rio de Janeiro stock market channeled investment into various activities through the issue of both debt and equity, but the overall level of activity remained low until the 1880s.

The sources of railroad investment from within Brazil were diverse, as the experience of the early railroads suggests. In the case of the Dom Pedro II railroad, connecting the port of Rio de Janeiro to the interior Paraíba Valley, early investors were overwhelmingly urban. More than 90 percent of its shares in 1860 were held by institutions and individuals in the city.[31] The bulk of its investors each held 50 or fewer of the total of 60,000 shares issued up to that point, and only twelve investors held 500 or more shares. By contrast, the Companhia Paulista, organized and launched in the late 1860s, tapped mainly rural investors in the interior of São Paulo. Shares of stock for the Paulista were peddled virtually door to door in the interior of the province, using the reputational cachet of the local elite, along with a provincial dividend guarantee, as a means to reducing the risk perceived by investors. The very *fazendeiros* who stood to gain so much from the reduction of transport costs were prominent among the company's investors.[32] Although over the life of the company some individual investors held very large amounts of the company's stock, by 1900 its investors, including a large number of women, numbered more than 1,000 and most of these held appreciable if modest amounts of equity.[33] The Mogyana, another major São Paulo railroad, similarly began with local capital. Of its twenty-one founding shareholders, no fewer than seven were coffee planters, two were coffee brokers, three were merchants, and two more were lawyers, all in the region of Mogy-Mirim.[34]

On the British side investors in Brazilian railroads doubtless included the full range of people participating in the London stock market. Shareholder lists for the British railroads are even more scarce than those for Brazilian lines, and uncertainty attaches to assessing the degree of concentration of stock and bond ownership. Still, participation in the British capital market was more widespread than participation in Brazil. Typically, new issues of equity on Brazilian railroads were eagerly snapped up in London, no doubt made attractive by the guaranteed dividends. The initial public offer of a relatively small line, the Alagôas Railway Company, found the whole stock of capital subscribed in London almost immediately. Within three hours of its launching on the exchange, investors had requested five times the number of shares available.[35]

These initial subscribers to stock and bond offerings in London were, by definition, a critical source of finance, and ongoing equity holders were important because of the control they exercised as voting owners over each railroad's future plans and activities. Nonetheless, the typical shareholder was far removed from the day-to-day operation and business of any particular railroad. In this regard, more important were the concessionaires, entrepreneurs, and directors of these lines, themselves often important shareholders, who created, managed, and planned the future of each company. On both sides of the Atlantic, these men tended to be among the most active—and well-connected—in the business and political community. Their resources, access to information, and expertise were indispensable for organizing and running costly railroad projects.

The typical British railroad in Brazil began with its organizers purchasing an unexploited or undeveloped concession held by native Brazilian entrepreneurs. About the time a guaranteed dividend was bestowed by the Brazilian government, organizers would launch the company on the London exchange. British railroad organizers and directors formed a distinct group. By drawing a sample of the directorates (including ex-officio members) on all British-owned railroads in Brazil from business directories for 1867, 1873, 1880, 1887, and 1900, it is possible to assess the general characteristics of directors.[36] The total number of board positions in the sample comprised 139 seats. Three distinct patterns emerged. First, while there was appreciable overlap among the directors of the companies that worked lines in Brazil, the degree of interlock among directorates was not especially high. A second pattern revealed that, however little interlock existed *within* the directorates of British-owned railroads in Brazil, the degree of interlock *between* that group and the directorates of railroads elsewhere around the world was very high. While some directors of British-owned railroads in Brazil held no such similar position on any other line, and occupied their seat for only limited time, a good number of them headed up various other railroads in Britain, Europe, Africa, and India. Third, no fewer than seven of those directors were also members of the British Parliament. Though these men were chiefly "ornamental" directors, their presence made it clear that the political connections of the boards of foreign railroads in Brazil needed not be informal or veiled.[37] These men were well positioned to wield influence in the formal apparatus of British policy making.

In the early phase of British railroad investment, neither the directors of the San Paulo Railway, nor those of the Bahia and San Francisco, held seats on any other railroad anywhere in 1867, although two of the Bahia line's directors were members of Parliament (MPs).[38] The overseas interlocks of the directorate of the Recife and San Francisco, however, were extensive. In particular, the company's six directors in 1867 held among them an additional twenty-four directorships. Moreover, the overlap of directorships among these additional companies was virtually nonexistent. These directors indeed held widely scattered railroad interests. The largest portfolio was that of W. B. Greenfield, who sat on the board of no fewer than seven railroads in Britain, and another one organized to construct a line from Turin. With the gradual turnover of directors, the extreme degree of interlock on the part of the Recife line declined within a few years, but multiple directorships had become more common on the other railroads by 1873. The Bahia road retained an MP, representing Marylebone Common in the House of Commons, as director. By 1887 the Conde D'Eu and the Great Western railroads shared three directors in common, the greatest degree of interlock among directorates in Brazil found in the sample. During the 1880s and 1890s, Frank Parish, a director of the Great Western Brazil Railway linking Recife to Limoeiro, served also on the board of the Conde D'Eu line in Brazil. He further directed three Argentine railroads and two Uruguayan lines. By 1900, one year before the Brazilian government bought up many of the British-owned lines, no less than fourteen men of the thirty-seven who occupied directors' positions on British-owned Brazilian railroads also held numerous seats on other railroads headquartered in London.[39]

In short, two types of directors served on the boards of British-owned companies. The first, likely younger directors, held no other positions on railroads anywhere, but might well have sat on the boards of banks, public utilities, and other companies that do not appear in the published railroad directories. The second type was that of the experienced capitalist holding multiple important positions in a variety of British and overseas railroads, and perhaps occupying an elected political post as well. These entrepreneurs comprised a cosmopolitan class of men with special expertise in overseeing the operations and strategies of railroads at home and abroad. Both types of directors necessarily held relatively large amounts of the company's stock, and as such were important investors in their own right.

Less typical of Brazil's overseas railroad investors before 1914, but indicative of the rise of new corporate interests abroad, was Percival Farquhar and his paper behemoth, the Brazil Railway Company. Farquhar burst upon the scene in 1907, but was forced out of the Brazilian railroad business following the onset of the Great War. The Brazil Railway Company was but one of Farquhar's many vehicles for investment throughout South America.[40] Yet the company did surprisingly little. By 1913, the Brazil Railway Company owned outright or held controlling interests in some 40 percent of Brazil's total railroad track, mostly in São Paulo, but had only built one new railroad. That line, the Rio Grande–São Paulo, exploited the only concession left over from the Empire to carry with it extensive grants of land.[41] Funded by French, U.S., British, and Belgian investors, Farquhar's company devoted much of its efforts to raising more money overseas. Its operations were short-lived; by heavily leveraging the company and engaging in a large amount of debt financing, Farquhar left the firm highly vulnerable to the slightest shock. The disruption to financial markets in Europe from the outbreak of World War I quickly revealed this untenable debt load when the Brazil Railway failed to meet its bond payment, forcing the company into receivership.

Especially important in early railroad development were Brazilian entrepreneurs. Like their British counterparts, the promoters, organizers, and officers of Brazil's domestically owned railroads were men of means, connection, and influence, and their entrepreneurship manifested itself as much politically as economically. Indeed, Brazil's first steam-powered railroad was established by the most tireless (if not the most successful) of Brazil's mid-century entrepreneurs, Irineu Evangelista de Sousa, the Visconde de Mauá, in 1854. As one of the Empire's most prominent businessmen, Mauá held interests in international banking, Brazilian iron works, railroads, and a steam shipping company he founded in London for the purpose of plying the Amazon, supported by government subsidy.[42] Lacking elite origins, Mauá arrived in Rio de Janeiro and apprenticed for several merchants, including a British firm in which he ultimately became a partner.[43] With his British mentor he soon created a banking firm in Manchester, and a few years later started an iron foundry across the bay from Rio.[44] Using his own resources, a loan he obtained through his ties to government officials, and a contract obtained from the Minister of Empire to provide water pipes to Rio, the foundry initially flourished behind a wall of tariff protection. Mauá further leveraged his political connections to acquire the franchise for gas lighting in Rio de Janeiro. In a maneuver he regularly executed deftly, he soon sold that concession at an impressive profit. He did the same years later with his franchise to link Brazil to Europe by telegraph, though in the latter case his real payment was the award of the title Viscount by Brazil's Emperor. By building upon his success and branching into gas lighting and shipbuilding early on, Mauá effectively integrated vertically his iron works and his other operations, making for himself a good deal of money in the process.

Mauá organized Brazil's first railroad linking the edge of Rio de Janeiro's bay to the foot of the *serra* by exploiting a concession he acquired from the provincial government of Rio de Janeiro. He then created a joint-stock company, placing his friends as fellow directors. Mauá raised initial financing by tapping not only investors in Rio de Janeiro, but also his partners in England, along with his own wealth. The line proved a moderate financial success, boosted by government aid along the way.[45] Its operations were limited by its extension, and it mainly carried passengers from the city to the wagon road running into the *serra*, and hauled coffee descending on mule-back from the other direction. Mauá's little line was soon dwarfed by larger railroads emanating from Rio. Nonetheless, he helped put together the initial deals creating what would later be predominantly British-funded lines in São Paulo and Pernambuco, and his bank handled the accounts of the British-owned Bahia and San Francisco Railway.[46]

Francisco de Paula Mayrink was typical of Brazil's railroad promoters, defining as much as Mauá the stereotype of a Brazilian politico-economic entrepreneur. A native of Rio de Janeiro, he established a successful career in a wide variety of business activities. In the 1880s he was simultaneously president of both the Companhia Estrada de Ferro Bahia a Minas and the Estrada de Ferro Sorocabana, one of São Paulo's major railroads.[47] All the while he also headed one of Brazil's largest banks, the Banco de Crédito Real, whose capital in 1886 was second only to that of the Banco do Brazil.[48] His links to big banking in Rio later extended to the Banco Predial, the Banco Constructor, and the Banco dos Estados Unidos do Brazil. He did not limit himself to cultivating connections and business ties, but translated his success into political advance as well. Linked to the Liberal Party under the Empire, he served as a member of the Republican Congress through the turn of the century.[49] Outside of the relatively big businesses of railroads and banking, his other activities encompassed agricultural interests and two different cotton textile mills.[50]

In São Paulo, the Prado family's political and business ties epitomized the notion of political and entrepreneurial dynasty. Descendants of the Barão de Iguape, the brothers Antônio and Martinho da Silva Prado held myriad properties and political offices. Both trained with the elite in São Paulo's renowned Law School. And both were directors of the Companhia Paulista das Estradas de Ferro, the largest privately owned Brazilian railroad by the turn of the century. Antônio further served a long stint as company president. The brothers' early involvement with the railroad stemmed from the massive amounts of coffee land and large numbers of slaves the family held in the districts the railroad served. Antônio's sons, cousin, and brother-in-law, among other relatives, also served as directors of the railroad at various times. Antônio and Martinho held additional merchant and financial interests as founders and partners of a major coffee brokerage and export firm. In 1890 Antonio Prado created the Banco de Comércio e Indústria de São Paulo, which soon became São Paulo's leading bank, and of which he served as president until 1920. Martinho served as director of São Paulo's Sociedade Promotora da Immigração. An eleventh-hour abolitionist, Antônio Prado enjoyed a stellar political career as a Conservative, serving as Deputy in four different legislatures, and was appointed to the Senate by the Emperor in 1887. He also served in two cabinets, first as Minister of Agriculture, then later as Minister of Foreign Relations. Under the Republic, he was again elected to Congress. Martinho Prado was heavily involved in provincial politics under the Empire and also attained a seat in the Republican Congress.[51]

Thanks to their comfortable status as political insiders, their respective roles as major players on the business scene, and their diverse portfolios of wealth, the Prados, Mauá, and Mayrink, like all of Brazil's leading railroad developers, held the power to leverage government aid if necessary, and knew how to use those favors when they received them. Unlike the later immigrant-entrepreneurs who concentrated in São Paulo, or the merchant-industrialists of Porfirian Mexico, Brazil's leading railroad men tended to be native sons.[52] As citizens, they were eligible for public office and could exercise substantial influence directly. Mauá, Antônio and Martinho Prado, and Mayrink all served at some point in the Imperial Parliament or Republican Congress. Their position and connections no doubt gave them privileged access to valuable information, and they were poised to do battle when necessary with opponents in both the political and business realms. Personal wealth, power, and connections proved indispensable for the success of these men in garnering the concessions and the financing necessary for the development of Brazil's railroads. Together with their contemporaries in Britain they played a central role in tapping savings and channeling investment to railroads.

Government Railroads

While the private sector remained a key source of railroad finance, its importance in funding Brazil's railroad expansion diminished with time. The driving force in the railroad sector became the state. As arbiter of concession, and promoter through subsidy, the public authorities maintained control over railroad projects. However, government, in a far more direct fashion, also took on a growing share of the burden of constructing and operating Brazil's railroad enterprises. Public authorities (both national and provincial) increasingly played a more direct role in railroad development as owners and operators. A direct stake in individual railroad projects on the part of government began under the Empire with financial schemes to shore up the price of railroad stock by exchanging government bonds for shares of British-owned railroads and the Dom Pedro II in the early 1860s.[53] By the late 1860s, the Imperial government had taken over the financially troubled Dom Pedro II railroad. Increasingly thereafter, government undertook new railroad projects directly, not only extending the Dom Pedro II on a continuous basis, but also constructing lines in Brazil's north. Policy debates in the 1880s foreshadowed the Republican policy of buying up individual railroads that, in spite of providing benefits via cheap transport, had net operating revenues so low as to consistently require the guaranteed dividend payment from the Treasury in order to pay out dividends to shareholders.[54]

The Republican government that replaced Brazil's constitutional monarchy granted many fewer dividend guarantees, yet expanded dramatically the state's role as a railroad owner and operator.[55] It bought up many British-owned lines at the turn of the century, leasing them back out in most cases to British companies. As Brazil's stake in railroad expansion grew, so did the share of the railroad sector owned by government. After 1900, with the state owning most of the railroad sector, Brazil resembled Tsarist Russia; in leasing out a good deal of what it owned, however, it also leaned toward the French system.

The Imperial government undertook direct construction and operation of railroads in the 1870s and 1880s. There were two principal reasons behind

Table 3.1

Growth of Extension of Railroad Track in Service in Brazil, 1854–1913

Year	Kms of track	Kms added each year	% increase each year	Year	Kms of track	Kms added each year	% increase each year
1854	15	—	—	1884	6,302	949	16
1855	15	0	0	1885	6,930	628	10
1856	16	2	11	1886	7,586	655	9
1857	16	0	0	1887	8,400	814	10
1858	109	93	191	1888	9,321	921	10
1859	109	0	0	1889	9,583	262	3
1860	223	113	71	1890	9,973	390	4
1861	251	28	12	1891	10,590	617	6
1862	360	108	36	1892	11,316	726	7
1863	428	69	17	1893	11,485	169	1
1864	474	46	10	1894	12,260	775	7
1865	498	24	5	1895	12,967	707	6
1866	513	15	3	1896	13,577	610	5
1867	598	85	15	1897	14,015	438	3
1868	718	120	18	1898	14,664	650	5
1869	737	19	3	1899	14,916	251	2
1870	744	7	1	1900	15,316	401	3
1871	869	125	15	1901	15,506	190	1
1872	932	63	7	1902	15,680	174	1
1873	1,129	197	19	1903	16,010	330	2
1874	1,284	155	13	1904	16,306	296	2
1875	1,801	517	34	1905	16,781	475	3
1876	2,122	322	16	1906	17,243	462	3
1877	2,388	266	12	1907	17,605	363	2
1878	2,709	321	13	1908	18,633	1,028	6
1879	2,941	232	8	1909	19,241	608	3
1880	3,398	457	14	1910	21,326	2,085	10
1881	3,946	548	15	1911	22,287	961	4
1882	4,464	518	12	1912	23,491	1,205	5
1883	5,354	889	18	1913	24,614	1,123	5

SOURCE: IBGE, *Repertório Estatístico do Brasil*, 46.

NOTE: All distances rounded to the nearest kilometer; all percentages rounded to the nearest whole number.

this direct government role. The first involved extensions to extant lines, often British-owned, over which the company owning the initial segment had chosen not to exercise an option for extension. In these cases, the companies did not garner dividend guarantees over the extensions and opted out of additional investment. Where the government grew impatient with capital markets, it undertook railroad extensions on its own account, operating the completed lines as property of the state. The second type of direct government involvement included initial concessions where the government either chose not to wait for private investors or felt a pressing need to create the projects to alleviate local conditions, as in the case of drought-afflicted regions.[56] The Imperial government on several occasions relied on railroad construction projects to shore up economic conditions in drought-stricken areas of the northeast.[57] These cases, combined with the expansion of the government-owned Dom Pedro II through the 1870s and 1880s, meant that by the fall of the Empire in 1889 the central government owned 34 percent of the nation's railroad mileage.[58]

The tendency toward increasing government ownership accelerated greatly under the Republic. The expansive monetary policies of the new regime in the 1890s, and the resulting price inflation, weakened the Brazilian currency dramatically in international markets.[59] Since dividend guarantees to British investors were fixed in sterling, the principal side effect of exchange depreciation was a tremendous increase in the share of tax revenues devoted to paying railroad dividend guarantees. This weighed most heavily on Brazil's Treasury at precisely the moment when officials sought to correct the problem of currency inconvertibility. Outright financial crisis erupted in 1898, and as part of Brazil's debt accord it was forced to pay those railroads receiving subsidies in discounted bonds. In 1901 Brazil "recaptured" those lines that, thanks to its own monetary and financial policies, had burdened the Treasury so heavily.[60] Most of the lines the government purchased were soon rented out to other companies, so that while the government remained the owner, the task of operation fell to private firms. By 1914 the central and state governments together owned 61 percent of the railroad routes in Brazil, but operated outright only 20 percent.[61]

The process by which the government increased its ownership through recapture, while limiting its operational oversight by leasing many of those same lines to foreigners, has been characterized as "expropriation" followed by "alienation."[62] In fact, it was neither, if one understands expropriation to mean the forcible denial of ownership, and alienation to mean the loss of control. Had foreign owners been expropriated, they would have lost their investment. Instead, the Brazilian government paid them in accordance with

Table 3.2

Incremental Additions to National Rail Track for Various Intervals,
1854–1913

Interval	Track kilometers added
1854–1860	208
1860–1870	521
1870–1880	2,654
1880–1890	6,575
1890–1900	5,343
1900–1910	6,009

SOURCE: Table 3.1.

conditions stipulated in their original guarantees of subsidy.[63] Had the government then alienated those same lines, it would have given up effective control. Instead, government regulated the newly leased franchises in accordance with standing law and procedure, setting rates, defining standards of service, and providing full-time oversight. The principal outcomes of the state's actions were an increase in the national railroad capacity that was publicly owned, and an increase in the fiscal costs of public ownership.[64] Ironically, the "recapture" policy increasing government railroad ownership, designed and implemented to aid in alleviating fiscal deficits and external imbalance, due to its very success ended up costing the government more in the long term than had the previous guarantee system. Even so, the leakage abroad of foreign railroad remittances was small relative to the net benefits these railroads created in Brazil.[65]

Railroad Development

After 1852 Brazilians, foreigners, and the government all invested in railroad projects, and the expansion of the railroad sector proceeded apace. The growth of Brazil's railroad system from its first year of operation through 1913 is presented in Table 3.1. In addition to annual figures on the length of track in service, the table presents the first difference of that series to reveal the annual incremental increase, and the annual percentage increase. From

Table 3.3

Opening Dates of the First Railroads in Each State, 1854–1900

State	Year
Rio de Janeiro	1854
Pernambuco	1858
Município Neutro	1858
Bahia	1860
São Paulo	1867
Minas Gerais	1869
Alagôas	1873
Ceará	1873
Rio Grande do Sul	1874
Rio Grande do Norte	1881
Paraiba	1883
Paraná	1883
Santa Catarina	1884
Pará	1884
Espírito Santo	1887
Maranhão	1895

SOURCE: Pessôa, *Guia da Estrada de Ferro Central do Brasil*, 89.

only about 15 kilometers of track in the mid-1850s, the system expanded to a length of more than 24,000 kilometers at the end of 1913. The largest percentage increases on an annual basis came in the first decade of operation, when modest absolute additions to low levels of extant track made for big proportional jumps. In contrast to the large percentage increases in the 1860s, the early twentieth century witnessed the largest absolute increases in track.

Table 3.2 traces the contours of railroad expansion over longer intervals of time. From 1854 to 1880, railroad construction proceeded gradually. After 1880, much larger sections of track opened to operation each decade. The acme of growth in trackage came in the period 1910–1913, when more than 3,000 kilometers entered service in only four years. The annual average increase in the size of the railroad system from 1854 to 1913 was almost 11 per-

Table 3.4

Regional Distribution of Brazilian Rail Track, 1860–1910

Year	Center–South	Northeast	South	North
1860	112 (64%)	64 (36%)	— (—)	— (—)
1870	450 (62%)	271 (38%)	— (—)	— (—)
1880	2,655 (78%)	590 (17%)	43 (1%)	125 (4%)
1890	5,962 (62%)	2,142 (22%)	1,167 (12%)	377 (4%)
1900	9,212 (63%)	2,695 (18%)	2,020 (14%)	720 (5%)
1910	13,778 (64%)	4,003 (18%)	2,736 (13%)	1,144 (5%)

SOURCE: Wileman, *The Brazilian Year Book, 1909*, 612.

NOTE: Parenthetical figures are percentage shares of total Brazilian trackage. All distances rounded to the nearest kilometer. Values for 1910 are extrapolated from 1907, assuming constant regional shares. The center-south is composed of Rio de Janeiro, Côrte/Federal District, Espírito Santo, São Paulo, and Minas Gerais. The northeast includes Bahia, Pernambuco, Alagôas, Rio Grande do Norte, and Paraiba. Ceará, Maranhão, and Pará make up the north, while Rio Grande do Sul, Paraná, and Santa Catarina comprise the south.

cent per year. Thereafter, however, expansion slowed. Annual incremental additions of track fell off dramatically after 1913 with the cutoff of imported inputs and capital brought about by the Great War. By the 1920s, Brazil had come to rely increasingly on motor roads for transport services, and while the length of railroad track grew continually for decades thereafter, it did so only at a reduced pace.

Not all of Brazil benefited equally or simultaneously from the expansion of the railroad sector. Table 3.3 shows the opening dates of the first railroad in each province or state through 1900. Areas that were relatively well served by river, such as the Amazon, had nary a kilometer of track at the turn of the century. Unsurprisingly, those areas that had been most influential in Imperial politics, such as the province of Rio de Janeiro, the Côrte, Pernambuco, and Bahia all had railroads by 1860. Other provinces were required to wait their turn, and as of 1900 five of Brazil's twenty states still had no railroad.

The Brazilian Parliament crafted the Railroad Law of 1873 with the intent not only of attracting more railroad investment to Brazil, but also to redress, at least in part, the early stark concentration of railroads in only a few provinces of the center-south and northeast. The law certainly had the desired effect, although Brazil's regional distribution of rail track remained skewed through the turn of the century. Table 3.4 presents figures on track in service, aggregated for Brazil's major regions, for the period 1860–1910. While the totals for all of Brazil differ slightly from those in Table 3.1, due to small differences among sources, they are nonetheless very close. Importantly, trackage remained relatively concentrated in Brazil's center-south for the entire period, and much of that came to be concentrated in São Paulo. In 1910, with 64 percent of total route trackage, the center-south possessed the same share of railroads as it had fifty years earlier. By contrast, the proportion of total track located in the northeast had declined by half over the same period, thanks to the slower pace of railroad expansion in that area. Once it had its first railroads, the relative share of total track accounted for by the northeast remained steady. It was Brazil's far south that had the most rapid increase in construction after 1880. The south's share of track rose from 1 percent to 13 percent of the Brazilian total in thirty years. By the end of the first decade of the twentieth century, the bulk of total trackage was heavily concentrated in the thriving agricultural zones and the rapidly growing manufacturing centers of Brazil's center-south and far south.

While late in coming and slow to start, railroads expanded impressively in Brazil after 1880. As a result, most of the new technology's impact on the economy is concentrated in the period circa 1880–1913. Estimates of the total output of the Brazilian railroad sector over this interval, unfortunately, do not exist. It is not possible to trace reliably the increase in the production of railroad transport services on an annual basis for the entire period before 1914. The output of the companies comprising the sample elaborated in Chapter 4 does not provide a representative indicator for the sector as a whole because of the varying share of capacity among them over the period of study, and because of differences in utilization rates. A reasonably complete and reliable estimate of the revenues of all Brazilian railroads, developed in Chapter 6, puts the value of railroad output at some 250 million milréis in 1913. At that level, railroad transport services equaled approximately 4.3 percent of gross domestic product that year.[66] While that figure is a correct measure of the share of railroad revenues in GDP, it is a sorely deficient indicator of the contribution of the railroad to the Brazilian economy. Because the railroad served precisely to improve the poor transport conditions outlined in the previous chapter, its contribution to the level of economic activity must be understood in the context of the resources it saved. A measure of the railroad's material significance can come only through an assessment of the role it played in reducing transport costs. That question is pursued in some detail in the following two chapters.

Chapter 4

The Direct Gains from
Railroad Freight Services

The costs of shipping freight overland were high in Brazil in the pre-rail era. The introduction of railroads stood to create considerable savings on those costs. The value of the resources previously devoted to transport that the railroad released to other activities reveals the railroad's importance to Brazil. By 1913 the savings on freight transport costs accounted for a large share of Brazilian national income. An extensive literature on the economic impact of railroads has shown that in countries possessing relatively efficient pre-rail transport, often navigable inland waterways, the technological advance embodied in the railroad did not create particularly large savings on transporting freight. By contrast, in Brazil, where relatively inefficient and costly technologies characterized the pre-rail transport system, the economic benefits conferred by steam-powered locomotion were proportionally greater. The material benefits that railroad freight services made possible in late-nineteenth- and early-twentieth-century Brazil boosted the level of economic activity and dramatically accelerated the pace of economic growth. With hindsight, it is clear the railroad's gains created a peculiar contradiction for the course of the economic change. By generating such large increments to total output, the railroad made it possible for Brazil to attain much improved growth without having to undertake a wider range of measures that might have altered the institutional arrangements governing economic organization. As such, railroads allowed Brazil to improve overall resource allocation, but they did so on the cheap.

This chapter estimates the contribution of railroad freight services to the Brazilian economy in 1913. It does so by elaborating a range of measures of the resources released from transport to other sectors of activity. Resource savings stemmed directly from the reduction in freight costs that railroads made possible. Concretely, those savings arose through improvements in the integration of product markets. The first section considers the market-integrating effects of the railroad. The second section details the course of the fall in the costs of transport by assembling evidence on the volume of freight services and revenues in the railroad sector between 1858 and 1913. The third section draws on these new data series to assess the importance of railroad freight services to the level of economic activity in 1913 by measuring the direct social savings. The measure of the railroad's social saving is then subjected to several tests to determine how sensitive it is to alternative specifications of the economy's responsiveness to cheap transport. The fourth section measures the social return on the capital employed in the railroad sector. There, the estimated resource savings make it possible to determine whether or not Brazilian policies had channeled too much or too little capital into railroads by 1913. Given the strong assumptions required to measure the social rate of return, the results of the section necessarily remain more suggestive than conclusive. Nonetheless, the issue of their validity raises a series of questions that are addressed more fully in Chapter 7, where the implications of subsidy, foreign ownership, and the state's role as owner and operator are explored in greater detail. The concluding section of this chapter recasts the estimates of resource savings in terms of their importance in Brazil's transition to dramatically improved economic growth in the early twentieth century.

Resource Savings and Market Integration

Railroads saved resources because of the relative efficiency with which they produced freight-transport services.[1] Because they required less capital and labor than pre-rail modes of overland transport to produce a given level of transport output, the unit cost of shipment by rail was less than other modes. Those lower costs were reflected directly in lower freight charges to the consumers of freight-transport services. The decline in the price of transport shrank the economic distance between geographically separate markets because fewer resources were required to traverse that space. Railroads permitted formerly isolated regions to trade with one another, and regions already in contact to trade with lower transactions costs. Exchange, in turn, made it possible for those regions to specialize in the production of the goods and services for which they were best suited. The resulting gains to the economy from trade and specialization translated into higher levels of output and income in the regions involved.

Conceptually, the gains from local and interregional trade and specialization that resulted from transport cost reductions equal the output derived from the resources released to the economy by substituting the railroad for pre-rail transport modes. Those gains comprise the social surplus—or more commonly, the "direct social saving" of the railroad. The social saving measure is, of course, an accounting convention, and it is important that the *measure* of the railroad's social saving not be confused with *how* that saving arises. As a measure, the social saving captures the magnitude of the transport cost savings provided by the railroad sector to the economy. The direct social savings on railroad freight services equal the gains arising from improved market integration under two assumptions: (1) there are constant returns to scale across all sectors of the economy, and (2) the economy is characterized by perfect competition. As long as those two assumptions roughly hold, the direct social saving effectively measures the magnitude of the gains from trade and specialization that arise from the reduction in transport costs that railroads make possible.[2] The more efficient allocation in the economy that railroads created came about through the redeployment of capital and labor previously tied up in the production of transport services to other activities.[3]

The bulk of the resource savings from Brazilian railroads resulted from lower charges paid directly by shippers. But the savings in overall transport costs that railroads wrought had additional components. Railroads not only moved goods to market at lower prices. By rail, those goods moved to markets a great deal more quickly and securely than they did by mule or cart. As a result, there was less risk of spoilage of the product or loss en route. Trips that previously had taken days were reduced to hours by rail. Observers at mid-century placed the top speed of mule trains at three leagues (18.6 kilometers) a day. The average rail freight journey in 1913 for all Brazil was 134 kilometers. For that distance, roughly the trip from Santos to Jundiaí in São Paulo, freight would take more than seven days to get to market on the backs of mules, yet less than a day at most by rail.[4] Mule speeds in the mountainous interior, with its precarious trails and roads, were as slow as one-and-a-half to two leagues a day.[5] The railroad reduced other costs as well. Shippers and carriers confronted less risk of loss in route by rail. While torrential tropical rains regularly washed out sections of rail track, the likelihood of frequent interruption and extended delay by rail was much reduced over what it had been when merchandise went to market on roads. The consequence of the improvement in speed, reliability, and coordination attributable to the railroad was a reduction in inventory requirements across all transportable-goods-producing activities. The gain arising from reduced inventories amounted to the interest and depreciation charges that were saved by not holding merchandise on the farm, or by having it pile up at the factory. Unfortunately, so little information bearing on these inventory costs survives that, for the present analysis, they are ignored, and only the direct costs of shipment figure in here.

By reducing the cost of freight shipment, railroads shrank the wedge that transport costs drove between producers and consumers. That wedge is directly observed in the gap between prices for the same product in different localities. In Brazil the spread between prices in geographically distinct markets had been long apparent. Commodity prices among Brazil's regions in the mid–eighteenth century exhibited large gaps.[6] The limited extent of market integration in regions not served by railroads persisted well into the nineteenth century because of the poor overland-transport conditions there. In the 1880s price dispersion prevailed in areas not yet served by railroads, such as the north of Minas Gerais:

> In Ouro-Preto the price of corn runs between 2$200 and 2$500 for fifty liters in a good year, and iron 3$000 per arroba; but in the Gravatá basin corn is between $700 and $800 for fifty liters . . . while iron is 7$000 to 8$000 per arroba, and everything else in the same proportion. The cultivator sells his products at a low price, and having to buy items of first necessity at a high price, the result is fatal.[7]

An improvement in transport that decreased the cost of transport would reduce the gap between the prices of corn in Ouro Preto and the countryside, and would do the same for iron. The price that the farmer would receive for corn would rise, while that for the consumer would go down. The same would hold true for iron, along with all other transportable commodities. Both the producers and the consumers of those goods would benefit from transport improvements. The outcome would be an improvement in the inter-regional terms of trade, and a net increase in income.

Declining transport costs in Brazil further permitted more effective arbitrage between geographically separate markets. Rural producers, laboring under newly reduced transport costs, altered their crop mixes, inventories, and effort accordingly. The shift in relative prices and costs between suppliers and purchasers was not limited in its impact to *fazendeiros* and *sitiantes* (resident laborers) alone. Factory owners were able to locate (or locate anew) where they would acquire the profit-maximizing combination of inputs, given the distance to both the markets for those inputs and markets for consumers. The resulting reorganization of production led in the aggregate to increasing output and incomes across the economy.

The process of market integration generates testable implications; the most clear-cut of those is the convergence of prices for the same commodity in distant markets. That the market-integrating mechanism which gave rise to resource savings on the part of the railroad was actually at work in Brazil may be readily inferred from commodity price data. Coffee prices at the *município* level for thirty-six counties in São Paulo in 1854 and 1906 provide a unique opportunity to test for this effect in Brazil. Information on local coffee prices reveals improvements of intra-regional market integration. Since railroads were first operated in São Paulo in 1867, and continued to expand through the turn of the century, the improvements in intra-regional product market efficiency that are detectable over fifty years are mostly (and perhaps completely) attributable to the decline in freight rates brought about by the new transport technology. Computing the coefficient of variation (the standard deviation divided by the mean) of these prices reveals that local price dispersion in São Paulo fell from 0.27 in 1854 to 0.14 in 1906.[8]

In comparative terms, this decline in intra-regional price dispersion for coffee in São Paulo was similar to the decline in the inter-regional dispersion of prices of rice, jowar, cotton, and wheat in India, and of the prices for rye and wheat in Russia, over roughly the same period.[9] Since coffee possessed a relatively high value-to-weight ratio, and was widely commercialized in the province before the arrival of railroads, the impact of improved product market integration was likely much less in the coffee sector than for other crops that could not bear the high cost of pre-rail transport. For those other goods, the relative gains arising from cheap railroad transport were much larger.[10] In any case, one can be sure that the gain to the coffee sector in São Paulo is chiefly attributable to railroad expansion. A corollary of falling transport costs and the gains from trade and specialization was rising agricultural land values. Contemporary reports described increases in real farm values in São Paulo as high as 20 percent per year during the 1860s and 1870s.[11]

The Growth of Railroad Freight Services

The strength of the long-term market integrating effect of railroads depended on three variables in pre-1914 Brazil. The first was the decline in the unit charge for freight-transport services between the 1850s and 1913. The greater the fall in the cost of shipment brought about by the railroad, the greater the benefits to the producers and consumers of each unit of freight that was shipped. The second was the share of the transportable-goods-producing sector in the economy's total output. The greater the share of the economy's resources devoted to transportable commodities, the more important was the reduction in the costs of shipment to the economy as a whole. The third was the responsiveness of the commodity sector to the decline in transport costs. The economy's response to the reduced cost of shipment was itself a function of the pace at which those cost reductions became available to a greater number of shippers. That pace was set by the reach of the railroad. Freight charges fell for an increasingly larger number of Brazilian shippers as a result of the rapid expansion of the railroad system beginning in the 1880s. Falling transport charges not only provided immediate benefits, but also signaled new opportunities to farmers, merchants, and industrialists alike.

While the length of track in service for all Brazilian railroads is known, the course of freight charges for the entire railroad sector is difficult to trace. Complete figures on freight output and revenues for the railroad sector do not exist.[12] For the earliest years of operation, the sector was sufficiently small that estimates of revenues, output, and the like could be constructed. But from the 1870s until the late 1890s a complete accounting is possible for only a few benchmark years, largely because the original records required to do so were neither reprinted in government reports nor preserved in an accessible form.

Thanks to the appearance in 1898 of railroad statistical volumes, published by the central government and containing operating data for lines it conceded, the series of freight output and revenues from 1898 to 1913 encompass the vast bulk of the railroad sector. Because similarly complete measures are not available for the period before 1898, a sample of major railroads, in place of the sectorwide data, indicates the course of railroad freight charges for the period 1858–1897. The tonnage, freight service, and revenue series presented in this chapter are based on reconstructions that rely largely on primary source materials. When necessary, they also make judicious use of statistical estimating procedures; the interested reader will find a discussion of these in Appendix B. While there are clear limits on the uses to which the sample may be put, it proves to be invaluable in tracing the time path of the reduction in freight-transport costs in Brazil.

Table 4.1 lists the eleven railroads comprising the sample and the year that each first began operation. The sample lines represent the mix of ownership and regional distribution across Brazil. The Central do Brazil was the country's second railroad, and the largest, running from Rio de Janeiro into the Paraíba Valley, and from there into São Paulo and Minas Gerais. The San Paulo, Paulista, Mogiana, and Sorocabana e Ituana lines mainly served the state of São Paulo. Several British-owned lines are included. The San Paulo

Table 4.1

Sample Railroads, 1858–1913

Railroad	Year of Opening
Dom Pedro II (Central do Brazil)	1858[a]
Recife and San Francisco	1858[b]
Bahia and San Francisco	1860[c]
San Paulo (Santos a Jundiaí)	1867
Paulista	1872
Leopoldina	1874[d]
Mogiana	1875
Sorocabana e Ituana	1876[e]
Great Western of Brazil	1881[f]
Southern Brazil Rio Grande do Sul	1883[g]
Brazil Great Southern	1887[h]

NOTES:

[a]The Dom Pedro II absorbed the São Paulo–Rio de Janeiro railroad after 1885.

[b]The Recife and San Francisco became part of the Great Western network after the government buyout of the line at the turn of the century.

[c]The Bahia and San Francisco was included in the Bahia state railroad network after the government buyout of the line at the turn of the century.

[d]The Leopoldina absorbed numerous other lines in Rio de Janeiro, Minas Gerais, and Espírito Santo in the 1880s and 1890s.

[e]The Sorocabana e Ituana includes the Ituana line, with which it merged. The Ituana opened in 1873, but there is little useful data for the first three years of its operation.

[f]The Great Western of Brazil included most of the railroads in Brazil's northeast by the first decade of the twentieth century.

[g]The Southern Brazil Rio Grande do Sul joined with the Rio Grande do Sul state network after 1905.

[h]The Brazil Great Southern joined with the Rio Grande do Sul state network after 1905.

railway was the most heavily trafficked of Brazil's British-owned lines. The Great Western of Brazil began as a modest line in Pernambuco but expanded steadily and later came to own or operate most of the lines in the northeast located north of Bahia. The Recife and San Francisco railway was one of the first to begin operations in Brazil, but was bought up by the government at the turn of the century and incorporated into the Great Western's network. The Bahia and San Francisco line was British, and like the Recife line was bought by the government and combined with the publicly owned state network in Bahia. The Brazil Great Southern Railway was a British line that served the far southern state of Rio Grande do Sul. It, like the Southern Brazil Rio Grande do Sul railroad, was bought up by the government in 1905 and consolidated into the Rio Grande do Sul network. The Central do Brazil began as a mixed government and private enterprise, but came to be owned by the government soon after it began operations. The Leopoldina began as a Brazilian company, but became British-owned in the 1890s under a debt settlement. Financial difficulties on the Sorocabana led to a portion of it falling under government ownership. The Mogiana and Paulista remained privately-owned Brazilian firms, financed primarily by Brazilian capital markets.

The representativeness of the sample firms can be assessed by comparing the sample data series to the full sectoral series for the years in which the latter exist. Table 4.2 uses the extension of track in service to provide a rough measure of the total capacity accounted for by the sample lines. It presents the length of sample track in operation and compares it to two different measures of total Brazilian rail track. The "A" series of total track derives from the standard secondary source materials on transport in Brazil, found in Table 3.1. Using it as the denominator, the sample companies account for varying shares of total track in operation between 1858 and 1913. The sample share rises somewhat when considered against the "B" series of total track. That series derives from the lines comprising the "full-sector" estimates constructed here, and is built up directly from the company reports and government surveys. The discrepancy between it and the "A" series of track stems from the fact that the former excludes a number of smaller provincial lines for which no operating information has been located, even after 1898. It is possible that the "A" series overstates the length of track in service in the later decades. Its documentary origin is unclear, and it may include sidings, along with double- and triple-tracked segments of trunk line, as components of total route-mileage. The fact that the sample railroads include the most intensively trafficked lines in Brazil suggests that they can reliably reveal the trend in freight charges for the sector as a whole.

Capacity, when expressed as track in service, says nothing about utilization. Freight density was much greater on the eleven sample lines than for the sector as a whole. Table 4.3 shows this by contrasting the tonnage carried by the sample railroads with total tonnage. For the early decades, the "total tonnage" derives from the major railroad studies of that era.[13] Given the difficulties the government encountered in enforcing its reporting requirements, even railroad specialists of the time had difficulty piecing together basic data series, especially when the sector expanded after the mid-1870s. In the first decade the sample tonnage frequently exceeds, by a large margin, the total tonnage figures. Total tonnage comes from contemporary sources that

Table 4.2
Sample Track as a Share of Total Track, 1858–1913

Year	Sample Track (km)	Total track "A" (km)	Total track "B" (km)	Sample share "A" (%)	Sample share "B" (%)
1858	83	109	—	75	—
1859	94	109	—	85	—
1860	156	223	—	70	—
1861	270	251	—	108	—
1862	279	360	—	78	—
1863	347	428	—	81	—
1864	373	474	—	79	—
1865	386	498	—	77	—
1866	424	513	—	83	—
1867	575	598	—	96	—
1868	585	718	—	82	—
1869	603	737	—	82	—
1870	609	744	—	82	—
1871	699	869	—	80	—
1872	756	932	—	81	—
1873	807	1,129	—	71	—
1874	890	1,284	—	69	—
1875	1,049	1,801	—	58	—
1876	1,481	2,122	—	70	—
1877	1,609	2,388	—	67	—
1878	1,852	2,709	—	68	—
1879	1,864	2,941	—	63	—
1880	1,978	3,398	—	58	—
1881	2,055	3,946	—	52	—
1882	2,196	4,464	—	49	—
1883	2,390	5,354	—	45	—
1884	2,587	6,302	—	41	—
1885	2,978	6,930	—	43	—
1886	3,529	7,586	—	47	—
1887	3,863	8,400	—	46	—

Table 4.2 (cont.)

Year	Sample Track (km)	Total track "A" (km)	Total track "B" (km)	Sample share "A" (%)	Sample share "B" (%)
1888	4,319	9,321	—	46	—
1889	4,599	9,583	—	48	—
1890	5,228	9,973	—	52	—
1891	6,013	10,590	—	57	—
1892	6,440	11,316	—	57	—
1893	6,576	11,485	—	57	—
1894	6,645	12,260	—	54	—
1895	6,904	12,967	—	53	—
1896	7,066	13,577	—	52	—
1897	7,123	14,015	—	51	—
1898	7,034	14,664	11,504	48	61
1899	6,857	14,916	11,575	46	59
1900	6,914	15,316	11,901	45	58
1901	7,604	15,506	12,362	49	62
1902	8,034	15,680	12,391	51	65
1903	8,796	16,010	12,629	55	70
1904	9,177	16,306	14,028	56	65
1905	9,373	16,781	14,078	56	67
1906	10,357	17,243	14,431	60	72
1907	10,804	17,605	15,008	61	72
1908	11,276	18,633	15,798	61	71
1909	11,532	19,241	16,540	60	70
1910	12,252	21,326	18,297	57	67
1911	12,645	22,287	19,561	57	65
1912	13,405	23,491	20,214	57	66
1913	13,914	24,614	21,805	57	64

SOURCES AND NOTES: Sample track is the length of track in service at the end of year for the eleven railroads comprising the sample, reported in Table 4.1. The "A" measure of total track is taken from Table 3.1. The "B" measure of total track is the sum derived from the annual statistical volumes and company reports after 1898. The "B" series misses some of the smaller lines, and as a result the sample is a larger share for it than it is for the "A" series.

Table 4.3

Tonnage Carried by Brazilian Railroads, 1858–1913

Year	Sample tons	Total tons	Sample share of total (percent)
1858	9,729	—	—
1859	37,078	39,425	94
1860	53,269	55,045	97
1861	76,080	54,261	140
1862	67,618	43,448	156
1863	70,248	44,636	157
1864	77,496	74,230	104
1865	114,003	102,432	111
1866	126,434	117,412	108
1867	187,079	119,108	157
1868	213,562	208,473	102
1869	308,904	284,022	109
1870	292,004	300,587	97
1871	329,586	306,158	108
1872	353,304	375,428	94
1873	405,491	420,972	96
1874	473,332	492,297	96
1875	543,168	537,657	01
1876	573,571	539,960	106
1877	665,122	663,169	100
1878	736,596	755,135	98
1879	798,988	830,150	96
1880	856,314	957,899	89
1881	983,801	1,113,231	88
1882	1,013,657	1,007,235	101
1883	1,162,071	—	—
1884	1,210,865	—	—
1885	1,330,978	—	—
1886	1,371,865	—	—
1887	1,405,008	1,979,737	71
1888	1,632,828	—	—
1889	1,889,177	—	—

Table 4.3 (cont.)

Year	Sample tons	Total tons	Sample share of total (percent)
1890	2,037,176	—	—
1891	2,567,553	—	—
1892	2,886,786	—	—
1893	3,091,950	—	—
1894	3,415,791	—	—
1895	3,732,071	—	—
1896	4,199,422	—	—
1897	4,298,754	—	—
1898	3,874,962	4,716,803	82
1899	3,870,750	4,779,932	81
1900	3,969,194	4,922,373	81
1901	4,902,792	5,651,519	87
1902	5,263,864	5,917,692	89
1903	5,157,932	5,748,158	90
1904	5,209,455	5,830,137	89
1905	5,418,397	5,994,319	90
1906	6,487,158	7,052,824	92
1907	6,724,445	7,323,869	92
1908	6,656,803	7,259,691	92
1909	7,511,960	8,235,801	91
1910	7,624,790	8,432,178	90
1911	8,532,613	9,561,376	89
1912	9,774,453	10,962,332	89
1913	11,198,179	12,698,652	88

SOURCES: For sample series and total series from 1898, see Appendix B. Total series for the period 1859–1882 is drawn and adapted from Costa, *Viação Ferrea*, 1–425; MACOP, *Relatório . . . 1886*; and MACOP, *Relatório . . . 1887*.

Table 4.4
Railroad Freight Service, 1858–1913

Year	Sample (ton-kilometers)	Total (ton-kilometers)	Sample share (percent)
1858	689,941	—	—
1859	1,660,188	—	—
1860	2,274,043	—	—
1861	3,773,519	—	—
1862	4,207,110	—	—
1863	5,120,159	—	—
1864	6,150,865	—	—
1865	8,849,247	—	—
1866	11,282,589	—	—
1867	17,157,508	—	—
1868	20,295,551	—	—
1869	30,366,285	—	—
1870	33,271,960	—	—
1871	38,558,644	—	—
1872	40,052,597	—	—
1873	45,131,500	—	—
1874	52,851,480	—	—
1875	61,681,009	—	—
1876	64,850,483	—	—
1877	77,218,839	—	—
1878	83,138,642	—	—
1879	96,538,734	—	—
1880	103,132,304	—	—
1881	120,088,007	—	—
1882	124,225,086	—	—
1883	135,149,399	—	—
1884	136,689,464	—	—
1885	161,226,316	—	—
1886	162,088,148	—	—
1887	164,249,333	221,115,655	74

Table 4.4 (cont.)

Year	Sample (ton-kilometers)	Total (ton-kilometers)	Sample share (percent)
1888	191,224,350	—	—
1889	208,447,652	—	—
1890	239,496,662	—	—
1891	271,090,630	—	—
1892	321,998,235	—	—
1893	345,803,639	—	—
1894	373,498,395	—	—
1895	425,050,412	—	—
1896	506,232,040	—	—
1897	530,556,812	—	—
1898	523,625,270	585,847,372	89
1899	576,318,552	634,342,037	91
1900	566,558,827	619,819,895	91
1901	713,646,869	775,754,351	92
1902	694,458,569	747,121,998	93
1903	736,240,561	797,114,074	92
1904	687,880,364	756,710,017	91
1905	702,261,487	772,305,736	91
1906	854,525,180	918,610,908	93
1907	939,599,507	1,004,155,911	94
1908	936,981,188	1,010,316,736	93
1909	1,073,545,944	1,165,366,703	92
1910	1,076,323,776	1,191,697,485	90
1911	1,138,967,179	1,284,619,330	89
1912	1,287,648,275	1,449,253,470	89
1913	1,475,076,568	1,697,321,018	87

SOURCE: See Appendix B.

Table 4.5
Railroad Freight Revenues, 1858–1913

Year	Sample freight revenue (current milréis)	Total freight revenue (current milréis)	Sample share (percent)
1858	220,781	—	—
1859	528,184	—	—
1860	680,294	—	—
1861	927,703	—	—
1862	922,917	—	—
1863	989,675	—	—
1864	1,197,771	—	—
1865	1,829,427	—	—
1866	1,910,608	—	—
1867	3,485,274	—	—
1868	4,077,847	—	—
1869	6,132,142	—	—
1870	5,992,528	—	—
1871	7,342,378	—	—
1872	7,130,523	—	—
1873	8,487,195	—	—
1874	10,298,697	—	—
1875	11,186,634	—	—
1876	11,230,451	—	—
1877	13,213,930	—	—
1878	15,407,093	—	—
1879	16,483,241	—	—
1880	16,711,618	—	—
1881	19,896,884	—	—
1882	20,281,814	—	—
1883	20,407,975	—	—
1884	20,618,175	—	—
1885	22,806,923	—	—
1886	23,109,243	—	—

Table 4.5 (cont.)

Year	Sample freight revenue (current milréis)	Total freight revenue (current milréis)	Sample share (percent)
1887	21,119,657	27,225,424	78
1888	25,373,880	—	—
1889	27,865,590	—	—
1890	28,432,414	—	—
1891	34,379,878	—	—
1892	41,025,523	—	—
1893	49,736,252	—	—
1894	63,847,454	—	—
1895	71,660,404	—	—
1896	82,495,214	—	—
1897	85,837,623	—	—
1898	84,071,463	95,506,161	88
1899	83,521,880	97,261,821	86
1900	85,834,338	103,071,325	83
1901	106,423,687	118,001,096	90
1902	100,401,765	109,519,342	92
1903	94,456,065	104,430,564	90
1904	88,049,476	99,117,254	89
1905	88,869,736	99,621,410	89
1906	114,254,628	125,062,562	91
1907	110,148,178	121,084,859	91
1908	104,209,361	114,625,247	91
1909	118,629,530	131,108,473	90
1910	105,338,440	119,472,383	88
1911	114,384,585	131,929,443	87
1912	128,101,133	148,860,659	86
1913	142,204,724	165,367,102	86

SOURCE: See Appendix B.
NOTE: All values are in current milréis.

Table 4.6
Unit Freight Charges, 1858–1913
(in milréis)

Year	Sample unit charge— nominal	Sample unit charge— deflated	Total unit charge— nominal	Total unit charge— deflated
1858	0.32	0.68	—	—
1859	0.32	0.66	—	—
1860	0.30	0.63	—	—
1861	0.25	0.54	—	—
1862	0.22	0.47	—	—
1863	0.19	0.45	—	—
1864	0.19	0.41	—	—
1865	0.21	0.39	—	—
1866	0.17	0.30	—	—
1867	0.20	0.34	—	—
1868	0.20	0.30	—	—
1869	0.20	0.31	—	—
1870	0.18	0.25	—	—
1871	0.19	0.29	—	—
1872	0.18	0.25	—	—
1873	0.19	0.27	—	—
1874	0.19	0.27	—	—
1875	0.18	0.28	—	—
1876	0.17	0.25	—	—
1877	0.17	0.24	—	—
1878	0.19	0.26	—	—
1879	0.17	0.25	—	—
1880	0.16	0.26	—	—
1881	0.17	0.26	—	—
1882	0.16	0.25	—	—
1883	0.15	0.24	—	—
1884	0.15	0.24	—	—
1885	0.14	0.23	—	—
1886	0.14	0.24	—	—
1887	0.13	0.22	0.12	0.22

Table 4.6 (cont.)

Year	Sample unit charge— nominal	Sample unit charge— deflated	Total unit charge— nominal	Total unit charge— deflated
1888	0.13	0.24	—	—
1889	0.13	0.21	—	—
1890	0.12	0.18	—	—
1891	0.13	0.15	—	—
1892	0.13	0.13	—	—
1893	0.14	0.12	—	—
1894	0.17	0.14	—	—
1895	0.17	0.16	—	—
1896	0.16	0.14	—	—
1897	0.16	0.12	—	—
1898	0.16	0.11	0.16	0.12
1899	0.14	0.11	0.15	0.11
1900	0.15	0.12	0.17	0.13
1901	0.15	0.14	0.15	0.14
1902	0.14	0.15	0.15	0.15
1903	0.13	0.14	0.13	0.14
1904	0.13	0.13	0.13	0.13
1905	0.13	0.15	0.13	0.16
1906	0.13	0.15	0.14	0.15
1907	0.12	0.12	0.12	0.13
1908	0.11	0.11	0.11	0.12
1909	0.11	0.13	0.11	0.13
1910	0.10	0.11	0.10	0.12
1911	0.10	0.11	0.10	0.11
1912	0.10	0.10	0.10	0.10
1913	0.10	0.10	0.10	0.10

NOTE: In 1913, 1 milréis exchanged for US$.32. Deflated charges adjusted to 1913 levels by use of the price index are discussed in the text.

in several cases did not report freight volume. As a result, the total series systematically understates the quantity of freight, while the sample uses estimating techniques to impute likely levels of freight service. The total tonnage series re-emerges in 1898, thanks to the composite measure made possible by both the major company reports and the appearance of government statistical volumes. The share of total freight tonnage accounted for by the eleven sample lines is quite high, comprising the majority of total freight shipped in the latter period. From 1898 onward, the relatively more complete information provided in the company reports and government railroad censuses instills much greater confidence in the reliability of the sectorwide series. Growth in freight tonnage was faster than the growth of the economy as a whole for two reasons. The first was a substitution effect, through which the railroad's lower charges for shipment steadily pulled traffic away from muleteers and carters as the extension of track in service increased. The second was an income effect, whereby lower transport costs reverberated through the economy, increased incomes, and fed back into expanding markets for transportable goods. Increases in traffic levels thus came about as a response to falling transport costs that both supplanted non-rail modes of shipment and induced a shift in the demand schedule for transport services.

Information on the tons of freight shipped reveals the total quantity of physical output carried by rail. It does not, however, lead directly to a measure of the output of railroad freight services. Some of those tons may have been hauled only a few kilometers; others may have traveled hundreds of kilometers by 1913. Moreover, by 1913 over-counting of tonnage was inevitable. A ton of freight that was transferred from one railroad, at its terminus, to another, would appear twice in the operating data. Because of the differing lengths of haul by commodity, converting tons into a consistent measure of output requires multiplying tonnage by the average length of haul per ton. Table 4.4 presents the sample series of freight output in units of ton-kilometers. The absence of information on the average length of haul in the early decades makes it difficult to convert the tonnage series into measures of total ton-kilometers. From 1898 onward, almost every railroad reported either output in ton-kilometers, or the average length of haul for freight. Before 1898, every sample line failed to do so for at least several years. In those cases, simple interpolations and extrapolations of the average length of haul, or the unit freight charge, were employed in constructing the ton-kilometer output series.[14] The estimates of freight-service output are quite reliable from 1898 to 1913. The likely margin of error in the sample output series generally increases as one moves further back from the 1890s. The most notable feature of this series is its trend over time. In particular, the increase in the volume of freight services after 1898 was impressive. Freight output nearly tripled between 1898 and 1913.

Estimates of freight revenues similarly derive from the company reports and statistical volumes. Reporting of revenues by sample lines was virtually complete, and few interpolations were required to construct the data series. Dividing the output series from Table 4.4 into their respective freight revenues reported in Table 4.5 gives the average unit freight charge by rail for each year. Annual average unit freight charges derived in this manner appear in Table 4.6. To make those charges comparable over time, they must be adjusted for inflation. Both sample and total unit charges are adjusted to 1913 prices, using the extended wholesale price index described below. The real unit freight charge on the sample lines declined nearly sevenfold from 1858 to 1913, from 680 réis per ton-kilometer to only 100 réis. Comparing the sample series to that for the sector as a whole in 1898–1913 reveals only occasional differences. The "total" unit freight charges tended to be slightly higher than those in the sample series, as a result of including a number of smaller railroads that did not have freight rates as low as those on the large companies dominating the sample. Unit revenues fell from 1858 to 1870, then fluctuated between $210 and $290 through 1889. Accompanying the spurt of inflation that began in 1889 was another decline in real freight charges. Between 1891 and 1913 average revenue per ton-kilometer never again rose above $160.

Because real freight charges fell in an almost uninterrupted fashion while the capacity of the railroad sector continuously expanded, an increasingly large share of the Brazilian economy confronted newly reduced transport costs over the course of more than a half-century. In this context, the increase in freight services, particularly strong after 1898, implies that the total resources saved by rail freight transport grew appreciably. The magnitude of these savings depended on the cost of transporting freight by the next best alternative to railroads. Had Brazil been deprived of its railroads, and forced to shift resources from other activities in order to carry the same amount of freight over the same distances, the losses would have been large. Explicating that counterfactual yields the measure of the economic impact of the railroad's freight services.

Direct Social Savings on Freight Services

The resources Brazil saved by shipping freight on railroads comprised a hefty share of national income by 1913. The social saving equals the difference between the cost of shipping freight by rail in a given year and how much it would have cost to ship that freight by the next best alternative mode of conveyance if the railroad system was closed. This approach partitions the economy into two sectors—the transport sector and the non-transport sector—and assesses how changes in the transport costs bear on changes in GDP.[15] However, some strong assumptions implicit in this approach to measuring the benefits accruing to the economy from cheap transport give cause for concern that the impact of the railroad is not fully measured. In particular, the direct social savings concept excludes the dynamic gains that railroads can create by increasing the economy's stock of resources. This scenario is broached in Chapter 6 and addressed in Appendix A. Excluding, for the estimates of the present chapter, the railroad's dynamic impact merely understates the railroad's already large direct influence.

Estimating the freight social savings in 1913 Brazil requires information on three variables: the level of railroad freight services, the cost to carry freight by rail, and the costs that shippers would have faced in the absence of the railroad. Before the construction of railroads this freight would have moved overland in Brazil on the backs of mules or, where possible, by cart. These were precisely the modes of transport that were supplanted following the construction of railroads.[16] A concern is whether railroads were substitutes mainly for roads, or whether such substitution transpired between railroads and coastwise shipping. Railroads would only partly substitute for coastwise shipping if they replaced muleteers who, instead of carrying freight directly to the final market (or port), carried it to a nearby port, where it was then shipped by boat to the final destination in Brazil. Coastwise shipping charges were substantially lower than rail charges. The cost to carry freight by water from São João da Barra, in the northern part of Rio de Janeiro province, was less than one-half the cost of shipment by rail.[17] Such routing by mule and boat would occur whenever and wherever that particular combination minimized the total outlay on transport charges for agents sending goods to market. In Brazil, where freight most often came from the interior along routes that were perpendicular to the coast, the substitution of joint mule-water transport by railroads would arise only for a limited number of specific commodities and lengths of haul. In those cases, however, railroads might indirectly substitute for coastal carriers. There, some increment of freight and passenger services produced by rail would, in the absence of the railroad, have been produced instead not only by muleteers and stagecoaches, but also by water shippers.

Were such substitution present in an appreciable degree, the analysis would need to take into account not a single overland alternative to the railroad, but a mix of alternate modes of shipment. Additional complications for measuring the benefits of the railroad would immediately arise, since determining the least-cost combination of multiple substitute modes of shipment invokes a complex linear programming problem.[18] Nonetheless, for Brazil, the main indicators of substitution between modes, namely the changing mix of rail and water arrivals of some key commodities at major ports, suggests that water-rail substitution was not especially important.

Scattered data on freight arrivals by mode of shipment for two main ports, Recife (Pernambuco) and Rio de Janeiro, make possible a partial assessment of the degree of water-rail substitution. The pattern of sugar arrivals in Recife after 1883 suggests that substitution between rail and water shipment was trivial.[19] The rising share of sugar delivered by rail between 1883 and 1909 came largely at the expense of arrivals by pack animals rather than arrivals by water. The share of total sugar freight arriving in Recife by water in 1909 had declined to 40 percent of its 1883 level. By way of contrast, the share of sugar arriving on the backs of pack animals declined to less than 6 percent of its 1883 level by 1908, and to less than 1 percent of its 1883 level by 1909. As one might expect, the animal-borne arrivals of sugar in Recife were much more sensitive to the expanding rail system than were shipments by water.

Less detailed information on coffee arrivals in Rio de Janeiro suggests the same story. There, the share of coffee arriving by water actually increased over time, although the categories in which this data are reported are not sufficiently disaggregated to provide for in-depth analysis. Considering only those water shipments arriving by *cabotagem*, the ratio of railroad deliveries to coastwise arrivals of coffee remained steady at 3 to 1 from 1876 to 1892, but rose thereafter to about 6 to 1 in 1909.[20] Summing railroad arrivals of coffee with "*barra dentro*" deliveries causes the railroad share of arrivals to rise even more, from 3.5 to 1 in 1876 to 13 to 1 in 1909. The origin of coffee arrivals in the "*barra dentro*" ("within the bar") category was Niterói, where coffee arrived by several modes, most of it by rail. From there it was carried by boat across the bay. The timing of the falling share of coastwise deliveries of coffee to Rio suggests that the apparent substitution between coastal shipping and railroads includes a statistical artifact. Two features of the changing coffee economy of late-nineteenth-century Brazil help explain at least part of the "substitution" by railroads in Rio for coastal shipping before 1909: (1) the spread of coffee cultivation into the south of Minas, and (2) the dramatic growth of cultivation in western São Paulo and the rise of Santos as a major coffee port in its own right. The first phenomenon would raise the relative share of rail deliveries to Rio, since it moved the frontier of cultivation in the Rio zone far from secondary ports; the Minas coffee region was linked to Rio solely by rail. The second feature would reduce any coastwise transshipment of coffee because those cargoes increasingly departed Santos directly for Europe and North America. The absolute level of coffee arrivals in Rio changed little between 1890 and 1909, but the origin of that coffee likely changed a great deal. Both factors worked to raise the ratio of railroad deliveries to coastwise deliveries in Rio.

Although ultimately the degree of substitution between coastal shipment and rail in Brazil cannot be known with complete certainty, it is not likely that it was large. However, that it was present at all potentially imparts a bias of unknown magnitude to the measures of the economic impact of the railroad that base themselves solely on overland alternatives. Nonetheless, the countervailing biases present in the measure of the railroad's economic impact should prove sufficient to offset any upward bias resulting from the lingering mis-specification of substitute modes. The estimate here relies on a counterfactual that admits the possibility that, if deprived of railroads, Brazilians would have devoted considerable effort and resources to improving the non-rail transport system, namely by constructing a network of improved wagon roads. Based on maximum freight density estimates of wagon-road capacity, 1 kilometer of improved road would have been required for each 16,500 ton-kilometers of freight service.[21] Carrying Brazil's 1913 level of railroad freight would have required more than 100,000 kilometers of wagon road. Moreover, assuming that each mule made fifteen trips each year, with each trip equal to the railroad's average haul, Brazil would have required at least six million additional mules.[22] It is not clear that the counterfactual economy would have been able to supply that many pack animals and still keep the unit costs of shipment as low as they actually were in the pre-rail era. The assumption that a Brazil that was deprived of railroads would have improved its wagon roads to accommodate 1913 freight levels potentially imparts a substantial downward bias to the railroad's impact.

The cost of pre-rail overland freight services was nonetheless high even where good wagon roads were found. Table 4.7 presents scattered observations of the cost of transporting freight in the immediate pre-rail era for various regions of Brazil. To render them comparable, they are all adjusted to 1913 values using a common price index. These charges exhibit a large amount of variation. The differences between rates stem from several sources. Many of these charges are "spot" observations, and thus reflect the prevailing local and seasonal conditions at the time and place they were recorded. Others were recorded by contemporaries, who were instrumentally rhetorical in their complaints over high pre-rail charges. The lowest rate, that for Pernambuco, is not indicative of costs because it comes from a period in which the region suffered from a severe drought and disruption within the local economy. Most of the charges in the table are for shipment by mule or horse, although the average rate for São Paulo reflects freight charges on wheeled-vehicle traffic as well. Because the working hypothesis of this chapter is that

Table 4.7

Non-Rail Overland-Freight Charges
in Nineteenth-Century Brazil
(per ton-kilometer)

Location	Year	Rate at current prices	Rate at 1913 prices
Alagôas	1888	$570	1$018
Bahia	1855	$540	1$148
Minas Gerais	1883	$800	1$251
Paraná	1869	$753	1$172
Pernambuco	1864	$528	1$117
Pernambuco	1886	$251	$421
Rio de Janeiro	1855	$573	1$220
Rio de Janeiro	1854	$919	2$088
Rio de Janeiro	1856	1$111	2$264
Rio de Janeiro	1865	$675	1$278
Rio de Janeiro	1859	$441	$916
São Paulo	1856	$430	$876
São Paulo	1864	$393	$832

SOURCES: For Alagôas in 1888, see Alagôas Railway Company, Ltd., *Petição e Memoria Justificativa,* 11–12; for Bahia in 1855, see GBPP, 1856, LVII, 14; for Minas Gerais in 1883, see Bovet, "A Indústria Mineral na Província de Minas Gerais," 51–52; for Paraná in 1869, see Rebouças, *Tramway,* 10; for Pernambuco in 1864, see GBPP, 1865, LIII, 53–54; for Pernambuco in 1886, see Coutinho, *Estradas de Ferro do Norte;* for Rio de Janeiro in 1854, see *O Agricultor Brasileiro* 1 (December 1854), 13–15; for Rio de Janeiro in 1856, see EFDPII, *2d Relatório,* 1857, 32, and EFDPII, *3d Relatório,* 1857, 49; for Rio de Janeiro in 1859, see Companhia União de Indústria, *Relatório,* 1860; for Rio de Janeiro in 1855, see MI, *Relatório,* 1855, 42; for Rio de Janeiro in 1865, see MACOP, *Relatório . . . 1866,* Annexo P: "Exploração do Rio Hyapurá e do Rio Araguaya," 47; for São Paulo in 1856, see Dean, *Rio Claro,* 40; for São Paulo (dry- and wet-season rates) in 1864, see *Correio Paulistano* and *Diário Official do Império do Brasil.*

NOTE: Rates adjusted to 1913 levels using the extended wholesale price index for Rio de Janeiro, described in the text. Where contemporaries give a range of rates, the table presents only the lowest figure in that range.

railroad freight savings in Brazil were large, the rates used in the analysis are selected in such a way as to bias downward the magnitude of those savings.

The social savings estimate employs dry-season overland charges in São Paulo from 1864. Table 4.8 presents these charges. A number of important theoretical and historical criteria dictate this choice. All of them work against

Table 4.8
Dry-Season Unit Freight Charges
in São Paulo, 1864 (in current milréis)

Route	Unit charge
São Paulo–Santos	0.290
Rio Claro–Santos	0.357
Capivary–São Paulo	0.317
Itú–São Paulo	0.374
Campinas–Santos	0.378
Average charge	0.343

SOURCE: Rates are taken from *Correio Paulistano* and *Diário Official do Império do Brazil*, various issues, 1864. Pre-rail route distances are taken from the map in Müller, *Ensaio d'um Quadro Estatístico da Província de S. Paulo.*

NOTES: Unit charge is for 1 ton-kilometer freight service by mule and cart, based on average of monthly spot rates during the dry season for each route, expressed in milréis. When converted to 1913 prices, the average charge here is less than one-third of the simple average charge for all Brazil, derived from Table 4.7.

overstating the costs of pre-rail transport in Brazil. First, the São Paulo charges are based on market quotes for a competitive industry rather than anecdotes of parties with an incentive to make costs appear high. Second, since rate quotations are available every couple of weeks, it is possible to control for wet- and dry-season variation.[23] Third, common roads in São Paulo were generally better than those elsewhere in Brazil, where contemporaries complained not only of poor road conditions but the absence of roads altogether. By the 1860s the road linking São Paulo to Santos had been paved with macadam. Moreover, in 1864 a new, improved route down the *serra* to Santos was completed, and the rates from that year reflect cost savings made possible by the upgrade, along with new competition from wheeled carriers.[24] Fourth, using freight rates from a period in which the impact of the war with Paraguay had not yet registered avoids potential distortions that would make those rates unrepresentative of normal conditions, for two different reasons. All else being equal, the relative price of mule freight service would rise after 1864 in response to the increased demand for pack animals by the army in the south. Also, the spurt of inflation arising from wartime deficit spending shows up in varying degrees and with varying lags in the price indices after 1865. The delays in picking up the inflation among the different price indices potentially distorts any freight charges from the later 1860s, once they are adjusted to values for other years. Fifth, the rate on the São Paulo–Santos route is low. The charge in 1864 is for shipment along the newly improved and slightly shorter route. However, the distance employed in converting that charge to a ton-kilometer basis is the one used for the old road. This understates the prevailing unit charge. Sixth, the fact that an appreciable volume of transport services was already being supplied by railroads elsewhere in Brazil alone would have reduced aggregate demand for mules in 1864 (albeit perhaps only slightly), and thereby lowered the relative price of competing, non-rail modes of shipment. As such, the 1864 mule freight charges in São Paulo may already have declined in response to lower demand for pack animals in regions already served by rail. Finally, by 1913 nearly one-half of all railroad freight services in Brazil was generated along these same trade routes in São Paulo. The conditions and charges on the pre-rail routes in the region are those required for estimating the resource savings. Where prevailing charges were probably higher, as in Minas and in the northeast, the use of the São Paulo rates understates the unit savings on shipment. All of these considerations, along with the exclusion of all hidden or indirect cost arising from slower speed of shipment in comparison with the railroad, work to understate actual pre-rail freight costs. The direct savings on railroad freight services apply the average of the dry-season rates from the five major routes in São Paulo to all of Brazil.

Employing the rates charged by commercial freight handlers in an analysis of the railroad's transport-cost savings raises what is often a troublesome issue in relatively backward economies. Depending on conditions elsewhere in the economy, using the market rates for pre-rail freight service potentially overstates the non-rail costs of shipment, and thus imparts an upward bias to the unit-transport-cost savings. Farmers, for example, seeking to avoid high outlays on pre-rail transport, could carry their own goods to market using their own animals, slaves, and hired hands. If the labor and capital applied in transporting that freight lacked alternative uses, and became underemployed once the railroad was constructed, then the market rates for pre-rail commercial shipment would overstate the true opportunity cost of those resources. Indeed, many Brazilian farmers did not purchase transport services, preferring instead to carry their products to market themselves. This raises the possibility that the labor, capital, and time invested in pre-rail transport would have been idled by the railroad. In that case, the benefits of cheap transport would be much reduced, because the railroad would not release resources previously devoted to transport, but would instead leave them unemployed.

The concern over underemployed resources and their consequences for estimating the resource savings of the railroad is inapplicable in Brazil for two reasons. First, it is unlikely that railroads idled labor and capital, and similarly unlikely that resources were systematically underemployed.[25] Rather, railroads increased the demand for slave labor in the regions of heaviest railroad development before 1888. In the late nineteenth century, railroad expansion would prove equally important in attracting new flows of immigrant labor to Brazil.[26] Second, so long as both the pre-rail transport sector, and farming in general, were activities relying on inputs priced competitively in factor markets, the rates charged by muleteers accurately reflected the opportunity cost to the economy of farmers' providing their own transportation. Qualitative evidence suggests that Brazil's pre-rail overland-transport sector was quite competitive; it is highly unlikely that anything resembling monopoly rents were ever garnered by mule drivers. Indeed, muleteering met the classic requirements of a competitive industry. There were many commercial carriers, since muleteers typically operated on a small scale relative to total economic activity. Information on mule freight rates was widely available. This made for a large number of independent transport firms, no single one of which could influence the market price of freight services. Each perceived the demand for their transport service as highly elastic. As a result, they would have set their prices in accordance with their costs, with an extra margin to compensate for the time, risks, and entrepreneurship of the muleteer.

Whether *fazendeiros* and other shippers purchased their transport services in a market, or provided those services themselves, the costs to the economy were the same. The owners of rural estates in Brazil who hauled their own goods had to invest in mules, and grow or purchase feed. They also had to divert slaves and hired hands from farm work to take crops to market. They either had to pay someone to manage their farming operation, or simply stop farming altogether, during such lengthy trips. Contemporaries understood quite well the degree to which providing one's own transport services drained resources from farming activities. In the mid-1850s commentators indicted Brazil for having failed to improve transportation and stated succinctly the consequences for agriculture:

> The farmer, when caught between losing goods in storage houses, or becoming an agent of transport, puts together a "*tropa*," diverting himself from farm work, taking from there the best workers, and creating pastures and grains for mules. The results soon appear: farming suffers, and the perfection of the crop is set back or stationary.[27]

That microeconomic anecdotes at the farm-level match perfectly the social savings identity used here is not surprising. In nineteenth-century Brazil it was clearly understood that railroads would release capital and labor for other uses by replacing relatively inefficient forms of transport. That producers would enjoy real resource savings, either by not having to hire expensive muleteers to carry goods to distant markets, or by not having to maintain mules to carry goods themselves, was not merely wishful thinking. Railroads made it possible for agricultural producers in Brazil to escape the costs arising from "the numerous workers occupied in handling the *tropa*, and the even greater number employed in degrading the best lands to produce crops for feeding the same *tropa*."[28] In noting that the Recife and San Francisco Railway provided transport for over two hundred sugar mills, the public works engineer for the province of Pernambuco pointed out that "the personnel of these mills who had previously been employed in transporting the harvest to market are now used in planting cane and cereals, and the capital employed in animals and transport accessories now reverts to the farmers and is employed in production."[29] In short, mules, oxen, carts, wagons, and pasture were not without cost to Brazilian *fazendeiros*. Nor were the slaves, hired help, or the farmer's own time and labor that might be devoted to transport. Under prevailing practices, all of the inputs into transporting freight were priced in markets. Assigning costs to those inputs based on the charges of commercial carriers, as is done here, values those inputs correctly in nineteenth-century Brazil.[30] Commercial freight charges for non-rail transport may thus be confidently employed in the analysis.

The São Paulo freight charges from 1864 embody more than the costs of the historically relevant alternative to railroads. They also imply pre-rail transport conditions that were substantially better than what much of Brazil actually possessed at the time. The social saving measured below assumes that all of Brazil would have had roads as good as São Paulo's in the absence of the railroad. The São Paulo rates thus approximate a technological best-practice alternative to the railroad for Brazil in this period. Non-rail freight charges were typically much higher in other regions where roads were not as good.

To make the pre-rail rate comparable with the 1913 railroad freight charge requires adjusting it for inflation. The absence of a price index suited to adjusting the 1864 pre-rail freight charge to 1913 levels complicates the computation of the unit savings on freight transport. Ideally, that adjustment would use an index composed of the prices of the main inputs into the pre-rail transport sector—mules, carts, labor, feed, and harnesses. No such index exists. At the same time, the abundance of competing price indices for other bundles of goods bedevils the adjustment of money values in nineteenth-century Brazil. No single one of those indices is uniquely appropriate for the task at hand. There are no indices of the general price level before 1900.

Those series put forward in the literature as GDP deflators rely either on British wholesale prices run through the pound–milréis exchange rate, or hybridize overseas prices with fragments of other indices from Brazil. Since pre-rail overland-transport services were not internationally tradable "goods," and virtually none of the inputs in the pre-rail transport sector came from abroad, adjusting pre-rail freight charges to 1913 levels by overseas price indicators has little meaning.

Because the magnitude of the social savings is sensitive to the choice of a price deflator for freight costs, the estimate of the social savings relies on two distinct price indices, thereby providing a sensitivity test on the results. For the first of these (measure "A"), the pre-rail freight charge is adjusted to 1913 levels using a consumer price index (CPI) for Rio de Janeiro. That index is based on the prices of nine items representing a mix of internationally traded goods and domestic agricultural commodities.[31] However, the version of the index using 1856 budget weights rises more than sevenfold between 1864 and 1913. Using it to adjust the pre-rail freight charges for inflation risks considerably overstating the costs of non-rail transport in 1913. The 1919 version of the CPI weights some other items more heavily, namely butter, sugar, and wheat flour. It exhibits a more modest rise, increasing slightly more than fourfold between 1864 and 1913.[32] Of the CPIs for Rio de Janeiro it rises the least, and thus presents less risk of overstating inflation.

For the second estimate of the social savings (measure "B") several potential deflators remain. The other available indices exhibit less dramatic increases before 1913 than do any of the Rio de Janeiro CPIs. For the "B" measure of the social savings estimate, only Brazilian price indices were considered.[33] The wholesale price index for Rio de Janeiro has the broadest product coverage of any of the available indices, although it begins only in 1870.[34] Here, it is manipulated statistically and extended backward for six additional years. This is accomplished by regressing it on the 1919-weighted CPI for Rio.[35] The predicted values of the wholesale price index for the period 1864–1870 provide the necessary extrapolation. This "extended" index exhibits slightly less increase than the export price index, rising some 113 percent from 1864 to 1913. The second estimate of freight social saving relies on this index to adjust pre-rail charges to 1913 levels.[36] Adjusting the pre-rail freight charges by the two price indices gives rates in 1913 equal to 1.388 and 0.727 milréis per ton-kilometer, respectively.

The large difference between the two inflation-adjusted non-rail freight charges (almost 100 percent) might be thought to yield equally divergent measures of the social savings. But the latter further depend on the quantity of freight services. The quantity of railroad freight services produced in 1913, and the average rail freight charge, come from two types of sources. For railroads conceded by the central government, total freight output and revenue figures are available in the railway inspectorate's 1913 statistical volume.[37] In São Paulo a number of major railway companies operated several important lines that were not federally conceded and thus partly escaped the central government's reporting requirements. For the three largest of these companies—the Companhia Paulista, Companhia Mogiana, and Companhia Sorocabana—the reports of inspectors, appended to respective shareholder reports, provide the desired coverage and detail. The partial information on those lines presented in the inspectorate's statistical volume was replaced by the complete output and revenue figures from the company reports. Similarly, the output and revenue figures of other major railroads that operated only a share of their lines under federal concession, such as the Leopoldina and the Great Western, were supplemented using the information in their company reports.

Table 4.9 presents railroad freight service and revenue in 1913. In that year, Brazilian railroads comprising 89 percent of the nation's total track carried almost 1.7 billion ton-kilometers of freight, at a total cost of 165 million milréis, or $097 per ton-kilometer. This output figure excludes livestock and parcels. This imposes the assumption that in the absence of railroads, all livestock would have been driven to market on the hoof, with no loss along the way beyond that actually found in rail shipment. It also assumes that parcels would have been carried by passengers, courier, or simply not been sent at all. These assumptions are unlikely to hold in practice, and they serve to reduce the measured benefits of the railroad. Whenever possible, the output figures exclude all construction materials and other freight in the service of the line. None of that would have been carried absent the railroad. Only commodity freight and merchandise enter into the freight output figures.

Table 4.10 employs the output and cost measures to derive the social savings on railroad freight services. These estimates assume that, in the absence of railroads, all rail freight in 1913 would have been carried over the same distances and along the same routes by muleteers and carters.[38] In the first estimate of the social savings (estimate "A"), railroads generated a surplus to the Brazilian economy equal to 2.15 billion milréis. The lower half of the table presents the second estimate (estimate "B"). Adjusting the pre-rail freight charge by the wholesale price index puts the resources released to the economy by railroads in 1913 in excess of 1 billion milréis. Both figures warrant one further adjustment. Because both the central government and the provincial governments regulated freight rates, the railroad freight charge in 1913 may not represent the full cost to the economy of freight services. Given the influence of landowners and industrialists in the polity, they likely

Table 4.9
Freight Output and Revenue, 1913

Railroad	Freight output (ton-kilometers)	Freight revenue (milréis)
Madeira–Mamoré	3,133,347	4,210,149
Rede Ceará–Baturité	13,106,393	1,375,257
Rede Ceará–Sobral	3,281,050	403,793
Central do Rio Grande do Norte	2,432,064	72,992
Rede Bahia São Francisco and Branch	39,472,485	1,481,615
Rede Bahia–Central da Bahia	5,648,802	522,926
Rede Bahia–Bahia e Minas	7,907,100	791,408
Rio do Ouro	3,195,423	142,122
Rede Sul Mineira	47,046,470	2,811,256
Oeste de Minas	27,888,582	2,538,934
Formiga a Goyaz	2,045,245	199,208
Araguary a Catalão	1,062,736	174,933
Paraná	43,598,174	4,790,361
Dona Thereza Christina	745,664	65,840
Santa Catarina	324,478	61,409
Viação Ferrea Rio Grande do Sul	155,006,377	8,447,538
Itaqui a S. Borja	731,198	56,841
Prolongamento da E. F. Maricá	39,017	8,197
Caxias a Cajazeiras	351,010	64,390
Vitória á Santana dos Ferros	5,597,408	1,021,308
Curralinho á Diamantina	816,133	108,197
Baurú a Itapura	8,701,246	802,056
Quarahim a Itaquy	3,017,886	216,031
São Paulo–Rio Grande Itararé a Uruguay	26,074,795	1,712,290
São Paulo–Rio Grande Linha de S. Francisco	4,414,710	451,450
Great Western	80,081,948	7,497,105
Central do Brazil	359,931,486	20,916,928
Companhia Paulista	236,054,054	25,391,470
Sorocabana	137,520,736	12,347,898
San Paulo Railway	265,649,458	27,623,875
Companhia Mogiana	154,085,223	19,368,000
Leopoldina Railway	58,360,320	19,691,325
Total	1,697,321,018	165,367,102

SOURCE: See Appendix B.

succeeded in exercising significant downward pressure on railroad rates. Indeed, the regulated rail rates led to freight charges that were less than costs on many railroads. In that case, using the average revenue to proxy the unit resource cost of railroad services to the economy overstates the unit savings, and the social savings estimates would be too large.[39] An adjustment is perhaps warranted to correct for that bias in the estimates. At the same time, the advisability of such a correction can be questioned in light of the various biases already built into the calculations to ensure that the unit savings are not overstated.

Both calculations in Table 4.10 deduct from the gross benefits of railroad freight services subsidies of various types, including payments made to railway companies as profit guarantees by the Brazilian government in 1913. Sources vary in the level of profit guarantees disbursed for 1913. One source puts guarantees at 8.8 million milréis, while another reports 11.8 million milréis paid out in the *garantias de juros*.[40] In addition to these profit guarantees, the Brazilian government paid interest in 1913 on loans it had contracted to buy up railroads and build new ones. Together with the higher figure on profit guarantees, these payments comprise fixed charges not reflected in the railroad revenues, and as such, are costs to the economy of producing transport services. The value of the total "missing" capital costs comes to 36.9 million milréis, and that figure is deducted from both variants of the social savings in Table 4.10.[41] Charging all of those capital costs against freight services overstates the extent to which railroad freight charges departed from true costs, since railroads also carried passengers, animals, and the like, and a portion of capital charges would have to be assigned to these other categories of service.[42] Estimate "A" of the social savings, adjusted in this fashion, equals 38 percent of Brazilian GDP in 1913, while estimate "B," similarly adjusted, exceeds 18 percent of GDP.[43]

These magnitudes should be considered an upper-bound on the "true" measure of freight social savings.[44] By fixing railroad output at 1.7 billion ton-kilometers, the estimate assumes that the same level of freight service would have been demanded, and produced, at the much higher pre-rail freight charges. It implies that the production of transportable goods in Brazil was unresponsive to the fall in freight shipping costs. It takes the demand for freight services as perfectly inelastic over a large change in the price of that service, and the supply of freight service as perfectly elastic over a large range of output. The net bias in the social saving that results from this assumption is unknown, because there are potentially offsetting factors in both directions. One of them is a price effect, and the other is a quantity effect.

On the one hand, it is possible that the pre-rail charges for freight service at this level of output are not just low, but much too low. This is because us-

Table 4.10
Direct Social Savings on
Railroad Freight Services, 1913

Estimate "A"

1. Railroad freight output	1,697,321,018 ton-km
2. Railroad freight revenues (at $097 per ton-km)	165.4 million milréis
3. Cost of pre-rail shipment (at 1$388.5 per ton-km)	2,356.7 million milréis
4. Direct social savings (line 3 minus line 2)	2,191.3 million milréis
5. Brazilian government profit guarantees	36.9 million milréis
6. Adjusted direct social savings (line 4 minus line 5)	2,154.4 million milréis

Estimate "B"

1. Railroad freight output	1,697,321,018 ton-km
2. Railroad freight revenues (at $097 per ton-km)	165.4 million milréis
3. Cost of pre-rail shipment (at $727.1 per ton-km)	1,234.2 million milréis
4. Direct social savings (line 3 minus line 2)	1,068.8 million milréis
5. Brazilian government profit guarantees	36.9 million milréis
6. Adjusted direct social savings (line 4 minus line 5)	1,031.9 million milréis

---

SOURCES: For freight output, see Tables 4.4 and 4.9; for freight revenues, see Tables 4.5 and 4.9; for non-rail freight charge, see Table 4.8.

ing the pre-rail freight rate assumes constant unit costs in the old transport sector over a very large range of output. This implies that the supply of inputs into the pre-rail transport sector was itself perfectly elastic. If that were not the case, then the resource savings estimated here would be too low. The pre-rail economy never witnessed levels of transport demand anywhere near that exhibited once railroads were in place. Confronted with a vast increase in demand, unit costs might well have risen spectacularly in the absence of the railroad, well beyond the observed pre-rail charge. Diverting mules, labor, materials for carts, and resources for road construction from other activities might have quickly pushed freight charges well above their 1864 levels. A large amount of capital and labor would have to be shifted from the rest of the economy to the non-rail transport sector in order to produce 1.7 billion ton-kilometers of freight service, and that is precisely what the social savings measures. It is, in fact, not at all clear that the pre-rail transport sector could have provided this much freight service without moving to a point on the industry's cost function where the average cost of transport was rising. At that level of output, the costs of providing transport services in the absence of railroads may well have risen above the pre-rail rate and the social savings would be understated. Altering the assumption of constant pre-rail costs would simply increase the estimated resource gains due to the railroad.

On the other hand, holding constant the quantity of freight services demanded at the higher, pre-rail freight rate creates an offsetting bias. This bias stems from assuming that the demand for railroad freight services in Brazil was perfectly inelastic over a large range of freight charges. Indeed, the assumption that the demand for freight services in nineteenth-century Brazil was perfectly inelastic with respect to price, and that all of the freight carried in 1913 would have been carried in the absence of railroads, is unlikely warranted. Given the large change in the unit cost of transport, in Brazil's pre-rail economy many fewer goods would have traveled to market. In the absence of railroads, Brazil would have had much-reduced margins of feasible cultivation, just as it had in the pre-rail era. Crop choices at the level of the farm would differ, and specialization by region would have been limited to a greater degree. In manufacturing, the less efficient textile mills and iron forges would have continued to operate with the natural protection afforded by transport costs, and relatively more efficient firms would be unable to exploit the gains from trade and product specialization. Transport demand no doubt expanded considerably in the decades before 1913. Since the unit-cost savings on shipping freight were so great, forcing the "non-rail" counterfactual economy to operate with the 1913 levels of transport output effectively guarantees that the measured social saving is large. A separate counterfactual case or cases may be just as plausibly specified. In order to do so, the Brazilian economy is permitted to adjust its level of freight output, in accordance with the sensitivity of the demand for freight services to changes in the unit price of those services. Under such conditions, the social savings in Brazil would be smaller, since the diversion of resources from other sectors to transport would be less than in the case where the full 1913 level of transport services was produced. Since the actual margins of feasible cultivation, and the marketing perimeters of factories, were direct functions of the cost of transporting those goods to market, the degree to which the demand for freight services was reduced at higher transport charges can be estimated from evidence. Then the level of that demand, and even total output in the economy, can be adjusted accordingly.

Adjusting the social savings to allow for a smaller transport sector is accomplished by letting the demand for freight service vary with its price. This permits the price elasticity of demand for freight services to take on values

Table 4.11

Freight Social Savings for
Alternative Values of the Price Elasticity of Demand
for Freight Services

Elasticity of demand	Estimate "A" (milréis)	"A"/GDP	Estimate "B" (milréis)	"B"/GDP
0.00	2,154,436,330	0.38	1,031,991,151	0.18
−0.25	1,359,886,696	0.24	738,271,436	0.13
−0.50	880,944,119	0.16	535,948,741	0.09
−0.75	586,868,154	0.10	394,980,928	0.07
−1.00	402,487,678	0.07	295,527,105	0.05
−1.25	284,157,875	0.05	224,406,558	0.04
−1.50	206,258,361	0.04	172,806,822	0.03
−1.75	153,562,944	0.03	134,794,602	0.02
−2.00	116,897,608	0.02	106,344,733	0.02

NOTE: Proportions of social savings in GDP are rounded to the nearest hundredth. The direct savings estimates are adjusted by varying the elasticity of demand for two different cases. Where $\phi \neq -1$, the lower-bound social savings are:

$$LBSS = \int_{P_R}^{P_N} DP^\phi \, dp - G = D \left[\frac{P_N^{\phi+1} - P_R^{\phi+1}}{\phi + 1} \right] - G$$

while for the case in which $\phi = -1$:

$$LBSS = \int_{P_R}^{P_N} DP^\phi \, dp - G = \left[D\ln\left[\frac{P_N}{P_R} \right] \right] - G$$

other than zero. How much smaller the social savings would be in this case depends directly on the elasticity, which is the sensitivity of demand for freight service to the change in the cost of transport.[45] Estimates of social savings derived with non-zero price elasticities of demand provide measures of the social savings less than the upper bound. Table 4.11 presents alternative measures of both the "A" and "B" estimates of the resource savings for non-zero values of the price elasticity of demand, and Figure 4.1 presents the same information graphically. At any elasticity between 0 and −1, the social savings decline, but still exceed or remain comparable with the upper-bound estimates for the late-nineteenth-century United States. Beyond that point, however, the savings falls off to levels that are considered insignificant by

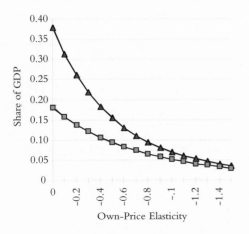

Figure 4.1. Sensitivity of the direct social savings on railroad freight services to the own-price price elasticity of demand for transport in Brazil, 1913.

much of the literature on railroads. The more sensitive the demand for transport is to the change in transport costs, the smaller the lower-bound social saving becomes.

By directly inferring the sensitivity of demand from observable features of the market for freight-transport services, it is possible to assess the validity of these adjustments. It turns out that although demand was not perfectly inelastic, as assumed by the upper-bound social savings, the demand for transport was indeed *relatively* inelastic. One regular commentator on railroads in Brazil's northeast during the 1870s and 1880s held that if rail rates on sugar were halved, the result would be roughly a 40 percent increase in the volume of sugar shipped. The arc elasticity of demand implied by this was −0.85.[46] Because transport is an intermediate input, the elasticity of demand for transporting sugar is itself a function of both the elasticities of farm-gate supply and market demand for sugar in Brazil, and the share of the delivered price of sugar accounted for by transport costs. Since these elasticities and proportions vary widely across commodities, the evidence from one market alone is insufficient for concluding that the demand for all freight services was inelastic. Fortunately, evidence beyond the impressions of contemporaries discussing markets for a single good is available. Econometric analysis of the market for freight services establishes a plausible range of elasticities of demand.[47]

Table 4.12 presents the results of this analysis. Annual time-series data from 1898 to 1913 for the entire railroad sector make it possible to estimate

Table 4.12

Alternative Specifications of the Demand for Freight Transport Service in Brazil, 1898–1913

[I]

$$\ln Q_D = -13.2 - .37 \ln P + .72 \ln GDP + 0.82 \ln POP + 0.2 \ln T - .03 \ln COAL$$
$$\quad\quad (-.9) \quad (-1.7) \quad\quad (1.9) \quad\quad\quad (.6) \quad\quad\quad (0.2) \quad\quad (-0.1)$$

$R^2 = 0.96$ D.W. = 2.4

[II]

$$\ln Q_D = -10.2 - 0.55 \ln P + 1.2 \ln GDP$$
$$\quad\quad (-8.2) \quad (-6.8) \quad\quad (22.9)$$

$R^2 = .90$ D.W. = 2.3

[III]

$$\ln Q_D = -10.3 - 0.59 \ln P + 1.23 \ln GDP$$
$$\quad\quad (-5.5) \quad (-4.3) \quad\quad (15)$$

$R^2 = .96$ D.W. = 2.7

NOTE: Q is the level of freight service in ton-kilometers, P is the price of that service in deflated milréis, GDP is real income, COAL is the deflated price of coal, POP is the population, and T is the extension of track in service. For data sources and assumptions behind the different specifications, see text. The price elasticity of demand for freight transport service, ϕ, is given by:

$$\phi = \frac{\partial \ln Q_D}{\partial \ln P}$$

which is the parameter estimate of $\ln P$ in the demand functions. Parenthetical figures are t-statistics.

the price elasticity of demand for freight services for several different specifications of the market for transport services. The partial coverage of the sample series in the years before 1898 precludes extending the analysis further back in time. All of the estimating equations employ logarithmic transformations of the data series so that the coefficients may be interpreted directly as elasticities. For all equations, t-statistics are reported in parentheses.

The first specification treats the demand for freight service (Q), in units of ton-kilometers as a function of the real unit freight charge (P), GDP, track, the price of coal, and population.[48] Applying ordinary least squares (OLS) regression yields a price elasticity of demand of -0.37. This specification of the market is valid only if one assumes that the prices for freight services were completely exogenous. Rate regulation by the government means that, at least in the short run, rates were indeed set exogenously, and themselves did not vary with the quantity of freight services demanded. However, since most railroads by the late 1890s had their regulated rates set to "slide" with the exchange rate, the exogeneity of freight charges cannot be pushed too far. Therefore, the second specification reported in the table uses instrumental variables to control for supply-side shifts in the market. Population, track in service, the real price of coal, and a time trend serve as the instruments. The demand for freight service is modeled as a function of its own price, and GDP. The resulting elasticity (-0.55) is higher in absolute value, and takes on greater statistical significance than that estimated in the first specification. A third specification, again based on instrumental variables, employs as instruments the time trend, track, and population. The demand equation looks solely at price and income effects. The elasticity there increases slightly in absolute value (-0.59), and again takes on statistical significance.

It would be imprudent to claim that any of the estimated elasticities represents the true measure, for two reasons. First, these specifications of the demand function are admittedly crude, and exclude variables that might be important simply because no information on them is available. Second, there is in fact no one true elasticity of demand, but rather a continuum of elasticities, ranging from the very short run to the very long run. The parameters obtained here are reassuringly robust to different specifications of the demand function. Based on the measured elasticities, the demand for freight services in Brazil was relatively inelastic, at most lying in the interval running from -0.6 to -1.0. Figure 4.2 portrays the position of the demand curve when the elasticity is -1.0. If the social saving is adjusted accordingly, it ranges between 5 and 15 percent of GDP in 1913. While the magnitude of the social savings measure proves quite sensitive to varying assumptions about the price elasticity of demand for freight services, at the highest elas-

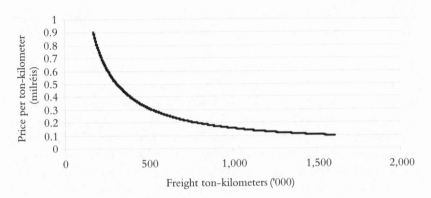

Figure 4.2. Demand for freight transport services in Brazil, 1913.

NOTE: The right-most point of the demand curve is the unit freight charge and level of railroad freight service in 1913. The demand curve is of constant elasticity, parameterized by a price elasticity of demand equal to −1.0.

ticity measured the saving remains large, between 8 and 16 percent of GDP in 1913.

Major implications emerge from these adjustments to the social savings. First, it is unlikely that any other single technological or institutional innovation offered such gains to the Brazilian economy before 1914. As such, the railroad conferred on Brazil benefits that probably exceeded, by far, those stemming from the other major changes in economic organization in this period, such as the capital market reforms of the early 1890s, or the changes in the definition and enforcement of property rights in land under Republican state governments.[49] Second, in comparison with other countries for which similar estimates exist, the gains from railroads in Brazil were proportionally greater than in countries at roughly similar stages of development. Table 4.13 presents estimates of freight social savings for a variety of cases. Comparison with the results for railroads elsewhere is rendered problematic by the differing counterfactual specifications employed in obtaining those results. Reference to those results makes it clear that in Brazil the gain to the economy from cheap transport provided by railroads was quite large. In most other countries where such estimates have been constructed, the results were lower than that.

The main complication involved in comparing Brazil with other cases arises from the specification of the counterfactual mode of shipment. In the Fogelian model of the United States, the economy is permitted to adjust to using the technological second-best mode of shipment in the absence of the railroad by constructing an elaborate network of canals to tie in with natural waterways. In the Fishlovian specification, the economy relies upon the historically relevant alternative modes of shipment that were in place. The Brazilian counterfactual lies between these two alternatives. On the one hand, this admits that overland shipment by some mix of cart and mule was the historically relevant alternative to railroads in Brazil. These were the modes that were put out of business when the railroad was constructed. On the other hand, it employs a freight charge from a region where improvements had made roads significantly more trafficable than elsewhere in Brazil. It approximates, in that regard, a second-best specification of the alternative transport technology.

Directly comparing the Brazilian results with those of the advanced economies is most appropriate in the case of the antebellum U.S., which was at a roughly similar stage of railroad development.[50] Fishlow found the *upper*-bound direct savings in 1859 to be in the range of 4 percent of national income, under the assumption of inelastic demand for freight services.[51] In 1913 Brazil, the *lower*-bound freight savings was at least that much, and probably greater. By contrast, for the late-nineteenth-century U.S., Fogel put the direct savings on freight services at 8.9 percent of GNP at the very most.[52] In Tsarist Russia, Metzer put freight social savings at 4.6 percent of GNP in 1907.[53] Both of these are *upper*-bound estimates. The analogous measure for Brazil, the upper bound of the second variant, is, in proportional terms, four times larger than the savings in Russia, and double the savings in the United States. Similarly, in England and Wales in 1865, the direct social savings was around 4.1 percent of national income.[54] Only in Spain and Mexico do the resource savings from railroad freight services rival the Brazilian estimates. In Spain, railroads saved between 19.2 and 23.7 percent of GNP in 1912.[55] For Mexico, similar measures are greater still, ranging between 24.9 and 38.5 percent of GDP in 1910. This result is due in large part to the extraordinary share of freight services that depended wholly on the contiguous U.S. market, a unique circumstance in the extreme.[56] The implication of geographic propinquity for the magnitude of Mexico's social savings was no doubt huge. By way of illustration, if the social savings for the United States and Mexico are estimated simultaneously, Fogel's results for the United States would be little changed, since a relatively small share of freight services in the United States depended on commerce with Mexico. But the estimated Mexican social savings would be vastly reduced, falling off perhaps by more than 50 percent.[57] As such, the size of the social savings the railroad created in Mexico depends critically on the direct connection by rail to the much larger U.S. economy.

Table 4.13

Estimates of Freight Social Savings for Various Countries

Country	Year	Social saving as a share of GDP
England and Wales	1865	4.1
England and Wales	1890	11.0
France	1872	5.8
Germany	1890s	5.0
Spain	1912	23.7
Belgium	1865	2.5
Belgium	1912	4.5
Russia	1907	4.6
China	1933	0.5
United States	1859	3.7
United States	1890	8.9
Argentina	1913	26.0
Colombia	1927	7.9
Mexico	1910	38.5
Brazil	1913	18.0

SOURCES: For Argentina, see Summerhill, "Profit and Productivity on Argentine Railroads"; for Brazil, see Table 4.10; for Colombia, see Ramirez, "Railroads and the Colombian Economy," table 3; for Mexico, see Coatsworth, *Growth Against Development*, 113–19; for China, see Huenemann, *The Dragon and the Iron Horse*, 228; for all others, see O'Brien, "Transport and Economic Growth," 336–67.

Nineteenth-century Brazil was a relatively backward economy with a similarly backward pre-rail transport sector, where little of its freight service depended on connections to neighboring countries. Reallocating its freight shipments in 1913 to animal-drawn, wheeled vehicles, even with good roads, would have created stunning economic losses. The expansion of railroads between 1854 and 1913 drove down the cost of transport, which in turn redounded through the economy and allowed producers to expand output to service ever-widening markets, thereby creating hefty social savings. Brazil garnered a large share of its national income from the resource savings that railroad development afforded.

From Social Savings to Social Returns

The large direct contribution of the railroad to the economy does not reveal whether Brazil received a good return on the investment it made in securing those benefits. If the railroad created large social savings, but required inordinately large amounts of capital to do so, then its contribution might well have been negative when considered in light of alternative investments. Indeed, whether or not the payoff from railroad capital represented a large return depended on the returns to investments in other forms of capital. Such an assessment requires an estimate of the social rate of return, converting the "stock" of railroad benefits into a flow. In practice, social rates of return suffer from interpretive difficulties that stem from theoretical and methodological ambiguities. The social rate of return is nonetheless the best available measure indicating the return to the economy from having undertaken an investment in railroads. Table 4.14 presents estimates of the average and marginal social rates of return to the capital employed in Brazil's railroads in 1913.[58] The average social rates of return apply two distinct estimates of the lower-bound direct social savings from Table 4.11, summed with net railroad operating revenues. Those benefits are divided by a measure of the stock of capital employed in producing all railroad transport services that year. Construction costs, representing real, reproducible, physical capital of Brazilian railroads, are used as the denominator in the calculation. While the resulting average social rates of return are based on downward-biased measures of freight benefits, they are nonetheless large, ranging from 17.9 percent to 23.1 percent in 1913. Using the upper-bound measure of the social saving would raise the return higher still.

The average social rate of return reveals whether the benefits from railroad capital exceeded its costs. However, it does not show whether or not "too much" or "too little" had been invested in the rail sector.[59] Benefit-cost analysis in this form must be performed in terms of the marginal rate of return. The marginal rate of return indicates the benefit to Brazil from additional milréis invested in the railroad system. Marginal rates of return are rarely observable in practice and must be inferred from other indicators. Interpreting any particular estimate of the marginal social rate of return can be unclear in the absence of estimates from a variety of alternative investment activities. The bottom portion of Table 4.14 presents two estimates of the marginal social return to the Brazilian rail sector. In doing so, it necessarily invokes several assumptions that some scholars find problematic in similar measures for the United States, namely that the railroad sector enjoyed constant returns to scale, that there was strict proportionality between the social

Table 4.14

Average and Marginal Social Rates of Return to the Brazilian
Railroad Sector, 1913

---

1. "Non-appropriale" social benefits (lower-bound estimates of
freight social savings where the elasticity equals −1.0)

    (a) Estimate "A" (7 percent of GDP)   402.5 million milréis

    (b) Estimate "B" (5 percent of GDP)   295.5 million milréis

2. Total rail revenues   250.0 million milréis

3. Net rail revenues   73.3 million milréis

4. Total social benefit (social savings plus net rail revenues)

    (a) Estimate "A"   475.8 million milréis

    (b) Estimate "B"   368.8 million milréis

5. Construction cost of railroads   2.053 billion milréis

6. Average social rate of return for estimate "A" (line 4(a)/line 5)   23.1%

7. Average social rate of return for estimate "B" (line 4(b)/line 5)   17.9%

8. Share of capital earnings in revenues (line 3 + G/line 2 + G,
where G is government subsidy payments plus interest)   0.381

9. Marginal social rates of return, 1913

    (a) Estimate "A" (product of line 8 and line 6)   8.81%

    (b) Estimate "B" (product of line 8 and line 7)   6.82%

SOURCE: See Table 4.11 and text.

and private output of the sector, and that the economy was marked by constant returns and competition throughout.[60] Under those admittedly tight assumptions, the average social rate of return converts to the marginal rate through two additional steps. The first infers the output elasticity of capital from the share of capital earnings in total costs. In a constant-returns-to-scale activity, the share of capital costs in total revenues equals the elasticity of private output with respect to capital.[61] For this purpose, the capital earnings in the railroad sector in 1913 include both the net revenues of the sector and the government's outlays on interest and guaranteed dividends. Those capital earnings in 1913 were 38.1 percent of total railroad revenues plus guarantees. The second step simply applies this scaling factor to derive the marginal social rate of return. Multiplying the average social rates of return by this figure yields the marginal social rate of return, which is the "social productivity" of an additional investment in the railroad sector.

The results of those manipulations in Table 4.14 show that the marginal social rate of return of railroad capital in Brazil in 1913 was between 6.8 percent and 8.8 percent, under the assumptions outlined here. The social rates of return on alternative projects in Brazil remain unknown in the absence of supplementary research. If the capital market is well integrated, the marginal social return on capital across the economy equals the private return to capital. As such, these figures may be compared with private rates of return (profits) elsewhere in the economy. To do so, the private rate of return to the railroad sector itself is first calculated from total outlays on reproducible physical capital, and the railroad's capital earnings (net revenues plus guarantees). That ratio comes to 5.32 percent in 1913. The return to other activities for which securities traded on stock markets is revealed by the earnings-price ratios on their stocks and bonds. The earnings-price ratio on Brazilian government gold bonds in 1913 was around 5.1 percent.[62] The earnings-price ratios on stocks and bonds for a sample of publicly traded Brazilian cotton textile firms were higher, ranging from 7.0 to 8.5 percent in 1913.[63] However, the financial measures of profit exceeded the returns on the physical capital in these textile firms because they embodied some risk. The average annual returns on Brazilian government debt investments in London ranged from 6.91 percent to 9.21 percent.[64] The upshot of this comparison is that it was highly unlikely that Brazilians had somehow overinvested in railroad technology. These downwardly biased measures of the average social return, converted by plausibly inferring the output elasticity of capital in the railroad sector, yield results that equal or exceed the market rates of return, and the private rate of return on the rail sector itself. If one permits the unappropriable social benefits (taken to equal the social savings) to increase, by assuming a value of the price elasticity of demand between 0 and −1, the marginal rate of return to railroad investment rises spectacularly.

On the surface, it may well be the case that the Brazilian economy could have done better with still more railroads, and that the strategies pursued in regulating rail companies stifled investments in transport that would have raised Brazilian GDP even higher in 1913. Upon closer examination, however, the return to the economy from railroad investments in *particular* railroad projects grows considerably more cloudy. The results of Table 4.14 obscure important details because they are highly aggregated, treating all of

Table 4.15
Marginal Social Rate of Return on Railroad Capital, 1913

Railroad	Marginal social rate of return	Railroad	Marginal social rate of return
Madeira–Mamoré	-0.008	Viação Ferrea do Rio	
Baturité	0.064	Grande do Sul	0.097
Sobral	0.019	Itaqui a S. Borja	0.015
Central do Rio Grande do		Caxias a Cajazeiras	0.016
Norte	0.016	Recife a Limoeiro	0.138
Natal a Itamatahy	0.019	Vitória á Santana	0.020
Conde d'Eu	0.033	Curralinho á Diamantina	0.017
Central de Pernambuco	0.054	Leopoldina	0.144
Recife a São Francisco	0.140	Ramal do Sumidouro	0.011
Ribeirão a Cortez	0.020	Prol. da Barão de	
Sul de Pernambuco	0.066	Araruama	0.021
Central de Alagôas e		Carangola e Ramais	0.156
Ramal	0.038	St. Eduardo a Itapemirim	0.077
Paulo Affonso	0.002	Central de Macaé	0.009
São Francisco e Ramal	0.071	Leopoldina–Norte	0.093
Central da Bahia	0.024	Sul do Espírito Santo	0.013
Bahia e Minas	0.027	Caravelas e Ramal	0.011
Central do Brazil	0.125	Santos a Jundiaí	0.233
Cruzeiro a Tuyuty e		Sorocabana	0.152
Ramais	0.056	Bauru á Itapura	0.071
Muzambinho a Posses	0.017	Paulista	0.204
Formiga a Goyaz	0.018	Mogiana	0.131
Araguary a Catalão	0.014	Quarahim a Itaquy	0.044
Paraná	0.121	Itararé a Uruguay	0.037
D. Thereza Christina	0.008	Linha de São Francisco	0.020
Santa Catarina	0.005		

NOTE: These lines provide the greatest disaggregation possible of the railroad systems of Table 4.9.

Brazil's railroads as a single project. Table 4.15 repeats the procedure of Table 4.14 in estimating the marginal social rate of return, but on a line-by-line basis for all of the railroads that possess complete information on costs, capital, and freight output and revenues for 1913. The main difference between the two tables is that in Table 4.15 the social saving for each line is calculated at one-half of the upper-bound "B" measure of social savings, under the assumption that each line confronted linear demand for its services and that, at the pre-rail rate, no freight would have been carried. Disaggregating the sector in this fashion suggests that most of Brazil's railroads did not generate social returns at the margin in excess of what could have been earned on low-risk securities. In short, while the sector as a whole manifested an impressive social return, many of the sector's lines did not represent an effective economic application of capital.[65]

This apparent contradiction is intelligible in light of Brazilian policies, including low tariffs on railroad inputs, government dividend guarantees, and outright subsidies on government-owned lines, which channeled many railroad investments to areas where production possibilities were poor. Just how costly such policies were in 1913 can be roughly gauged in light of the results in Table 4.15 in the following manner. Collectively, the railroads that generated marginal social returns in excess of 5.1 percent (which may be taken as the opportunity cost of capital) achieved more than 13 percent at the margin. If the capital in railroads that performed poorly had been directed instead to regions or activities that did as well as the top performers, it would have increased the lower-bound freight social savings by 65.3 million milréis, or some 22 percent, and the upper-bound social savings by more than 6 percent. Since the good-performing railroads did not rely on poor-performing feeder lines for a large share of their freight, the more than half a billion milréis that Brazil sank into these poorly performing railroads could have been diverted to other income-enhancing uses without reducing the gains on the remaining railroads. The benefits such a diversion could have created for Brazil could easily have been quite large. By way of example, while there has been relatively little study of schooling and education in Brazil under the Old Republic, low levels of literacy indicate that investments in human capital were lacking. Had some or all of the poor-performing railroad capital been redirected to education, Brazil might well have garnered handsome returns, the magnitude of which can only be guessed at.[66]

This, then, was the essence of "order against progress": policies that promoted sorely needed transport, or improvements in general, also promoted overinvestment in individual railroads that did poorly. Accompanied by underinvestment in other forms of social overhead capital, the opportunity

Table 4.16

Upper-Bound Estimate of Direct Social Savings (DSS)
on Railroad Freight Service in Brazil, 1869–1913

Year	Freight service (millions of ton-kilometers)	Cost for non-rail carriage (milréis)	Rail freight revenues (milréis)	DSS (milréis)	GDP (milréis)	DSS/GDP (percent)
1869	32.7	15.3	6.13	9.13	516	1.8
1887	221.1	92.1	27.2	78.4	658	9.9
1898	586.0	601.6	95.5	506.1	3,262	15.5
1907	1,004.0	685.8	121.0	564.8	3,655	15.4
1913	1,697.0	1,234.2	165.4	1,068.8	5,679	18.8

SOURCES AND NOTES: These estimates revise the original figures produced in Summerhill, "Transport Improvements and Economic Growth in Brazil and Mexico," 104. The figures do not adjust for subsidy payments from the government. The DSS figures here correspond to the "B" estimate of Table 4.10. All values expressed in millions, in prices of that year. The non-rail unit freight charge employed in establishing the cost of carriage is from Table 4.8 and is adjusted to the respective price level for each year using the Rio de Janeiro wholesale price index.

costs of misallocation may well have approached the magnitude of the benefits Brazil did obtain from railroads.

Railroads and the Growth of the Brazilian Economy

In Brazil an expanding railroad sector carried an increasingly larger quantity of freight from 1858 to 1913. Simultaneously, the cost of shipment by rail declined. As a result, the savings to the economy grew steadily, becoming quite large by 1913. The importance of the large direct social saving from railroads in 1913 can be recast in terms of the economy's growth. This is because the saving comprises not only a portion of Brazil's output, but is also a share of the total increase in economic activity over the relevant interval of time. In 1869 Brazil's railroad sector was still small, consisting of only six lines. Most of the gains that railroads brought the Brazilian economy came well after that, most likely following the railroad boom in the 1880s. Table 4.16 presents estimates of the freight social savings from 1869 through 1913. Between 1885 and 1913 Brazil's GDP rose from some 1.53 million contos to 5.68 million contos de réis at 1913 prices, an increase in output of 4.15 million contos. Over the same interval, Brazil's population grew from 12.9 million persons to 23.7 million. The implied gain in productivity across the economy was 1.56 million contos. The *lower*-bound "B" measure of social saving, when evaluated at a price elasticity of demand of −1, comes to almost 19 percent of the productivity gain, and more than 7 percent of the total increase in GDP. The upper-bound "B" measure of social saving accounts for 66 percent of the gain in productivity per capita, and almost 25 percent of the total change in output. By dramatically reducing the cost of freight-transport services, railroads accounted for a large share of the overall growth of the Brazilian economy in the late nineteenth and early twentieth centuries, precisely in the period when Brazil effected a dramatic traverse to much improved economic performance. To the extent that Brazil failed to reap the full potential of the investments in railroads, it was not because the notion of progress shared by Brazilian elites under the Empire and early Republic embodied a blind support for imported technology and capital. Rather, political arrangements proved responsive to demands for railroads in regions where economic prospects did not warrant them. The Brazilian form of Order, so necessary for economic growth, brought with it an associated set of costs and incentives that ironically may well have worked to inhibit long-term material progress.

Chapter 5

Railroad Passenger Benefits

In the same way that railroads reduced the costs to the economy of shipping freight, they could also make passenger travel more affordable, since they were cheaper than other commercial alternatives. However, in Brazil, pre-rail travel was largely by foot or on the backs of animals. A minority of travelers enjoyed the relative luxury of stagecoaches. In light of the railroad's large social savings on freight services, one might expect the same for passenger travel. In the North Atlantic economies, for example, passenger social savings rivaled those obtained on freight services, contributing a large increment to the total gains that the railroad created.[1] In Brazil, the resources released by substituting railroad passenger services for traditional modes contributed relatively less to the overall benefits from railroads. This chapter examines the impact of railroad passenger transport by deriving measures of those passenger benefits in Brazil. The savings that this economy received by having its passengers travel by rail depended on the value of the resources released in shifting away from the prevailing archaic modes of travel. Railroad passenger benefits had two sources, the first of which was the direct savings on travel fares, and the second of which was the value of the passenger travel time that the railroad saved. If passenger benefits in Brazil were low, it was not because too few Brazilians traveled. In fact, Brazilians traveled more frequently than their contemporaries in Mexico and Russia. Rather, passenger benefits were limited in Brazil mainly because walking was a viable low-cost substitute for second-class railroad passengers (and indeed for the bulk of the population), and because the value of the time saved in traveling by rail for both classes of passenger service was low. Walking sacrificed comfort and speed, but involved negligible cash output.

While data on pre-rail freight service are difficult to obtain, even less information on pre-rail passenger travel survives. As a result, the estimates of passenger social savings must be considered more tentative than those for railroad freight services. Some of the assumptions required to measure those benefits work to elevate the passenger savings, while a number of assumptions, derived from the known features of the Brazilian economy, work to keep those measures down. Although the passenger social savings estimates are clearly subject to reassessment and revision as additional information becomes available, it is highly unlikely that such revisions will raise the passenger benefits to anywhere near the level of the freight social savings.

The measure of passenger social savings to the Brazilian economy parallels that of the estimate of freight savings. The ramifications of travel for the level of economic activity depended on two things. First, travel was a consumption good. When the cost of travel fell, travelers enjoyed a consumer's surplus. The benefit was independent of whether the purpose of their travel was leisure, business, or commuting to work. Second, when the speed of conveyance increased, there were additional gains to travelers that resulted from the savings on travel time. The unit savings on passenger travel thus consisted of two elements. The first was the direct travel charges, or fares, saved by traveling on the railroad. This is analogous to the unit savings on freight services in Chapter 4. The second element is the value of the time saved traveling on the railroad. Trains were much faster than pre-rail modes of travel. The passenger travel time saved is analogous to the savings on inventory costs on freight, which were ignored in Chapter 4. For the estimate of the passenger social savings, where the working hypothesis is that passenger benefits were low, incorporating the value of time saved works against producing an estimate of total passenger benefits that is predestined to be small. Just as was the case with freight, where the social saving captured the gains of product market integration and specialization, passenger savings similarly capture the gains of improved labor-market integration. However, unlike the case of product markets, labor-market integration is difficult to detect through declining "price" dispersion—or more appropriately—wage dispersion. Since labor is a factor input into production, the commodity price convergence that arises from product market integration can cause real wages to appear to converge across regions, even though no laborer might ever move from a low-wage to a high-wage area, and no independent improvement in labor-market integration transpires.

Table 5.1
Railroad Passengers by Class, 1913

Railroad	First-class passengers	Second-class passengers
Madeira–Mamoré	4,737	17,737
Rede Ceará–Baturité	103,916	131,193
Rede Ceará–Sobral	19,126	33,735
Central do Rio Grande do Norte	11,507	21,905
Rede Bahia São Francisco and Branch	229,344	619,863
Rede Bahia–Central da Bahia	34,242	81,931
Rede Bahia–Bahia e Minas	1,353	5,267
Rio do Ouro	19,755	124,351
Rede Sul Mineira	92,987	461,240
Oeste de Minas	118,064	247,122
Formiga a Goyaz	7,779	15,132
Araguary a Catalão	7,131	18,696
Paraná	65,047	170,592
Dona Thereza Christina	4,788	48,944
Santa Catarina	1,990	31,361
Viação Ferrea Rio Grande do Sul	727,680	232,993
Itaqui a S. Borja	5,197	4,000
Prolongamento da E. F. Maricá	1,131	5,380
Caxias a Cajazeiras	3,334	3,367
Vitória á Santana dos Ferros	16,736	63,016
Curralinho á Diamantina	2,396	8,115
Baurú a Itapura	12,463	83,007
Quarahim a Itaquy	10,728	11,603
São Paulo–Rio Grande Itararé a Uruguay	32,810	86,145
São Paulo–Rio Grande Linha de S. Francisco	8,812	77,400
Great Western	887,538	1,996,466
Central do Brazil	11,267,462	23,479,527
Companhia Paulista	555,554	1,857,217
Sorocabana	272,841	1,217,759
San Paulo Railway	968,019	2,543,087
Companhia Mogiana	635,436	2,266,551
Leopoldina Railway	2,181,934	3,923,516
Total passengers	18,311,837	39,888,218

SOURCES: See text and Appendix B.

Travelers fall into two groups: leisure travelers and working travelers. Leisure travelers include those not traveling for purposes of work or business, whereas working travelers are those whose movement is directly related to labor or commerce. The passenger social savings estimated for Brazilians in the workforce thus provide a unique way of incorporating the gains in labor-market efficiency that resulted from improved overland travel.

The volume of passenger services in Brazil was relatively small. Table 5.1 presents information on the number of railroad passengers in Brazil in 1913. Brazilian railroads carried more than eighteen million first-class passengers, and almost forty million second-class passengers that year. Although Brazilians traveled by rail with reasonable frequency, they did not travel for long distances. Given a population in 1913 of slightly less than twenty-five million persons, the average Brazilian traveled by train about twice a year. The figure is surprisingly high for a relatively backward economy at the time, although it no doubt masks considerable variance across individuals. In Mexico and Russia the average person traveled by rail only once a year in the early twentieth century.[2] In advanced industrial economies people traveled by rail more frequently. In 1890 North Americans traveled on the railroad about eight times per year, while in 1870 the English and Welsh traveled by rail more than thirteen times per year, six times as often as Brazilians more than forty years later.[3]

The number of railroad journeys does not address the length of a typical trip. In spite of a frequency of rail travel in Brazil two times greater than that in Mexico and Russia, Brazilian railroads did not produce a proportionately greater level of passenger services. That is because Brazilian rail journeys were shorter in length. Table 5.2 presents the level of passenger service by class on Brazil's railroads in 1913. Dividing the total passengers of Table 5.1 into the passenger-kilometer figures of Table 5.2 reveals a good deal of variance in the length of the average passenger journey by railroad. That the average length of journey for the sector as a whole masks these differences in Brazil is due chiefly to the large volume of travel on commuter trains around Rio de Janeiro and São Paulo.[4] Overall, first-class passengers typically traveled only about thirty-three kilometers per trip, while second-class passengers traveled only twenty-five kilometers. Brazilians traveled in 1913, on average, shorter distances than their counterparts in 1910 Mexico and 1907 Russia.

The predominant alternative to railroad travel for most Brazilians was either walking or riding. For the most part, traveling by foot or on a mount was virtually a free good that required comparatively few scarce inputs. In the industrializing countries, the estimates of railroad passenger savings revealed that an important component of those savings was the value of time

Table 5.2
Railroad Passenger Service Output, 1913

Railroad	First class (passenger-km)	Second class (passenger-km)
Madeira–Mamoré	414,636	2,026,391
Rede Ceará–Baturité	6,647,787	7,614,133
Rede Ceará–Sobral	1,278,783	2,176,092
Central do Rio Grande do Norte	478,662	931,793
Rede Bahia São Francisco and Branch	10,742,377	21,357,318
Rede Bahia–Central da Bahia	583,167	3,373,376
Rede Bahia–Bahia e Minas	401,433	1,016,531
Rio do Ouro	1,244,565	7,834,113
Rede Sul Mineira	5,033,662	18,293,050
Oeste de Minas	7,859,821	7,452,213
Formiga a Goyaz	499,786	882,452
Araguary a Catalão	455,858	1,000,484
Paraná	6,777,596	12,952,026
Dona Thereza Christina	174,233	1,283,661
Santa Catarina	55,097	816,218
Viação Ferrea Rio Grande do Sul	48,691,882	26,663,822
Itaqui a S. Borja	335,010	232,195
Prolongamento da E. F. Maricá	26,578	129,120
Caxias a Cajazeiras	187,065	177,267
Vitória á Santana dos Ferros	1,024,114	3,379,533
Curralinho á Diamantina	168,325	793,210
Baurú a Itapura	1,392,248	6,898,406
Quarahim a Itaquy	693,243	590,123
São Paulo–Rio Grande Itararé a Uruguay	4,422,400	9,256,884
São Paulo–Rio Grande Linha de S. Francisco	647,216	3,962,276
Great Western	26,990,918	46,824,515
Central do Brazil	271,769,633	439,400,055
Companhia Paulista	43,771,132	98,874,930
Sorocabana	24,664,870	70,205,973
San Paulo Railway	45,118,048	90,628,605
Companhia Mogiana	36,718,809	74,366,763
Leopoldina Railway	55,922,968	50,606,686
Total passenger-kilometers	605,191,923	1,012,000,214

SOURCES: See text and Appendix B.

saved on the journey. In Brazil the value of the time saved in traveling by rail was low because low labor productivity plagued the economy. Poor productivity and a relatively elastic supply of labor kept wages down. Since wages reflected the opportunity costs of travel time for many Brazilians, the unit savings on travel time were relatively low. While railroad passenger services no doubt improved the efficiency of Brazilian labor markets by making laborers geographically more mobile, the magnitude of that gain would be limited by the structural conditions of the economy and by low wages confronting most of the workforce in the early twentieth century.

The savings afforded by railroad services had two components. The first was the travel fares saved, while the second was the savings on travel time. Because relatively little information is available on the nature of passenger travel in pre-rail Brazil, measuring the impact of rail passenger service necessarily involves imposing a number of assumptions. These follow directly from the general features of work and travel in Brazil. With respect to non-rail travel fares, the relevant alternative modes of travel are taken to be the *diligência* (diligence, or stagecoach) for first-class travelers. The unit savings on fares thus equal the difference between the charge to travel by stagecoach and the charge to travel by rail. For second-class passengers, the alternative to the railroad was either walking or riding. The high travel charges by rail, and even higher travel charges for the non-rail commercial alternatives, would have been prohibitively costly for most Brazilians. And the assumption finds support in anecdotal evidence from the nineteenth century. For example, the manager of one of the largest railroads in Brazil's northeast in the 1870s noted with some frustration that his passenger trains operated with a large number of vacancies, yet the dirt roads alongside the tracks were full of people walking from town to town.[5] For the many Brazilians who were already unable to afford diligence travel, even the train proved too expensive and they were left to travel on foot, if they traveled at all.

Empirical studies of the markets for modern passenger-transport services show that demand is quite sensitive to changes in passenger fares.[6] Small increases in fares tend to drive passengers off of one mode of travel and onto another. In pre-1914 Brazil the situation was no doubt quite similar, if not even more extreme. Overall demand for passenger services was likely quite elastic with respect to price. Quantifying this elasticity is complicated by the unique attributes of the railroad as a mode of travel. The demand for passenger services may be partitioned into two distinct components: the demand for basic transport and the demand for luxury and comfort. Increases in the price of passenger transport typically lead to both a reduction in the level of demand, and a shift to cheaper, less comfortable classes of travel. Gauging the extent of such reductions in passenger demand, substitutions to other modes of travel in Brazil would be ideally established through an econometric analysis of rail passenger data. The heterogeneous nature of rail passenger output, and the dearth of data on fares for the sector as a whole, render such an analysis unfeasible at present. Nonetheless, an inference from contemporary comment is that slight increases in the price of travel in the nineteenth century were sufficient to reduce demand and cause major shifts in the distribution of passengers. Indeed, observers noted that the demand for passenger services declined noticeably with the imposition of a transit tax in 1880 on the country's railroads. Those persons who continued to travel on the Pernambuco routes and on Brazil's largest railroad, the government-owned Dom Pedro II, in the wake of the fare increase were recorded as having preferred lower-class tickets, with "first class being nearly empty."[7]

Substantial uncertainty thus attaches to the precise sensitivity of first-class demand to fares. To accommodate a range of elasticities of demand for passenger services, two estimates of the savings on first-class passenger charges are constructed. The first assumes that, in the face of the higher stagecoach fares that would have prevailed in the absence of railroads, many fewer people would have paid to travel in first-class. Following other studies of passenger social savings, as well as various studies of modern passenger demand, this first estimate (estimate "A") of the savings on direct charges for first-class passengers starts from the assumption that the demand for those services was unit-elastic.[8] This captures the feature that it is unlikely that all first-class rail passengers would have traveled by stagecoach. Few of those persons able to afford first-class would have gone so far as to walk. Many, particularly men traveling alone (given the customs of the era) would have ridden on horseback or on mules.[9] Travel by mount would have required no additional time beyond that for travel by stagecoach, but would have saved the travel fare for those travelers who already owned horses and mules.[10] To test the sensitivity of the estimated savings on travel fares to this assumption, estimate "B" alters it by assuming perfectly inelastic demand. Under this specification, in the absence of the railroad all of its first-class travelers would choose to travel by stagecoach, even when confronted with the much higher ticket price.

The second component of passenger benefits—the savings on travel time—requires separating the productively employed passengers from those whose time had little or no value at all. National income accounting encompasses the income of labor, but does not value the time of leisure travelers, children, the elderly, and other persons who are not employed in the conventional sense. As a result, a money metric of the time saved in traveling by rail is appropriate only for those rail passengers who were in the labor force. Even among working travelers, a good number were probably on trips unrelated to work, or they were individuals who worked but whose labor was not compensated based on their time on the job on any given day, such as military men and public employees. Brazil's railroad passenger statistics provide no information on the number of children, workers, soldiers, and the like. The best that can be done is to assume that rail passengers were in the labor force in the same proportion as the Brazilian population. The amount of time saved by these "working" passengers further depended on the relative speeds of the rail and non-rail modes of transport. Assigning value to the time saved by "working" passengers in Brazil follows work on the value of passenger travel time in various modes of conveyance in the late twentieth century.[11] For the purposes of estimation, the value of time saved by "working" first-class passengers is taken to be twice the wage in their respective employment sectors. It exceeds the valuation of travel time by late-twentieth-century commuters, and thus constitutes a likely upper bound on the value of time saved by traveling on railroads. It nonetheless does not capture the other welfare-enhancing gains that do not enter into GDP accounting, such as increased leisure time, comfort, safety, and the like.

Estimates of the savings on second-class services adhere to some different assumptions. In contrast to the parameters assumed for first-class travel in Brazil, the savings on second-class passenger fares take the demand for second-class services as perfectly inelastic with respect to the price of travel in general, but with strong intermodal substitution. This implies that with any increase at all in travel fares, everyone who traveled in second-class would have instead walked. While at first blush the assumption may seem severe, it concords with the admittedly limited information available on passenger travel in nineteenth-century Brazil. This assigns to the railroad tremendous importance in saving passenger travel time. However, for the travel-fare component of second-class passenger benefits, a similarly generous assumption is untenable. Indeed, fare savings for second-class railroad passengers are actually negative under this assumption. If those passengers would all walk, they would spend nothing on travel charges in the absence of railroads. Just as in the case of first-class passengers, without the railroad it might be the case that many fewer second-class passengers would have traveled. But, if they traveled at all, most, if not all, of the railroad's second-class passengers would have traveled by foot (or at best, by mount) before railroads were constructed, an activity that required little or no money expenditures on their part. Nonetheless, traveling by rail still saved a good deal of time for second-class travelers. It was precisely such time savings that motivated people to pay to use the railroad. In particular, the time saved by working passengers in traveling by rail instead of walking could be very significant in the aggregate if the value of that time was sufficiently large. The value of travel time for "working" second-class passengers is estimated from wages, as in the case of first-class passengers. However, the value of the typical second-class passenger's time was doubtless a good deal less than that of the first-class passenger. Though it is not possible to infer the actual value these workers placed on their travel time, for the purpose of estimation the value of the time saved by "working" second-class passengers equals the wage in their respective sectors of employment.[12]

The sum of all the savings on passenger charges and the value of travel time comprises the direct social savings on railroad passenger services.[13] The actual values of the variables and parameters used in estimating these passenger savings come from a number of sources. Data on the volume of passenger services for both classes come directly from information reported by railroad companies, either to their shareholders or to the Brazilian government.[14] Direct observations of actual passenger charges by class exist only on the lines for which company reports are available, and which further reported to their shareholders those unit revenues by class of service. For 1913 this is limited to seven of thirty-two railroads for which passenger-kilometer data exist. There are two possible approaches to deriving the passenger rail fares in the absence of direct figures. The first of these is to use statistical procedures to estimate them for the entire railroad sector. The second is to take them from the direct evidence in the available company reports, and then apply those to the rest of the railroads in Brazil. Both approaches are combined here to establish railroad passenger charges.

The average charges for first- and second-class passenger services are first distilled by assuming that the average charge by class of service for all lines equaled the marginal revenue by class. Estimating the marginal revenue involves exploiting the following identity:

$$TR_{PAX} = R_1 + R_2$$

where TR is total passenger revenues, R_1 is first-class passenger revenue, and R_2 is second-class passenger revenue where R_1 equals $P_1 Q_1$ (the product of price and quantity) and R_2 equals $P_2 Q_2$. The imputed fare equals the average revenue per passenger-kilometer, which is the same as the "mean price" for that class of service. The marginal revenues for each class of service are equated to average revenues by substituting and taking partial derivatives:

$$\frac{\partial TR}{\partial Q_1} = P_1$$

and

$$\frac{\partial TR}{\partial Q_2} = P_2$$

In practice, the marginal revenue for each class of service is derived from a straightforward statistical regression of total passenger revenues on first- and second-class passenger-kilometers for thirty-two railroads in Brazil in 1913. In the first specification the constant term is constrained to 0, while the second specification removes this constraint (t-statistics are in parentheses):

Specification I:

$$TR_{PAX} = .040Q_1 + .016Q_2$$
$$\quad\quad (1.82) \quad (1.2)$$

$$R^2 = .91$$

Specification II:

$$TR_{PAX} = 555777 + .041Q_1 + .012Q_2$$
$$\quad\quad (2.96) \quad\quad (2.13) \quad\quad (1.02)$$

$$R^2 = .90$$

The estimate of the marginal revenue per first-class passenger-kilometer ranges between $040 and $041, while the marginal revenue per second-class passenger-kilometer runs between $012 and $016. This is certainly consistent with the notion that first-class service cost a good deal more than second-class. However, in both of the equations the estimated marginal revenue of second-class passenger services (the coefficient on Q_2) is statistically insignificant. The problem stems from the fact that second-class fares varied widely across railroads. The second-class category encompassed both longer-distance travelers and a large share of mainly local—and shorter distance—commuters. That differential fares by length of journey were in effect is apparent in the weakness of the estimate on second-class marginal revenues.

To give a degree of confidence to the estimated fares, the marginal revenues by class of service sector may be compared to the average passenger charges on seven railroads for which they are directly observed.[15] In 1913, these seven lines accounted for 83 percent of Brazil's first-class passenger services, and 86 percent of all second-class passenger-kilometers. The average charge on those seven "sample" railroads for first-class service was $044 per passenger-kilometer, while the charge for second-class service was $025 per passenger-kilometer. The former figure accords well with the estimated marginal revenue (being within 10 percent of the estimate), but the latter distinctly diverges. As a test on the applicability of the rates from the sample railroads to the sector as a whole, the product of the sample rates and the quantities of passenger service by class for all railroads are summed across classes to obtain the estimated passenger revenues. The resulting total is compared to the known total passenger revenues for the sector as a whole. Actual passenger revenues in 1913 exceeded the revenues estimated in this manner by about 7 percent. This justifies boosting the average charges on the sample roads by 7 percent so that the rates more closely reflect those implied by the total passenger revenues for all of Brazil. The implicit unit charges approximated in this manner are $046.8 and $026.5 per first- and second-class passenger-kilometer, respectively. Direct savings on passenger services in 1913 use $046.8 as the basis for the railroad fare per first-class passenger-kilometer, and $028.8 for the second-class passenger-kilometer charge.

For travel by diligence, relatively little information is available, partly because of the paucity of surviving sources and partly because of the scarcity of roads adequate for stagecoaches. The first-class rail charges were well below those for travel by stagecoach. The cost of stagecoach travel need not be estimated or inferred. Advertised fares in 1865 for travel from the city of São Paulo to the port of Santos were 15$000 per person.[16] Converted to a passenger-kilometer basis, this charge equaled $190 in milréis of 1865. Adjusting this rate to 1913 levels using the wholesale price index for Rio de Janeiro gives a passenger-kilometer charge of $360, an almost eightfold increase in real terms over the first-class passenger rail charge that year. The railroad offered very large savings to the passengers in first class who would have taken the stagecoach if travel by rail were not available.

It proves slightly more difficult, however, to measure the value of first-class travel time saved by the railroad. Given that the share of working passengers was not reported by the railroads, the savings on the time spent traveling assumes that people traveling by rail participated in the labor force in the same proportions as Brazil's entire population. Since no direct labor-force figures are available for 1913, the sectoral labor-force shares used here are interpolated values from the censuses of 1900 and 1920.[17] The share of the population working in agriculture in 1913 was roughly 34.5 percent, while 17.2 percent worked in "non-agricultural" activities (manufacturing, mining, and services). Hence, slightly less than half of the total railroad passengers in 1913 are treated as "unproductive" travelers in the context of measuring the time savings.[18] The value of these time savings was a function of how much those travelers could have earned in those hours.

Representative wages in agricultural and non-agricultural sectors of employment, used to value the travel time for working passengers, are also not directly available for 1913. The agricultural wage employed here is a simple average of the daily wages of farm workers throughout Brazil in 1911.[19] In order to be consistent with the travel-time savings estimated in work on modern passenger transport, it would be desirable to have a manufacturing wage from 1913 to use for the "non-agricultural" wage. Although there are no wage series for manufacturing workers for Brazil in this period, observations of daily wages do exist for various manufacturing jobs in the major urban centers of Rio de Janeiro, São Paulo, Curitiba, and Porto Alegre in 1913.[20] Daily wages in both agriculture and manufacturing are converted to an hourly basis by assuming a ten-hour workday, and the agricultural wages are further adjusted to 1913 levels by assuming that wages moved together with the wholesale price index from 1911 to 1913. The average daily wage in 1911 for farm workers in all of Brazil was 1$609. Adjusted to 1913 hourly levels, this gives a real wage equal to $141 per hour in farming. Other sources show that in rural São Paulo in 1913 the daily wage in spot-labor markets was 2$500, or as much as $250 per hour.[21] However, given the higher productivity of agriculture in that region of the country, the wage there is not particularly representative. Wages for skilled workers in manufacturing in Rio de Janeiro, São Paulo, Curitiba, and Porto Alegre in 1913 typically ranged from 3$000 to 15$000 per day, depending on the occupation. Taking 10$000 per day as the manufacturing wage implies an hourly wage of 1$000. This wage is not likely representative of all manufacturing jobs and purposively overstates the value of time for the estimates derived here. In any case, gaps between urban and rural wages are unsurprising. Although a fair amount of labor-market "failure" is to be expected, especially between city and countryside, the rural-urban wage differential that this figure implies is extreme. Agriculture-industry wage gaps are to be expected, and are common even in economies with relatively well-integrated labor markets. The degree to which they reflect imperfect labor markets, or imperfect adjustments for country-city differences in purchasing power, remains unknown in Brazil. The fully sevenfold gap between the manufacturing and farming wages employed here suggests a likely upward bias in the former. As such, the savings on travel time for those working travelers considered to be employed in manufacturing is overstated.

Table 5.3
Time Savings on First-Class Rail Passenger Services, 1913

1. Passenger-kilometers	605,191,923
2. Passenger-kilometers by agricultural workers (34.5% of line 1)	208,791,213
3. Passenger-kilometers by non-agricultural workers (17.2% of line 1)	104,093,011
4. Time required for agricultural workers to travel by stagecoach (at 13 kilometers per hour)	16,060,863 hours
5. Time required for non-agricultural workers to travel by stagecoach (at 13 kilometers per hour)	8,007,344 hours
6. Time required for agricultural workers to travel by rail (at 39 kilometers per hour)	6,317,584 hours
7. Time required for non-agricultural workers to travel by rail (at 39 kilometers per hour)	2,669,115 hours
8. Travel-time savings for agricultural workers (line 4 minus line 6)	9,743,279 hours
9. Travel-time savings for non-agricultural workers (line 5 minus line 7)	5,338,229 hours
10. Value of time saved in agriculture ($169 multiplied by line 8)	1,648,563 milréis
11. Value of time saved in non-agriculture (1$ multiplied by line 9)	5,338,229 milréis
12. Total first-class time savings ([line 10 + line 11] multiplied by 2)	13,973,584 milréis

Travel speeds in both the pre-rail and railroad eras could vary considerably. The travel time required by non-rail first-class passengers is derived by assuming that the average speed of non-rail, first-class travel equaled that of the stagecoaches that ran between the cities of São Paulo and Santos. In 1913 the length of the average first-class passenger rail journey was only 33.05 kilometers, while the speed implied by the advertised travel times by *diligência* from São Paulo to Santos in the 1860s was about 13 kilometers per hour. Travel times on the União e Indústria road were similar, with a reported speed of a little less than 15 kilometers per hour.[22] Based on scattered observations of typical train speeds, along with published trip schedules, 39 kilometers per hour serves as the typical speed of passenger travel by rail in 1913.[23] The time that would have been required for a stagecoach to complete the average first-class rail journey in 1913, running over a reasonably trafficable road, was 2.5 hours. By rail, this same trip was accomplished in slightly less than 1 hour, leading to a time savings of the railroad over the stagecoach of 1.7 hours per first-class passenger journey.

For second-class passengers the time saved by rail was much greater. The average trip by rail for a second-class passenger was only 25.4 kilometers in 1913. That journey was well less than an hour, on average, when traveling on the railroad. By foot it would have taken a good deal more time to travel that same distance. No information on the typical speed of foot travelers in Brazil has yet been located and present-day parameters must suffice for the assessment here. Infantrymen in the late twentieth century are expected to maintain a moderate road speed of around 5 kilometers per hour for lengthy (i.e., 30 kilometers or more) marches. Travelers in nineteenth-century Brazil would have moved more slowly than that, given both the travel conditions and the mix of people making the journey (children and elderly persons, for example, would maintain a slower speed than young adults traveling alone). To avoid understating the amount of time saved by second-class rail passenger travel, 3 kilometers per hour serves as a best guess at foot-travel velocity in Brazil. At that walking speed the average second-class railroad trip in 1913 would have required 8.5 hours by foot, which meant that taking the train saved 7.8 hours per passenger trip.

Using these travel speeds, Table 5.3 derives the first-class passenger time savings for Brazil in 1913. The time saved by first-class working passengers in using the railroad came to 15 million hours in 1913. When valued at twice the sectoral hourly wages, that time savings was worth almost 14 million milréis. Table 5.4 presents two separate estimates of the direct savings on travel fares for all first-class travelers. The first one assumes that the demand for service was unit-elastic. This means that a 10 percent increase in the price of first-class travel would lead to a 10 percent falling off of demand for that service. To the extent that first-class travel accommodations might have been viewed as a frivolous luxury in the face of higher stagecoach fares, many fewer Brazilians might have opted for such comfort in the absence of the railroad. In that case, the direct savings on first-class tickets comes to almost 58 million milréis. Combined with the time savings of Table 5.3, the value of resources released through railroad first-class passenger travel equals almost

Table 5.4
Total Savings on First-Class Fares and Time

Rate Differential (A)

1. First-class rail passenger-kilometers in 1913   605,191,923
2. Passenger-kilometers at higher stagecoach price
   (assuming unit-elastic demand)   79,011,168
3. First-class passenger rail revenues
   ($047 multiplied by line 1)   28,44,020 milréis
4. Savings on travel fares, given by:

$$\int_{P_R}^{P_D} Qdp = D\left[\frac{\ln P_D}{\ln P_D}\right]$$

                                                                57,910,786 milréis
5. Total savings on fares and time for first-class passengers
   (line 4 plus bottom line from Table 5.3)   71,884,370 milréis

Rate Differential (B)

1. First-class rail passenger-kilometers in 1913   605,191,923
2. Stagecoach passenger revenues
   (at $360 per passenger-kilometer)   217,869,092 milréis
3. First-class passenger rail revenues
   ($047 multiplied by line 1)   28,444,020 milréis
4. Savings on travel fares (assuming inelastic demand)
   (line 2 minus line 3)   189,425,072 milréis
5. Total savings on fares and time for first-class passengers
   (line 4 plus bottom line from Table 5.3)   203,398,656 milréis

72 million milréis. The second estimate of the direct savings on travel fares in Table 5.4 is based on inelastic demand. If the appropriate counterfactual specification for Brazilian travel is one in which all of the railroad's first-class passengers would have shifted to stagecoaches, the total savings on first-class fares rise by a good deal, coming to 189 million milréis. In that case, the fare savings and time savings sum to 203 million milréis in 1913.

The benefits for second-class railroad passengers were much less than those for first-class. Table 5.5 shows the derivation of the travel time saved on second-class services. Given the assumption that all second-class passengers would have walked or ridden mounts in the absence of railroads, savings on travel fares are necessarily negative. Even still, those passengers in second class who were classified as "workers" in accordance with the procedure described above would have saved 161 million working hours, thanks to the higher speed of rail travel in 1913. These net savings were worth some 45 million milréis to the economy.

The importance of the overall social savings afforded Brazil by railroad passenger services is revealed by their share of Brazilian national income for 1913.[24] In the case where demand is taken to be unit-elastic, first-class rail passenger services saved about 1.3 percent of GDP in travel charges and working time in 1913. However, assuming inelastic demand, which is the likely upper bound on the true measure, the combined fare and travel-time savings rise to 3.7 percent of GDP. Second-class passenger services saved a good deal less, at only one-third of 1 percent of GDP in 1913. As in the case of freight services, comparing the passenger social savings in Brazil to that for other countries is difficult because of the differing specifications elaborated in each case. In Mexico the first-class passenger savings (assuming unit-elastic demand) came to but one-half of 1 percent of GDP in 1910. With inelastic demand they would rise to only 1 percent of GDP. Savings on second-class services in Mexico, derived in the same manner as here, came to one-third of 1 percent of GDP.[25] In Tsarist Russia the value of travel fares and time saved by rail for all classes of passenger service in 1907 was about 1.2 percent of GNP.[26] In the late-nineteenth-century United States, where waterways would have substituted for a large share of the railroad's passenger services, railroad passenger savings still came to 2.6 percent of GNP under the assumption of unit-elastic demand. Taking demand to be inelastic almost doubles that figure.[27] In England and Wales in 1865 railroad passenger benefits were similarly large, equaling 5.8 percent of GNP under an assumption of inelastic demand and no time savings.[28]

The value of railroad passenger services in Brazil in terms of the resources they released was, even by the lower-bound measure, appreciable, if not particularly large. At the upper bound, roughly 4 percent of GDP in 1913, those savings begin to take on important significance for the overall level of economic activity.[29] In 1913 Brazil's railroad passenger social saving probably exceeded (in proportional terms) that for Mexico and Russia, but was less than the levels encountered in the United States and England and Wales. Passenger savings in Brazil were greater than in Mexico and Russia because of the greater unit savings on first-class services, and because of the larger volume of passenger services per capita. Passenger-transport savings in Brazil were less than that in the North Atlantic economies because the volume of ser-

Table 5.5

Savings on Second-Class Rail Passenger Services, 1913

---

1. Second-class passenger-kilometers	1,012,000,214
2. Passenger-kilometers by agricultural workers	
(34.5% of line 1)	349,140,074
3. Passenger-kilometers by non-agricultural workers	
(17.2% of line 1)	174,064,037
4. Time required for agricultural workers to travel by foot	
(at 3 kilometers per hour)	116,421,742 hours
5. Time required for non-agricultural workers to travel by foot	
(at 3 kilometers per hour)	58,042,144 hours
6. Time required for agricultural workers to travel by rail	
(at 39 kilometers per hour)	8,951,990 hours
7. Time required for non-agricultural workers to travel by rail	
(at 39 kilometers per hour)	4,463,021 hours
8. Travel-time savings for agricultural workers	
(line 4 minus line 6)	107,469,752 hours
9. Travel-time savings for non-agricultural workers	
(line 5 minus line 7)	53,579,123 hours
10. Value of time saved in agriculture	
($169 multiplied by line 8)	18,162,388 milréis
11. Value of time saved in non-agriculture	
(1$000 multiplied by line 9)	53,579,123 milréis
12. Total second-class time savings	
(line 10 plus line 11)	71,741,511 milréis
13. Second-class rail passenger revenues	
($026.5 multiplied by line 1)	26,818,006 milréis
14. Total second-class passenger savings	
(line 12 minus line 13)	44,923,505 milréis

---

vices in Brazil was not as large comparatively, and because travel time was more valuable in the United States. Without the railroad, Brazilian labor markets would have been less well integrated, direct outlays on fares would have been higher for many of those traveling commercially, and first-class travelers in particular would have been worse off in pecuniary terms.[30] The costs to the economy of a technologically less-efficient mode of passenger travel would be perceptible. Yet if deprived of railroad passenger services in 1913, Brazil would have lost a portion of income equal to only about two weeks' worth of annual GDP. As limited as the railroad's passenger benefits were, they likely flowed disproportionately to the higher-income sectors of the Brazilian population.

The modest passenger benefits afforded by the railroad follow directly from both stylized and observed features of the Brazilian economy that the measure embodies. The demand for passenger transport in Brazil was probably elastic with respect to the price charged. At fares higher than those charged by rail, many people would have opted out of travel completely, or at least traveled less frequently. Second-class passengers in particular would have largely abandoned commercial modes of travel. Nonetheless, the unit savings on first-class fares that railroads provided in Brazil were remarkable. At the upper bound, the savings that railroads created on travel time were large in terms of hours per passenger journey. Given the level of efficiency to which labor was consigned by Brazil's overall economic structure, that time was not worth very much. In the words of a commercial envoy who visited the country in the 1880s and discussed the torpor of travel in Brazil's pre-rail regions, "The axiom 'Time is Money' did not yet embody a truth."[31] Given the classic tradeoff between "time" and "money" in low-income economies, travelers often spent the former to economize on the latter. In the early twentieth century, most Brazilians had plenty of time but precious little money, and modes of conveyance requiring large cash expenditures were simply beyond their reach.

Chapter 6

Railroads and Brazilian Economic Structure

Historians have long emphasized the role played by railroads in strengthening Brazil's ties to the world economy in the nineteenth century. The presumed consequences of Brazil's export orientation include increased dependence on foreign finance, product markets, and technology.[1] Corollaries to this canonical process of "growth toward the outside" on the part of peripheral economies include a weak stimulus to domestic industrialization and a concentration of resources in the production of agricultural goods for export. This chapter examines the strength and form of the connection between Brazilian railroads, domestic production, and the international market by exploring the railroad's structural impact before 1914. Its findings hold relevance for many of the *dependentista* characterizations of the process of economic change in Brazil between 1850 and 1914 because they explicitly examine the connection between Brazil's railroads and Brazil's ties to the world economy.[2]

Railroads posed important implications not only for the size of the Brazilian economy, but also for the nature of growth. Absent a discussion of the differential impact of transport-cost reductions across different sectors of economic activity, the estimates of social savings are, at best, incomplete indicators of the effects of the railroad on the economy. The role of the new transport technology in altering the output mix and the underpinning structure of production eludes the concept of the social savings employed in the two preceding chapters.[3] Assessing the structural consequences of railroads for Brazil entails a focus on three issues.[4] The first is the strength of the derived demand for railroad inputs, or the "backward linkage" from railroads to other sectors of the economy. In Brazil, few of those inputs were supplied domestically. The bulk of the resources required to build and operate railroads came from abroad. The prevailing wisdom in much of the historiography is that the costs of provisioning the railroad sector that resulted from the outlays on overseas inputs were high.[5] The second issue relates to the character of the railroad's "forward linkage," namely the tie between railroads and qualitative features of the economic expansion of the late nineteenth and early twentieth centuries. Railroads strengthened Brazil's comparative advantage in export agriculture, a process that putatively left the country excessively vulnerable to the vagaries of the world market.[6] The third area examines a resource-savings linkage between railroads and the nascent manufacturing sector that transcends the measure of direct social savings in Chapter 4. It engages directly the possibility that the railroad made a unique contribution to industrialization by inducing economies of scale in transport-using manufacturing activities, and investment in new manufacturing enterprises.

Investigation of these areas of inquiry leads to three findings about the structural impact of Brazilian railroads. First, the strength of the impulse to Brazilian industry that resulted from the demand for inputs into railroad construction and operation was weak. In the industrializing North Atlantic economies railroads contributed to an expanding industrial sector by consuming part of its output. Major inputs into the railroad sector, such as rails, rolling stock, locomotives, and the like were relatively intensive in their use of iron, steel, and coal, products that were mainstays of early industrialization. Early in the railway age, Britain provisioned not only its own railroads, but also supplied expanding railroad sectors of most other countries. Yet the United States, Germany, and other industrializing nations soon came to produce their own railroad inputs domestically. By way of contrast, Brazilian railroads met their need for inputs by importing the very products that elsewhere comprised the core of industrialization. By exporting these potential output and employment effects, Brazil possibly weakened the impetus to growth embodied in backward linkages, diverting it abroad. What is of interest in this chapter is the magnitude of that "lost" stimulus. The answer varies with one's assumptions about exactly how railroads might have stimulated the growth of the industries provisioning them. Under any historically plausible specification of alternatives, that loss was small. It was the absence of an independently developing manufacturing sector in the early years of railroad construction and operation, not the weak stimulus from railroads per se, that explains Brazil's weak impulse to develop "heavy" industry.

The second key finding is the distribution of the benefits of the reduced cost of freight transport across different sectors of economic activity. Railroads in other Latin American economies are viewed as having promoted export-led growth.[7] While that characterization is often extended to encompass Brazil, it turns out that Brazil's experience ran in a different direction. The expansion of the Brazilian railroad sector is closely associated with the rise of the export economy, particularly in the coffee regions.[8] However, it turns out that an increase in agricultural production for domestic use, along with an expanding market for domestic manufactures, generated an especially pronounced response to the transport-cost reductions made possible by railroads in Brazil. This effect swamped the more palpable features of a growing export sector.

Third, the cheap transport services that railroads provided Brazil created a different stimulus to manufacturing output. They did so, not by enabling industries to attain scale economies that would have been otherwise unrealized. Rather, railroads impelled the establishment of new factories, using capital of more recent vintage, and hence of higher productivity. Such gains from railroads surpass those that arise solely from the transport-cost reductions in shipping the manufacturing output. They entered the economy through the way in which the reduced cost of transport induced investment and created scale economies in transport-using activities. Yet, beyond integrating the markets for manufactures, in the very same way they did for agriculture, railroads also offered some dynamic gains for industry in Brazil.

Railroads and the Demand for Inputs

This section examines the backward linkage from railroads to other sectors of the economy. Outlays on railroad construction and operation created both aggregate effects *and* sector-specific resource demands. Aggregate impacts, such as the influence on the business cycle and the railroad's role in total investment, cannot be evaluated because of a dearth of evidence that would shed light on these interactions.[9] The focus here shifts from the direct gains established in the preceding chapters to the indirect impact that arose from the demand for the inputs into railroad construction and operation.[10] Railroad construction and operation required iron, steel, coal, lumber, skilled labor, and finance. In Brazil, as in other "peripheral" economies, this backward linkage from railroads to other sectors, particularly industry, was highly attenuated. A large share of the railroad matériel, capital, technical knowledge, and skilled labor was not supplied within Brazil, but rather came from abroad. As a result, the magnitude of indirect benefits to Brazil attributable to backward linkages from railroads was no doubt small. Sources permit neither a full nor precise appreciation of the strength of the backward linkage as it was actually realized before 1914. Nonetheless, it is possible to approach the question from a different direction, and gauge the magnitude of the indirect benefits that were *foregone* as a result of Brazil's reliance on overseas inputs.[11] Historians have implied precisely such an analysis. Indeed, they have even gone so far as to claim that "while it is true that large sums of investment capital and loans entered Latin America from the North Atlantic nations and were basic to the shaping of local economies, it is equally true that large amounts of money flowed in the opposite direction as profits and interest rates. . . . More than a little evidence exists to suggest that the net capital flow probably favored the North Atlantic nations."[12] The poverty of evidence bearing on this issue means that it is far from a settled question. This section operationalizes and tests that hypothesis by elaborating a measure of the railroad-induced leakage from the economy, providing a first approximation of the losses attributable to railroads. It should be emphasized that this approach to assessing the indirect savings differs markedly from that of the direct savings of Chapter 4. The direct savings captures the net gains accruing to Brazil from cheaper transport. These are exactly identical to the benefits of market integration arising from the reduction in transport costs. What is measured here, instead, are the costs to Brazil of importing its railroad inputs rather than producing them domestically. The particular measure employed is an upper bound on the magnitude of the indirect savings that escaped Brazil, flowing to the coffers of bankers, financiers, shareholders, and suppliers in the North Atlantic economies.

Three categories of imported inputs into the Brazilian railroad sector are readily identifiable: financial services; materials needed to construct, maintain, and operate railroads; and skilled labor. From the outset, Brazilian railroads imported the bulk of their physical inputs from Britain. Many of these entered Brazil duty-free under the terms of railroad concessions.[13] The arrangements that enabled the organizers of Brazilian railroad projects to procure financing often depended heavily on capital markets overseas, particularly in the City of London. By the turn of the century, the United States had supplanted Great Britain as the preeminent supplier of materials and locomotives. The ongoing purchase of inputs from overseas ensured that an increment of Brazilian national income arising from railroads continued to flow abroad. The payments for these services and goods are resources that "leaked" from the Brazilian economy because of the way in which railroads were financed, built, and operated.[14] Had the institutional, technological, and resource arrangements been very different in Brazil, the financial services and material imported from abroad might have been supplied domestically. All other things being equal, the Brazilian industries and institutions that could

Table 6.1
Railroad Dividend Payments Abroad, 1913

Railroad	Value of outstanding shares	Share type	Dividend rate (percent)	Dividend (in milréis)
Brazil Great Southern	£82,400	debenture	6.0%	74,160
Brazil Great Southern	£99,869	debenture	6.0	89,882
Brazil Great Southern	£200,000	debenture	6.0	180,000
Brazil Great Southern	£225,000	preferred	7.0	236,250
Brazil North-Eastern	£350,000	debenture	6.0	0
Brazil Railway	£32,000,000	stock	0.0	0
Brazil Railway	$4,997,700	preferred	6.0	967,297
Brazil Railway	$15,002,300	preferred	6.0	2,903,671
Brazil Railway	£3,835,200	bonds	4.5	2,588,760
Brazil Railway	£2,000,000	debenture	5.0	1,500,000
Great Western	£306,250	debenture	6.0	275,625
Great Western	£1,668,800	debenture	4.0	1,001,280
Great Western	£750,000	preferred	6.0	675,000
Great Western	£1,250,000	stock	6.0	1,125,000
Leopoldina	£5,690,690	stock	3.0	2,560,811
Leopoldina	£2,845,340	preferred	5.5	2,347,406
Leopoldina	£4,495,300	debentures	4.0	2,697,180
Leopoldina and Terminal	£1,000,000	debentures	0.0	0
Madeira–Mamoré	£1,000,000	bonds	6.0	900,000
Madeira–Mamoré	£1,600,000	bonds	5.5	1,320,000
Mogiana	£2,500,000	bonds	5.0	1,875,000
San Paulo	£3,000,000	stock	14.0	6,300,000
San Paulo	£1,000,000	preferred	5.0	750,000
San Paulo	£750,000	debentures	5.5	618,750
San Paulo	£250,000	debentures	5.0	187,500
San Paulo	£1,000,000	debentures	4.0	600,000
Sorocabana	£31,750,000	debentures	4.5	21,431,250
Southern San Paulo	£900,000	debentures	5.0	675,000
Compagnie Auxiliaire de Chemins de Fer au Brésil	Fr130,419,300	various	various	1,783,021
Total				55,662,842

SOURCE: *IMM*, November 1913, 637–39; *Annex au Moniteur Belge*, 18 July 1914, 365.

NOTES: Pounds sterling converted at 15 milréis (15$000) per pound; U.S. dollars converted at US$0.31 per milréis; French francs converted at 0.589 milréis per franc.

have possibly supplied those inputs, along with the economy as a whole, would have been bolstered as a result.

Just how much "leakage" did railroads inflict on Brazil due to the international nature of the backward linkage? Given the extent to which railroad inputs came from abroad, a reasonable working hypothesis is that a large share of the revenues paid into the sector flowed right back out to pay for foreign materials and foreign finance. This hypothesis may be tested using information on the railroad sector's derived demand for inputs in 1913. Of the three types of inputs, only financing and materials can be assigned values with the available sources. The magnitude of the wages of foreign workers that might have flowed back to their home countries, as either remittances or through the purchase of imported consumer goods, defies measurement. No information on the share of foreign workers in the rail sector, their incomes, or their propensity to remit and purchase imports has been located. Anecdotal evidence on strike activity by workers on the largest British-owned railroad in the northeast suggests that most of the employees were Brazilian and most of the wage bill likely remained in Brazil.[15] Excluding the wage and remittance element likely leads to a very small reduction in what will already comprise an overstated measure of leakage.[16]

The flow of financial payments abroad took two forms. First, interest and dividends paid out by railroads on debt and equity issued in Europe remunerated the overseas shareholders and creditors who had purchased stocks, debentures, and bonds in Brazilian railroad companies. Second, because the Brazilian government directly owned and operated railroads, it often financed them through overseas loans on which it, too, paid interest. Those payments flowed to the holders of government debt. The measure constructed here assumes that both categories of interest and dividend payments accrued entirely to foreigners. Such an assumption overstates, perhaps heavily, the degree of foreign ownership in the rail sector. The reorganization of the Leopoldina railroad in the 1890s, for example, revealed that a large share of the outstanding bonded debt was held not by foreigners, but rather in Brazil. Should the owners and creditors of other "British-owned" lines prove to be similarly mixed in nationality, then the leakage of payments abroad as derived here is well overstated.

Table 6.1 presents estimates of the interest and dividend payments from Brazilian railroads listed on the London Stock Exchange in 1913.[17] The City of London was home to the bulk of the foreign finance that had been tapped by Brazil since the middle of the nineteenth century. Yet, by 1913, many of the Brazilian railroad debt and equity issues found there were no longer unique to the London stock market, as they were traded in both North America and Continental Europe. When listed on other exchanges, the se-

Table 6.2

Brazilian Overseas Payments on Government Railroad Debt, 1913

Government debt and year of issue	Outstanding value	Dividend rate (percent)	Dividends (in milréis)
Railway rescission bonds (1902)	£12,495,160	4	7,497,096
Railway loan (1908)	Fr100,000,000	5	2,945,000
Railway loan (1910)	Fr100,000,000	5	2,945,000
Railway loan (1911)	Fr60,000,000	4	1,413,600
Railway loan (1911)	£2,400,000	4	1,440,000
Total			16,240,696

SOURCE: *IMM*, November 1913, 624; "Quadro de Titulos da Bolsa do Rio de Janeiro," JC (7 December 1913); IBGE, *Reportório Estatístico do Brasil*, 133.
    NOTE: French francs converted at 0.589 milréis ($589) per franc; pounds sterling converted at 15 milréis (15$000) per pound.

curities typically appeared in the same quantities and denominations as in London. As a result, the total debt and equity reported on the London stock exchange very likely captures the company totals for those particular issues. The list in Table 6.1 excludes one French company, the Chemins de Fer Federaux de L'est Bresilien, which was the lessee of the network of government-owned lines in the state of Bahia, known in Brazil as the Viação Geral da Bahia.[18] There is some double counting in the table, since the Brazil Railway and the Compagnie Auxiliaire were fundamentally the same company, with various issues of debt and equity spread across European and U.S. stock exchanges. The Brazil Railway Company's equity and debt encompassed most or all of the publicly issued assets and liabilities of the Belgian railroad.[19] Any overstatement of dividends and interest necessarily imparts an upward bias to the estimated leakage.

    The sum of all dividends and interest paid on all of Brazil's foreign-owned and -financed lines comes to nearly 56 million milréis in 1913. To this figure must be added the leakage of debt payments on loans taken out by the Brazilian government to finance new railroad construction and to pay for the *resgate* ("recapture") of unprofitable roads at the turn of the century.[20] The former shareholders of a number of the companies that owned and leased track in Brazil held government rescission bonds that were issued in the railroad buy-back scheme. This introduces additional likelihood of double-

Table 6.3
Leakage Overseas of Interest, Profits, and Payments
for Merchandise Imports, 1913
(in milréis)

Dividends and Interest	
Railroad dividends and interest	55,662,842
Interest on government railroad debt	16,240,696
Total railroad capital payments overseas	71,903,538
Merchandise Imports	
Coal	26,379,582
Axles, wheels, etc.	3,705,187
Tracks	34,705,949
Locomotives	10,583,534
Wagons	28,358,084
Total overseas payments for materials	103,732,336
Total Leakage on Capital Payments and Materials	175,635,874

SOURCES: Tables 6.1 and 6.2; Ministério da Fazenda, *Commércio Exterior do Brasil*; and estimates discussed in text.

counting the payments that flowed abroad. Interest on the rescission bonds held by those companies accrued to them as revenues, which they then used to make dividend and coupon payments on their own equity and liabilities. Such overstatement of leakage goes uncorrected here. Table 6.2 presents the five outstanding issues of government railroad debt on which interest was paid in 1913, along with those payments. The total interest on Brazilian government railroad debt comes to more than 16 million milréis in 1913. The top half of Table 6.3 aggregates the government and private categories of interest and dividends, making for a total of nearly 72 million milréis in Brazilian railroad capital payments overseas that year.

Beyond the outflow of profits and interest on railroad debt, there was also the value of the merchandise and materials imported for use by the railroad sector. These imports were employed for both new construction and for producing freight and passenger services in 1913. The inclusion of capital goods in this figure is consistent with the circular-flow-of-income model that underpins the notion of leakage used here. The bottom half of Table 6.3 reports the value of all axles, carriages, track and accessories, locomotives, and wagons imported to Brazil in 1913.[21] While some share, likely small, of the goods in these categories undoubtedly went not to railroads but rather to streetcar companies and central sugar mills, they are all taken here as inputs into producing rail transport services.

Prominent among the imported inputs was coal, although some fuel substitution on railroads was still possible in this period. The reporting of the price of wood fuel by a number of major railroads suggests the continued importance of such substitution.[22] Brazilian railroads employed a mix of coal and wood in their locomotives well into the twentieth century.[23] Nonetheless, most rail service was fueled by coal, and most, if not all, of the coal was imported. The coal deposits in Brazil's south that contemporaries hoped to exploit proved unsuitable for use in steam locomotives, and the railroad line constructed to tap these deposits went wanting for freight.[24] Coal imports to Brazil in 1913 were worth some 60 million milréis, and while most of that coal was bound for the transport sector, all of it cannot be charged against railroads. Coal fueled a wide variety of activities. Steamships involved in the coastwise trade, along with riverboats on the Amazon and its tributaries and on the Rio São Francisco, potentially used large amounts of coal. The Brazilian government used coal as well to fuel the ships of its navy. Industry further consumed imported coal in this era.

Given the uncertain division of coal imports among various activities, the level of imported coal consumption in the railroad sector was derived in two steps. First, direct measures of railroad coal use were obtained for a sample of lines in 1913. It is assumed that all of the coal used on these railroads was in fact imported to Brazil. Forty-one lines or branches under federal concession reported the quantity of coal burned per locomotive-kilometer run in 1913. Multiplying that figure by the locomotive-kilometers run on each line yielded coal consumption by line. Coal consumption was then regressed on ton-kilometers of freight service, by line.[25] Estimated levels of consumption, based on the regression equation, were almost 25 percent above the reported levels of coal use for those railroads, overstating actual coal requirements and imparting an upward bias to the estimate of materials leakage. The second step extended the estimated consumption per freight ton-kilometer to all railroads in Brazil to derive total coal consumption for the sector as a whole. The resulting quantity, when multiplied by the unit price of imported coal, yields a value of railroad coal consumption in 1913 in excess of 26 million milréis.

Summing this upwardly biased measure of the value of coal imports that can be charged against railroads with the value of other imports gives a merchandise leakage estimate of almost 104 million milréis. Together with the overseas capital payments, this made for the outflow abroad of almost 176 million milréis in 1913. Total railroad revenues that year, estimated in Chapter 4 using the company reports and the government statistical volumes, come to 250 million milréis. Remitted profits, interest, and material imports combined thus yield an estimate of leakage abroad equal to 70.4 percent of railroad revenues in 1913. However, just as the contribution of railroads to the economy in 1913 went well beyond the revenues of the railroad sector itself, the leakage of indirect savings must be considered in a larger context. Ignoring for the moment both the benefits that railroads created, and the injections to the Brazilian economy from exports that the railroad made possible, leakage "cost" Brazil less than one-half of 1 percent of its GDP in 1913. Doubling the capital remittances to account for amortization of bonds would grossly overstate the aggregate leakage, but would still come to less than 1 percent of GDP. If by some bizarre twist the value of the missing remittances and import consumption on the part of railroad workers somehow doubled this figure, the total leakage would still be quite small in comparison with the railroad's benefits.

The meaning that can be assigned to this value varies directly with the assumptions one chooses to make about what the Brazilian economy would have looked like if this flow had been stanched. On the one hand, this result bears little resemblance to the picture painted in the historiography about the net flows running against Brazil. Counterbalancing this leakage were the social savings measured in Chapters 4 and 5. However, the leakage measure may still understate the costs of reliance on overseas inputs. Consider for a moment the possibility that the railroad sector could have been provisioned domestically. Under that scenario this leakage would have been eliminated, and the demand for railroad inputs would have instead been redirected in a way that stimulated Brazilian coal mining, industry, and capital markets.[26] It is possible that the resulting gains might have been much larger than the magnitude of the leakage suggests. This is because the needs of the railroad sector for iron, steel, and coal might well have rippled through the economy, stimulating a wide variety of activities marked by historically declining marginal costs and powerful inter-industry linkages. Moreover, the financial requirements of railroads might have induced profound and far-reaching changes in the institutions governing the Brazilian capital market, leading to greater efficiency across a wide variety of activities for which borrowing and lending were especially important. Under this particular counterfactual specification, the opportunity costs of importing these railroad inputs from abroad might have been far greater than indicated by the leakage estimate presented above.

International and historical comparisons quickly call into question the reasonableness of such a counterfactual. Successfully tapping the backward-linkage potential of railroads would have required one of two things that Brazilians did not have. The first was the perfect foresight, and the political will, to impose simultaneously both heavy restrictions on the import of rail-road equipment, and the subsidies for iron- and steel-making investments that would have been required to substitute away from foreign inputs. While such a policy could have been pursued, it lies well beyond any analytical form of counterfactual specification because it lacks historical precedent ei-ther in Brazil or elsewhere in Latin America during this period. As an assess-ment of the Spanish case suggests by analogy, the likely delays in railroad con-struction and the diffusion of cheap transport into the interior that would result from such a protectionist development strategy would pose a steep op-portunity cost in terms of the share of the social saving that would have been sacrificed.[27]

A second condition might have enabled Brazil to better exploit potential backward linkages from railroads. A resource endowment and array of insti-tutions providing for an independently growing industrial sector and a flex-ible and responsive capital market on the very eve of the railway age could have permitted the backward linkage to blossom. Britain and the United States possessed precisely such conditions, although the input requirements of their railroad sectors served largely to bolster processes of growth already well underway in industry and in the financial sector. Even in these ad-vanced, industrializing cases, the backward linkage was weaker than one might anticipate. Expecting railroads to spark industrialization in Brazil through their use of manufactured inputs assigns to them a role that they failed to play even in the most successful cases of industrial development. In-deed, one recent summary notes that "the backward linkages are a disap-pointment to those convinced that the railroad was crucial to nineteenth-century American industrial development."[28] Although the postbellum railroad sector came to absorb the majority of Bessemer steel output through the 1880s, that stage in the sequence of industrial evolution came only after several decades during which the railroad sector was but one of a number of activities requiring industrial outputs. The early vibrancy of industry in En-gland and the new North American republic owed relatively little to the de-mands of an expanding railroad sector. In proximate terms, it was the absence of nascent industry in the pre-rail era that diverted Brazil from the path of industrial evolution that elsewhere fueled strong ties between railroads and manufacturing in later stages of development.[29]

One final caveat about the limits of the meaning of the leakage measure is in order. The magnitude of the payments that leaked from the Brazilian income stream do not comprise an additional cost of Brazilian railroads that has, in the analysis so far, gone unexplained and unmeasured. The resource-savings estimates of Chapters 4 and 5 are already net of the capital subsidies to overseas shareholders and the costs of inputs to the rail sector in 1913. Rather, the leakage measure simply suggests the strength of the impact of railroads along a different dimension—that of derived demands for inputs. Leakage is employed instrumentally here as an excessively narrow and incomplete measure of the railroad's impact. That narrowness serves to overstate the costs to Brazil of dependence on foreign suppliers. Expanding the definition of leakage used thus far to include the offsetting income injections that railroads made possible changes the face of things considerably. For every unit of income that leaked from Brazil because of its railroads' reliance on overseas inputs, there was an injection into the Brazilian income stream from abroad in the form of payments from overseas consumers of Brazilian goods. The offsetting leakages and injections attributable to the railroad are nothing more than the railroad's contribution to Brazil's balance of payments. Net leakage was thus considerably less than the gross measure established here. Indeed, in most years it was not a leakage at all, but a net injection. The very export of those products generating the injections was, of course, greatly facilitated by the railroads that carried the exports to port. That the gross level of leakage was high relative to railroad revenues in no way renders evanescent the gains measured by the social saving. They represent two distinct facets of the railroad's overall impact on the economy. Whether there was an export bias in the railroad's contribution to the income stream through resource savings is taken up further in the next section. That the leakage of indirect benefits dominated the backward-linkage effect indicates that the strength of that linkage from railroads to other sectors of the Brazilian economy was small through 1913. Only if the relatively limited demand for inputs by the railroad sector could somehow have sparked a flowering of domestic industry can the modest leakage here even be viewed as an indicator of opportunity costs to the Brazilian economy at all. The magnitude of that leakage suggests that the stimulus to industry that escaped Brazil was probably not terribly great. The "net flows" of costs and benefits between Brazil and the North Atlantic economies heavily favored the former.

Railroads and the Position of Exports

The second component of the structural impact of the railroad addressed in this chapter provides a more qualitative measure of the strength of the railroad's forward linkage. It also addresses the character of that linkage in light of the sectoral distribution of the freight social savings. All areas of economic activity did not benefit equally from cheap transport. This section examines the hypothesis that railroads differentially favored the export sector, making for export-led growth. Differing elasticities of supply by sector of production, and the uneven distribution of regional endowments across Brazil, made for highly variable responses to the new opportunities arising from the dramatic reduction in transport costs that railroads made possible. Early railroad construction in Brazil was justified in the eyes of contemporaries in terms of facilitating the movement of export goods to port, and early on, export goods comprised the lion's share of freight. It has long been held that railroads in Brazil forged a special tie between agriculture and the world market that benefited the export sector disproportionally, perhaps to the detriment of the economy as a whole.[30] A typical characterization of the nature of the "export-led" growth process that unfolded with the construction of railroads holds that "the plantation and mine to port pattern of Latin American railroad construction did little to provide political integration, to serve local, regional, or national markets, and to encourage industrialization. Rather it further integrated and subordinated Latin America within the North American economy."[31]

The market-integrating impact of the railroad within Brazil was clearly established in Chapter 4. A testable implication of the assertion quoted above is that the railroads in Brazil integrated the markets for export goods to a greater degree than they did the markets for domestic goods, thereby privileging the export sector of the economy. For Brazil, the close tie between railroads and the expansion of Brazilian coffee production is especially prominent. Disentangling completely the multiple forces bearing on the relationship between railroads and exports is not feasible, and the railroad's dynamic consequences pose a challenge to identifying all of the causal mechanisms linking transport-cost reductions to differential gains in a transportables-producing sector of the economy. A thorough assessment of the linkage from railroads to exports would require detailed information on the production technology of all transportable goods and the elasticities of supply and demand in their respective markets. Without this information, the hypothesis of railroad-induced export-led growth must be approached less directly.

Even though the component processes of export expansion in the face of declining transport costs cannot be fully operationalized, the realized outcomes still can be observed. The mechanism linking railroads to the changing share of exports in the economy's output mix may thus be reasonably inferred. Partial measures suffice to indicate the principal nature and strength of the relationship between railroads and the export sector. The finding of this section suggests that the singular contribution of railroads in Brazil was not one in which the export sector was favored over the other transportable-goods-producing sectors of the economy. Rather, Brazilian railroads effectively fostered the disproportionate growth of the internal sector of the economy in the second half of the nineteenth century, while simultaneously attracting new labor and capital into export activities.

The notions of "export growth" and "export-led growth" in Latin America are easily conflated. The former is simply an observable rise in the level of the volume and real value of exports. Given data on exports, the hypothesis that a country enjoyed export growth can be summarily tested. The testable implications embedded in the latter concept are less clear. Several elements comprise a process of export-led growth. One is that production for export was a relatively high-productivity enterprise. The average product of labor and land in that case would be higher in exports than in the production of non-export crops. The shift of inputs into export production would raise total agricultural output, and output for the economy as a whole, all else being equal. If railroads, by integrating product and labor markets, contributed to the shift of resources into export production, then they played a central role in "export-led" growth. Moreover, in extending the margin of cultivation, and in attracting immigrants and capital, the railroad's dynamic consequences might have further skewed the economy's output mix in the direction of exports. So few details are yet available on the relative shares of exports and domestic-use production in agricultural output that even this elementary hypothesis cannot be tested. Agriculture was only one sector of Brazil's economy, and one of the more salient features, beginning in the 1880s, was the steady growth of manufacturing. The scattered wage data discussed in Chapter 5 suggest that industry was a relatively high productivity sector. Output gains within agriculture resulting from a shift of resources into export production might well have been overshadowed by even greater productivity gains in manufacturing.

Because of the constraints imposed by missing details, the relationship between railroads and the export economy has to be approached in a relatively aggregated manner. This treatment of the sectoral distribution of the railroads' forward linkage relates closely to several tests for "export-led growth" devised by Irving Kravis.[32] Kravis hypothesized that a growth process that was "led" by the export sector would reveal itself in at least one of several different ways. The two hypotheses tested here involve a rising share of exports in gross domestic product, and a rising share of export freight in shipments, along with a concentration of foreign capital (financed, of course, by export earnings) in export activities or enterprises closely related to them. These characterizations about how export-led growth might emerge are more de-

Table 6.4

Quantity of Coffee Shipped and Share of Coffee in Total Freight,
Selected Railroads

Railway and year	Total goods shipped (tons)	Total coffee shipped (tons)	Coffee share (percent)
Central do Brazil			
1870	151,458	85,698	57
1875	245,194	118,273	48
1880	328,053	139,471	43
1885	429,888	172,153	40
1890	483,685	82,432	17
1895	734,892	98,864	13
1900	830,979	104,894	13
1905	917,692	94,299	10
1910	1,246,730	67,446	5
1913	1,520,956	64,846	4
San Paulo Railway			
1871	93,890	28,731	31
1875	122,746	45,440	37
1880	177,482	67,725	38
1885	304,706	112,397	37
1890	607,309	146,515	24
1895	1,107,358	214,272	19
1900	1,164,959	390,994	34
1905	1,512,410	425,986	28
1910	2,019,978	516,012	26
1913	3,104,708	669,485	22

scriptive than analytical, and perhaps gloss over finer points that could be applied in a critical test of the hypothesis of export-led growth. In the absence of richer data, these criteria do give a rough set of benchmarks against which Brazil may be compared in order to determine the extent to which exports drove the late-nineteenth-century growth process. Tailoring these tests to the Brazilian case makes it possible to offer the most rigorous global assessment to date of the hypothesis that railroads made for export-led growth in Brazil.

Table 6.4 (cont.)

Railway and year	Total goods shipped (tons)	Total coffee shipped (tons)	Coffee share (percent)
Companhia Pualista			
1881	111,888	64,270	57
1885	175,278	97,977	56
1890	300,671	132,764	44
1895	615,847	175,693	29
1900	659,768	338,453	51
1905	725,400	356,396	49
1910	1,050,493	437,237	42
1913	1,541,263	532,951	35
Leopoldina Railway			
1875	14,121	9,741	69
1880	38,124	22,190	58
1885	86,470	51,210	59
1890	—	—	—
1899	361,523	118,897	33
1903	479,667	163,878	34
1907	594,477	162,172	27
1910	686,808	122,966	18
1913	1,065,451	148,537	14

SOURCES: Company reports as described in Appendix B.

Coffee was by far the most important of Brazil's exports before 1914. Available time-series data and extensive anecdotal evidence make clear that the Brazilian coffee economy underwent a veritable boom in the nineteenth century. The degree to which this is true is revealed by the position of coffee relative to all Brazilian exports, along with Brazil's share of the world coffee market. In fiscal year 1850 coffee accounted for 48 percent of total Brazilian export revenues. By 1913, coffee's share had risen to some 62 percent.[33] Sugar, the next most important export in 1850, accounted for 23 percent of Brazilian export earnings that year, but by 1913 had plummeted to one-tenth of 1 percent of export earnings. Rubber, the commodity second in importance to coffee in 1913, had experienced a meteoric tenfold rise in its share of export revenues since 1850. Because rubber was produced largely within the Amazon, almost none of its growth depended on the supply of railroad transport services. By 1913, rubber exports were in relative decline, falling from a high of 32 percent of exports in 1905 to only around 16 percent in 1913. Of all of Brazil's agricultural exports, it was coffee that maintained the steadiest rise and accounted for the largest share. Brazil's unique position among the world's coffee producers was evident in the increase in its share of the international coffee market. It already claimed 52 percent of world production as its own in the quinquennium 1855–1859, well before the widespread diffusion of railroads in either Brazil or any other coffee country. By 1905–1909, Brazil's share had risen to 77 percent of the world market.[34]

Because Brazilians constructed railroads precisely to carry goods such as coffee, sugar, cotton, and tobacco from interior to port, it is not surprising that the expansion of the rail sector and the rise of coffee exports are tightly bound.[35] The volume of coffee that Brazil exported was a function of both supply and demand. The reduction of transport costs made possible by railroads came to bear heavily on the supply-side of the market. Were railroads important to the expansion of exportable production, then Brazil should have experienced detectable shifts in coffee output, and the rising volume of coffee exports should be visible in the rail shipments. That is precisely what happened, and available data show that railroads were important to the growth of the coffee sector in Brazil.

In particular, railroad expansion in São Paulo pushed out the extensive margins of agriculture, attracted large-scale immigration from abroad, and stimulated investments in the form of improvements to land.[36] Such increases in the stock of the economy's resources generated dynamic gains that escape the social savings estimates.[37] These gains appeared in the increase in output that was due to the newly acquired factors of production. However, even accounting for dynamic gains, railroads need not offer the coffee sector differentially large benefits. Focusing on the relative gains to coffee growers and export producers more generally reveals that while the export sector benefited from railroads unambiguously, it did not benefit disproportionately.

Coffee shipments by rail, when considered as a share of total freight, show that while coffee growers undoubtedly gained tremendously from the reduction in transport costs made possible by railroads, over time the differential strength of the impulse to coffee production from cheap transport diminished. Table 6.4 presents the data on coffee shipments for several of the major "coffee railroads," starting when disaggregated freight shipments first

Table 6.5
Sectoral Distribution of Railroad Freight, 1887

Commodity	Freight (tons)	Share of total (percent)
Export Freight		
Coffee	302,748	20
Sugar	177,624	11
Cotton	24,026	2
Hides	10,309	1
Tobacco	34,285	2
Total export freight	548,992	36
Non-Export Freight		
Cereals	42,243	3
Salt	91,143	6
Diverse	865,340	56
Total non-export freight	998,726	65
Total Freight	1,547,718	101

SOURCES: MACOP, *Relatório . . . 1887*; EFDPII, *Relatório*, 1887.
NOTE: The figures in the table are for twenty-nine different railroads that reported freight by category in 1887. Total exceeds 100 percent due to rounding error.

become available. These lines demonstrate very different experiences with respect to the volume of coffee they carried. However, on most of them it is readily apparent that the share of coffee in total freight declined over time. The volume of coffee freight on the Central do Brazil peaked in 1881, then enjoyed a brief resurgence right after the turn of the century. Yet coffee's share declined steadily from 1869 to 1913, as a wide variety of other categories of freight came to dominate total shipments. A similar pattern is evident, though less pronounced, on São Paulo's thriving Companhia Paulista. The Paulista served zones that were the most heavily oriented toward coffee cultivation of any place in Latin America. It nonetheless exhibited a perceptible decline in the share of total shipments accounted for by coffee between 1881 and 1913. A similar decline is clearly evident on the Leopoldina. Only on the

San Paulo Railway would it seem that such a characterization might be in doubt. A rising share of coffee freight there would not be surprising; virtually all of the coffee leaving the highland plateau of São Paulo passed over this line en route to port. Nonetheless, regression analysis of annual time-series data on the share of coffee in total freight tonnage reveals that, here too, the share fell, declining at a rate of 1 percent per year during the very decades of the region's coffee boom.[38]

Brazil's export sector consisted of more than coffee, and it is natural to turn to the results for the sector as a whole. The distribution of export-sector freight on Brazil's railroads during the period of "export-led" growth is presented in Tables 6.5 and 6.6. In 1887 the five major enumerated exports on twenty-nine lines reporting to the central government comprised 35 percent of total freight shipments. In 1913 that share had actually fallen to 18 percent of the total tonnage shipped on the same lines or on the regional systems into which they had been integrated. Two biases actually serve to understate the intensity of the downward trend in the share of freight accounted for by agricultural export goods on these lines. The first is that the level of exports is understated in 1887. Goods such as rubber and *mate* (South American tea) were not enumerated, and are thus reported in the "diverse" category as non-export freight that year. The second bias results from the fact that the level of export freight is overstated in the terminal year. Those same goods excluded in 1887 are enumerated and included as export freight in 1913. Additionally, all sugar shipped is treated as if it were headed overseas, when in fact the vast share of sugar produced and shipped in Brazil by 1913 was bound for the domestic market. These assumptions make the increase in the share of non-export freight in 1913 look smaller than it actually was, and thus understate the fall in the export share of total rail freight shipments from 1887 to 1913.

The changing composition of rail freight followed from the shifting forces of supply and demand in the markets for transportable goods. Railroad transport services were only one among several factors influencing these markets. The available evidence on the structure of freight rates reveals one way that Brazilian railroads favored changes in the economy's output mix. In contrast to Mexico, where railroad freight charges heavily favored shipments of export products, Brazilian freight charges discriminated *against* export goods.[39] The case of coffee is particularly telling in this regard. Table 6.7 compares the published charge for shipping coffee in the first trimester of 1909 with the average charge for all categories of freight on each of Brazil's major railroads that year. The average charges for all freight are based on revenue per ton over each of the railroads' respective average length of haul. The rates for coffee are based on the charge to ship 1 ton a distance of 200 kilometers, with the

Table 6.6

Sectoral Distribution of Railroad Freight, 1913

Commodity	Freight (tons)	Share of total (percent)
Export Freight		
Coffee	1,084,276	12
Rubber	717	0
Mate	55,519	1
Sugar	380,937	4
Cotton	100,002	1
Tobacco	34,073	0
Hides	36,853	0
Total export freight	1,692,377	18
Non-Export Freight		
Cereals	362,370	4
Aguardente	47,946	1
Textiles	41,348	0
Xarque	143,707	2
Salt	209,868	2
Lumber	154,039	2
Diverse	6,596,861	71
Total non-export freight	7,556,139	82
Total Freight	9,248,516	100

SOURCE: MVOP, Inspectoria Federal das Estradas, EEF, 1913.

NOTE: Figures are for twenty-seven railroads or regional systems corresponding to the twenty-nine railroads for 1887 in Table 6.5.

exception of the San Paulo Railway, where the original charges are for a haul of 100 kilometers and here have been doubled to facilitate comparison. With only two exceptions, published coffee rates were well above the average charge actually collected on all freight. On none of the major coffee railroads was the charge to carry coffee less than the charge for all other freight.

Table 6.8 compares the freight rates on a wider array of goods. The charges for shipping Brazil's major exports exceed the charges on shipping textiles and domestically produced food crops.[40] The major export crops enumerated in the rate schedules include coffee, cotton, sugar, rubber, hides, tobacco, and *mate*. Because a growing share of Brazilian cotton and sugar production came to be consumed domestically in this period, rates for shipping those goods on some lines bear a closer resemblance to the rates on foodstuffs than they do to rates on the other exports. The prominent agricultural commodities and products that were consumed domestically include wheat flour, corn, rice, manioc flour, beans, and potatoes. On every railroad the rates on those goods were significantly lower than for the traditional agricultural export commodities. Freight-rate discrimination against export goods may well have worked like an optimal export tax, aiding in ensuring that the terms of trade did not run against Brazil.[41] In short, the freight-rate structure, set and revised by the state and central governments since the earliest days of railroads in Brazil, worked strongly in the same direction as the shifting composition of railroad freight in this period.[42] Both effects moved in the same direction as the shifting output mix of the economy as a whole.

While Brazil's export sector grew in an almost uninterrupted fashion before 1914, the best available indicators reveal that its expansion was surpassed by that of the rest of the economy. Using macroeconomic series to chart aggregate performance from 1861 to 1913 makes it possible to illustrate the position of exports in the Brazilian economy. Two different income series exist for this period. Unfortunately, neither is based on directly observed levels of GDP in the nineteenth century, given the absence of economic censuses. Instead, income series for the period have been constructed using statistical techniques carefully selected to provide plausible backward projections of income levels. Table 6.9 presents figures from the two series at various intervals and compares them to the nominal level of exports for those same years. While the two nominal income series differ in their respective levels and trends, the share of exports in both declined over the period before 1914. Estimating the annual trend in the export share in GDP using time-series data indicates that the position of exports in the economy diminished at an average rate ranging from seven-tenths of 1 percent to 1.5 percent each year.[43] The results clearly call into question the notion that the growth of production for export dominated all other types of economic activity. In short, the rise of exports in Brazil was not the same as "export-led" growth, if by the latter one means an increasingly important role for the export sector in the economy. That railroads provided important gains to the economy by integrating product markets, as shown in Chapter 4, is unsurprising, given the

Table 6.7
Average Unit Charge and Coffee Rates
on Major Railroads, 1909

Railroad	Unit charge per ton-km for all freight (in milréis)	Published coffee rate per ton-km (in milréis)	Percentage difference
Baturité	0.170	0.240	41
Sobral	0.175	0.195	11
Viação Geral da Bahia	0.093	0.130	40
Victória–Diamantina	0.219	0.240	10
Goiás	0.154	0.180	17
Leopoldina	0.191	0.263	37
Oeste de Minas	0.151	0.187	24
Central do Brazil	0.052	0.113	117
Paulista	0.139	0.175	26
Sorocabana	0.119	0.211	77
Mogiana	0.143	0.183	28
San Paulo Railway	0.144	0.185	28
Noroeste do Brazil	0.101	0.200	98
São Paulo–Rio Grande	0.088	0.088	0
Paraná	0.148	0.100	-32
Dona Thereza Christina	0.143	0.160	11
Viação Ferrea Rio Grande do Sul	0.074	0.093	26

SOURCES: Unit charges are the average unit freight revenue for each railroad in 1909, drawn from MVOP, Inspectoria Federal das Estradas, *EEF*, 1909, and company reports, where appropriate. Coffee freight rates are found in MVOP, *Relatório . . . 1909*, 14–64 for the first trimester of 1909, adjusted as discussed in the text.

backward state of the pre-rail transport technology. Perhaps more unexpected is the evolving sectoral distribution of the forward linkage from the expanding rail sector suggested here. However, even though rates favored the shipment of domestically consumed goods, it is still possible that exports benefited disproportionately from cheap transport if those exports were increasingly "railroad intensive." The degree of railroad intensity is indicated by the share of total sectoral output that is carried to market by rail. At first blush, exports certainly appear to have been relatively railroad intensive. With

Table 6.8
Freight Rates per Ton, 1909
(in current milréis)

	Railroad								
Commodity	Great Western	Leopoldina	Central do Brazil	Paulista	Sorocabana	Mogiana	San Paulo Railway	Viação Ferrea–Rio Grande do Sul
Coffee	46.25	52.50	30.75	34.90	45.00	36.50	37.00	21.00
Cotton	32.50	30.00	9.00	49.40	47.00	36.60	41.20	23.00
Sugar	20.90	12.75	9.00	49.40	48.00	46.80	41.20	21.00
Rubber	46.25	—	9.00	49.40	48.00	46.80	41.20	23.00
Hides	34.40	75.00	31.00	49.40	48.00	46.80	41.20	21.00
Tobacco	34.40	62.50	37.00	49.40	48.00	46.80	41.20	—
Mate	46.30	50.00	20.00	49.40	48.00	46.80	41.20	21.00
Textiles	46.30	30.00	45.00	49.40	48.00	46.80	41.20	30.00
Wheat Flour	21.00	17.50	9.00	18.50	18.50	18.50	20.00	21.00
Corn	12.80	3.20	6.40	9.25	8.00	9.25	10.00	10.00
Rice	21.00	3.20	6.40	9.25	9.25	9.25	10.00	10.00
Manioc Flour	12.80	3.20	9.00	9.25	9.25	9.25	10.00	10.00
Beans	12.80	3.20	6.40	9.25	9.25	9.25	10.00	10.00
Potatoes	9.00	6.00	9.00	9.25	9.25	9.25	10.00	19.00

SOURCE: MVOP, Relatório . . . 1909, 15–64.

NOTES: Leopoldina Railway Company rates are for the Rêde Mineira line; Viação Ferrea–Rio Grande do Sul rates are for the Porto Alegre–Novo Hamburgo line. All are rates for a 200-kilometer haul, except for the San Paulo Railway, where original rates are for 100 kilometers (doubled here for easy comparison).

the exception of rubber, which traveled largely by boat, the vast majority of Brazilian export tonnage went to port by rail. Railroads carried much less of Brazil's total production of non-exported transportable goods. Yet it is not the case that export freight in Brazil was more "railroad-intensive." Because they were bound for distant markets, export goods were in fact more transport-intensive in general. With respect to the specific mode of shipment, it was freight that was bound for the domestic market that was relatively more railroad-intensive in character. This is precisely what Tables 6.5 and 6.6 reveal. Because of this, a growing share of the gains from cheap transport made possible by railroads accrued to non-export activities. This process made for exactly the kind of observable change in the division of total output between exports and non-exports that occurred before 1914. Railroad development and the export economy were related in Brazil, but the feedbacks between them did not fall outside of realm of the ordinary.

Railroads and Transport-Using Industries

Railroads similarly stimulated manufacturing in Brazil to an important degree, but the bulk of that stimulus came about in the normal manner, through the resources saved as a result of product market integration. The evidence on freight rates presented above suggests that while manufactures, like exports, most certainly gained from cheap transport, they did not receive a particularly strong differential stimulus to production. Textiles, for example, paid freight rates on par with, or even greater than, some of the export goods. But there were other ways in which railroads could offer additional gains to industry. One way in which railroads could do so that has important implications for both the structure of the economy and its long-term success is by creating economies of scale in transport-using activities. This could occur if the reductions in the cost of transport brought about by railroads permitted a manufacturing industry as a whole to operate at a lower average cost of production. A key assumption of the social savings model employed in the previous chapters is that railroads did *not* cause transport-using activities to enjoy economies of scale. If railroads did in fact create scale economies at the industry or sectoral level, the resulting benefits are not fully captured in the direct social savings estimates.[44] This is especially important for changes in economic structure involving manufacturing. Again, it may be inferred from the scattered wage data for Brazil discussed in Chapter 4 that productivity, and hence value added per worker in manufacturing was higher than in agriculture. The same held true in the classic cases of industrial development, such as the United States and Britain. Should part of the railroads' social savings accrue to increasing-returns-to-scale manufacturing activities that en-

Table 6.9

Share of Exports in Brazilian Gross Domestic Product, 1861–1913
(in millions of current milréis)

Year	Value of export production	Nominal GDP "A" series	Nominal GDP "B" series	Export share "A" series	Export share "B" series
1861	120.7	408.5	273.2	0.30	0.44
1870	168.0	744.8	491.6	0.23	0.34
1880	231.0	930.9	615.9	0.25	0.38
1890	280.7	1,293.2	864.6	0.22	0.32
1900	850.3	4,645.8	3,122.2	0.18	0.27
1910	939.4	4,415.6	4,821.6	0.21	0.19
1913	981.8	4,661.4	5,678.6	0.21	0.17

SOURCES: For Exports, see IBGE, *Repertório Estatístico do Brasil*, 68–69, adjusted from fiscal to calendar years through 1887; for nominal GDP—"A" series, see Contador, "Crescimento, Ciclos Econômicos e Inflação"; for nominal GDP—"B" series, see Contador and Haddad, "Produto Real, Moêda, e Preços."

NOTE: Export share is the value of exports divided by GDP. To avoid difficulties arising from the choice of deflator for these series, all are expressed in nominal values. While the levels of exports and GDP are thus not comparable over time, the trend of the export share in GDP can be correctly traced.

joy higher levels of output as a result, they would contribute to accelerating the expansion of the industrial sector. This would then, in turn, hasten the "pull" of resources into industry, where their returns and productivity were higher, further raising national income.

This section considers the possibility that the railroad created such additional benefits through economies of scale in Brazilian industry. It does so by first examining the textile sector. Then it extends the analysis to all manufacturing in Brazil. Economies of scale exist when an industry is able to operate at a lower point on its average cost curve. A declining schedule of average cost per unit of output represents a technology that lends itself to greater efficiency at higher levels of output. By reducing the costs of transportable inputs to the industry as a whole, railroads may actually create the scale economies in particular activities. Moreover, by extending and integrating product markets, railroads have the potential to permit that industry to realize scale economies that are internal to the firm, further enhancing productivity in that sector. In the latter case, however, those gains are captured in the direct savings estimates of Chapter 4. The former case is quite

Table 6.10

Benefits Accruing to the Textile Industry Under the Assumption of
Railroad-Induced Scale Economies

Textiles transported by rail in 1913	43.3 thousand tons
Average haul for all rail freight	133.7 km
Ratio of textile haul to average haul for all freight (on Central do Brazil)	1.5
Average length of haul for textiles (1.5 multiplied by 133.7)	200.6 km
Level of textile freight service by rail, 1913	8.68 million ton-km
Cost of shipping textiles by non-rail mode ($343 per ton-kilometer in 1864, adjusted to 1$390 in 1913)	12.1 million milréis
Cost of shipping textiles by rail (at $097 per ton-kilometer, the average charge for all freight in 1913)	0.84 million milréis
Direct savings	11.23 million milréis
Value of textile industry output, 1913	192.1 million milréis
Direct savings on textile freight as share of textile output	5.8%
Elasticity of scale in the Brazilian textile industry, 1915	1.042
Direct and indirect savings from shipment by rail under the assumption that scale effect is attributable to rail road, as share of sectoral output in 1913	$1 - (0.942)^{1.042} = 0.06$
Indirect savings on shipping textiles by rail as a share of sectoral output in 1913	$0.06 - 0.058 = .002$

SOURCES: See text.

different. If railroads did indeed induce economies of scale at the supra-firm level, then these benefits escape the social savings model and the estimates presented in the preceding chapter miss what may be an especially important part of the contribution of railroads to changing the relative share of industry in total output.[45]

In Brazil, such additional benefits, to the extent that they existed at all in this period, were small and of second-order importance when compared to the measured social savings. Relatively little is known about the existence or degree of scale economies in Brazilian industry as a whole in this period. Scale economies are inferred in practice by estimating production functions that relate an industry's output to its inputs using firm-level data. Econometric work focusing on the Brazilian cotton textile industry suggests that it enjoyed mildly increasing returns to scale in the early twentieth century.

Denslow's estimates of production functions by region for the Brazilian textile industry in 1905 yield scale coefficients ranging from 1.012 to 1.042.[46] Haber's more recent estimates for all Brazil using the cotton textile census of 1915 likewise give an elasticity of such scale equal to 1.042.[47] Estimates below provide a slightly higher elasticity of scale for textile manufactures in 1907. The presence of scale economies does not indicate their origins. The extent to which the economies of scale in Brazilian textile manufacturing were external to the textile firms themselves is not revealed by the estimates of the scale elasticity. The difference is important because scale economies at the firm level would not be related to the impact of transport-cost reductions across all firms. However, for the purpose of the present analysis all of the scale economies in textiles are treated as if they were at the level of the industry, resulting solely from the reduction in transport costs that followed the construction of railroads. This assumes from the outset an overstated role for railroads in creating this effect.

Measuring the additional benefits from railroad-induced scale economies requires, first, an estimate of the direct savings on textile shipments by rail. The railroads that specified the tonnage hauled on a commodity-by-commodity basis in 1913 enumerated a total of 43.3 thousand tons of nationally produced textiles transported that year. Converting the tonnage shipped to ton-kilometers further requires a measure of the average haul for a ton of textiles. The available information on the length of haul for textile freight shows that it was greater than the typical haul for all freight. For example, on the Central do Brazil, the country's largest railroad, the average haul for a ton of nationally produced textiles in 1913 was 356 kilometers, while the average haul for all freight was 237 kilometers.[48] Assuming that this ratio of the average haul for a ton of textiles to the average haul for all freight was the same for all railroads permits the derivation of the overall level of textile freight service in 1913. The average haul for all freight in Brazil was 133.7 kilometers, leading to an estimated average haul for textiles of 201 kilometers. Applying this factor (1.5 x 133.7) to the textile tonnage shipped in 1913 leads to an estimate of 8.7 million ton-kilometers of freight service. Table 6.10 uses these figures to derive the direct social savings on textile shipments by rail.

The direct savings measure for textiles is likely overstated to a substantial degree because of the manner in which it is derived. It assumes perfectly inelastic demand for freight service, and it exaggerates the unit savings on shipping that freight. The average charge for all freight in 1913 ($097) is employed as if it were the rate charged for shipping textiles, despite indications that the rail transport charges on textiles were positioned toward the high end of the rate schedule, as seen in Table 6.8 above. Realized unit charges, rather than published rates, reveal the same disparity; unit revenues on textiles shipped over the Central do Brazil were almost three times greater than the average charge for all freight in 1913.[49] Using the average charge for all freight thus works unambiguously to overstate the savings on the unit cost of transporting textiles. The average dry-season rate in the interior of São Paulo in 1864, as presented in Chapter 4, adjusted to 1913 levels by the Rio consumer price index, provides the basis for computing the unit savings.

Leaving intact the assumptions that overstate the gains on shipping domestically produced textiles by rail, the upper-bound measure of the direct social saving on textile freight equals 11.2 million milréis. In 1913, the value of cotton textile production came to some 192.1 million milréis.[50] The savings on textile shipments equal 5.8 percent of the value of the output of the Brazilian textile industry in 1913. In other words, absent railroads, the resources employed to produce 5.8 percent of textile output in 1913 would have to be diverted to transporting the remaining output of the industry. Textile output would be reduced to 94.2 percent of its actual 1913 level to allow for the higher costs of its shipment. This serves as an upper-bound measure of the direct contribution of railroad transport services to the industry.

This direct measure provides the basis for measuring the additional gains that would have resulted if railroads created economies of scale in the industry. The steps involved in revealing the magnitude of the additional "indirect" gains from railroads, assuming that scale economies in the textile sector resulted solely from cheap transport, are presented in Table 6.10. The result there shows that if all of the scale economies in the textile industry were attributable to the reduction in transport costs made possible by railroads, then the decline in the scale of industry output that would obtain in the absence of railroads leads to an additional loss to the economy equal to less than three-tenths of 1 percent of the value of the output of the textile sector. It may be reasonably inferred that, in the presence of railroad-induced scale economies, the extra, or "unmeasured," benefits to the Brazilian textile industry made possible by railroad-induced scale economies would amount to less than 385 thousand milréis, a minuscule share of GDP in 1913.

When considered in terms of the textile sector's value added, rather than total output, the indirect gain from induced economies of scale is appreciably greater, but not by much. Applying the ratio of value added to output in textiles from the census of 1919 to the textile output estimate here gives a value added in cotton textiles in 1913 of 84.5 million milréis.[51] Following the same procedure used in Table 6.10, the direct savings on textile shipments as a share of value added is 13.3 percent; the combined direct and indirect benefits through economies of scale are $[1-(.867)^{1.042}]$, or 13.8 percent of value added.[52] Indirect benefits from railroad-induced economies of scale provided a negligible increase over the direct gains.

Though scale effects in one sector of manufacturing cannot be imputed to the economy as a whole, ignoring the possibility of such effects potentially understates the railroad's contribution to industry. Extending the measured scale economies of the textile sector to Brazilian industry as a whole provides a rough check on the possible extent of that bias. The value added in all industry in 1913 was 815 million milréis.[53] Applying the ratio of indirect benefits to the value added derived above for textiles, 0.005, to Brazilian industry as a whole produces an upper-bound measure of the additional indirect gains provided by railroads to manufacturing. Under these assumptions, the maximum "missing" gains to industry that are attributable to railroads in 1913 would be 4.1 million milréis, less than one-tenth of 1 percent of GDP.

It should be reemphasized that these gains do not take explicitly into account any "special" stimulus to capital formation in manufacturing from railroads, beyond the impetus running through the increased demand for products, which resulted from the market-integrating effect of the forward linkage. Dynamic consequences such as new investment and changes in the savings rate could have run from railroad expansion forward to industry. Railroad expansion extended the market, which in turn induced investment in the activities benefiting from lower transport costs. New investment made itself apparent not only in the expansion of manufacturing capacity and output, but also in new locations. In the 1860s all of Brazil's textile firms were located in coastal areas, where they could exploit cheap coastal shipment for inputs and outputs and simultaneously locate in urban markets.[54] By the 1880s modern textile manufacturing had spread to the interior, especially Minas Gerais.[55] Up-country expansion continued through the turn of the century. Industrial investment, as indicated by imports of machinery and capital goods, increased spectacularly in the 1880s, contracted precipitously during the generalized recession of the 1890s, and experienced explosive growth again after 1900.[56]

The railroad's additional boost to textile manufacturing, with expansion of new mills and new machinery into inland areas, appears in productivity differentials between coastal mills and up-country mills after the turn of the century. Taking textile output as a function of inputs and a shift (productivity) parameter, the production function is given by:

$$Q = AK^{\alpha}L^{\beta} \quad (6.1)$$

where Q is output, A is the index of total factor productivity, K is the capital stock, L is the labor input, and α and β are the elasticities of output with respect to capital and labor. Linearizing the function by taking logarithms and adding a variable for inland location of firms gives the functional form:

$$\ln Q = a + \alpha \ln K + \beta \ln L + \delta INLAND \quad (6.2)$$

where INLAND is a dichotomous, or "dummy," variable that equals 1 if the textile mill was located inland, and 0 if it was near the coast. Textile production figures for 1907 provide data on inputs, output, and location.[57] The results of an ordinary least squares regression on this specification gives:

$$\ln Q = 4.2 + 0.72 \ln K + 0.37 \ln L + 0.34 \text{ INLAND} \quad (6.3)$$
$$(6.4) \quad (6.6) \qquad (4.4) \qquad (2.9)$$

$$R\text{-squared} = .812$$
$$F = 246.7$$
$$N = 172$$

The elasticity of textile output with respect to a firm's up-country status, which is a proxy for the firm's age and capital vintage, is given by:

$$\varepsilon = (e^{\delta} - 1) = 0.4. \quad (6.4)$$

The elasticity result means that, for a fixed level of capital and labor, being inland raised a firm's output by a full 40 percent, on average. The result shows that newer firms, made possible by the railroad's expansion in the last decades of the nineteenth century, were systematically more productive than the industry average.

Roughly half the textile industry's output came from these high productivity firms located up-country from the coast. If those firms were to remain in existence in the absence of the railroad, but at the lower levels of productivity typical of coastal firms with their older vintage of capital, the sector's output would decline by nearly 20 percent. If the same relationship held across all Brazilian manufacturing, the additional costs to the economy deprived of its railroads would come to some 2.6 percent of GDP. The expansion of manufacturing inland from the coast is scarcely imaginable without railroads, and hence one of the dynamic consequences not captured by the social savings estimate was not only an increase in the quantity, but also the average productivity of manufacturing capital brought about by railroad development.

Despite the additional unique gains to industry from railroads estimated here, they are so small that it appears unlikely that the magnitude of any such effects would be large in relation to GDP or the direct social savings already measured. Though they in no way diverted resources or otherwise inhibited manufacturing, railroads can be ascribed little special role in promoting structural change in Brazil through industrialization.

Conclusions

Railroad development in Brazil altered the structure of the economy, but did so in an unexpected way. There is little to suggest that railroads promoted export monoculture. Instead, Brazil effected a transition to modern economic growth in a way that made it less dependent on its traditional agricultural exports. As demonstrated above, the share of agricultural exports in rail freight shipments declined between 1887 and 1913. The fall in the share of agricultural export freight is likely understated, given the nature of the biases in the measure used. However, the fact that most all of the agricultural exports (with the exception of rubber) were carried to port by rail in 1913 might suggest that export goods were somehow especially railroad-intensive. That obscures the point that exports were not so much railroad-intensive as they were transport-intensive more generally. Already bound for overseas markets, each unit of freight that was exported benefited relatively less from the reduction in transport costs that railroads offered than did freight bound for the domestic market. Moreover, the export sector manifested a relatively weaker response to those transport-cost reductions. All things otherwise being equal, the supply response of these other products in the face of falling transport costs and preferential rate discrimination was far more pronounced.

The character of railroad linkages in Brazil intersects with and bears heavily on the issue of "export-led" economic growth and "dependency." The share of rail freight accounted for by coffee declined on the major coffee railroads up through 1913. The share of export freight for the rail sector as a whole declined as well. The export sector declined in importance in the overall output mix of the economy, albeit erratically, over the period 1861–1913. But the trend of the share of Brazilian GDP accounted for by exports, using the best available indicators, unmistakably fell at a rate between seven-tenths of 1 percent and 1.6 percent a year. By this measure, economic growth in Brazil cannot be considered to have been "led" by exports. This was in sharp contrast to Mexico and even the United States, countries where the export share in GDP grew during the same period.[58]

A second test for export-led growth, namely the close relationship between foreign capital and export-related activities, remains to be considered in brief. The presence of foreign-owned railroads would seem to provide the strongest case for linking railroads to export-led growth in Brazil. Indeed, those railroads were built to haul export goods, and their investors expected that the export sector would manifest sufficient vitality to pay profits to the railroad companies. Even though the share of exports in freight shipments declined, it was still Brazil's export earnings that ultimately paid for the imports of capital goods and materials, the railroad profit dividends, and the interest on bonded debt. On the one hand this would seem to present overwhelming support for an irrefutable connection between railroads and export-led growth. But any such claim is based on a tautology. The conclusion arises directly from the fact that Brazil imported most of its rail inputs. By definition, imports, be they of railroads or fine china, are financed in the long run with export earnings. Railroad inputs were clearly a high-payoff import, given the magnitude of the resources they saved Brazil. In this regard, Brazil was little different from the United States and Germany during their early phases of railroad expansion, when they too relied heavily on overseas inputs to invest in projects that provided resource savings.

What was different in the U.S. and German cases was that accompanying the expansion of the rail network was the rise of a manufacturing sector. The railroad's backward linkages in both cases involved the use of an appreciably significant if modest amount of the output of this sector. Yet even in the United States, railroads cannot be assigned a major role in the early development of the iron industry. It is unrealistic to expect them to make an even more dramatic contribution in Brazil, given the institutions, policies, and interests that comprised the political economy of the country in the middle of the nineteenth century. Perhaps had Brazil pursued an aggressively protectionist policy, going so far as to exclude foreign railroad inputs, it might indeed have stimulated industry. But such actions would have reduced dramatically the pace and scope of the expansion of Brazil's railroads by raising the costs of their construction and operation. Brazil could have done this only by delaying growth, falling further behind, and sacrificing the resource savings that railroads made possible.

By relating railroad development to the mix of activities comprising the economy in Brazil in the way that this chapter does, it becomes possible to grasp some of the implications of the new transport technology for changes in the economy's structure. It also permits some tests of the rather more intuitive specifications of the concept of economic dependency. It may be the case that none of the hypotheses explored here suffice to provide a rigorous test. But that is because the analytical content of dependency rests on whether it is a mere label that underscores certain general features of economic growth in the context of relative backwardness, or whether it is viewed as a process of underdevelopment over time. Though much of the literature that originally elaborated the concept did so in the latter vein, dependency has been more frequently invoked in the sense of the former usage. The latter specification, that of "dependency-as-process," is in fact rich in testable implications and leading hypotheses which, to date, are not fully explored for most of Latin America. It is regrettable that the notion has been so infrequently employed in that way in applied work.

Identifying and assessing the more prominent links between railroads and structural change certainly sustains some of the long-held suppositions about the ways in which railroads made a difference in Brazil and the ways in which they did not. But the results do not readily lend themselves to conclusions that support *dependentista* interpretations. The call to "reflect further [on] whether rising exports really indicate a growing economy or only reveal the growth of one sector of the economy counterbalanced perhaps by declines elsewhere" is answered in this chapter with evidence that turns the standard dependency narrative inside out.[59] Export growth in Brazil was overshadowed and surpassed by the rise of the internal market, which was greatly facilitated by the increase in the supply of transport that railroads made possible. That most inputs into the rail sector came from abroad suggests that Brazil missed out on an important opportunity to industrialize only if one chooses to ignore the dire need for transport improvements outlined in Chapter 2. Had early-nineteenth-century Brazilian policymakers and elites come to understand that, a century down the road, the economy might be better off with a large and vibrant manufacturing sector, then they might well have opted to import fewer rails and devote more resources to adapting and reproducing industrial manufacturing processes in Brazil. The normative character of such ex-post speculation indicts contemporaries, not for having the wrong motives, but for not possessing perfect foresight. Were railroads constructed in Brazil under different historical circumstances and institutional arrangements, they might indeed have provided a powerful impulse to domestic industry. But many of those circumstances were wholly exogenous and alien to Brazil, namely, Britain's virtually absolute advantage in industrial manufactures. That Brazil failed to experience even more rapid industrial growth before 1914 suggests more about the importance of understanding the long-standing constraints on manufacturing in Brazil before the railway age than it does about any unique way in which railroads made for dependence on overseas inputs. One implication of this realization is that the historical origins of unfavorable and regressive political and social outcomes that are so often believed to be rooted in "dependency" may best be sought in other dimensions of the political economy of growth and distribution in Brazil.

Chapter 7

Dividing the Surplus:
Subsidies, Regulation, and Profits

Railroad companies in Brazil had very mixed experiences in terms of profitability. Two themes related to profits occupy this chapter. The question of profits is important, first because of its implications for the magnitude of the gains that railroads created and, second, because of its implications for the distribution of those gains. In accordance with several legislative acts and Imperial decrees beginning in the 1850s, Brazil's central and provincial governments, seeking to attract investment, supplied profit guarantees to railroad companies in the manner outlined in Chapter 3. By doing so, the government sought to ensure that investors in those roads received a minimum dividend payment each year. Generally, the government made good on these arrangements, paying the guarantee in years when those lines failed to achieve profits equal to a predetermined dividend rate. Had the government not devised and implemented such a plan, Brazil would have received much less railroad investment than it did. Whether or not those guarantees were actually needed in order for those companies to earn profits that were competitive is an important issue of public policy in nineteenth-century Brazil. The profit levels realized by the railroads that operated under those guarantees aid in revealing whether or not the guarantee policy was in fact necessary.

This chapter explores the consequences of Brazilian railroad policy by providing a detailed evaluation of the efficacy of the guarantee scheme. It constructs measures of both the profitability of the guaranteed lines, and the larger economic consequences for the regions they served, in order to assess the need for subsidies. It does so by developing estimates of the private and social returns on six major railroads for which annual operating and financial figures survive. The chapter addresses four main questions about the working of the guarantee scheme. First, how profitable were investments in guaranteed railroads for the firms that undertook to construct and operate them? Second, how important were government-guaranteed dividend payments to the financial success of each company? Third, were the economic benefits these railroads created in the form of lower transport charges sufficiently greater than the costs of securing them to justify the policy? Finally, did the nature of ownership have any bearing on the observed differences in performance among railroads?

The question of who captured the profits that railroads created in Brazil addresses a critical distributional issue. Three different types of ownership arrangements prevailed in Brazil: private ownership by foreigners, domestic private ownership, and Brazilian government ownership. Foreign-owned railroad companies, particularly British firms, were prominent in Brazil from the outset and were typically constructed with government guarantees. Whether or not they succeeded in earning high profits reveals the extent to which they might have directly contributed to Brazilian underdevelopment by siphoning off resources. On the other hand, Brazilian privately owned railroads, like the British companies, received government profit guarantees as well. The extent to which the Brazilian companies enjoyed profits that were higher than those received by foreigners indicates the degree of preferential treatment they may have received at the hands of their government. The Brazilian government itself owned and operated some railroads. The level of profits on those lines helps reveal whether they served as revenue-generating instruments of fiscal policy, or instead generated economic rents for the shippers who used them.

The connection between the profits of individual companies, and the overall economic gains made possible by each railroad, raises to the fore the inherently interrelated nature of the private and social returns to railroad investment. Even though railroads potentially created large social returns, realizing those projects required a mechanism that would serve to reduce the gap between those social returns and the expected private return to investors. The state provided this mechanism.[1] Railroad technology brought with it the potential to reduce transport costs in Brazil by an impressive degree. Whether or not that potential was actually realized turned in large part on the rates that each company charged to carry freight. Companies that charged very high rates might succeed in capturing handsome profits for themselves, yet simultaneously reduce the total gain to the economy. The Brazilian government regulated the rates on these railroads, in an attempt to keep the benefits to consumers of freight-transport services high, yet it also supplied the dividend guarantees that allayed investor concerns and ensured them a portion of the benefits. Considered together, the issues of guarantees, regulation, and profits tie together the main features of the distributional and income-creating aspects of the government's involvement in the railroad sector in Brazil.

The argument of this chapter runs along the following lines. Landowners were a preeminent political constituency under the Monarchy and, at the very least, an important political actor under the Republic.[2] Central and provincial governments in Brazil worked to satisfy landowners' demands for cheap transport by offering guaranteed minimum dividends to railroad investors. That scheme succeeded in attracting railroad projects to Brazil. However, in many cases government guarantees proved unnecessary when considered on an ex-post basis. Profits on some lines proved surprisingly high soon after construction. For railroads that were less successful, the government-guarantee scheme may be seen as a requisite measure for supplying landowners with the benefits of cheap transport. Irrespective of the private financial success of each railroad project, the sharp decline in transport costs that railroads occasioned meant that Brazilian farmers, manufacturers, and consumers obtained, in varying degrees, the long-hoped-for gains from these investments.

Within Brazil the experiences of railroads that operated under the guarantee scheme varied widely. Some companies performed so well as to need the guarantees for only a few of their early years of operation. Other lines received such payments every year. While Brazil's use of the guaranteed dividends, and their presumed role in attracting railroad investment, is well known, there has been relatively little assessment of that policy.[3] Villela and Suzigan, in a major study of economic policies, raise the possibility that government railroad guarantees in the late nineteenth and early twentieth centuries impelled the building of lines in regions where traffic conditions and prospects did not warrant them. They concluded that the integration of national territory by railroads constructed under this policy came at "a high social cost."[4] Fendt ventured a comparison of the costs of securing railroad investment in Brazil using guaranteed dividends with the costs that would have prevailed had the Brazilian government obtained loans in London and built the railroads itself.[5] However, Fendt's was a cost analysis of a purely private character, not a benefit-cost analysis.[6] He considered none of the social benefits to Brazil of the cheap transport services that railroads afforded, nor how those benefits might have varied under different arrangements of ownership. Railroad subsidies suffer further indictment for presumably having attracted foreign investment that did little good and much harm to Brazil.[7]

Criticisms of Brazilian railroad policy stand on a meager empirical base. This chapter reassesses those characterizations by providing the first detailed evaluation of the efficacy of the guaranteed dividends. In Brazil, all six of the major railroads built under the guarantee scheme generated large gains to the economy through 1913. While the government's subsidy scheme was effective in tapping domestic and overseas savings, not all of the railroads built with guarantees needed subsidies to attain profit levels sufficiently large to secure investment. Among the railroads constructed under the guarantees, foreign-owned companies did not fare disproportionately well in terms of profits. Regulation pushed charges down on all of the roads, but relatively less so on the privately owned Brazilian lines. High social rates of return on guaranteed railroads, and the varying profit experiences across lines, stemmed from the political factors that gave rise to the guarantee policy in the first place. In particular, the manner in which the public-goods problem was solved by Brazilian political institutions favored Brazilian constituencies over British investors in railroad projects.

Closely related to the guarantee scheme was the government's regulation of freight and passenger rates. Because the private success that each railroad company experienced, as well as the benefits accruing to the region it served, hinged on the rates it charged, the mechanism by which rates were regulated in Brazil is critical. Unfortunately, little is known of the specific arrangements through which rates were determined, either within the Ministry of Agriculture, the Legislature, or at the provincial level. What is known is that rates were regulated by the government from the outset, and they could vary across lines and commodities. In this context, ownership made a big difference when it came to the division of the surplus made possible by the investment. For example, the Central do Brazil typically had "poor" profits. Because it was government-owned, it was the railroad most subject to direct pressure for rate reductions and thus proved to be a useful tool for politicians seeking to reward prominent constituencies. On the other hand, British-owned railroads like the San Paulo Railway and the Great Western enjoyed respectable if not stellar profits. Brazilian-owned firms such as the Mogiana and the Paulista fared better still. No doubt, a number of elements account for these differences in profitability. The "degrees of freedom" required to disentangle all of those factors are not available when considering only six cases. Nonetheless, even after taking into account regional differences, politics and ownership emerge to the fore. The political "distance" that separated each company's shareholders from the regulatory apparatus of the Brazilian state offers considerable explanatory power in understanding the differing profit experiences of these roads. That Brazilian shareholders in domestic railroads comprised an important political constituency suggests that they enjoyed some success at resisting downward pressure on rates. British share-holders were likely less effective in this regard because they had less direct representation within the political system.

Irrespective of their degree of private financial success, each of the major railroads in Brazil generated impressive rent streams. Economic rent is that sum of resource savings and redistributed benefits created by the railroad and received by the consumers of transport services.[8] Much of this rent, if not all of it, consisted of the social savings that the railroad created by reducing transport costs, as discussed in Chapter 4. Some increment of that rent com-prised redistributed income. To the extent that the immediate distribution between railroads and shippers was skewed in Brazil, it was foreign share-holders who drew the short straw. Indeed, in contrast to the view of railroads in Brazil held by adherents to dependency interpretations, the bulk of the rent generated by railroads remained in Brazil.[9]

In posing answers to the questions raised above, this chapter proceeds in the following manner. The first section discusses the general policy problem of establishing railroads in a way that allowed for the greatest gains to the economy. It outlines the main features of government railroad policy and how that policy related to each of the six railroads considered here. The sec-ond section presents estimates of the private profits realized by each of those companies in Brazil through 1913. It contrasts the profits that were actually earned with the profits that each company would have received in the ab-sence of the subsidies implicit in the guarantee scheme. Section three ex-pands the measure of profits to include a conservative estimate of the bene-fits each railroad created by reducing transport costs in the region it served. Such a measure makes it possible to reconsider the necessity of subsidy ar-rangements in light of both the level of private profits and the externalities generated by each railroad. The conclusion discusses the implications of the results derived here for current understanding of the Brazilian political econ-omy before 1914.

Railroad Subsidies in the Brazilian Setting

The general problem of government subsidies to railroads has two distinct yet related components. First is the need for any sort of subsidy at all. The second is the most effective means or form of the subsidy, if one is required. Evaluating in retrospect the need for subsidies involves two criteria. The first is that the market rate of return exceed the private return to the railroad, with the subsidy being just enough to equate the private rate to the market rate. The second is that the social rate of return on the railroad exceed the market rate of return. Railroads that met these two criteria were desirable because they increased economic activity. Yet such projects were difficult to implement if investors expected to do better by placing their funds elsewhere. Subsidies pulled the expected private rates of return closer to the social returns from the railroad, prompting investors to undertake the project. There were other ways of getting an investor to build a railroad, prominent among them being outright government ownership. The Brazilian government often constructed its own railroads. While the share of the railroad sector owned by the government grew steadily though 1913, relatively few lines were actually initiated under government ownership. More typically in Brazil, the government used guaranteed dividends as the preferred means of promoting railroad investment.

The second element bearing on the need for subsidies is the role played by regulated transport rates. The prices charged by the railroad, and thus government rate regulation, were integrally linked to both the social benefits that railroads made possible and the profits earned by those railroads. High company profits could imply low gains to farmers and manufacturers. Railroads, unlike most firms, were the archetypal natural monopoly. The potential for monopoly pricing on the part of the railroad implied very high transport costs to producers. Only if the railroad could perfectly discriminate in setting prices, and if the railroad itself owned all of the land that would benefit from lower transport costs, would its monopoly power not lead to a loss in external benefits. In that case the railroad could set price equal to marginal social cost, since the railroad would receive all of the land rents that cheap transport made possible.[10] In that scenario the railroad internalized the externality it created. In a highly modified manner this "land grant" option was the one that was employed to encourage railroad construction in the United States. For uniquely Brazilian reasons, outlined in Chapter 3, land-grant railroads were rare.[11]

Railroad subsidies in Brazil worked to overcome two types of negative perceptions on the part of investors. First, subsidies aided in attracting investment in cases where those investors feared that, because of its high fixed costs and large, indivisible capital, or rate regulation, the railroad would not earn a return that covered more than its operating expenses. Second, subsidies helped get railroads to build lines where it was feared that construction might be ahead of demand and that the company could not bear the costs of the maturation period. Because both of these perceptions by investors work like an imperfection in the capital market, subsidies reduced the perceived risk and permitted the railroad either to obtain capital that it would not have received, or to obtain it more cheaply than would be otherwise possible.[12]

Profitability was an enduring concern, both for investors and for frugal statesmen. One prominent contemporary opponent to subsidies averred that "had the railroads that were desired fallen from the sky, ready to operate, the revenues would still have been insufficient to cover the costs."[13] Such sentiments illustrate well the pessimistic extreme of the ex-ante view of railroad profitability. Indeed, those contemporary concerns about the prospects for private success of railroad companies underscore the very rationale for government subsidies in Brazil.

Brazilian policymakers were sensitive to the need for subsidies, as well as the potential problem of monopoly pricing. Protecting landowners from high rail charges led the government to guard against such monopoly power. To ensure that Brazilian shippers reaped the full benefits of cheap transport, individual railroad concessions prescribed the maximum allowable rates for freight and passenger services. The features of Brazil's first concession, outlined in Chapter 3, are telling. That concession set passenger and freight rates but offered no guarantees to investors. No railroad was ever built under its original terms. The rates prescribed for it may well have been close to the social optimum. But given the large capital indivisibilities inherent in railroads, potential investors feared that they would have never earned anything remotely close to the opportunity cost of that capital under the established rate structure. The Brazilian government, seeking to guarantee high returns to consumers of railroad services, failed to ensure that shareholders in that railroad could reasonably expect to enjoy a share of those returns. The government policy early on guaranteed, ironically, that no railroad would be built. It was only after attaching a minimum guaranteed dividend to such concessions that railroads were constructed in Brazil.[14]

Whether or not shareholders in Brazilian railroad companies needed the guarantee scheme to achieve competitive rates of return may be assessed through two related measures of profits. The first is the private profits of the railroads, both inclusive and exclusive of guarantee payments. This measure permits a test of the hypothesis that the unaided private rate of return employed by investors in the railroad would have been less than the market rate of return on other investment projects. It reveals the extent to which the investment project actually required, ex post, a subsidy. Investors in Brazilian railroads would anticipate low profits if they believed that insufficient demand for rail services existed. Or, they might fear that government regulation would permit shipping constituencies to treat the railroads' services as an appropriable quasi-rent, an above-normal profit that could be captured for shippers via low freight rates. The presence of these concerns, or any other factor that worked like a capital market imperfection, made it difficult to attract needed investment funds and created the need for a subsidy in order to obtain the rents generated by cheap transport. The presence of such externalities in the form of benefits and costs not bearing on the railroad's investors suggests the desirability of using a second measure of project success as the ex-post vehicle for evaluating the overall efficacy of the guarantees. Two variants of such a measure are developed and used here: the social rate of return and the benefit-cost ratio. These measures include not only the profits to the railroad, but also the larger set of gains, or rents, to the regions served by them.

The sample of six major railroads is particularly well suited for the purpose at hand. The companies within the sample represent the diversity of regional distribution and ownership arrangements prevalent before 1914. The "British-owned" railroads in the sample include the San Paulo Railway (SPR), the Great Western of Brazil Railway (GW), and the Leopoldina Railway Company. The Brazilian lines considered are the government-owned Central do Brazil (formerly the Estrada de Ferro Dom Pedro II), the Companhia Paulista, and the Companhia Mogiana. Constructing the estimates required to assess the necessity and efficacy of the government's subsidy policy requires data series for several variables. Annual estimates of operating revenues, operating costs, capital stock, freight service, and government profit guarantees and repayments for each company have been compiled for the years before 1914. For the most part, this information is taken directly from company reports. For the three British-owned lines, these are the semester and annual reports issued to shareholders.[15] For the Brazilian-owned lines, similar information is appended to reports filed by government-appointed inspectors, or "fiscal engineers."[16] Semester and annual reports were supplemented where necessary by government studies and the contemporary railroad press.[17]

Of the six companies, three (the Mogiana, Paulista, and San Paulo) operated wholly or predominantly within the state of São Paulo, which is roughly proportional to the overall concentration of rail track and rail-transport services in that region. While the government-owned Central do Brazil also partly served São Paulo, via the old São Paulo–Rio de Janeiro line running up the Paraíba Valley, it operated largely within the states of Rio de Janeiro and Minas Gerais, as did the Leopoldina Railway, which also extended northward into the state of Espírito Santo. The Great Western in fact served Brazil's northeast, running from the coast inland, and ultimately operating lines that it either owned or leased from the federal government in the states of Pernambuco, Alagôas, Rio Grande do Norte, and Paraiba. Importantly, these companies first constructed their rail lines under one of several government arrangements for guaranteed dividends. All six companies eventually came to own or operate lines that were initially constructed under legislation from both the pre- and post-1873 periods. The Central do Brazil, Mogiana, and Paulista railroads, along with the San Paulo Railway Company, originated under early project-specific guarantee laws, but later incorporated lines that had been established with guarantees provided by the more general 1873 legislation. The Great Western participated in the guarantee policy under the 1873 law, but went on to incorporate some lines that had been established through earlier, project-specific guarantees, along with some government-owned lines.

Guarantee arrangements differed across railroads. The first of these six roads to be constructed was the Estrada de Ferro Central do Brazil, known originally as the Estrada de Ferro Dom Pedro II. Designed to connect the port of Rio de Janeiro with the fertile Paraíba Valley, its promoters constructed it with a guaranteed minimum dividend of 7 percent, 5 percent of which came from the Imperial government, with 2 percent from the province of Rio de Janeiro. Construction of the initial section on-line began in 1855, and it first entered operation in 1858. Extensions proved prohibitively expensive for the company, as it had to traverse the Serra do Mar by means of costly cuts involving extensive tunnel blasting and excavation. Even with its guaranteed dividends, the Central found it difficult to obtain the steady flow of investment from the Rio de Janeiro capital market that was needed to construct traffic-increasing extensions in the Paraíba Valley. In 1865, with the company facing the prospect of bogging down completely and failing, the Imperial government intervened, buying out the shareholders and taking over the financing of the railroad.[18] Thus, after 1865 the Central had the advantage of raising capital at interest rates paid by the government. It remained the largest railroad in Brazil well into the twentieth century. Beyond serving as a significant improvement over the old pre-rail modes of transport, the Central do Brazil remained for the rest of the century the object of an enduring conflict over its potential use as a revenue-generating instrument of fiscal policy versus its role as a rent-generating machine of private-wealth accumulation.[19] The gulf between its profits and social returns, revealed below, shows that the latter role was the one it ultimately played.

A contrasting case is that of the British-owned San Paulo Railway Company (SPR). It was first organized in 1860 in London to construct and operate a line from the port of São Paulo, Santos, terminating at the interior market of Jundiaí. In a manner similar to the Central, the SPR was constructed with a 5 percent guarantee from the Imperial government and an additional 2 percent from the province of São Paulo. The terms of its original concession dictated that net profits above 8 percent had to be divided with the provincial government, and profits above 12 percent would result in rate reductions on the line. This effectively established a rate-of-return band for the company's profits, so long as it at least covered its own operating expenses. The line opened officially in late 1867 and collected guaranteed dividends from the government through 1873.[20] Those payments brought the company's net revenue up to the level of a nominal 7 percent dividend on the par value of its stock. Performance improved after 1873 and the company split its profits above the 8 percent level with the government in accordance with the guarantee repayment scheme. By 1887 the company had repaid all of the guarantees; profit-splitting payments finally ended in 1889 when the SPR renounced its claim on any future guaranteed dividends.[21] The SPR never extended its own line beyond Jundiaí, expanding only in 1904, when it acquired one small line, the Companhia Bragantina.[22] However, all the other major inland railroads in São Paulo fed into the San Paulo Railway. This "monopoly" position did not, in contrast to claims by historians, translate into either differentially high profits or "ransom."[23]

Rail service from Jundiaí was extended into the interior by the Companhia Paulista. The Paulista's guaranteed dividend of 7 percent came wholly from the provincial government, since it neither linked a major population center to the coast nor crossed a provincial border.[24] The company began to collect its guarantee payments well before completion. So heavy was the demand for its services that it almost immediately proved not to need the guarantees when it opened in 1872. Half of its profits in excess of 10 percent went to the provincial government through 1876. Soon thereafter its contract with the government was modified to raise the government's share to half of the company profits in excess of 8 percent. The Paulista quickly renounced its claim on provincial guarantees and repaid the guaranteed dividends from 1874 to 1882. Beyond laying its initial lines, the company expanded continually, constructing new track and acquiring a British-owned railroad, the Rio Claro Railway, in 1891.[25]

The Companhia Mogiana, by way of contrast, had more complicated guarantee arrangements. At Campinas the Mogiana branched off from the Companhia Paulista and ultimately extended to the border with Minas Gerais. The Mogiana's early guaranteed dividends came from the provincial government on two of the lines that it operated. It also received central-government guaranteed dividends stipulated in the Imperial railroad legislation of 1873.[26] By 1886 it had completely repaid the dividend guarantees it had received from the provincial government, through profit splitting.[27] Thereafter, some of its constituent lines continued to be worked with guarantees from the central government. In the case of its Rio Grande and Caldas branch, the Mogiana received guarantee payments through 1913. For the purposes of the analysis below, those payments are treated as if they were never repaid to the government.

The Great Western of Brazil, which constructed and operated the line from Recife to Limoeiro, was also established with guarantees created under the 1873 legislation. It opened to traffic in 1881 and, like most of the railroads in Brazil's northeast, received guaranteed dividends every year that it operated through the turn of the century.[28] Because of the fiscal burden arising from paying guarantees in gold in the context of monetary policies that made for an ever-worsening exchange rate, at the turn of the century the Brazilian government began to purchase railroads in the northeast that had never turned a profit.[29] Among these was the older, British-owned line, the Recife and San Francisco Railway. Because of its poor financial performance and constant need for guarantee payments, it, like a number of other financially troubled lines, had long been under consideration for government "recapture."[30] The Great Western was one of the few companies in the region that was not bought up by the government, and it found itself in the position of leasing many of these lines, along with lines that had been owned and operated by the government itself since the 1880s.[31] As part of these arrangements, the Great Western renounced its claim on dividend guarantees after 1900.[32] By 1909 it had incorporated the lines operated by the defunct Imperial Brazilian Natal and Nova Cruz Railway Company, the Alagôas Brazilian Central Railway and its branch line, the Central de Pernambuco, the Recife and San Francisco Railway, the Paulo Affonso line, the Sul de Pernambuco, and the Conde d'Eu line.[33]

The final case, the Leopoldina Railway, began in a very different fashion. The Leopoldina started out as a Brazilian company whose first line operated under a concession that provided a choice between a subvention per kilometer of line or a dividend guarantee from the province of Minas Gerais.[34] Opting for the subvention, the road first opened to traffic in 1874, and later incorporated several smaller lines through the 1880s.[35] Saddled with an untenable debt load by the late 1880s, the Leopoldina reorganized and renamed itself in 1891.[36] By 1892 it had failed, and was placed in receivership by the courts.[37] Negotiations in 1896 and 1897 led to a complete restructuring of the company. Bondholders of the Leopoldina, the Rio de Janeiro and Northern, and the Macahé and Campos railroads in London and Brazil hammered out a reorganization agreement and the Estrada de Ferro Leopoldina was reborn as the Leopoldina Railway Company in 1898.[38] The new company operated with guarantees from both the federal government and the state of Minas Gerais. Lines within the new system included, in Minas, the original Leopoldina lines; in Rio, the Príncipe do Grão Pará, the Cantagallo, the Sumidouro, the Carangola, the Macahé and Campos, and the Barão de Araruama lines; and in Espírito Santo, the São Eduardo ao Muniz Freire, the Sul de Espírito Santo, and the Caravellas line.[39]

It is possible to obtain a rough idea of the representativeness of the sample by reference to the entire railroad sector. By 1913 the lines owned and leased by the six sample companies used here accounted for the bulk of the output of the railroad sector, producing almost 70 percent of Brazil's freight service (measured in units of ton-kilometers). However, freight density, measured in units of freight service per kilometer of track, was much greater for the sample here than for the sector as a whole. The implications of possible sample selection bias in this regard are further discussed below.

The Record on Profits

Estimates of the crude accounting rates of return reveal that all of the railroads clearly were profitable, in the sense that before 1914 they typically enjoyed positive profits. Most roads earned negative or small but positive profits only in the early years of their operation. The Central, SPR, Mogiana, and Paulista railroads all moved to higher profit levels within just a few years of operation. They quickly and successfully tapped both the shipments of extant coffee growers, along with the freight generated by those farmers who had cleared land and planted coffee groves in response to the plans to build those lines. On the Central, however, the unaided profits slumped again soon after recovering, and following the government takeover in 1865 profits were never again at the levels of the early 1860s. In the later decades in question the British-owned Leopoldina suffered the ill-effects of competition from the government-owned Central Brazil, keeping its traffic levels and profits lower than they would have otherwise been.[40] On the three São Paulo railroads profits generally remained high through the rest of the period. The Great Western, serving a relatively depressed area in Brazil's northeast, did not fare as well before 1900. Its unaided profits were unusually low in comparison to the major British-owned line in São Paulo. While it is beyond the scope of the present analysis to sort out all of the macro- and micro-determinants of profits on these lines, it is important to note the financial performance of roads during the episode of rapid inflation and exchange-rate depreciation that occurred in the early 1890s.[41] At that time, profits fell badly on the São Paulo lines as well as on the Central, with the Paulista suffering the least.[42] Unaided profits also fell on the Great Western. During the 1890s all railroads sought to raise their rates in response to skyrocketing inflation. British lines petitioned to put freight schedules on a sliding scale tied to the milréis–Sterling exchange rate for several consecutive years before the government provided any relief. Eventually, all of the São Paulo lines were permitted to employ such sliding schedules.[43] The low profits obtained by railroads in the early years of high inflation represent what were effectively income transfers to the consumers of freight services, made possible by regulated rates and rising inflation.

Interpreting just how profitable these lines actually were is complicated by both the need to convert the annual profits to "average" figures for a longer time period, and the choice of the appropriate alternative with which to compare the rates of return. Four factors militate against relying solely on the accounting measure of profit. The first is the peculiarities of nineteenth-century railroad accounting in Brazil, and these were several. Railroad capital was rarely depreciated, leading to an overstatement of the capital stock. Operating costs included replacement expenditures and new capital outlays, both of which should have appeared in the capital account. That they did not leads both to an understatement of net revenues and to further distortions in the measures of capital. The second factor is the very nature of the cost and earnings profiles of railroads. Railroads were investments that could be long in maturing. The impulse to new production in the regions served by the railroad, and the associated rise in the volume of traffic over time, meant that profits in early years could be consistently low or even negative, yet quite high in later years. Such "construction ahead of demand" can indicate the developmental impact of the railroad. But when a company has very different annual rates of return across the years, annual profit measures make it difficult to assess correctly the "average" profitability of the line for the period under consideration. Third, the working of the Brazilian guarantee scheme distorts the annual measures of profit. Lines that proved privately successful in the long term and repaid their dividends to the government in effect enjoyed a subsidy in the form of an interest-free loan. This makes their profits appear high when they are receiving subsidies and low in the years that they repay them. Railroads that did not repay their guarantees until many years after they had initially received them (or that, in some cases, never repaid them at all) clearly came out ahead by having to repay no more than the nominal value of the guarantee. Finally, in addition to the practical difficulties in accounting for profits on Brazilian railroads, it turns out that the very measure of the annual accounting rate of return (and the market rate of return) is inherently biased in an indeterminate direction.[44]

The internal rate of return avoids these problems.[45] This provides the correct summary measure of the "average" profitability in the period before 1914 because it properly discounts and weights each year's revenues, costs, and capital outlays, and takes into account the value of the railroad at the end of the period. The internal rate of return is the level of profitability for which the present value of the railroad is zero:

$$PV = \sum_{t=0}^{T} \frac{(R_t - C_t - I_t)}{(1 + r_i)^t} + \frac{V}{(1 + r_i)^T}$$

(7.1)

where PV is the present value of the railroad, R is operating revenues in each year, C is operating costs, I is capital expenditures, t is a time subscript indicating the year of operation, T is the time period corresponding to the final year considered (in this case, 1913), V is the value of the railroad in the terminal period, and r_i is the internal rate of return.[46]

Revenues (R) and costs (C) for the six railroads are taken directly from company reports and deflated by the wholesale price index for Rio de Janeiro.[47] The accounts of the British-owned roads, kept in pounds sterling, were converted to milréis, taking care to use the companies' accounting rates of exchange for the period 1885–1894, during which accounting rates departed from the market rates. The annual investment expenditures (I) for each company are obtained from end-of-year measure of the capital stock for each railroad, adapted from the total assets reported in each company's balance sheet. Assets and liabilities in these accounts potentially contain a number of sources of "water." Securities, particularly on the Brazilian-owned lines, were often issued at discount and may have been used on occasion as payments to contractors, although no evidence exists to suggest that shares or bonds were frequently used to pay dividends. To avoid distortions, I derive the capital figures as outlays on construction and physical assets. The railroads' book values were thus converted to capital-stock levels by summing the reported value (typically, the acquisition cost) of all track, road, structures, rolling stock, furniture, and the like, while excluding all obviously inappropriate or non-earning assets (e.g., stock put up by the firms' directors) and assets of dubious value (unpaid debts to the company). These adjustments proved impossible on the San Paulo Railway, and its book value had to be employed for the capital stock. Since its book value changed to reflect the doubling of track and the acquisition of the Bragantina line, it likely provides a reliable measure of investment expenditures. To convert these normal estimates of the capital stock to real annual investment expenditures, the first difference of the annual capital series was deflated by the Rio de Janeiro wholesale price index. For all railroads, both operating expenditures (C) and investment expenditures (I) in these reports include part of the capital outlays. Replacements and new investment often appeared, in varying degrees, under operating costs. However, since both categories of expenditures appear in the numerator of equation (7.1), the total capital expenditures, irrespective of accounting category, enter into the identity in the proper manner.

Unlike the accounting ratios measures of profit, this approach permits a ready and unambiguous comparison between profits bolstered by subsidy and hypothetical "unsubsidized" profits. Removing the guarantee payments makes it possible to estimate what the internal rate of return would have been had these railroads been constructed and operated without the guarantee scheme. The unaided rate of return differs from the aided rate by stripping from the net earnings stream both the government guarantee payments and, where appropriate, repayments by the firms. The difference between the aided and unaided rates equals the subsidy implicit in the guarantee program. As sketched out above, these payments varied widely across lines. In the case of the Central, the guarantees paid by the government in the first decade of the company's life were never "repaid" following the government's purchase of the line. Estimating those hypothetical profits without the guarantees gives those subsidy payments back to the government, treating them as if they never existed. By way of contrast, the SPR's contract stipulated not only repayment of guarantees as soon as dividends rose above a certain level, but actual profit sharing with the province of São Paulo. The SPR was not relieved of this requirement until 1890, when it renewed its contract. Here, those additional payments to the government are "returned" to the company. To estimate the hypothetical unaided internal rate of return, equation (7.1) above is modified as:

$$PV = \sum_{t=0}^{T} \frac{(R_t - C_t - I_t - G_t)}{(1 + r_i)^t} + \frac{V}{(1 + r_i)^T}$$

(7.2)

where G is the stream of net guaranteed dividend payments in any period (guaranteed dividends received from the government minus dividends repaid to the government). Table 7.1 presents the estimates of the aided and unaided internal rates of return computed in this way, by railroad.

As the net accounting measures of profits suggested, all of these companies had positive rates of return on average.[48] Whether or not the unaided internal rates of return on these railroads would have been sufficient to attract the needed capital depends on the opportunity cost of those funds, as indicated by the returns to other similar investments. In Brazil a limited range of long-term investment options was available in this period. A lucrative, albeit risky, investment until 1888 was slaveholding. The average annual real rate of return on a male prime field slave in Rio de Janeiro during the period 1873–1885 was high, ranging from 11.5 to 15 percent.[49] The ever-present possibility of slave flight, the rise of abolitionist sentiment and political activity, and the Free Birth Law of 1871 combined to create a great deal

Table 7.1

Aided and Unaided Internal Rates of Return
on Brazilian Railroads

Railroad	Period	Unaided internal rate of return (percent)	Aided internal rate of return (percent)
Estrada de Ferro Central do Brazil (Dom Pedro II)	1855–1913	4.60	6.40
San Paulo Railway Company	1867–1913	7.87	8.36
Companhia Mogiana	1875–1913	9.03	10.16
Companhia Paulista	1872–1913	12.70	12.90
Great Western of Brazil	1880–1913	4.30	7.30
Companhia Leopoldina	1874–1888	5.00	7.05
Leopoldina Railway Company	1874–1913	-1.00	2.00

NOTE: Unaided rates of return are the average profit of the railroad in the absence of guaranteed dividends from the government. The aided rates of return are the average profits including those guaranteed dividends. The rates of return are computed for each railroad in accordance with the procedure outlined in the text.

more risk in slaveholding in this period than one would encounter in holding government bonds, and such additional risk is reflected in these high returns. The return on slaves thus may not provide the best comparison with the returns on railroads; the return on relatively riskless assets is better suited to the question at hand. Government debt, issued both in Brazil and in Europe, was a relatively low-risk alternative. Observations of the earnings-price ratio for various Brazilian government bonds from 1854 to 1913 indicate the instantaneous rate of return on relatively riskless alternatives to railroads.[50] Rising returns on bonds whose dividends were paid in paper in the 1890s reflect the increase in risk inherent in them that resulted from high inflation. Gold bonds better reflect the return on relatively more secure assets in this period. Although there was some variability in the bond returns, particularly during the financially unstable 1890s, the typical rate hovered between 5 and 7 percent per annum.

Comparing the returns on bonds with the unaided returns on railroads makes it clear that only the Great Western, Leopoldina, and Central do Brazil demonstrated an obvious need for subsidies of some sort. After 1865 the Central was a government-owned line, and it did not really "need" any particular return. None of the government-owned lines were run for profit, and the Central suffered intermittent periods of negative operating revenues.Yet it concentrated the benefits of cheap transport in one of the politically most important regions.The degree to which its rate of return diverged from that of the privately owned lines is an index of the success that shippers had in extracting differentially low freight rates from the government. The other three roads enjoyed unaided profits that exceeded the market rates of return on bonds. Their average earnings were sufficiently large to make subsidies unnecessary when considered ex post.The excess of the subsidized rate over the unsubsidized return was inefficient, but relatively small. The "unnecessary" nature of the guaranteed dividends on most of these roads in no way diminishes their role. Guaranteed dividends settled the nerves of investors who were confronted with an opportunity to undertake projects of unknown prospects. While the payments to the railroads by the government were redundant in these cases, the commitment to make them served an important purpose at the outset. It assuaged investor concern, attracting railroad investment that Brazil would otherwise have had to pay much more to obtain, or failed to obtain at all.Whether or not the subsidies to railroads led to a net loss to Brazil depended not on the private returns to railroad capital, but rather on the social rates of return created by these lines.

From Private Profits to Social Returns

Gauging whether a subsidy was warranted requires that the market rate of return exceed the profits of the railroad, and that the railroad's social rate of return exceed the private benefits enjoyed by its owners.The internal rate of return presented in the previous section provides a measure of the "average" profitability for the firm over the period under consideration. However, it misses the larger set of benefits created by the railroad through the reduction in transport costs.To remedy that omission, two measures of the social benefit for each railroad are estimated: the average social rate of return and the social benefit-cost ratio. Both add to the private profits of the railroad the social savings due to reductions in transport costs. The inclusion of the social savings means that the social rate of return encompasses both of the streams of producers' and consumers' surplus created by the railroad. Deriving social rates of return in this manner, using the "social saving," is not without problems.[51] However, the difficulties inherent in measuring social rates of return are common to all benefit-cost analyses, be they of railroads or any other activity.The usefulness of the approach may be inferred from a voluminous historical literature that has employed it to offer new insights on the consequences of specific transport projects.[52]

Whether or not "too much" or "too little" was invested in these particular government railroads is not taken up here, though a cursory assessment along the lines pursued in measuring the marginal social rate of return in Chapter 4 suggests that the major railroads did not suffer overinvestment. For the present analysis, the average social rate of return suffices to indicate the magnitude of the gains generated by the railroad relative to the costs of obtaining those benefits. The second measure of the return to specific railroads used here is the benefit–cost ratio, which differs from the average social rate of return in that it uses the market rate of interest to discount returns, profits, and outlays over time. Benefit–cost ratios greater than 1 indicate that the railroad was a project that could be justified, based on the gains it made possible. Benefit–cost ratios less than 1 reveal a project that cost the economy more than it was worth.

The average social rate of return on the capital invested in a railroad is given by r_s when the present value of the railroad is set to zero:

$$PV = \sum_{t=0}^{T} \frac{(R_t - C_t - I_t - G_t + B_t)}{(1 + r_s)^t} + \frac{V}{(1 + r_s)^T}$$

$$(7.3)$$

It adjusts equation (7.2), the private internal rate of return, to include the measure of social benefits B from equation (7.5); r_s is the social rate of return, and all other variables are the same as in equation (7.2) above. No attempt is made here to render a social valuation of V. Table 7.2 presents the social rates of return by railroad.[53]

The second means of expressing the social benefits is through the benefit–cost ratio, which applies the social rate of discount to the streams of social benefits, private profits, and investment outlays. The benefit–cost ratio is calculated as:

$$\frac{B}{C} = \frac{\sum_{t=0}^{T} \frac{(R_t + B_t)}{(1 + r_d)^t} + \frac{V}{(1 + r_d)^T}}{\sum_{t=0}^{T} \frac{(C_t + I_t + G_t)}{(1 + r_d)^t}}$$

$$(7.4)$$

where r_d is a measure of the social rate of discount each year. In spite of conceptual ambiguities involved in determining the social rate of discount, the estimate in equation (7.4) uses the government bond rate.[54] Government dividend guarantees are treated as a cost assigned to each railroad. Benefit–cost ratios greater than 1 indicate that the railroad was a project that was jus-

Table 7.2

Average Social Rates of Return on Brazilian Railroads, 1855–1913

Railroad	Period	Unaided social rate of return— "A" (percent)	Unaided social rate of return— "B" (percent)
Estrada do Ferro Central do Brazil			
(Dom Pedro II)	1855–1913	18.0	—
San Paulo Railway Company	1867–1913	15.4	—
Companhia Mogiana	1875–1913	27.5	—
Companhia Paulista	1872–1913	26.6	—
Great Western of Brazil	1880–1913	15.0	11.4
Leopoldina Railway Company	1874–1913	6.8	—

NOTE: The social rate of return adds an estimate of social benefits to the measure of the internal rate of return in Table 7.1. Social rate of return "A" employs the prevailing pre-rail freight charge in computing the social benefits. The "B" measure of the social rate of return uses a drought-era, non-rail freight charge to compute those benefits in the relevant region. Figures for the Leopoldina Railway cover the firm's operations during both the era of Brazilian ownership and the later period when the line was British-owned.

tified in terms of the gains it made possible. Benefit-cost ratios less than unity show that the railroad cost the economy more than it was worth. Table 7.3 presents the social benefit-cost ratios by railroad.

The social benefits on individual railroads (B_t) were the resource savings of transport cost reductions, and their estimation confronts the same problems raised in Chapter 4 for the sector as a whole. Two approaches to measuring the magnitude of social benefits from specific railroads are prominent in the literature. The first treats most of the gains of cheap transport as accruing to the agricultural sector of the economy. In that case, the social benefits equal the increase in the value of farmland in the regions served by rail. Railroads shrink the transport-cost "wedge" between suppliers and consumers. The resulting rise in farm gate prices shows up in the relatively scarce factor of production, and the increase in agricultural producers' surplus reveals itself in higher land values.[55] Estimating the social benefits in this manner for Brazil is prohibitively difficult. The second tack is to measure the magnitude of the total savings on shipping freight for each railroad, in the manner of Chapter 4.[56] Given the information that was recorded on freight shipments in Brazil, and the ability to estimate the unit-cost savings on transporting freight, this second approach provides a more workable manner of incorporating the streams of producers' and consumers' surpluses created by the railroad.

As in Chapter 4, the magnitude of the social benefits depends first on the unit cost savings and second on the volume of freight service produced.[57] Because the unit savings on transport costs provided by railroads in Brazil are so large, a rather conservative estimate of the social benefits is employed in order to reduce the risk of overstating the gains each railroad created. Those benefits are computed in the following manner. The unit–cost savings each year is equal to the difference between the ton-kilometer charge for carrying freight by rail and the prevailing best-practice freight charge in the immediate pre-rail era. The rail charge is taken as the average freight revenue per ton-kilometer. The pre-rail charge comes from contemporary sources in Chapter 4. Railroad profits, estimated in the preceding section, indicate that rail rates departed systematically from costs. This poses little problem for the analysis here, since most rail charges were an overstated measure of cost and using them has the effect of further understating the social benefits. On the Great Western, Leopoldina, and the Central the regulated freight charges may have been less than cost, overstating somewhat the unit savings. In that case, private profits would be low because shippers extracted rents through regulation, in addition to gaining through resource savings.

The second factor bearing on the magnitude of social benefits is the level of freight services. This, in turn, depends first on the volume of freight service actually supplied by rail, and secondly on the volume that would have been shipped in the absence of railroads. Actual levels of service derive from rail reports and government surveys, just as in Chapter 4, on a line-by-line basis for each year that the company operated. The volume of freight service that would have prevailed in the absence of those railroads at each point in time in the areas they served is unobservable. However, they can be reasonably inferred by specifying the counterfactual.[58] The social benefits for each Brazilian railroad are estimated here by assuming that the demand schedule for freight services in the market served by each line was linear and that at the prevailing pre-rail freight charge absolutely no freight was shipped. The resultant equation is:

$$B_t = \frac{1}{2} Q_t (P_M - P_R)$$

(7.5)

where Q_t is ton-kilometers produced by rail in year t, P_M is the ton-kilometer charge for pre-rail shipment, and P_r is the rail charge per ton-kilometer.

All of the freight carried by rail is thus treated as if it resulted from the reduced cost of shipment. While this is obviously "wrong"—substantial freight

Table 7.3
Benefit–Cost Ratios on Brazilian Railroads, 1855–1913

Railroad	Period	Benefit-cost ratio— "A"	Benefit-cost ratio— "B"
Estrada de Ferro Central do Brazil (Dom Pedro II)	1855–1913	2.42	1.65
San Paulo Railway Company	1867–1913	3.18	2.17
Companhia Mogiana	1875–1913	2.73	2.30
Companhia Paulista	1872–1913	3.33	2.71
Great Western of Brazil	1880–1913	1.49	1.09
Leopoldina Railway Company	1874–1913	2.61	7.44

NOTE: Benefit-cost ratios derived as described in text. The "A" ratio assumes a social rate of discount of 4.59 percent. The "B" ratio takes 8.18 percent to be the social rate of discount. Leopoldina Railway encompasses both Brazilian and British ownership, as described in Table 7.2.

was shipped at pre-rail rates in Brazil, and that is precisely why those rates are available—it is a useful restriction to impose. It ensures that the resulting social benefits stream is not overstated. In fact, such a strong assumption potentially does serious damage to magnitude of the estimated benefits on a line-by-line basis. That they prove to be quite significant under such restrictive conditions inspires some confidence in the argument that benefits on the lines that were constructed under the guarantee scheme were sufficiently large as to justify the policy.

Unit charges on each railroad are adjusted to 1913 levels, and for the São Paulo lines (the SPR, Paulista, and Mogiana) the pre-rail rate used to compute the unit-cost savings is that derived from the major pre-rail trade routes for São Paulo (see Table 4.8), but differs slightly in that it averages both wet- and dry-season changes. That rate comes to 0.832 milréis per ton-kilometer in 1913 prices. The pre-rail rates cited by contemporaries for the regions served by the Central and the Leopoldina lines are particularly high, so the São Paulo pre-rail rate is employed there as well, under the assumption that it is a reasonable lower-bound estimate of the cost of transport for all of Brazil's center-south, using the historically relevant best practice pre-rail technology. For Brazil's northeast, fewer pre-rail freight quotations are available. Contemporary observers, including the British consuls and Brazilian government officials, noted a wide range of charges. To mitigate the risk of overstating these costs, the São Paulo dry-season charge from Table 4.8 is used here to calculate unit savings on freight shipped on the Great Western's lines. Special conditions in the region served by the Great Western warrant additional consideration. Through the 1870s and 1880s Brazil's northeast was hit by successively severe droughts, profoundly disrupting the regional economy. If drought conditions rendered the region's labor and animal resources underemployed for part of this period, the pre-rail freight rates may not reflect the alternative costs of freight shipment. Social opportunity costs, or "shadow prices," diverge from market rates in the context of underutilized resources. To adjust for this possibility, a second measure of social benefits for the Great Western uses the recorded non-rail freight charges during the drought period.[59] The freight rate used for that calculation, when adjusted to 1913 levels, is 0.421 milréis.

Unit savings obtained in this way are calculated for each railroad. For all lines, rail freight tonnage in each semester or year was usually taken directly from company reports. Where necessary, these figures were reduced to exclude freight shipped on the railroads for constructing extensions or otherwise in the "service of the line." Creating measures of the level of freight services, in units of ton-kilometers, posed a significant challenge given the relative paucity of information on the average length of haul (ALH). For many early years, and all of the years after 1898, the average length of haul was readily available. For every line in earlier years, at least part of the series of ALH had to be either interpolated or extrapolated, as detailed in Appendix B. Whenever the average haul had to be derived in this way, it was done so in a manner that reduced the chances of overstating the level of freight service.

The social rates of return presented in Table 7.2 reveal that the gains made possible through cheap transport on each of these railroads were large and positive. All exceed the private internal rates of return to these same railroads presented in Table 7.1 and the market rates of interest. On the São Paulo railroads, the presence of both strong profits and high social rates of return confirm the general vibrancy of the region's economy in this period. They also suggest the onset of a more generalized pattern of economic growth in the interior of the state. High social returns in the context of low private profits, such as the case of the Central, serve as an insightful measure of the extent to which the government-owned railroad was subject to "holdup" in the political arena by shippers seeking cheap freight rates. What is striking here is that, in spite of a number of assumptions imposed to make the social returns on all of these lines low, most are still quite large.

The social returns on the Central do Brazil and San Paulo Railway, while high, are less than encountered on the Mogiana and Paulista. Both the San Paulo Railway and the Central had lengthy segments that had been double-

and triple-tracked in the latter decades of the century. Their respective levels of physical capital were relatively large in relation to output levels before 1914, reducing somewhat the detectable social rates of return. The capital-output ratio was also somewhat high on the Central because of the relative decline of agriculture in much of the region it served. The Leopoldina, serving in part the same region, had relatively lower social returns. Competition from the Central worked at times to push the Leopoldina's rates down, the former road succeeding in pulling away some of the traffic that had been carried by the latter. The social returns on the Great Western are effectively no lower than those of the vibrant San Paulo Railway, so long as one assumes that the pre-rail charge in the northeast is the appropriate element to use in calculating the unit-transport-cost savings. Even if the drought-era, non-rail freight rate is the more appropriate alternative, the social returns indicate benefits of an impressive magnitude to the region. All of these estimates for Brazilian railroads compare favorably with similar calculations for railroads in the United States, Canada, Australia, and Mexico.

The benefit-cost ratios for each of the railroad projects, presented in Table 7.3, mainly serve to support the implications derived from the social rates of return. Because of the uncertainty over which of the government bond yields to employ as the social rate of discount, Table 7.3 presents two separate benefit-cost ratios for each road, based on the extreme values of gold-bond yields for the decades under study. The first, ratio "A," discounts both the numerator and denominator of equation (7.4) using a social discount rate of 4.59 percent, the lowest non-gold-bond yield estimated in the period 1856–1913. The second, ratio "B," repeats the same calculation but uses instead a discount rate of 8.18 percent, the highest observed yield. The two extreme bond rates test the sensitivity of the benefit-cost ratios to widely divergent values of the social rate of discount. The resulting benefit-cost measures all exceed unity, irrespective of the discount rate employed. Even though the measure of benefits is understated, the gains these railroads created were still as much as three times as great as the outlays of the railroad. Benefit-cost ratios are highest for the São Paulo railroads, which had the greatest overall traffic densities. Benefits relative to costs were somewhat lower for the Leopoldina and Central, and only on the Great Western did the ratio edge down toward the social "break-even" point. Since the government-guaranteed dividend payments are excluded from the benefits stream, the social rates of return of Table 7.2 and the benefit-cost ratios of Table 7.3 are unsubsidized, and thus are net of the direct transfers that might inflate their magnitudes. All of these investments paid for themselves, some at least several times over.

Whether or not the investments in railroads brought the highest social return possible to Brazil is unknown in the absence of measures of social rates
of return on alternative projects—realized or foregone—in this period.
Other activities that received guaranteed dividends in the late nineteenth
century, such as central sugar mills, likely had social returns that were quite
low or even negative. The government guarantee policy in those cases facilitated redistribution rather than an improvement in allocative efficiency. Although guarantees on investments in central sugar mills provide apt historical comparison, they may not be an appropriate referent in terms of
benefit-cost analysis. Irrespective of the returns to real or hypothetical alternative investments, when the social rates of return on these railroads are
compared with bond yields and their own private profits, all six of the railroads made for impressive material gains in the regions they served. The
guaranteed dividends supplied by the Brazilian government, along with the
regulation of freight rates, conjoined to create an income-enhancing outcome for Brazil. The result was one in which the guarantee arrangements ultimately succeeded in attracting investments in specific railroad projects that
made an important contribution to the Brazilian economy. Only if one
could specify an historically feasible alternative investment project with
higher returns could any of the railroads here be considered to have been a
drag on the Brazilian economy in any way.

Railroads that were smaller and carried less traffic than the six considered
here quite possibly had very different experiences. Despite the claim to a certain amount of representativeness on the part of these larger companies,
based on their share of total freight output, smaller lines probably had lower
social rates of return, as suggested by the cross-sectional results for 1913 in
Table 4.15. The British-owned railroads that were integrated into the Great
Western after the turn of the century had poor profit records before 1900.
Unsatisfactory financial performance, even with guaranteed dividends, was a
perennial source of complaint from shareholders in some companies.[60] At
times, those companies encountered regulatory conflicts with the government, which could reduce their allowable charges under the guarantee program.[61] Some smaller companies operated lines in regions where sufficient
traffic levels never developed.[62] At the same time, some of those troubled
companies may have labored under unrealistic expectations. Many held the
San Paulo Railway in envy, noting that "it has paid dividends that would
make the mouths of shareholders of many of the English railways water."[63]
The same source went on to attribute the poor location of these unprofitable
lines to Brazilian political influence in locating the concessions for foreign-
owned railroads. Lines with low profits, and low traffic levels, may well have
had low social returns. If correct, the regional-distributional intent of the

Railroad Law of 1873 worked to benefit relatively few shippers of freight, at a high social opportunity cost. But that result—one in which foreigners lost out, and the average Brazilian shipper gained relatively little as well—is quite different still from the outcome hypothesized by dependency interpretations. Testing this "low social return–low private return" hypothesis for that subset of railroads of lesser importance requires a more extensive analysis than can be supplied here. The results of Table 4.15, with respect to railroad lines that had poor returns, suggest that the hypothesis has merit.

Freight Rates, Regulation, and the Polity

Disentangling completely all of the factors accounting for differential profitability on the guaranteed railroads is not possible. Nonetheless, even after taking into account differences stemming from regional location and endowments, the interrelated questions of politics, regulation, and ownership emerge to the fore. The private success that each railroad company experienced and the benefits accruing to the region it served hinged on the rates charged. Left unregulated, most railroads in Brazil would have been textbook natural monopolies. Railroads charging very high rates could succeed in capturing handsome profits for themselves, yet simultaneously reduce the total gain to the economy. From the outset, Brazilian policymakers were sensitive to the potential problem of monopoly pricing, and protecting landowners from high rail charges led the government to guard against such monopoly power. Regulating the rates on these railroads was an attempt to keep the benefits to consumers of freight-transport services high. Supplying the dividend guarantees in the context of regulation allayed investor concerns and ensured them a portion of the benefits. Individual railroad concessions prescribed the maximum allowable rates for freight and passenger services, and rate regulation was a key determinant of profitability.

Considered together, profits, guarantee payments, and rate regulation provide insight into the main distributive and income-creating aspects of the government's involvement in the railroad sector. Rates were regulated from the outset by a legislature that set rates directly in many cases, and by Ministries authorized by the legislature to adjust rates within certain guidelines in the other cases. The analysis of rate regulation here assumes that legislators chose policies that garnered for them electoral support.

Policies adopted by legislators need not necessarily correspond to any criteria of economic efficiency.[64] Only in the case where market failures are widespread would regulation improve efficiency. In Brazil both the high cost of pre-rail transport and the need to regulate railroad rates were sufficiently pervasive that government policies would be likely to create real gains. An efficient policy, x, would maximize social surplus; that is, it would be one where the marginal benefit of regulation would equal the marginal social cost of the policy, as expressed by,

$$P(x) = B(x) - C(x)$$
(7.6)

and where the most efficient policy, x^* would be set thus:

$$B'(x) = C'(x)$$
(7.7)

Politicians did not share the economy's efficiency criterion. Rather, in seeking to garner electoral support, they might easily adopt policies that departed from the most efficient ones. Politicians considered not just benefits and costs, but the incidence of the various components of costs and benefits in their respective constituencies. A simple variant of this electoral support model first disaggregates benefits into those internal and external to the district. It also disaggregates the costs into those received as payments within the district, those received outside the district, costs within each district that arise as negative externalities, and the tax burden of outlays. An elected politician considers how these bear on his political support in choosing x, a regulatory policy. Thus,

$$N_i(x) = B_i(x) - C_i(x)$$

(7.8)

where $N_i(x)$ is the political support that legislator i expects from policy x, $B_i(x)$ are the benefits of the project within the district, and $C_i(x)$ are the indirect costs borne by the district.

In Brazil, the outlays on railroad regulation were negligible. In the case where the railroad was "over"-regulated, reducing its revenues below (total) cost, the government had to pay the guaranteed dividends, thus creating a tax burden from the policy. However, in that case the costs were spread across Brazil's tax base, and the district that benefited from regulating freight rates had to bear only a small part of the burden. The tax incidence is disregarded here.[65] For regulatory policies, then, the taxes and direct outlays are taken as negligible. The politician equates the marginal political gains from the policy to its marginal political costs. The key insight here is that indirect costs weighing on districts in Brazil varied with railroad ownership. For a railroad with predominantly Brazilian owners, the costs within the district were salient, since regulation reduced shareholder profits. In that case, the legislator would choose a smaller project—less regulation. For a railroad with predominantly British ownership (or complete public ownership), those costs were zero, and no such countervailing force on regulation existed, creating a scenario where tighter control of rates would prevail. With no railroad owners among the legislator's constituents, the indirect electoral costs arising from shareholders who receive lower profits would be of no concern to the legislator.

Guided by the internal rates of return above, and the simple model of policy choice, the hypothesis that emerges is that ownership and operation of railroads by either the state or foreigners is associated with lower freight rates. Indeed, it may be reasonably inferred that the political distance separating each company's shareholders from the regulatory apparatus of the Brazilian government accounts in large part for the differing profit experiences of these roads. That Brazilian shareholders in domestic railroads comprised an important political constituency suggests that they enjoyed some success at resisting downward pressure on rates. British shareholders were likely less effective in this regard because they had less direct representation within the political system. In this context, ownership could make a difference in the division of the surplus made possible by the investment. While the rates of return suggest this hypothesis is plausible, it must be completed via the linkage through freight rates. A rough test of the rate-setting hypothesis is specified in the following form:

$$RATE = \alpha + \beta_1 \, EXPORT + \beta_2 \, STATE + \beta_3 \, FOREIGN$$

$$(7.9)$$

where RATE is the railroad's charge to carry one ton for 100 kilometers on various agricultural commodities, EXPORT is a dummy on high unit-value products bound largely for export, STATE is a dummy for government ownership and operation, and FOREIGN is a dummy for foreign ownership or operation.

Table 7.4 presents the results of two regressions on this specification for two sets of railroads in 1909, one of the few years for which a cross-sectional survey of Brazilian freight rates exists. The six railroads studied in the preceding sections comprise the first set, while a broader sample of nineteen railroads comprises the second. In both regressions, foreign and state owner-

Table 7.4

Regression Results: Determinants of Agricultural Freight Rates on
Brazilian Railroads, 1909

	Six-railroad sample	Nineteen-railroad sample
	Dependent variable:	
	Charge per metric ton for 100-kilometer haul	
Independent variables:		
Constant	9.57	11.98
	(7.65)[a]	(15.50)[a]
EXPORT	14.70	12.40
	(11.20)[a]	(12.50)[a]
STATE	-4.13	-2.33
	(-2.14)[b]	(-1.43)[c]
FOREIGN	-1.52	-3.80
	(-1.04)	(-3.30)[a]
R_2	.61	.38
N	88	282

SOURCE: MVOP, *Relatório . . . 1909.*

NOTES: Rates are in Brazilian milréis. In 1909 the milréis exchanged for US$0.31. The six-railroad sample matches the six companies for which profits, social rates of return, and benefit-cost ratios are estimated in Tables 7.1, 7.2, and 7.3. The nineteen-railroad sample includes all lines for which rates were reported. EXPORT denotes commodities for which a large share was production for export: coffee, rubber, hides, *herva mate* (tea), cacao, and tobacco. Excepted are rice, beans, manioc flour, wheat flour, and corn, along with goods, such as sugar and cotton, which were traditionally exported but which by 1909 were largely produced for consumption within Brazil. STATE indicates railroads owned and operated by the government. FOREIGN is assigned to railroads either owned outright by overseas companies, owned by the government but leased to and operated by foreign companies, or some combination thereof. Parenthetical figures are t-statistics.

[a]Significant at the 1 percent level
[b]Significant at the 5 percent level
[c]Significant at the 10 percent level

ship are negatively associated with rates. The results support the hypothesis relating ownership to rates, and, implicitly, to profits, via the political choice of levels of rate regulation. Privately owned Brazilian lines enjoyed higher private returns in part because they had higher freight rates. British companies had less room for maneuver within Brazil's polity and could not effectively make demands on Brazil's legislature beyond the guaranteed minimum returns. With lower freight rates, the British railroad profits were less than profits on Brazilian-owned railroads. Rate regulation was an integral element of distributive politics in Brazil.

Conclusions

In the second half of the nineteenth century Brazil's guaranteed dividend policy attracted investments in railroads that the country had failed to obtain previously. If the requirement that the social returns on these investments exceed the market returns were the sole criterion for their evaluation, the subsidies would have been justifiable. Each railroad generated large benefits for the consumers of its services. With social rates of return that ranged from 7 percent to almost 28 percent per year, it is clear that the costs of railroad investment were amply rewarded. However, the second criterion—that private profits be less than market rates of return—reveals that several of Brazil's indispensable railroads enjoyed wholly dispensable subsidies. Few of these major railroads failed to attain levels of profitability equal to or in excess of the market rates. For the railroads that did not need subsidies, the guarantee payments were a "giveaway." Had they not been paid, those guarantees would have accrued to Brazilian taxpayers. However, the magnitude of those transfers was small in comparison to the conservative measures of social benefits. Given the inability to predict perfectly the future course of entire regions and economies, the gap between the subsidized and unsubsidized rates of return on those railroads indicates a modest prediction error made by the officials that devised the guarantees.

The distribution of the gains from the railroads that were established under the guarantee scheme may be considered in several dimensions. One is the national-versus-foreign division of the surplus produced by transport investment. The previous chapter explored this question for the Brazilian rail sector as a whole in 1913, as part of an examination of the structural impact of railroads. The results obtained in this chapter, using a sample of companies operating in various regions over a much longer period, support and strengthen those conclusions. The historiography of Latin America has devoted a fair amount of attention to the putatively negative implications of foreign railroad ownership for the national economy. The rather standard, blanket view of foreign railroads in Latin America to date has been one in which "more often than not foreigners built and owned them, and did so where they would best complement the North Atlantic economies rather than Latin America's."[66] Nowhere have those characterizations been subjected to a rigorous test until now. For Brazil, the picture that emerges here is one in which foreigners did not fare disproportionately well in the period before 1914. British-owned railroads, viewed as "holding a nation to ransom" because of their role as carriers of export goods, ironically failed to exercise undue power or control over the streams of benefits that they created for the Brazilian economy.[67] That is not to say that they did not desire that control. What influence they did possess did not, in contrast to previous claims, translate into unusually high profits relative to the returns enjoyed by Brazilian-owned lines.[68] It is thus unclear what meaning, if any, could be assigned to that power, if they possessed it at all. As claimants on the residual gains that their railroads created, British companies did not take home an especially large share. What little "power" they did exercise—the ability to earn a competitive rate of return on their investments—came not from a privileged position within Brazil, but rather from the efficiency of the London capital market, which demanded over the long run risk-adjusted profits equal to those available elsewhere in the world. The very efficiency of that capital market made it all the more easy for the Brazilian government to keep most of the surplus at home, since all it had to do was guarantee a minimum competitive rate of return. Brazilians were able to assure overseas investors that they would earn at least that, even with rate regulation, by offering security through guaranteed dividends. Regulation worked to capture the rest of the surplus and keep it within Brazil.

Indeed, because freight rates were set by Brazilian regulators, it was Brazilian-owned railroads that likely enjoyed greater success in counterbalancing downward pressure on those rates by shipping interests. Just like the Brazilian consumers of transport services, Brazilian shareholders formed an influential political constituency. British shareholders, on the other hand, had less direct access to the regulation process, since they had only a limited voice in Brazil's political arena. Where outright government ownership of railroads existed, as was the case with the Central, there was no mediating institution to protect the railroad from the continuous clamor for lower freight rates. With no defenses, there was little risk that it would ever be employed as a revenue-enhancing enterprise by the government, in the way that the National Prussian Railways were used.[69] In Brazil, predatory politics rather than predatory pricing kept returns to foreigners and to the government-owned line comparatively low.

Chapter 8

Conclusions

Brazil began its fourth decade as an independent nation virtually devoid of the institutional arrangements and technologies that had enabled the industrializing North Atlantic economies to secure so much in the way of material progress during the first half of the nineteenth century. Disjoint product and labor markets, low levels of overall activity, and even the economy's output mix reflected Brazil's relatively inefficient economic organization. Of the myriad impediments confronting the economy, none was more oppressive than the state of internal transport. The *conciliação*, Conservative, and Progressista cabinets that led the government from 1853 through 1873 ameliorated transport conditions by establishing an array of policies designed to attract investments in railroads. That groundwork paved the way for the establishment of a railroad sector that vastly reduced the costs of transport. Brazil's railroads contributed powerfully to boosting the pace of economic growth at the turn of the century.

The abolition of slavery, the supplanting of the Monarchy by the Republic, the coffee and rubber booms, and rising industrialization comprise the better-known changes of the last decades of the nineteenth century. Perhaps less immediately detectable was the profound traverse experienced by the economy as a whole. Evidence suggests that the 1880s and 1890s witnessed an enduring improvement in overall productivity growth; by 1900, that transition was in full swing.[1] The increase in per capita income from 1900 through 1913 was dramatic. Though set back by the First World War and the

Great Depression, the economy proved sufficiently resilient to rebound quickly. Between 1900 and 1980 Brazil was one of the fastest-growing economies in the Western world. No other country in the Americas rivaled its performance.

Brazil's experience with railroads involved more than merely implanting a new transport technology. Railroads intersect directly with the role of the state in the economy. Moreover, nineteenth-century railroad policies grappled with the problem of how to encourage foreign investment while simultaneously regulating it. In the same way that Brazil countenanced the challenges of attaining growth more than a hundred years ago, the problems it faces today involve redefining the role of both the state and foreigners in the economy in order to try and improve efficiency, put people to work, and raise incomes. The railroad experience may yet prove to be an apt historical referent.

The railroad's most important direct contribution came precisely through its impact on the pace and scope of economic activity. By moving freight and passengers at a lower cost than the old technology of overland transport, the railroad integrated product and labor markets, improving inter- and intra-regional terms of trade. Initially, the railroad's impact registered more heavily in the already growing export sector. However, in the longer term, the gains of market integration were relatively greater in the domestic sector of the economy. With lower transport costs, rural producers faced less risk of shortage, along with less local price variation, and could afford to devote fewer resources to insurance-like activities and more to the production of crops with a marketable surplus. Manufacturers could reach broader and deeper markets than ever before within Brazil. Cheap transport by rail enabled Brazilians to capitalize on the long-standing presence of coastal shipping, and thus intensified inter-regional commerce. Workers and businessmen alike found in the railroad a way to locate opportunities for employment and commerce that had previously been far removed from them. Railroads effectively brought distant markets for domestically consumed goods together for the first time. Freight and passenger movement by rail contributed powerfully to the formation of a national market.

By 1913, the last year of large additions to the nation's track, a conservative upper-bound measure of the value of the resources released from transporting freight ranges between 18 percent and 38 percent of gross domestic product. Adjusting those figures to permit the overall level of Brazilian economic activity to respond flexibly to the impact of lower transport costs reduces those results to between 8 percent and 13 percent of GDP. While smaller than the upper-bound measures, the lower-bound estimates remain large by international standards.

The contribution of the new transport technology to the Brazilian economy in the late nineteenth century was matched in few other regions of the world. The differing assumptions and specifications built into the analyses of railroads in other countries render comparison with Brazil difficult. Nonetheless, the gains to the Brazilian economy from the new transport technology were likely much greater than in those nations, such as the United States, England, France, Belgium, and the Netherlands, that enjoyed relatively efficient and cheap pre-rail transport systems. While the railroad's impact in Brazil also exceeded that of several other backward economies, the degree of an economy's overall relative backwardness is in fact a poor predictor of the impact of railroads. Russia and Thailand were relatively backward economies in the second half of the nineteenth century. Both possessed affordable and navigable waterways; in neither did railroads create especially large gains. Factors other than transport carried greater weight in dampening economic growth in those areas. Only in the cases of Mexico and Spain did railroad freight services create gains of similar magnitudes as found in Brazil, although any country that did not enjoy cheap, efficient pre-rail transport would likely exhibit similarly large savings from the new transport technology. Even though the resource-saving estimates derived in Chapter 4 exclude several categories of benefits that railroads created, including the savings on inventory costs and livestock shipping losses, had Brazil not possessed its railroad sector in 1913 the additional costs of shipping freight would have made the economy much smaller. Even if the non-railroad counterfactual anchors the estimates to lower levels of transport output, the productivity-enhancing benefits that railroad freight services generated remained large in Brazil, and essential for late-nineteenth and early-twentieth-century growth.

The railroad created additional savings to the Brazilian economy through the reduction in the costs of passenger travel. Those gains were small relative to the benefits from railroad freight services. Nonetheless, rail passenger services contributed appreciably to the growth of the economy by improving the integration of the labor market. The passenger social savings derived in Chapter 5 measure exactly the gains to the economy from the enhanced labor-market efficiency that the railroad made possible. By reducing direct passenger outlays and the time involved in travel, railroads shrank the economic distance between workers and jobs. More frequent trips, the relative ease, safety, and comfort of rail travel, and the new flows of information about available work conjoined to give rise to new opportunities for those in the labor force.

Passenger benefits in Brazil ranged between 2 percent and 4 percent of GDP in 1913. Unmeasured benefits likely bolstered the overall impact of railroad passenger services. Government used railroads to subsidize immigration, effectively making the private costs of transport zero for many of those coming from abroad to work in Brazil. Cheap transport was a key ingredient in increasing the stock of labor. Leisure travelers enjoyed welfare gains from the railroad as well, although much of those escape the available resource-savings measures. Railroad passenger services possibly contributed to improvements in the flow of public news and private information, and to changes that led to cultural melding and that reshaped regional and class identities. Such consequences, though no doubt important, are analytically intractable in the absence of an axiomatically derived theory of cultural change, and lie outside the framework of this study altogether.

That the pecuniary measures of the railroad's direct resource savings for working passengers were not higher still was a result of three factors. First, the relatively short trips that Brazilians demanded arose from a concentration in short-haul services, especially in the market for commuter travel in and around the large urban centers of Rio de Janeiro and São Paulo. Brazilians also did not travel as frequently as their North Atlantic counterparts, and that reduced total passenger benefits as well. And, perhaps most importantly, the time that railroads saved for travelers was simply not worth very much in Brazil's low-wage economy.

Thanks to the innovation of the internal combustion engine and the rise of motor vehicles, the direct gains from railroad transport became less immediately relevant as the century progressed. However, the railroad still went far in laying the groundwork for Brazil's high rates of growth in the twentieth century. A good share of the investment in railroads that generated these gains was procured through the government's provision of dividend guarantees and its direct ownership of railroads. Dividend guarantees attracted a stream of foreign investment, largely British, into Brazil. Those policies circumvented some long-standing obstacles to capital formation posed by Brazil's thin financial markets, permitting the country to latch onto more efficient institutions abroad in order to hasten the pace of investment in transport infrastructure. In a set of policies brilliantly calculated to limit the foreign firms' ability to extract large profits, the Brazilian government maintained tight control over rates charged on railroads, guaranteeing that the fruits of cheap transport flowed to the very constituencies that had sought transport-cost reductions.

While the railroad's forward linkage was powerful, bringing in labor and capital, and opening new lands, strong backward linkages were conspicuously absent in Brazil. In contrast to the large gains from lower transport costs, the consumption by railroads of inputs from Brazilian manufacturing was small. Demands for coal, rails, and rolling stock were met largely by overseas suppliers. For many historians, it was the very success of railroads in reducing transport costs that bred the failure of backward linkages. In this view, the resolute ambition to obtain railroads quickly, combined with the absence of policies that would forge linkages backward to coal mining and metals production, meant that railroad development constituted an opportunity to industrialize that was foregone. That perspective, however, fails to square with either the comparative evidence on railroads and industrialization in the advanced economies, or the conditions inhibiting the rise of modern iron and steel production in Brazil. In the United States, for example, railroad construction and operation tapped extant manufacturing activities that depended only partly on the demands of the railroad sector. Brazil, by contrast, had weak backward linkages because railroad development came well before the rise of domestic industry. With nothing but primitive forges producing crude farmer's iron, Brazil relied on foreigners to supply it with rails and rolling stock.

Brazil's direct outlays on foreign railroad inputs were minuscule relative to the benefits of cheap transport, coming to less than one-half of 1 percent of GDP, at most, in 1913. Moreover, the opportunity costs of this reliance on foreign inputs were small. For Brazil, an import-substituting industrial strategy was not even remotely feasible in the nineteenth century. If that potential had been present, Brazilians would have pursued and exploited it just as vigorously as they did the forward linkages. The country simply lacked the resource endowment, namely ore and coal deposits of sufficient quality needed for a modern iron and steel industry. Had Brazil pursued protectionist strategies designed to forge backward linkages, railroad development would have ground to a halt in the 1800s, institutionalizing backwardness.

Also notable was the absence in Brazil of a number of effects attributed to railroads in the advanced industrializing economies. Although railroads benefited industry by reducing transport costs, they did not provide a particularly unique or special stimulus by creating economies of scale. If they did so, they brought about only very small resource savings beyond the direct benefits on freight and passenger services. The conclusion that railroads created even minuscule additional gains to industry rests on the assumption that the economies of scale detected in textiles were attributable entirely to cheap transport. However, in a dynamic framework such small gains might well compound in the long-term to create an important impetus to industrialize. If such an effect were present, it simply strengthens the conclusions here regarding the railroad's importance in fostering Brazilian economic growth.

In relatively backward economies railroads are often thought to exacerbate critical structural imbalances. Brazil's railroads did not alter the output mix of the economy in ways that made for "overspecialization" in agriculture or exports before 1914. The available indicators reveal that the decline in transport costs was associated with the rapid expansion of the internal sector of the economy. Moreover, the reduction in the costs of transport neither tilted relative prices against industry, nor did they promote a wholesale shift of resources into export agriculture. The agriculture-industry terms of trade within Brazil in 1913 were at the same level they had been in 1870.[2] At various intervals in the intervening decades, relative prices strongly favored manufacturing. The international economic ties that railroads strengthened did not worsen Brazil's terms of trade with Great Britain, its main overseas trading partner, from 1850 to 1914.[3] To the extent that railroads did alter inter-sectoral and international terms of trade, the consequences were not inimical to Brazilian industrialization or economic growth.

In terms of the railroad's rather unbalanced direct consequences, Brazil strongly resembles other relatively backward economies, such as Mexico and Spain. However, in Brazil the distribution of the direct gains differed markedly from that in Mexico, where cheap transport favored foreign-owned export activities. By contrast, Brazilian railroads, even when foreign-owned, served a growing and increasingly diverse economy characterized by Brazilian-owned industry and native-Brazilian and immigrant farming.[4] Regulation ensured that consumers of transport services reaped the bulk of the benefits, so that transport savings accrued to native producers. The government continuously pushed railroad rates down, and held them especially low for agricultural goods produced and consumed domestically. Foreign-owned railroad companies earned competitive profits, but rarely earned much more than that. Brazilian-owned railroads were better at opposing downward pressure on rates and earned slightly higher profits. Both kinds of railroads did receive some excess subsidies, but the losses from this extravagance were small. Because the government set especially low rates on domestic-use goods, the share of exports in total railroad freight declined steadily over time. So did the share of exports in Brazil's total output. In short, the benefits that railroads bestowed on Brazil went mainly to the domestic-use sector of the economy and not to the export sector or foreigners. The government's policy toward railroads helped to shift the economy's growth path dramatically upward and moved it away from the export "bias" of the early nineteenth century. New transport technology and government regulation formed a powerful combination in a country that had previously been starved of quick and affordable transport services.

Railroads in Brazil did give the Imperial state its first taste of active regulation of, and direct ownership in, an important sector of the economy. As already suggested, there was little that was neutral about the distributional outcome of that involvement. On the one hand, regulation, and ownership by the government, no doubt reduced efficiency within the railroad sector over what could have been achieved in the "first–best" scenario. That which is desirable is not always feasible, however, and Brazil's railroads, no matter how inefficient they might have been, proved to be a significant advance beyond the mule trains and carts that preceded them. By guaranteeing the dividends on some lines, owning others outright, and regulating the rates on all of those roads, the Brazilian state performed two classic functions. First, it solved "prisoners' dilemma"-like problems that markets did not solve alone. By securing investment, the state helped make for a permanent gain in efficiency for the economy as a whole. Second, it governed the distribution and redistribution of the benefits that railroads created. As the previous chapter demonstrated, in one dimension of distribution, government ensured that the consumers of railroad services enjoyed much of the gains that railroads brought to the economy. Neither the British shareholders, nor the government-owned lines, nor private Brazilian railroads made off with particularly large profits.

The results presented in the preceding chapters confirm the tremendous importance of railroads for relatively backward countries that had severe transport bottlenecks in the nineteenth century. They also call into question assumptions and leading generalizations about the roles of foreign investment and the state in Latin American economic development. In the Brazilian case, the claims emanating from dependency interpretations now appear exaggerated at best. When considered within the confines of conventional economic analysis, the railroad's accomplishment in Brazil was substantial. The government first subsidized and regulated railroads to reduce the burden of high transport costs for a rural elite that specialized in export agriculture. Foreigners invested in those railroads because they found the risks tolerable and believed they stood a chance of receiving good profits. Though built using foreign capital to link plantations to port, the railroads ultimately registered large gains for domestic markets, created new opportunities for immigration and industry, and put the country on the path to much-improved growth.

Beyond their overt impact, Brazilian railroads also created less visible benefits and costs that escape conventional notions of linkages. These effects lie beyond the immediate implications of the railroad for national income, and involve the interactions of the railroad with the country's institutional setting. These institutional externalities encompass some broader consequences of the railroad for the long-run trajectory of Brazilian development.

Railroad development altered the social, economic, and political map of Brazil, but did so differently than it did in other countries. The pattern of early railroad construction likely held important consequences for the institution of slavery. Because of the regional imbalance in the distribution of project concessions and subsidies, early railroads located disproportionately in the country's center-south. There, the first stage of railroad investment in the 1850s and 1860s contributed to an increase in the demand for labor, right after the foreign supply of enslaved Africans had been permanently interrupted by the British. Planters near railroad projects that were either planned or underway anticipated rising farm-gate prices and satisfied their demand for labor by buying slaves from northern provinces. This anticipatory accumulation of slaves was analogous to the anticipatory usurpation of Indian lands in Mexico and the anticipatory settlement of western lands in the United States, both of which transpired along planned railroad routes in those countries. In Brazil, the early phase of railroad development contributed to a new geographic concentration of slave ownership. This shift likely strengthened the political support for slavery in the center-south, but weakened it elsewhere. The regional redistribution of the slave population in the early decades of railroad development aided in undermining the status quo coalition supporting slavery in the Parliament.

The changes wrought by the railroad in the distributional realm do not reduce easily to one or two dimensions. One extreme possibility is that none of the benefits that railroads created remained in Brazil; all might have been siphoned off as part of the country's newly fortified integration into the world economy. Although railroad development unfolded during the very period in which the country's newly strengthened dependency is claimed to have given rise to a wide array of negative economic, political, and social consequences, Brazil before 1914 bears little resemblance to the standard caricature of a dependent, neocolonial Latin American economy. It is clear from the evidence of Chapters 6 and 7 that Brazilians, rather than foreigners, reaped the vast bulk of the benefits that railroads created. At the same time, the distribution of the benefits that railroads created might well have been highly skewed within Brazil. Much uncertainty attaches to any discussion of the distributional consequences of the railroad in the absence of reliable measures of the size-distribution of income and a model of how that distribution might be altered by cheap transport. Conventional measures of distribution would readily indicate "who won" and "who lost" in Brazil during the years of railroad expansion, as well as the pace and degree of distributional change. Unfortunately, that information is not available, and those measures remain beyond the historian's grasp for Brazil.

Given the predominance of agricultural goods in the mix of transportables for much of the period considered in this study, it is likely that a large increment of the resource savings that railroads created in Brazil accrued to landholders and consumers. In the countryside, rising land values potentially led to an increase in the concentration of wealth by two different avenues. The first is that the benefits of cheap transport may be so specific to a relatively small share of landholders that their wealth increases much more than the wealth of farmers less well served by railroads. The second way in which railroads can increase the concentration of wealth is the manner in which rising land values create an incentive to seize land from occupants who are less powerful. The evidence here is mixed, in part because property rights in land changed with the advent of the Republic. Property rights in land were traditionally poorly defined, and the Land Law of 1850 did little to make it easy to gain clear title to land. The Constitution of 1891 devolved the authority to define and enforce property rights in land to state-level governments. Thereafter, the history of landed property rights in Brazil becomes more complex because as many as twenty different policies were pursued. The study of immigrant farmers in São Paulo during the heyday of railroads reveals that there was ample opportunity for smallholders and new arrivals to gain access to land between 1905 and 1920.[5] It is also possible that agricultural colonists, responding to new opportunities created by railroads, may well have displaced extant occupants of the land.[6] One of the few areas where a railroad actually obtained land grants and established agricultural colonies was in the *contestado* region of southern Brazil. The outbreak of violence there in 1912 is attributed to the forces unleashed as a result of land expropriations by the railroad. Even if no body of evidence yet exists that demonstrates an increasing concentration of wealth in late-nineteenth-century Brazil, much less the role played by railroads in such a process, interest in the issue still serves to direct attention to how the railroad might have altered factor returns. No systematic evidence exists on the relative returns to either land or capital over the period of railroad development, though fragmentary data show that land values rose in regions served by rail. The ratio of unskilled wages to GDP per capita indicates the share of labor in national income.[7] Though the ratio fluctuated in the decades before 1913, there was no downward trend, despite heavy immigration that worked to keep wages from rising. As tentative as this measure is, it calls into question any belief that income distribution necessarily worsened in the era of railroad development.

Although the extent of distributional change induced by the railroad is unknown, the railroad's indirect consequences in other areas can be inferred. Railroads contributed in an unanticipated way to recrudescent local and provincial protectionism. This sort of interaction involved features far removed from the technology embodied in the railroad itself. Where the polity was potentially torn by centrifugal regional forces, as in Old Republic Brazil, the potential gains of cheap transport may be partly offset by the rise of new obstacles designed to protect groups that stand to lose from the creation of more efficient markets.

Inter-regional tariffs, tolerated under the Empire, flourished under the Republic, in spite of constitutional strictures on their collection.[8] Throughout much of Brazil, the market integration that railroads made possible was soon followed by the erection of barriers to inter-regional commerce. By way of contrast, in Mexico similar tariffs, known as the *alcabala*, had been largely eliminated by Republican government at mid-century. In the United States, taxes on internal trade were unconstitutional, and courts regularly struck down thinly disguised taxes that burdened the produce from other regions. In Brazil those tariffs emerged anew, not just to generate revenues and thus finance state-level expenditures, but also to protect constituencies who were less competitive than their peers in other regions of the country. Internal tariffs arose from the increased competition that farmers in one region faced from farmers in another—competition made possible by the transport-cost reductions of the railroad.

Market integration brought distant states, such as Rio Grande do Sul and Pernambuco, as well as immediate neighbors, such as Rio de Janeiro and Minas Gerais, into direct economic conflict because they had farmers and manufacturers who were in direct competition. This came about even when those regions did not share a rail connection.[9] Because the construction of railroads intensified inter-regional integration in product markets, and transmitted that integration via coastwise shipping, it brought far-flung hinterlands into competition with one another. Political barriers to commerce were a common source of complaint, particularly from merchant groups who saw valuable branches of trade fall off as a direct result of such barriers. The net result was that the stimulus arising from the resource savings of railroads, estimated in Chapters 4 and 5, was somewhat attenuated. The persistence of institutional arrangements of this rent-seeking and protectionist variety did not preclude Brazil from attaining improved economic performance in the early twentieth century. At the same time, institutional features were likely crucial in shaping the distributional path along which Brazilian growth proceeded after 1900.

Railroad development promoted the creation of a small but important new class of professionals in both the public and private sectors. Although foreign investment and state ownership remained prominent, several of the country's largest and most successful railroads were owned by joint-stock companies organized within Brazil. Just as they were in the United States, railroads were Brazil's first big business. The imperatives of modern production and coordination strengthened native entrepreneurship and business organization. The reliance on overseas investment and government subsidies to build the railroad sector had few, if any, negative effects on the development of the Brazilian capital market. Although government subsidies theoretically pulled away investments in other activities, in Brazil those subsidies worked to overcome investor perceptions that worked like capital market imperfections. By promoting railroad projects, they channeled investment into a sector of activity that gave rise to tremendous and direct positive externalities.

On the surface, Brazil's reliance on relatively efficient overseas capital markets and financial institutions stripped away the need for those same arrangements to evolve domestically. However, instead of stifling or diverting incentives to capital market innovations, railroads may well have strengthened them in two ways. The first was by extending and integrating product markets for manufactures within Brazil. Recognition of opportunities in those markets meant that entrepreneurs and investors stood to gain even more from institutional changes that would permit the formation of joint-stock companies and elaboration of long-term financial arrangements. The second was by requiring domestic intermediaries for Brazilian savers seeking to invest in railroads. As early as the 1880s no less than 25 percent of Brazil's railroad sector enjoyed domestic finance through equity and debt issues on stock exchanges in Rio de Janeiro and São Paulo. By 1900 railroad equities accounted for a greater share of the Rio de Janeiro and São Paulo stock markets than any other sector of domestic investment.[10]

In the case of government-owned railroads, the indirect effects were twofold. First, in the short term, the impact of government was no doubt positive. If nothing else, the dictates of effective administration created professional staff, managers, and planners in the public sector. And, the need to monitor the industry, especially the foreigners, created a shrewd and savvy group of regulators and railroad experts. Because less information is available on these effects, and measuring them defies present theory and method, gauging their impact is not possible. They may well be no less important in the long term than the direct consequences. Second, in the longer term, Brazil's experience with direct government railroad intervention likely proved negative. To the extent that heavy state involvement permitted Brazil to obtain foreign investment and capture a large share of the surplus, then the railroad's interaction with the polity proved extra-beneficial. Policies that channeled capital into railroads that generated low benefits pulled resources from areas where they likely would have created large gains, such as education. The experience with government regulation and ownership of railroads created important demonstration effects. State intervention in railroads increased the returns to lobbying for interventions in other arenas, including commodity and financial markets, many of which created no conceivable benefits. The costs of such interventions can only be guessed at. To the extent that the state's experience with railroads laid the groundwork for the grossly distorting and dissipating policy interventions of the twentieth century, the railroad may be held culpable in the same degree that it may be credited for creating direct gains.[11] As is so often the case for history, and for Brazil, these unanticipated consequences may prove to be the most profound.

AN	Arquivo Nacional [National Archives], Rio de Janeiro
CIB	Centro Industrial do Brasil [Brazil Industrial Center]
CM	Companhia Mogiana de Estradas de Ferro [Mogiana Railroad Company]
CP	Companhia Paulista de Estradas de Ferro [Paulista Railroad Company]
DSS	Direct social savings
EEF	*Estatísticas das Estradas de Ferro da União e das Fiscalizadas pela União* [Statistics of Railroads Owned and Inspected by the Federal Government]. Rio de Janeiro, 1898–1913.
EEH	*Explorations in Economic History*
EFCB	Estrada de Ferro Central do Brazil [Central Brazil Railroad]
EFDPII	Estrada de Ferro Dom Pedro II [Dom Pedro II Railroad]
EHR	*Economic History Review*
FEPASA	Ferrovias Paulistas, S.A.
GW	Great Western of Brazil Railway Company, Ltd.
HAHR	*Hispanic American Historical Review*
IBGE	Instituto Brasileiro de Geografia e Estatística [Brazilian Institute of Geography and Statistics]
IMM	*Investor's Monthly Manual*
JC	*Jornal do Commércio* [*Business Journal*]
LRC	Leopoldina Railway Company, Ltd.
MACOP	Ministério da Agricultura, Commércio, e Obras Públicas [Ministry of Agriculture, Commerce, and Public Works]
MI	Ministério do Império [Ministry of the Empire]

MVOP	Ministério da Viação e Obras Públicas [Ministry of Transportation and Public Works]
RSF	Recife and San Francisco Railway Company, Ltd.
SAJ	*South American Journal*
SPR	San Paulo (Brazilian) Railway Company, Ltd.
U.K.	United Kingdom (Great Britain)

Appendix A

Theory and Method of the Social Savings Approach

The study of railroads by new economic historians over the last four decades has left in its wake a rich array of methodological treatments by adherents and critics alike. Some of these provide philosophical explorations of the applicability of covering laws and counterfactuals in the context of historical questions.[1] Nearly all include applied technical discussions of the parameters of the markets for transport services and the usefulness of quantification. These detailed methodological statements provide in-depth assessments of the theoretical assumptions, practical pitfalls, and interpretive implications of econometric analyses of the railroad's impact.[2] The purpose of this appendix is to provide no more than a brief overview of the principal methodological concerns that bear on the analyses of Chapters 4 through 7. It highlights the more prominent biases involved in applying the social savings approach, the strengths and limitations of the treatment of the railroad's linkage effects, and the sensitivity of the study's main findings to alternate assumptions and parameters. More extensive treatments are available to the interested reader in the specialized literature cited in the Notes.

The substantive chapters of this work assess the railroad in terms of its direct effects and its principal linkages.[3] Direct effects are the social savings on railroad freight and passenger services. Linkages encompass the myriad connections and interactions between the railroad and other economic activities. The direct social savings concept is rooted in elementary benefit-cost analysis. The concept of linkage itself holds little analytical content and merely provides a categorical partition on a subset of the railroad's effects that renders them tractable for discussion. The analytic capability within the linkage framework rests with the application of price theory to key variables and parameters of the nineteenth-century Brazilian economy. In practice, the number and type of linkages is never predetermined. Rather, the investigative possibilities of more or less detailed configurations of possible linkages depend solely on the questions of interest to the investigator and on the historical circumstances of the process being investigated. In Chapter 6 the railroad's backward linkages include the demands for inputs generated by the railroad and the consequences of those demands. The forward linkage involves the stimulus to new activities from the railroad's reduction of transport costs and its increase in the supply of transport services, along with induced changes in the economy's output mix. Applying both the direct savings and linkage concepts to historical questions requires the use of counterfactuals to explore how some elements of the Brazilian economy might have been different in the absence of the railroad. Paradoxically, the use of such contrary-to-fact scenarios, which are at least implied by most historical statements worthy of deliberation, clarifies actual events and illuminates the processes of economic change before 1914.

In this appendix, the direct effects are outlined first, solely in terms of the railroad's freight social savings (the extension of the approach to passenger services follows analogously). A discussion of the conceptual issues surrounding the social rate of return on railroad capital follows. The theory of induced effects via the forward linkage, and the opportunity costs implied by the nature of the backward linkage, are outlined in a somewhat cursory manner since relatively less attention is devoted to those effects in Chapter 6. The appendix concludes with some general interpretive issues of the study's reliance on counterfactual analysis and with specific considerations bearing on its application to a relatively backward economy.

The Social Savings Concept

The social saving is defined as the difference between the actual cost of shipping freight by railroad in a given year and the cost of shipping the same amount of freight over the same distance without the railroad. It is necessarily counterfactual in nature by virtue of juxtaposing the Brazilian economy against a hypothetical economy deprived of its railroads. While the analysis is drawn from modern economic theory, nineteenth-century observers also expressed their assessments of the railroad's impact in terms that correspond directly to the social saving and social rate of return. One of the early directors of the Dom Pedro II railroad held that the line's freight rates in the 1860s

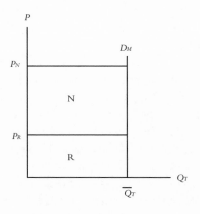

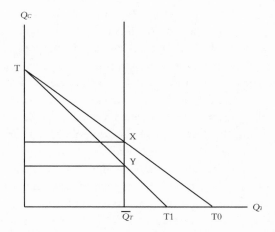

Figure A.1. The direct social saving. The upper half of the figure portrays the direct social saving in the market for transport; the lower half depicts the direct social saving in terms of the economy's output.

were but one-sixth of the rates that muleteers charged to carry freight. Noting that freight paid an average of 20 réis for an arroba to travel one league by rail, and that on the "backs of beasts" it paid six times that, "it follows that commerce and farming had a saving in shipping their products equal to 100 réis per arroba legua." He went on to compute the flow of the direct social savings each year from 1860 to 1868. By 1868, the social rate of return—the benefits to users of freight services and the net revenues of the line—was estimated at 40 percent.[4] In the late 1880s Antônio Prado, then Imperial Senator and Minister of Agriculture, referring to the railroads of São Paulo, "calculated that between 1880 and 1887 a saving had been effected by the province, by the use of their lines in preference to the old methods of carriage, which could not be estimated at less than £7,000,000."[5]

The upper portion of Figure A.1 presents the basic concept graphically by focusing on the market for freight-transport services. The quantity of transport services provided by the railroad, Q_T, is fixed. The demand schedule for transport services (D_M) is vertical and perfectly inelastic. The price of railroad transport is given by P_R. The total cost of freight services in the economy with the railroad is the product of this price and quantity, equal to the area of rectangle R. Without the railroad, the price of freight service is higher, as indicated by P_N. If the economy without the railroad uses the same amount of transport services as the economy that has the railroad, then the total cost of freight services equals the sum of rectangles R and N. The difference between the two total costs is rectangle N. Rectangle N is the direct social savings on freight services. It represents the loss in output from the value of the resources the economy would have to devote to transporting the same amount of goods over the same distances without the railroad.

While the upper portion of Figure A.1 illustrates the social saving as the cost reduction in the market for freight transport services, the lower portion depicts it as the direct gain in the economy's real income. The lower portion of Figure A.1 presents the economy's production possibilities curve, or transformation curve, representing all possible combinations of transport output and commodity sector output that can be produced from a fixed stock of resources. The upper transformation curve, T–To, corresponds to the output in the economy with the railroad, while the lower transformation curve, T–T1, represents the economy without railroads. To maintain the constant level of transport services in the absence of the railroad, resources must be reallocated from the commodity-producing sector to the production of transportation. The reallocation is costly, and the economy suffers a loss equivalent to the vertical distance from point X to point Y when railroads are removed.

The social saving can be expressed in terms of the amount of commodity output foregone as a result of not having the railroad. Referring to the economy's transformation curve in the lower portion of Figure A.1, the slope of each transformation function is the marginal rate of transformation between transport output and commodity output and is equal to the ratios of the prices of the two outputs,

$$- \frac{P_i}{P_C}$$

From the figure, the components of total output are related in the equation for a line:

$$Q_C = T - \frac{P_R}{P_C} \overline{Q_T}$$

for the economy with railroads, and

$$Q'_C = T - \frac{P_N}{P_C} \overline{Q_T}$$

for the economy using the non-rail transport technology. Designating the price of commodity output as numeraire, the difference between the level of commodity output with the railroad and without it is:

$$\Delta Q_C = \overline{Q_T} (P_N - P_R)$$

which is the expression for the social saving when measured in the transport market, as illustrated in the upper portion of Figure A.1.

The social saving calculated in the transport market corresponds identically to the increment to the economy's income that is derived from the resources no longer required to produce transport services once the railroad has been introduced. Underpinning Figure A.1 is the relationship between a fixed stock of resources and two different transport technologies. For simplicity of exposition, the economy is partitioned into two sectors: a transport sector and a non-transport sector, here called the "commodity-producing" sector. Both sectors generate output from capital and labor. Total output in the economy (national income, or GDP) is the sum of the final output of its two sectors[6]:

$$Q_Y = Q_T + Q_C$$

where Q_Y is total output, Q_T is the output of the transport sector, and Q_C is the output of the commodity-producing sector. The commodity sector produces goods and services by combining capital and labor in the C production function. The output of the transport sector may be produced using capital and labor with either one of two technologies, the railroad technology R, or the non-rail technology N:

$$Q_C = C(L_C, K_C)$$
$$Q_{TR} = R(L_R, K_R)$$
$$Q_{TN} = N(L_N, K_N)$$

The railroad technology is revealed to be more efficient in producing freight-transport services in Brazil, based on the observed unit costs of shipment in Tables 4.7 and 4.8. Brazilian railroads produced (a fixed level of) transport output using less labor and capital than required by the non-rail transport technology, so that:

$$L_N > L_R; \; K_N > K_R$$

for a fixed quantity of transport Q_T and

$$L_R + \Delta L = L_N$$
$$K_R + \Delta K = K_N$$

Substituting the N function for the R function (the non-rail transport technology for the railroad) diverts a portion of capital and labor from the commodity sector. For a given Q_T,

$$Q_Y = Q_C + \overline{R}(L_R, K_R)$$
$$Q'_Y = Q'_C + \overline{N}(L_N, K_N)$$
$$Q'_C = C(L_C - \Delta L, K_C - \Delta K)$$

That is, producing transport output using the non-rail transport technology requires more capital and labor inputs than are required by the railroad. Under the non-rail technology, those inputs are diverted from the commodity-producing sector, necessarily reducing its output, and hence GDP. The reduction in the economy's total output is:

$$\Delta Q_Y = Q_Y - Q'_Y = \Delta Q_C$$

which in the model is identical to the increase in total output, or GDP, achieved by substituting the railroad technology R, for the non-rail technology N. By algebraic manipulation, this equals:

$$\Delta Q_C = C(\Delta L, \Delta K)$$

and from above,

$$\Delta Q_C = \overline{Q_T}(P_N - P_R)$$

so that the direct social saving of the railroad equals the commodity output produced by the capital and labor released from transport when the non-rail technology is substituted by the railroad. This increase corresponds to the gains from the improved integration of markets for transportable goods and the resultant rise in regional and sectoral specialization that produces a reallocation of resources among activities within the commodity-producing sector. So long as the economy is characterized by constant costs and competitive conditions that equate marginal costs to prices, the total differential approximates the social saving:

$$\Delta Q_C \cong \frac{\partial Q_C}{\partial L} \Delta L + \frac{\partial Q_C}{\partial K} \Delta K$$

so that the social saving is the productivity of the increments of capital and labor released from transport by the introduction of the railroad.

These derivations correspond to an upper-bound measure of the social savings, for the amount of transport services is not allowed to vary no matter what the cost of non-rail transport services. For the upper-bound social saving the model relies on three assumptions: prices equal marginal costs in the transport sector; all costs are constant (i.e., there are no non-convexities in the economy's production surface); and the economy's stock of resources is unchanged by the railroad. The implications of departures from these assumptions for estimating the social savings are addressed below.

Variable Transport Output and the Lower-Bound Social Saving

The most severe assumption of the upper-bound measure of the social saving is that the same amount of freight would have been shipped over the same distances in Brazil in the absence of the railroad. Constructing the social savings estimate on an unchanging quantity of freight service, as done in the first assessment of Chapter 4, ignores the most likely counterfactual scenario—that is, had the economy faced a higher charge for freight service, the demand for such services would have been lower. The volume of goods produced in factories or farms dependent on location would plausibly and even likely fall with higher freight charges. Entrepreneurs might locate at distances from the market that were less than in the railroad-including economy. Distant producers might be eliminated altogether, or be pushed into other activities ill-suited to exploiting the opportunities for gains from regional specialization and trade made possible by lower transport costs. For these reasons, the total demand for freight services would be less in the counterfactual economy than they actually were in 1913. As Chapter 4 revealed, the magnitude of the social savings in Brazil was quite sensitive to changes in the quantity of freight service. The upper-bound estimate escapes this complication because it precludes any possibility of adjusting the quantity of transport downward in the face of higher transport costs. But it mechanically includes the saving on an increment of the economy's production that would vanish with the removal of the railroad. The upper-bound estimate thus overstates the railroad's direct impact.

If the counterfactual economy is modified to permit it to respond to higher freight charges by relocating production, and even eliminating out-right firms and farms in unfeasible regions, the demand for freight transport can no longer be assumed to be perfectly inelastic as it was portrayed in Figure A.1. A non-zero elasticity of demand has the effect of reducing the quantity of freight services at any charge higher than that of the railroad, since the demand curve passing through the 1913 level of transport services would be downward-sloping but no longer vertical. In the counterfactual economy the diversion of resources from the non-transport sector of the economy would be less, thanks to the flexible demand for transport. The level of GDP without the railroad is higher than it would be in the fixed-quantity formulation and the social savings is lower than in the upper-bound case. The effect of adjusting transport demand for the elasticity is to reduce the social saving because less freight is carried.

Considerable difficulty attaches to the estimation of a lower bound on the railroad's social saving. Adjusting the upper-bound social saving above requires changes to the model to enable it to establish the lower bound with variable demand for transport. Three additional simplifying assumptions must first be introduced to modify the model: society's economic well-being must be expressed by a social welfare function; market prices must equate with marginal social costs across the entire economy; and the introduction of the railroad must lower costs only in the transport sector.[7] The central complication of estimating a lower-bound social saving is not that the non-railroad counterfactual situation cannot be directly observed by the historian. Rather, the complication arises from the fact that there is not a unique measure of the transport demand curve resulting from the shift from the railroad-including transformation curve to the transformation curve of the economy without railroads. With no unique demand curve for transport, there is no single, "true" measure of the lower-bound social saving. Figure A.2 modifies Figure A.1 by permitting the quantity of transport services to vary with changes in the price of that service. It conceptually illustrates changes in the quantity of freight service by reference to the transformation curves. Each transformation line in Figure A.2 is associated with a social utility curve (U_1 and U_0), which represents all possible combinations of commodity output and transport services for which society's economic welfare is constant. The precise mix of transport output and commodity output in both cases is determined by the point of tangency between the transformation line and the associated utility curve. With the level of freight service no longer fixed, Figure A.2 shows Q_T falling to Q_N in the economy deprived of railroads. One

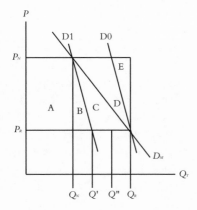

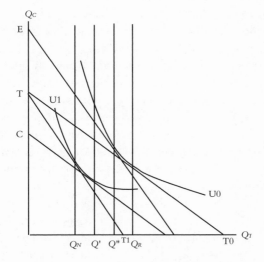

Figure. A.2. Lower-bound social saving. The upper portion of the figure portrays different concepts of the lower-bound social savings when measured in the transport market; the lower portion depicts the different concepts in terms of the economy's output.

measure of the social saving in the lower portion of Figure A.2 is the vertical distance between the two transformation lines at their respective levels of transport output, Q_R and Q_N. That difference is the change in commodity output between the railroad-including economy and the economy without railroads once the decline in the quantity of transport is taken into account. This measure corresponds in the upper portion of Figure A.2 to the sum of areas A, B, and C, the total area between P_N and P_R to the left of the transport demand schedule (D_M). Since the upper-bound social saving in Figure A.1 was given by the area of rectangle N, and rectangle N equals the sum of A, B, C, D, and E in Figure A.2, this new measure is clearly less than the upper-bound measure. Conceptually known as the consumers' surplus (CS), the sum of A, B, and C adjusts the social saving for a transport demand schedule that is no longer assumed to be vertical and inelastic.

The consumers' surplus captures not just the effect of the change in transport costs, but also income effects that influence the amount of transport services demanded. The transport demand schedule (D_M) in the upper portion of Figure A.2 warrants further correction for effects not strictly due to the change in the price of transport. The income effects of a shift between the railroad-including economy and the economy without railroads have an independent impact on the amount of transport demanded. The D_M curve does not control for those income effects and does not isolate the consequences due to the change in relative transport costs.

The consumers' surplus measure of the lower-bound social saving is modified to encompass only the effect of changes in the price of transport by modifying the demand curve for transport to exclude income effects. There is not a unique measure of this adjusted, or "compensated," transport demand schedule and no unique measure of the social saving as a result. The position of the compensated demand schedule depends on whether it is derived from the railroad-including transformation curve (T–To) or from the transformation curve of the economy without its railroads (T–T1). A compensated transport demand curve can be deduced from either pair of transformation and social-utility curves. There are transport demand curves for both the railroad-including level of society's economic welfare (Uo) and for that of the non-rail economy (U1). In the first case, the transport demand curve is traced by constructing a new transformation line tangent to Uo (the railroad-including level of economic welfare). It differs from T–To in that it is parallel to the transformation line of the economy without railroads (T–T1) and thus embodies the higher non-rail relative price of transport. This holds society's economic welfare constant at Uo and charts the change in the quantity of transport demanded solely as a function of the change in the relative price of transport. In Figure A.2 the increase in the relative price of transport from the removal of the railroad gives Q'' as the reduced quantity of transport, not Q_N, with Do as the compensated transport demand curve. Equally valid conceptually is the same procedure using the welfare level in the non–railroad economy (U1). Tracing a line tangent to the railroad-including transformation curve plots the effect on demand of the change in the relative price of transport. This, too, holds real income constant, but at the level found in the non-railroad economy, and determines the level of transport demand Q' at the railroad cost of transport. The resulting demand schedule in the upper portion of Figure A.2, D_1, is to the left of D_0. The two demand schedules differ from one another because they control for the income effect of the movement from the railroad economy to the non-rail economy using two different levels of economic welfare (U_0 and U_1). They also differ from D_M, which was derived without controlling for income effects.

Each of the compensated demand schedules implies its own measure of the social saving. For the D_0 demand curve, the adjusted social saving is the distance from T to E in the lower portion of Figure A.2, and the area given by the sum of A, B, C, and D in the market for transport services. The distance from T to E excludes the income effect on the quantity of transport and depends solely on the change in the relative price of transport. The distance from T to E is conventionally known as the equivalent variation (EV), and equals the amount of income the economy would need to remain at U_0 but with the higher cost of transport the economy confronts in the absence of the railroad. For the D_1 demand curve, the adjusted social saving is the distance from C to T in the lower portion of Figure A.2, and the sum of A and B in the upper portion of the figure. The distance from C to T is the compensating variation (CV) and conceptually expresses how much the economy would gain from remaining at U_1 but with a lower cost of transport. So long as transport services are a normal good (where the income effect reinforces the relative-price induced substitution between commodity output and transport services), the equivalent variation will never be less than the consumers' surplus. The latter, in turn, is equal to or greater than the compensating variation, so that:

$$EV \geq CS \geq CV$$

Only in a single instance will the market demand curve (D_M) correspond to either of the compensated demand curves (D_0 and D_1). If the social utility function underpinning the U_0 and U_1 curves is quasi-linear, there are no income effects and the three demand curves are the same. In that case, the three measures of the lower-bound social savings (EV, CS, and CV) are identical as well. Though convenient, there is no basis for claiming such a stringent condition necessarily prevailed in Brazil.

Chapters 4 and 5 addressed the social saving in the context of questions of *historical* interest, emphasizing the realized direct consequences of the railroad's reduction of transport costs. Since the impact of the railroad can be defined only in terms of the loss to the economy from removing the innovation, the compensated demand schedule that involves the actual levels of service from 1913 (D0) is the one best suited to the question at hand. The corresponding social savings concept is the equivalent variation. But the market demand, D_M, is the only schedule that can be estimated from actual evidence. The consumers' surplus, equal to the sum of A, B, and C, is the corresponding measure of the social saving computed from the terminal-period quantities. The use of D_M, rather than D0, is preferable not just because it can be inferred from evidence, but also because it understates the appropriate concept of social saving (since $CS < EV$). The problem of bias introduced by relying on the consumers' surplus actually serves a valuable purpose because it understates the desired measure and guards against exaggeration. In Chapter 4 the observed quantities and prices were used to trace out the freight transport demand schedule, giving a market demand curve (D_M) that was not compensated for income effects. The associated measure of the social saving applied there was the consumers' surplus. So long as the D_M curve that is established in practice (based on the 1913 levels of transport output) is not less elastic than D0, the consumers' surplus suffices as a lower bound on the railroad's direct impact.

Table 4.12 presented empirical estimates of the elasticity of market demand for rail freight services in Brazil using several different assumptions about the characteristics of that market and the best available quantitative evidence.[8] Freight transport demand was established as relatively inelastic, and the parameters estimated took on values between zero and −0.6. This finding for Brazil is consistent with results for Mexico, Colombia, and the nineteenth-century United States.[9] The sensitivity of the social savings to different values of the elasticity, presented in Table 4.11, did not depend on the estimates of Table 4.12, but rather considered a variety of elasticities, and the discussion focused on a more limited plausible range of elasticities (running from 0 to −1.0). If one assumes that the elasticity might have been in that range, the lower-bound freight social savings in Brazil was as much as, or greater than, the upper-bound estimates for Germany, France, the United Kingdom, Belgium, Russia, China, and the antebellum United States. In light of the fact that for a normal good the consumers' surplus concept used in Table 4.11 is always less than the equivalent variation, the lower-bound social saving for Brazil was probably higher still.

PRICES AND COSTS

Social savings are estimated accurately using freight charges only if those charges correspond to the real resource costs of producing transport services. If the actual and counterfactual transport sectors are characterized by full competition, prices and costs equate. Observed charges may then be used by the investigator with no risk of bias. However, should rates depart from ac-

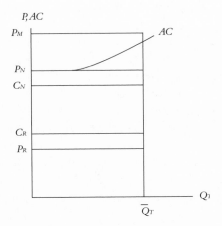

Figure. A.3. Potential biases from divergent prices and costs.

tual costs, bias is introduced into any social savings estimates employing observed charges. Depending on the circumstances, the charges of both the railroad, and the non-rail mode of transport selected for constructing the counterfactual transport sector, may depart systematically from resource costs. Were an unregulated railroad to enjoy a local or regional monopoly on transport services, its prices would exceed the unit cost of service. If at the same time the counterfactual mode of transport suffered from market and cost conditions that drove transport prices below marginal social cost, any social savings estimate based on observed charges would understate the true impact of the railroad. Conversely, if instead the railroad was regulated and subsidized, its charge for transport services might actually understate costs. If non-rail carriers enjoyed local monopoly power in their pricing, their charges would overstate the resource costs of shipping freight. Using the observed unit charges in such a case would exaggerate the social savings, erroneously including in the estimate both monopoly rents of non-rail providers and private losses by the railroad.

Figure A.3 illustrates this scenario and the resulting bias it creates. There, the charge for railroad freight service (P_R) is less than the unit cost (C_R) at all levels of output (assuming a highly stylized pair of railroad marginal revenue and cost curves). The charge for non-rail shipment (P_N) as depicted exceeds the cost (C_N). Using observed freight charges $(P_R$ and $P_N)$ in this circumstance overstates the actual social saving by the sum

$$\overline{Q_T} \, (P_N - C_N + P_R - C_R)$$

Discussions in Chapter 4 broached the possibility of price-cost divergences that could exaggerate the social saving estimate. Profits in the railroad sector, while by no means high, were not so low as to suggest that the sector as a whole charged rates that were appreciably below cost. Two allowances corrected for potential biases. First, the total cost of railroad freight services in 1913 was adjusted to incorporate capital subsidies paid by the government that year. Even that adjustment is unwarranted if one assumes that in the counterfactual economy the Brazilian government might have provided similar, or even greater, levels of roadway subsidy that would have pushed rates below cost. Second, the non-rail mode of shipment was selected so as to minimize the risk of overstating freight charges as a result of seasonal or other idiosyncratic factors. Both adjustments guard against exaggerating the social saving.

In both the upper- and lower-bound formulations, the social savings depend critically on the assumption of constant costs in the transport sector, whether actual or counterfactual. Railroads were quite capable of handling an increasing volume of shipments at constant, and perhaps even declining cost, given the relatively low freight service densities on even Brazil's most heavily trafficked lines. Whether the non-rail sector could have handled the 1913 level of railroad freight without confronting rising costs is another matter altogether. Accommodating 1.7 billion ton-kilometers of freight service using wagon roads and animals, as proposed in Chapter 4, quite possibly would have required a diversion of resources from other activities sufficient to raise the average cost of non-rail transport well above the observed rate in the 1860s. Figure A.3 portrays this as an average cost curve diverging upward from P_N. This possibility cannot be ruled out for Brazil. No evidence is yet available that would permit the estimation of a non-rail transport cost function, much less the extension of its parameters to an out-of-sample level of freight service as large as that for 1913. While the economic conditions of pre-rail Brazilian transport are of considerable historical interest, their consideration creates no need to alter the qualitative findings of Chapter 4 or Chapter 7 that depend on the magnitude of the social saving. The bias that would be introduced in the social saving from the assumption of constant non-rail costs would work against finding a large social saving.

Distortions within the commodity sector would bias the social saving estimate in an indeterminate direction, even if transport prices faithfully indicated the costs of the resources used in transportation. If monopoly, oligopoly, excessive government subsidy, or any other feature drives a wedge between the prices and costs of goods and services, resource allocation in the commodity sector and the aggregate economy will be suboptimal. The social savings will be over- or understated as a result. This can be envisioned in the lower portion of Figure A.1 as a change in the slope of the transformation curve corresponding to the divergence between market prices and resource costs in the commodity sector. The direction of the effect of the interaction of the railroad and such distortions cannot be determined. If the commodity sector suffered from non-competitive conditions or from a pervasive pre-capitalist mindset, then actual output levels could be below that indicated by the T–T1 transformation line. If any of those distortions were remedied by the introduction of a more efficient transport technology, then the railroad generated gains that it does not receive credit for in the social saving estimate. Conversely, if transport improvements somehow exacerbated or created non-competitive conditions elsewhere in the economy, output would be lower than indicated by the T–To line. Though the net bias from these possible distortions cannot be determined, the known features of the Brazilian economy, which while backward enjoyed by all accounts considerable competitiveness in nineteenth-century agriculture and manufacturing, suggest that the magnitude of such distortions would not likely be large.

The historian's choice of the counterfactual mode of shipment holds consequences for the costs of transport employed in the analysis beyond the biases from potential divergences between prices and costs in either the transport or commodity sectors. In the case of freight services, Chapter 4 defined the non-rail mode of shipment as overland carriage on improved roads by animal-drawn carts and competing pack animals. However, the predominant mode of shipment for much of Brazil on the eve of the introduction of the railroad was overland carriage on unimproved roads where the pack mule was the only feasible mode of transport. Table 4.7 presented non-rail transport charges that generally exceeded those on improved roads. The implication of the investigator's choice between these two counterfactual transport technologies can be envisioned in Figure A.3 as the difference between calculating the social saving using P_R and P_N, and calculating the social saving using P_R and P_M. Since P_M exceeds P_N, the social saving measured using the transport costs that prevailed throughout Brazil would be greater than the social saving measured under the assumption that all of Brazil would have had improved wagon roads. This difference corresponds to the key methodological divergence between the two pioneering studies of railroads in the United States. Fishlow's counterfactual involved the comparison between the cost of shipment on antebellum railroads and the costs that actually prevailed on the most likely substitute routes and modes.[10] Fishlow's counterfactual allowed for no improvements to the U.S. transport system in the absence of the railroad, and was thus historically quite feasible, relying on carriers in place in 1859. Fogel's counterfactual was, by contrast, more breathtaking, permitting the United States an entire system of canals that it did not actually possess (but which was technologically feasible) in 1890. Fogel's treatment of the problem had the effect of reducing the costs of non-rail carriage, by assuming that a wide array of transport improvements would have unfolded in the absence of the railroad. Fishlow's operational rendering of the social saving will always exceed Fogel's because of the way they each chose to define the counterfactual.

In the chapters above the counterfactual defined for Brazil combined features of both the historical alternative and the technological alternative mode of shipment. The non-rail rates for Brazil came from the carriers actually in operation in 1864, and thus might be viewed as providing a contrast between the costs to the economy of shipment by rail and the costs of shipment by the mode that was historically prevalent. However, the study's use of non-rail rates from São Paulo in effect gave the counterfactual economy a transport system that was rarely encountered elsewhere in Brazil, implying considerable investment and improvement to the existing mode of shipment. As such it is comparable with the technologically feasible counterfactual, of the variety that Fogel constructed. As Figure A.3 suggests, any departure from a Fogelian counterfactual (corresponding to P_N) toward a Fishlovian counterfactual (corresponding to P_M) in Brazil would simply increase the social savings. The rates reported in Table 4.7 suggest that such a change in the definition of the counterfactual would raise the upper-bound social savings by as much as 50 percent.

It bears repeating that, in the treatment of actual and counterfactual rates and costs (irrespective of general technological possibilities), historical and geographical parameters always inform and constrain the alternatives available to the investigator. For Brazil, the railroad's direct impact depended less on the choice among overland rates than it did on the fact that shipment over land, rather than over water, was the historically relevant alternative to the railroad. Had the United States been required to carry its railroad freight of 1890 overland by wagon alone, the social savings would have approached 25 percent of GDP.[11] Since the crux of the transportation revolution was the innovation of substitutes for pre-rail overland shipment, the revolutionary character of the railroad was magnified in regions that did not enjoy navigable waterways. As Chapter 2 stressed, waterways in Brazil could not duplicate the spatial pattern of freight services, and the high cost of overland shipment was alleviated only by the introduction of the railroad.

From Social Saving to the Social Rate of Return

The social saving reveals the direct impact of the innovation of the railroad on national income. It does not reveal the efficiency with which resources devoted to the railroad sector were used. Efficiency can only be gauged by comparing the gains the railroad provided with the costs of providing the railroad, and when considered against alternative uses of capital. The social rate of return provides a measure of efficiency by combining the "stock" measure of the railroad's social savings with the private profits of the railroad and converting the sum into a "flow" of benefits to the economy from the formation of railroad capital. Large social savings do not necessarily imply high social rates of return (and vice-versa). The amount of capital required to produce the social savings might in some cases be unjustifiably large. In other cases a high social return can result from small social savings on a modest amount of resources invested.[12]

The social returns to railroad investment can be expressed in two distinct ways. The average social rate of return considers the total benefits created by all the capital invested in the railroad. The marginal social rate of return considers only that incremental gain to the economy from investing in an additional unit of railroad capital. The two measures provide answers to distinct questions. If the investigator's interest is in whether the railroad generated gains sufficient to justify the expenditure of resources to modernize the pre-rail transport system, the average social rate of return suffices. If the question of interest is whether or not enough, or perhaps even too many, resources were invested in railroads, the marginal social rate of return must be used. Marginal social rates of return involve additional assumptions that complicate their measurement and interpretation, especially when comparing them to rates of return on alternative investments.[13] When those assumptions were imposed in Chapter 4 every attempt was made to purposively control for quantitative biases that might alter the qualitative findings.

The first step in measuring the social rates of return is establishing the total social surplus from railroad investments. The total social surplus has two elements: "unappropriable" benefits and "appropriable" benefits. The first of these is simply the freight social savings on the railroad sector as a whole (or on each individual railroad, depending on the unit of analysis). These are unappropriable because they are created by the railroads but not paid to the owners of railroad capital. Appropriable benefits equal revenues of the railroad net of the resource costs of labor and raw materials and represent the payment appropriated by the owners of railroad capital. In Chapter 4 the total social surplus was converted to the average social rate of return by dividing the surplus by the value of the physically reproducible capital of the railroad:

$$\frac{B + R - C}{K} = A$$

where B represents the unappropriable benefits, R the operating revenue of the railroad, C the railroad's operating costs, K the value of the railroad's physical capital, and A the average social rate of return. Chapter 7 employed a different formulation, in two respects. First, in estimating the social rate of return for individual railroads it applied an even more restrictive measure of the social saving. The transport demand curve was taken to be linear, intersecting the price axis at the non-rail transport charge. Second, it estimated the social rate of return over a span of time rather than in a single year. Additional detail on that estimate was presented in the chapter and is not repeated here.

Converting the average social rate of return to a marginal social rate of return involves additional assumptions. If the railroad's social output may be taken as proportional to its private output, then the private output elasticity of capital can be used to convert the average return to a marginal return. Moreover, under certain conditions the share of capital earnings in total revenues, inclusive of capital subsidies (G), equals the output elasticity of capital. The marginal social rate of return (M) is:

$$M = (A) \left[\frac{R - C + G}{R + G} \right]$$

where, by assumption:

$$\frac{\partial Q}{\partial K} \left(\frac{K}{Q} \right) = \left(\frac{R - C + G}{R + G} \right)$$

The result is the social return to an additional milréis invested in the railroad, expressed as a percentage.

The assumption that the share of railroad capital earnings in total revenue equals the output elasticity of capital is valid only if the railroad exhibits constant returns and is competitive. However, if the activity is non-competitive, or enjoys increasing returns to scale, then the two may not equate. For the purpose of Chapter 4 the output elasticity of capital was assumed to equal the share of capital costs in total earnings, even though the railroad industry was not strictly competitive and might have had increasing returns to scale. Though railroads are frequently invoked as a textbook case of economies of scale, modern studies of railroad production and costs reveal that increasing returns are mostly due to scope of operations (including density of traffic) rather than the size of the firm. While output was regulated rather than competitive, all of Brazil's railroad inputs—labor, raw materials, and capital—were priced by internationally competitive and increasingly integrated markets in the nineteenth century. Even under regulation the capital earnings on Brazil's railroads were within the range of rates of return found in the main capital markets at the time. The incorporation of guarantees into net revenues to infer the payments to capital is justified given that this was a supplement required by investors to render the profits from railroad projects competitive. Both of these assumptions were less important to the marginal rates of return in Chapter 4 than was the choice of unappropriable benefits. Using the lower-bound social savings imparts a potentially strong downward bias to the estimated average and marginal rates of return. Given that the results show Brazil had not overinvested in railroad capital, in the aggregate, the use of the lower-bound social savings to derive marginal rates of return actually favored a finding of excessive investment.

The marginal rates of return on a line-by-line basis in Table 4.15 were necessarily more conjectural than precise. Altering the assumptions used to construct them would change the value of the results, but would not change the rank-ordering of the railroads and would not alter the conclusion that many railroads were *relatively* poor performers in Brazil. The average social returns in Chapter 4, and especially in Chapter 7, prove less problematic in practice than the marginal rates of return.

Linkages

The static measure of the direct social saving captures the gains from trade and market integration brought about by lower transport costs.[14] It is an incomplete measure of the railroad's economic consequences because it does not isolate second-round effects of induced sequences of development, changes to the economy's optimal output mix, or increases in the economy's stock of resources. As Fogel pointed out, the social saving model was not designed to deal with these kinds of forward linkage effects.[15] The measure of the social savings is based on levels of transport demand and national income that were actually influenced, perhaps heavily, by the railroad's forward linkage. The direct social savings estimated for 1913 treated Brazil's stock of resources as if it had always been there, and as if its existence in Brazil had nothing to do with the preceding half-century of railroad development. Transport cost reductions induced changes in the stock of resources, unleashing a dynamic process embodied in opening up new lands for settlement and cultivation, increases in investment (both foreign and domestic), and inflows of labor from abroad. If changes in relative prices attract mobile factors of production responsive to new opportunities, increase the savings rate, stimulate concomitant accretions to the stock of capital from resources previously devoted to consumption, and even influence institutional trajectories, then the economic consequences of the railroad must be investigated using a dynamic rather than a static model. Only then can the forward linkage be rigorously assessed.

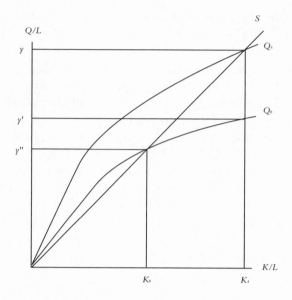

Figure. A.4. Forward linkage and "dynamic" social saving.

Figure A.4 provides a partial illustration of possible dynamic consequences of the railroad when the assumption of a fixed stock of factors is altered. The vertical axis measures output per worker, while the horizontal axis portrays the capital–labor ratio. The economy's aggregate production function with the railroad is the Q_A curve, while the production function in the counterfactual economy without the railroad is given by the Q_B curve. The line denoted S represents the steady-state growth condition of the economy under the assumption that the rate of growth of the labor force and the savings rate are constant. The intersection of Q_A and S determines the level of output per worker (y) in the railroad-including economy. Removing the railroad shifts the economy's aggregate production function down to Q_B, reducing output per worker to y' as resources are diverted from the commodity sector to transport. The social saving per worker is the difference between y and y'. An additional loss to the economy from removing the railroad appears when the capital stock is not assumed to be fixed, and its level is itself the result of railroad development. If the lower costs of transport attributable to the railroad induced capital formation, then Brazil's capital–labor ratio would be higher than what would prevail in the non-rail economy. Removing the railroad induces a fall in the capital–labor ratio from K_A to K_B, which in turn reduces output-per-worker farther, to y''. The dynamic effects that arise when there is a forward linkage from the railroad to new investment in other activities magnify the social savings, adding to them the difference between y' and y''. When the forward linkage is sufficiently strong, the difference between y' and y'' can far exceed the static social saving.

In some historical settings it has proven feasible to apply dynamic models to railroad development.[16] Because of constraints posed by data limitations, it is not yet possible to specify a dynamic model of the railroad's forward linkage for Brazil. While the dynamic impact may be difficult to estimate with precision, certain elements of the effect may still be identified and a crude sense of its contours established. Chapter 6 did so by reference to the close relationship between railroad development and agricultural expansion, inflows of immigrants, and changes in the economy's output mix. It also inferred the developmental consequences of lower transport costs for capital formation in Brazil's cotton-textile industry. The instances presented there are merely indicative of the induced effects of the railroad's forward linkage. In every instance, the forward linkage worked to increase the railroad's impact on Brazilian GDP.

The railroad's backward linkages have both direct and indirect components. The direct component was the actual demand for inputs. What was notable about the direct backward linkage in Brazil was its foreign character, which justified the focus in Chapter 6 on the leakage overseas of direct payments for inputs to the railroad sector. The indirect component was the likely impact on a counterfactual Brazilian economy if input demand had been constrained to rely only on Brazilian suppliers. Input requirements might have held appreciable consequences for the expansion of industry, even if their increment to total industrial demand was small. Where the counterfactual manufacturing sector exhibited average costs that declined at increasing levels of demand and output, the gains within industry could be large. In this scenario heavy reliance on overseas suppliers of capital, fuel, and materials could mean that the actual course of railroad development represented a lost opportunity for Brazilian manufacturing. A counterfactual Brazilian economy relying only on domestic suppliers could not be specified in Chapter 6. A survey of findings from other case studies pointed to the historical weakness of backward linkages in most countries. By implication, there were modest opportunity costs from overseas provision. The sole case where the counterfactual domestic provision of the railroad sector has been made operational and investigated demonstrated that Spain would have suffered considerable costs, rather than benefits, from substituting domestic inputs for foreign inputs.[17] The railroad's backward linkages in Brazil were weak, but were unlikely costly under either actual or counterfactual specifications of the economy. Rather, railroads directly and indirectly attracted long-term investment from abroad, augmenting considerably the total savings available for capital formation in Brazil.

Conclusion

Historians operate in actual and imaginary worlds simultaneously. The hypothetical portrait they employ, variations on it, and its key elements, inform deeply the characterizations they make about what actually transpired in the past. Historians choose whether to make their hypothetical portrait overt and accessible or to leave it implicit and relatively opaque. Counterfactuals and models are sufficiently valuable for the purposes of historical investigation that the present study made them explicit. The counterfactual Brazilian economy constructed to investigate the historical consequences of the railroad and to illustrate its linkages necessarily suffers from analytical limitations. One cannot investigate, for example, the direct impact of a transport innovation in nineteenth-century Brazil without holding constant the key parameters of its capital markets, its particular constellation of politics and institutions, and the occupational and sectoral distribution of the labor force. In history, many things change in tandem because of their fundamental interrelatedness, while other processes may appear to be related but in fact are wholly independent. Counterfactuals that address multiple independent changes and dependent interactions simultaneously defy investigation because of the inherent complexity the problem of specification presents to the historian. The purpose of the minimal rewrite of history dictum in applying counterfactuals is not to ignore the complexity of such interactions but rather deal with them in a tractable manner. An advantage of the model's application is that it serves to make clear what investigators can know, and what they are not yet able to know, and thereby highlights not the theoretical inadequacies of the social savings concept but rather the need to elaborate and apply other frameworks capable of engaging those questions of interest that are not well addressed by the social savings approach. Whatever their shortcomings, considerable insights remain to be made in reassessing key innovations, whether institutional or technological, by applying counterfactuals to the nineteenth-century Brazilian economy. Hypotheses regarding the country's economic history that masquerade as established propositions can no longer escape assessments that draw on axiomatic theory, simple models, counterfactual constructs, and systematically collected evidence. Fruitful revisions to our understanding of Brazilian economic development are most likely to flow from precisely these particular features of the process of historical investigation.

Appendix B

Financial and Operating Data: Sources and Method

Assembling the series of railroad financial and operating data used in this study proved challenging, even by the standards of fieldwork on historical statistics in Latin America. Unlike Argentina and Mexico, where government record keeping on railroad operations led to the compilation of extensive and thorough retrospective studies at the turn of the twentieth century, fully comprehensive reporting of railroad operating statistics in Brazil did not come about until well into the century. No central repository of the operating reports of individual railroads exists in Brazil. Instead, intermittent runs of reports for some of the country's largest pre-1914 railroads remain scattered throughout various Brazilian collections. Information on other major lines exists only in archival collections in London. Fortunately, operating data for the bulk of the sector can be reliably reconstructed from 1898 onward. Before the improved compilation of railroad statistics by the government, the sheer proliferation of individual railroad enterprises in Brazil complicated any attempt to assemble data series for the sector as a whole. Unlike Mexico and Argentina, where the bulk of transport service was heavily concentrated in relatively few firms, in Brazil a much larger number of independent routes and companies operated. Moreover, some of the most important Brazilian railroads had portions that escaped reporting their operations to central authorities because their initial concession derived from provincial and state governments.

Contemporaries complained regularly about the difficulties involved in obtaining railroad operating information. According to the terms of their concessions and ensuing legislation, all Brazilian railroads were required to report operating figures on a regular basis. The mechanisms for doing so, and the level of detail required, were poorly defined until the 1880s. Basic quantitative information appeared in the annual reports of the ministry in charge of monitoring railroads in Brazil. Through 1860 the cognizant ministry was the Ministério do Império, while from 1861 through the end of the Empire it was the Ministério da Agricultura, Commércio e Obras Públicas. Up through 1878 or so these are reasonably complete sources of very basic information on operations for the major railroads under central concession. Thereafter, however, the railroad sector grew faster than the government could monitor. Attempts to standardize the collection and reporting of operating figures found support among specialists and government officials at Brazil's first railroad congress in 1882.[1] By the late 1880s the quality and breadth of data collection had caught up, to the point that complete operating and financial information for virtually the entire sector became available for the first time in the annual report of the Ministry of Agriculture, Commerce, and Public Works.[2] Two supplementary studies that were particularly important, both of a quasi-official character, appeared in the 1880s, as the government sought to gather retrospective information about the growth of Brazil's railroads. These were Francisco [Barreto] Picanço [da Costa], *Viação Ferrea do Brazil* (Rio de Janeiro, 1884), and Cyro Diocleciano Ribeiro Pessôa Junior, *Estudo Descriptivo das Estradas de Ferro do Brazil* (Rio de Janeiro, 1886). Combined, the two sources provide revenues, numbers of passengers, and freight tons for Brazil's major railroads through the early 1880s. The Ministry of Transportation, newly created under Brazil's republican government, attempted to continue the practice, but coverage was so poor that constructing aggregate series was not feasible for most of the 1890s.

Compilations of data at the national level remained irregular until the appearance of annual railroad statistical volumes (*Estatísticas das Estradas de Ferro da União e das Fiscalizadas pela União*) beginning in 1898. These volumes provided extensive operating detail each year on all categories of railroad services.[3] However, coverage across railroads, while consistent, was incomplete. Railroad concessions were granted at both the central and provincial levels of government. When companies reported their operating figures, they typically did so only to the level of government that had granted their concession. This system of mixed concessions meant that sectoral coverage by the central government was partly truncated once it began publishing the reported figures in 1898. Many railroads simply reported little information to central authorities because they operated under state concessions.

Three types of source materials were employed in constructing both the sample series starting in 1858 and the sectorwide data set in 1887 and from

1898 forward. The first was contemporary railroad studies. These made it possible to fill in occasional gaps in material obtained from other sources. In addition to the two quasi-official surveys from the 1880s, the most important examples were the turn-of-the-century retrospective works on railroads in São Paulo.[4] The second source was the census-like summaries of railroads conducted by the central government. These appear only intermittently, and in varying detail, in the reports of the Ministry of Empire through 1860, and then those of the Ministry of Agriculture through 1891. From 1892 to 1897 somewhat more detailed, yet highly uneven reporting along these lines is found in the reports of the Ministry of Transportation and Public Works. From 1898 onward, almost complete coverage for all federally conceded railroads is found in the separate railroad statistical volumes, the *Estatísticas das Estradas de Ferro* (*EEF*), published by the office of the Inspectoria Federal das Estradas within the Ministério de Viacão e Obras Públicos. These volumes provided information on revenues, service and output by class, the volume of freight shipments, and costs. Even there, however, gaps were found. Inexplicably, the regular annual reports of the Ministry of Transportation and Public Works continued to provide partial yet occasionally more detailed data, entirely separate from the statistical volumes. Often the former source proved to be complementary to those statistical volumes, and numerous gaps could be filled as a result.

The third type of source used is the reports of the railroad companies, usually directed to shareholders. For the Brazilian-owned railroads these were often appended to the report of the government-appointed inspector, or "fiscal engineer," found in every head office. The shareholder reports contained financial data, whereas the reports of the fiscal engineers contained extensive operating figures. While the latter were required to be submitted to the central government, few entirely complete runs of reports have been located in public collections. More or less continuous runs of company reports for each of the eleven sample railroads in Chapter 4 were available. The reports for the British-owned railroads (the Recife and San Francisco, Bahia and San Francisco, San Paulo Railway, Great Western, Brazil Great Southern, Southern Brazil Rio Grande do Sul, and, after 1897, the Leopoldina) were produced by the directors of each company for their shareholders. They were filed either on a semester or annual basis with the London Stock Exchange. They lack the much more complete appended operating reports of the government-appointed fiscal engineers who oversaw the activities of railroads. British shareholder reports are located in the Guildhall Library, Corporation of London, and contain basic operating and financial data for those companies. The reports for the Brazilian railroads in São Paulo (Companhia Paulista, Companhia Mogiana, Companhia Sorocabana e Ituana) are located in the Arquivo do Estado de São Paulo and the library of the Ferrovias Paulistas, S.A. (FEPASA), in Barra Funda, São Paulo. A complete run of the reports for the Central do Brazil is scattered among the Biblioteca Nacional, the Arquivo Nacional, and the Biblioteca da Rede Ferroviária Federal, S.A., all in Rio de Janeiro. The reports of the Leopoldina from the period in which it was still under Brazilian ownership are found in the Biblioteca Nacional, and in the maintenance shops at Engenho de Dentro in Rio de Janeiro. Brazilian reports usually provided data on track, freight revenues, tonnage, ton-kilometers (once these came to be reported), capital stock, total revenues, operating costs, and government guarantee payments and repayments.

The *EEF* volumes, in combination with the individual company reports, make it possible to flesh out the entire railroad sector for 1898–1913. Those volumes contain operating data for about fifty constituent rail lines and branches each year. In some instances those lines were part of the railroads for which company reports existed, as in the cases of the Leopoldina and Great Western. For example, the Leopoldina Railway and the Great Western operated lines under both state and central government concessions. When those companies reported operating figures to the central government, they did so only for the centrally conceded lines within the system. In those firms' respective reports to their shareholders, they provided full coverage of their constituent lines but did so for far fewer data categories. The information for freight output in units of ton-kilometers, the average length of haul, or earnings per ton-kilometer was frequently absent from British shareholder reports through 1913. In those cases, the more complete series from the company reports were combined with the supplementary data in the statistical yearbooks.

The sample railroads (listed in Table 4.1) served two principal purposes. The first was to indicate reliably the course over time of railroad freight charges for the sector (see Chapter 4). The second was to provide time series data for the estimates of rates of return in Chapter 7. For the purposes of Chapter 7, the sample was restricted. The absence of reliable measures of the capital stock excluded the Sorocabana and Ituana from Chapter 7, but it remained in the sample for the specific assessment of freight services in Chapter 4. The Bahia and San Francisco, Southern Brazil Rio Grande do Sul, and Brazil Great Southern Railways were excluded from Chapter 7 for a different reason. By 1913, or even as early as 1900, their respective shares of railroad operations in Brazil were so small as to not justify their inclusion.

The railroads comprising the full sample for Chapter 4 were selected using three criteria: ownership arrangements, region of operation, and quantity of transport services provided. British investors, the Brazilian government, and native entrepreneurs all held significant portions of the railroad sector, and the sample lines reflect these diverse ownership arrangements. The sample further includes railroads operating in the northeast, center-south, and far south in very rough proportion to the geographic distribution of rail services. The sample also includes every major railroad from the first three decades of Brazil's railway age. Table B.1 presents figures from 1913 on freight tons, ton-kilometers of freight service, freight revenues, and the sectoral share of ton-kilometers accounted for by each railroad. By 1913 the sample lines (denoted in Table B.1 by asterisks) or the systems into which they had been recently integrated accounted for nearly 90 percent of Brazil's railroad freight services. If it had been possible to fully disaggregate the figures for the Southern Brazil Rio Grande do Sul, the sample share in 1913 would have been slightly less.

The most prominent exclusions from the sample by the end of the period under study were the Rede Sul Mineira, Oeste de Minas, Paraná, and São Paulo–Rio Grande systems. All four of these appear in the aggregate series from 1898 through 1913. The differences between the sample freight charge and sectoral freight charge, presented in Table 4.6, were so slight that excluding the four systems from the sample could not have made a major difference to the data series of freight charges. Several lines smaller than the ones excluded appear in the sample because of the regional representation they provided. The Bahia and San Francisco, Brazil Great Southern, and Southern Brazil Rio Grande do Sul Railways offered coverage of lines in Bahia and Rio Grande do Sul, regions not otherwise included in the sample. The remaining sample lines were Brazil's major carriers of freight and passengers. Chapter 7 provides additional discussion of their respective histories.

The sample time series data on track, the stock of capital, operating revenues and costs, government guarantee payments and subsidies, freight revenues, and freight tons originate with raw data in the reports of the railroad companies, along with government publications and quasi-official studies of railroad operations. Lacunae in the reported operating figures were common on the sample railroads. At various points at least some figures for each railroad required estimation techniques. Estimates mainly relied on simple interpolation and extrapolation of raw figures, or key ratios, to fill gaps in the data series.

Relatively minor difficulties arose in the course of creating the sample series of freight revenues and freight tons. Freight revenues were not always separated from total revenues in early reporting to shareholders and the government. On the Recife and San Francisco Railway detail on freight revenues was first reported in 1872. For the earlier years freight revenues were estimated at 68 percent of total operating revenues, which was the ratio that obtained in 1872. After 1890 the freight revenues implied by the company's reported figures in sterling diverge from the revenues in Brazilian currency re-

Table B.1
Freight Operating Results on Brazilian Railroads, 1913

Railroad	Freight ton-km	Freight tons	Freight revenues	Share of total ton-km	Cumulative share
*Central do Brazil	359,931,486	1,520,956	20,916,928	21.2	21.2
*San Paulo Railway	265,649,458	3,239,909	27,623,875	15.7	36.9
*Companhia Paulista	236,054,054	1,541,263	5,391,470	13.9	50.8
*Viação Ferrea Rio Grande do Sul	155,006,377	670,410	8,447,538	9.1	59.9
*Companhia Mogiana	154,085,223	1,133,606	19,368,000	9.1	69.0
*Companhia Sorocabana e Ituana	137,520,736	656,315	12,347,898	8.1	77.1
*Great Western	80,081,948	1,311,606	7,497,105	4.7	81.8
*Leopoldina	58,360,320	1,065,451	19,691,325	3.4	85.2
Rede Sul Mineira–Cruzeiro a Tuyuty and Branch	47,046,470	136,715	2,811,256	2.8	88.0
Paraná	43,598,174	311,763	4,790,361	2.6	90.6
*Rede Bahia São Francisco and Branch	39,472,485	193,864	1,481,615	2.3	92.9
Oeste de Minas	27,888,582	139,946	2,538,934	1.6	94.5
São Paulo–Rio Grande Itararé a Uruguay	26,074,795	143,677	1,712,290	1.5	96.1
Rede Ceará–Baturité	13,106,393	147,868	1,375,257	0.8	96.9
Baurú a Itapura	8,701,246	50,466	802,056	0.5	97.4
Rede Bahia–Bahia e Minas	7,907,100	26,537	791,408	0.5	97.8

Table B.1 (cont.)

Rede Bahia–Central da Bahia	5,648,802	66,074	522,926	0.3	98.2
Vitória á Santana dos Ferros and Branch	5,597,408	32,163	1,021,308	0.3	98.5
São Paulo–Rio Grande Linha de S. Francisco	4,414,710	48,726	451,450	0.3	98.8
Rede Ceará–Sobral	3,281,050	28,596	403,793	0.2	98.9
Rio do Ouro	3,195,423	50,721	142,122	0.2	99.1
Madeira–Mamoré	3,133,347	12,859	4,210,149	0.2	99.3
*Quarahim a Itaquy (Brazil Great Southern)	3,017,886	31,561	216,031	0.2	99.5
Central do Rio Grande do Norte	2,432,064	34,084	72,992	0.1	99.6
Formiga a Goyaz	2,045,245	26,532	199,208	0.1	99.8
Araguary–Catalão	1,062,736	15,141	174,933	0.1	99.8
Curralinho á Diamantina	816,133	17,662	108,197	0.0	99.9
Dona Thereza Christina	745,664	13,565	65,840	0.0	99.9
Itaqui a S. Borja	731,198	7,228	56,841	0.0	99.9
Caxias a Cajazeiras	351,010	12,840	64,390	0.0	100.0
Santa Catarina	324,478	8,881	61,409	0.0	100.0
Prolongamento da E. F. Maricá	39,017	1,667	8,197	0.0	100.0
Total	1,697,321,018	12,698,652	165,367,102	100.0%	—

NOTES: Freight revenues expressed in milréis. Asterisks denote railroads that make up the sample. The Recife and San Francisco Railway, though part of the sample, does not appear in the list because it had been subsumed under the Great Western's operations following the government purchase of the line. Because of the aggregation used in the government railroad statistical volumes, the Southern Brazil Rio Grande do Sul is subsumed in the Viação Ferrea Rio Grande do Sul in 1913.

ported in the annual reports of the Ministry of Transportation. The rapidly de-preciating exchange rate led several British companies to convert their Brazil-ian earnings to Sterling using an accounting rate of exchange different from the market exchange rates. The Recife and San Francisco was one of the com-panies that did so, and using the Brazilian-reported figures avoids the conver-sion distortion in the freight revenue series. Freight revenues on the Bahia and San Francisco from 1869 to 1873 were estimated at 57 percent of total oper-ating revenues, based on the observed ratio for 1874. From 1875 through 1886 straight-line interpolation of the ratio of freight revenue to total revenue served as the basis for the freight revenue series. The freight revenue series for the Leopoldina required similar interpolations in 1886, 1888, and 1897.

The Sorocabana's reports did not provide disaggregated figures on freight earnings before 1892. The ratio of freight revenue to total operating revenue in 1892 was 65.5 percent. This ratio was applied to the railroad's total earnings before 1892 to construct the series of estimated freight revenues. On the Great Western Railway the only adjustment required was to convert fiscal year rev-enues to a calendar year basis in the 1880s. This was accomplished by com-puting a simple average of the revenues reported for each two adjoining fiscal years, producing a two-year moving average of the revenues series. For a single year (1885) on the Southern Brazil Rio Grande do Sul Railway missing freight revenues were calculated by applying the following year's unit charge to the observed ton-kilometer figures. Wherever relevant, the overall sample freight revenue series excluded earnings on freight carried by water for railroad com-panies that had river subsidiaries, such as the Paulista and the Sorocabana. The series on freight tons and ton-kilometers, elaborated below, similarly excluded waterway operating results on these railroads. The freight revenue series for the sample lines is generally quite reliable, and especially so after the 1860s. From 1870 onward the share of sample freight revenues that were the result of in-terpolation or other indirect estimating procedures exceeded 10 percent in only three years, and was typically much less than that.

Company reports usually provided measures of freight tons for each year, though occasionally there was a need to estimate the tons carried when data were missing. Lacunae in the tonnage series were less common than in the freight revenue figures. As in the case of freight revenues, in only three years did interpolated freight tons exceed 10 percent of total sample tons. The most significant of these involved the Leopoldina. In 1892, 1897, and 1898 its freight tonnage figures were interpolated, accounting for around 10 percent of total sample tons each year.

Reconstructing figures on output in units of ton-kilometers proved con-siderably more difficult than the freight revenue and tonnage series. Output, when not reported outright, can be calculated directly from information on other key variables. Given information on freight revenue or freight tons, ton-kilometers for a given railroad can be derived with knowledge of either the average length of haul for freight carried by the line, or of the unit charge for a ton-kilometer of freight service. Total freight revenues (R) in a given year were the product of the number of tons carried on the railroad (T), the average distance each ton was carried or the average length of haul (ALH), and the unit charge per ton-kilometer (P):

$$R = T \times ALH \times P$$

When the company reported tonnage and the average length of haul, output (Q) in ton-kilometers is computed simply as the product of the reported haul and tons:

$$Q = T \times ALH$$

When the company reported the average freight revenue per ton-kilometer, output is given by the quotient of freight revenue and the unit charge:

$$Q = \frac{R}{P}$$

An acute challenge arises when no information on ton-kilometers of freight service is reported and data on the average haul per ton and the unit freight charge cannot be located. Six of the eleven sample lines failed to report their output in ton-kilometers (or provide other information that would permit its direct computation) at all in their first decade of operations. Even after the first decade of operation, most sample lines reported neither the unit charge nor the average haul for at least some years. Table B.2 indicates the availability of the data required to establish directly the levels of freight output for each sample line. In years where no data were available, estimating procedures were employed to fill lacunae in the data series. The Central do Brazil (originally the Dom Pedro II) was both the oldest railroad in the sample and the line with the largest level of freight service every year through 1913. The techniques employed to construct the ton-kilometer estimates for it are discussed first. Before 1870 the company did not report the average haul per freight ton. Published rate schedules revealed a wide range of charges across different classes of goods, eliminating the possibility of applying an estimated unit charge that would be valid for all freight on the line. From 1858 through 1869 the average length of haul (ALH) was set arbitrarily at one-half the length of track in service each year. The first reported average haul, in 1870, equaled 63 percent of the track in service that year. The ratio of ALH to track

Table B.2

Availability of Evidence for Establishing Ton-Kilometers of Freight Output for Sample Lines, 1858–1913

Railroad	Year									
	1858	*1859*	*1860*	*1861*	*1862*	*1863*	*1864*	*1865*	*1866*	*1867*
Dom Pedro II (Central do Brazil)	nd	nd	nd	nd	nd	nd	nd	nd	nd	nd
Recife and San Francisco	nd	nd	nd	nd	nd	nd	nd	nd	nd	nd
Bahia and San Francisco	—	—	nd	nd	nd	nd	nd	nd	nd	nd
San Paulo (Santos a Jundiaí)	—	—	—	—	—	—	—	—	—	nd
Paulista	—	—	—	—	—	—	—	—	—	—
Leopoldina	—	—	—	—	—	—	—	—	—	—
Mogiana	—	—	—	—	—	—	—	—	—	—
Sorocabana e Ituana	—	—	—	—	—	—	—	—	—	—
Great Western of Brazil	—	—	—	—	—	—	—	—	—	—
Southern Brazil Rio Grande do Sul	—	—	—	—	—	—	—	—	—	—
Brazil Great Southern	—	—	—	—	—	—	—	—	—	—

NOTES: nd = no data; — = line not yet in operation; x = data available.

Table B.2 (cont.)

	Year									
Railroad	1868	1869	1870	1871	1872	1873	1874	1875	1876	1877
Dom Pedro II (Central do Brazil)	nd	nd	x	nd	nd	x	nd	nd	x	x
Recife and San Francisco	nd	nd	nd	nd	nd	nd	nd	nd	nd	nd
Bahia and San Francisco	nd	nd	nd	nd	nd	nd	x	nd	nd	nd
San Paulo (Santos a Jundiaí)	nd	nd	nd	nd	nd	nd	nd	nd	nd	nd
Paulista	—	—	—	—	nd	nd	nd	nd	nd	nd
Leopoldina	—	—	—	—	—	—	nd	nd	nd	nd
Mogiana	—	—	—	—	—	—	—	nd	x	x
Sorocabana e Ituana	—	—	—	—	—	—	—	—	nd	nd
Great Western of Brazil	—	—	—	—	—	—	—	—	—	—
Southern Brazil Rio Grande do Sul	—	—	—	—	—	—	—	—	—	—
Brazil Great Southern	—	—	—	—	—	—	—	—	—	—

NOTES: nd = no data; — = line not yet in operation; x = data available.

Table B.2 (cont.)

Railroad	1878	1879	1880	1881	1882	1883	1884	1885	1886	1887
					Year					
Dom Pedro II (Central do Brazil)	x	x	x	x	x	x	x	x	x	x
Recife and San Francisco	nd	nd	nd	nd	nd	nd	nd	nd	nd	x
Bahia and San Francisco	nd	nd	nd	nd	nd	nd	nd	x	nd	x
San Paulo (Santos a Jundiaí)	nd	nd	nd	nd	nd	nd	nd	x	x	x
Paulista	nd	nd	x	nd	x	x	nd	x	x	nd
Leopoldina	nd	x	x	x	x	x	x	nd	nd	x
Mogiana	x	x	x	x	x	x	x	x	x	x
Sorocabana e Ituana	nd	nd	nd	nd	nd	nd	nd	nd	nd	x
Great Western of Brazil	—	—	—	nd	nd	nd	nd	nd	nd	x
Southern Brazil Rio Grande do Sul	—	—	—	—	—	—	nd	x	x	x
Brazil Great Southern	—	—	—	—	—	—	—	—	—	x

NOTES: nd = no data; — = line not yet in operation; x = data available.

Table B.2 (cont.)

Railroad	Year									
	1888	1889	1890	1891	1892	1893	1894	1895	1896	1897
Dom Pedro II (Central do Brazil)	x	x	x	x	x	x	x	x	x	x
Recife and San Francisco	nd	nd	nd	nd	nd	nd	nd	nd	nd	nd
Bahia and San Francisco	nd	nd	nd	nd	nd	x	nd	nd	x	nd
San Paulo (Santos a Jundiaí)	nd	nd	nd	nd	nd	x	nd	nd	nd	nd
Paulista	nd	nd	nd	nd	nd	nd	x	x	nd	nd
Leopoldina	nd	nd	nd	nd	nd	nd	nd	nd	nd	nd
Mogiana	x	x	x	x	x	x	x	x	x	x
Sorocabana e Ituana	nd	nd	nd	nd	x	x	x	x	x	x
Great Western of Brazil	nd	nd	nd	nd	nd	nd	nd	nd	nd	nd
Southern Brazil Rio Grande do Sul	nd	nd	nd	nd	nd	nd	nd	nd	nd	nd
Brazil Great Southern	x	x	x	x	x	x	nd	x	x	x

NOTES: nd = no data; — = line not yet in operation; x = data available.

Table B.2 (cont.)

							Year			
Railroad	*1898*	*1899*	*1900*	*1901*	*1902*	*1903*	*1904*	*1905*	*1906*	*1907*
Dom Pedro II (Central do Brazil)	x	x	x	x	x	x	x	x	x	x
Recife and San Francisco	x	x	x	x	x	x	x	x	x	x
Bahia and San Francisco	x	x	x	x	x	x	x	x	x	x
San Paulo (Santos a Jundiaí)	x	x	x	x	x	x	x	x	x	x
Paulista	x	x	x	x	x	x	x	x	x	x
Leopoldina	x	x	x	x	x	x	x	x	x	x
Mogiana	x	x	x	x	x	x	x	x	x	x
Sorocabana e Ituana	x	x	x	x	x	x	x	x	x	x
Great Western of Brazil	x	x	x	x	x	x	x	x	x	x
Southern Brazil Rio Grande do Sul	x	x	x	x	x	x	x	x	x	x
Brazil Great Southern	x	x	x	x	x	x	x	x	x	x

NOTES: nd = no data; — = line not yet in operation; x = data available.

Table B.2 (cont.)

| Railroad | Year | | | | | |
---	1908	1909	1910	1911	1912	1913
Dom Pedro II (Central do Brazil)	x	x	x	x	x	x
Recife and San Francisco	x	x	x	x	x	x
Bahia and San Francisco	x	x	x	x	x	x
San Paulo (Santos a Jundiaí)	x	x	x	x	x	x
Paulista	x	x	x	x	x	x
Leopoldina	x	x	x	x	x	x
Mogiana	x	x	x	x	x	x
Sorocabana e Ituana	x	x	x	x	x	x
Great Western of Brazil	x	x	x	x	x	x
Southern Brazil Rio Grande do Sul	x	x	x	x	x	x
Brazil Great Southern	x	x	x	x	x	x

NOTES: nd = no data; — = line not yet in operation; x = data available.

declined in a secular fashion thereafter. If that decline began right after the opening of the line, the estimated freight ton-kilometers before 1870 are understated as a result. Observed *ALH* data provide the basis for interpolating the ton-kilometer series between 1870 and 1873. The identical technique was used for the years between 1873 and 1876.

The Recife and San Francisco Railway, which like the Dom Pedro II began operations in 1858, did not report its average freight haul before 1885. For the first six years of operation virtually the sole available output measure was total revenue. Freight revenues for the line were derived in the manner described above, and output in ton-kilometers was established by assigning the estimated unit charge for 1864 to the preceding years and dividing it into freight revenues. The length of track in service never increased beyond that in operation in 1861 while the railroad was under the company's ownership. Given that the Recife and San Francisco served a limited area in which there had been substantial commercial activity before the opening of the line, there is little reason to suspect that the average haul before 1885 had risen appreciably over time. The reported average haul per ton in 1887 (89 kilometers) was slightly lower than the 1885 figure (99 kilometers). To minimize the possibility of overstating output, the 1887 figure was applied to tonnage figures reported from 1864 to 1884 to estimate freight service before 1885. The movement in the ton-kilometer series before 1885 is thus almost entirely due to annual variations in the tonnage shipped over the line. The reported average haul in 1898 (80 kilometers) was very close to the 1887 figure. For the intervening decade, linear interpolation of the average haul underpinned the freight output series.

For the Bahia and San Francisco Railway the average haul was reported for the first time in 1874 and then not again until 1885. Linear interpolation of the freight revenue per ton-kilometer yielded estimated unit charges for 1875–1884. Dividing these into the reported freight revenues each year gave the estimated output in ton-kilometers. Between 1887 and 1898 the *ALH* was occasionally interpolated to provide ton-kilometer figures. The average haul per freight ton on the San Paulo Railway failed to appear in either government sources or company reports until 1885. Like the Recife and San Francisco, the San Paulo Railway operated in a region with considerable freight traffic in the decades before the railroad, and during the nineteenth century the line in service never increased beyond its extension in operation at the time of its official opening in 1867. Most of its freight by the mid-1870s came from feeder lines in the interior of the province. From 1867 through 1884 the observed *ALH* for 1885 was used. The assumption of a constant average haul from 1867 through 1884 probably misstates the distance of the actual typical freight journey only slightly. Linear interpolation provided the imputed average haul between 1887 and 1893, and again between 1893 and 1898.

For the Companhia Mogiana the average length of haul was reported every year except the first of its operation. For 1875 the ratio of the average haul to track in service in 1876 served as the basis of extrapolation. The Companhia Paulista, another major road in São Paulo, did not report its average haul at all during the first thirteen years of operation. The ratio of *ALH* to track in service in 1885 (0.29) served as the basis for estimating the average haul before 1885. From 1887 through 1893 the average haul was estimated by interpolating between the observed values for 1886 and 1894. The same approach provided the average haul for 1896 and 1897.

The Leopoldina proved to be one of the most challenging of the sample lines for establishing estimates of freight service. What began as a modest interior railroad in Minas Gerais expanded during a quarter century to become Brazil's third most important railroad in terms of freight revenue by 1913. Most of its expansion came about through acquisitions and consolidations of small lines in Minas Gerais, Rio de Janeiro, and Espírito Santo. These acquisitions included the União Mineira, Sumidouro, Cantagalo, Carangola, Araruama, and Central de Macaé railroads, among others. In most cases the pre-acquisition operating results of these lines were not available and could not be included in the series for the years preceding their respective mergers with the Leopoldina. The company first reported its unit freight revenue in 1880. Estimates for 1873 through 1879 used the 1880 unit charge as the basis for deriving ton-kilometers from total-freight-revenue figures. The observed freight charge for 1884 was extrapolated through 1887 to give an estimated level of output. Financial turmoil afflicted the firm in the 1890s, and there was no reporting again of output levels until 1898. The solution in this case was quite crude: the observed unit charge from 1898 was applied to the preceding decade. That charge was nearly 40 percent higher than the one prevailing in the mid-1880s (260 milréis versus 190 milréis per ton-kilometer), with the result that its use likely underestimates actual freight service levels in the 1890s. Starting in 1898 the average haul was reported annually, but only for those branches of the line operated under concession from the federal government. For that portion of the tonnage carried on branches not reported in the government's operating figures the average haul required estimation. The technique applied simply extended the average haul on the federally conceded portion of the railroad to the tons carried on the rest of the Leopoldina's branches. If, instead, the average revenue per ton-kilometer on federally conceded sections of the Leopoldina had been used to derive ton-kilometers from total freight revenues on the remainder of the sections, the resulting estimate of freight ton-kilometers would be nearly triple the figure used for 1913. The figures employed in Chapter 4 and Chapter 7 are no doubt a considerable understatement of freight service in ton-kilometers on the Leopoldina from 1898 to 1913.

The Companhia Sorocabana e Ituana reported its average haul in 1903 and did so every year through 1913. Before 1903 no figures were located that could be used to reliably convert tons carried into ton-kilometers of freight service. Freight service overall, and the average haul in particular, depended on both the amount of time the line had been in operation and on the length of track in service. To derive the average haul before 1892, the observed haul from 1892 onward was expressed as a ratio of track in service each year. A statistical regression of the ratio on a time trend made it possible to extrapolate backward an estimated average haul that was a function of year and track kilometers. A second estimate of the average haul simply fixed the haul at 21.7 percent of track in service each year from 1876 to 1902, which was the ratio observed for 1903. Though more crude than the regression-based extrapolations, the second approach guarded against overstating freight output.

The Great Western Railway first reported its freight *ALH* in 1887, then again in 1894. To obtain ton-kilometer figures before 1887, and between 1887 and 1894, ordinary-least-squares regression of the observed *ALH* on the length of track in service each year provided a good statistical fit. The parameters of that regression were used to fill the lacunae in the ton-kilometer series, based on the length of track in use each year. The average freight haul for the Southern Brazil Rio Grande do Sul Railway was first reported in 1885 but not reported at all between 1887 and 1898. Both the reported *ALH* and the unit freight charge were quite stable over time. Both interpolated unit charges and interpolated measures of *ALH* were used to derive estimates of freight ton-kilometers, and both approaches gave nearly identical results. The series used in the sample was based on the interpolated unit charge. Finally, on the Brazil Great Southern a single interpolation of the average haul was required for 1894.

The techniques applied in filling lacunae in the sample series were selected first to provide the most reliable possible estimate, where that was feasible. All estimated data series were scrutinized carefully for consistency with related, directly observed series. When it was unclear which estimating technique might prove superlative, the one employed was designed to minimize the risk of either exaggerating output or understating revenues and costs. Because the hypothesis running through Chapters 4 and 7 is that each railroad's freight social savings was large, whenever estimating tons, ton-kilometers, or unit revenues the technique selected was designed to systematically control bias in a way that would understate the railroad's direct impact.

Notes

1. Brief outbursts of Loyalist activity in the provinces were quickly suppressed. See Barman, *Brazil*, 97–119, and Costa, *The Brazilian Empire*, 19–20; Bethell and Carvalho, "Empire: 1822–1850," 49–58.

2. On state building and formalizing the apparatus of government, see Carvalho, *A Construção da Ordem*.

3. IBGE, *Estatísticas Históricas do Brasil*, 32–33.

4. Leff, *Underdevelopment and Development in Brazil*, 32–34. For Brazil's comparative performance in the nineteenth century, see Coatsworth, "Economic and Institutional Trajectories in Nineteenth-Century Latin America," 26; and ibid., "Obstacles to Economic Growth," 82. The absence of economic censuses hampers national income-accounting for pre-1920 Brazil. Quantitative measures of nineteenth-century economic growth depend, as in Leff's case, on foreign prices and arbitrary assumptions about the income velocity of circulation, or, as in the cases of Contador and Haddad, and Haddad (before 1920), purely on statistical extrapolations using principal components analysis (see Leff, *Underdevelopment and Development in Brazil*; Contador and Haddad, "Produto Real, Moêda, e Preços"; and Haddad, *Crescimento do Produto Real no Brasil*). The tenuous nature of the estimates by Contador and Haddad, and Leff, have led others to reject their use (see Fishlow, "Conditionality and Willingness to Pay," 105 n. 23; and Catão, "The International Transmission of Long Cycles"). Leaving aside the even more conjectural revisions to Contador and Haddad by Topik ("The Economic Role of the State in Liberal Regimes," 129) and Goldsmith (*Brasil, 1850–1914*), the Contador and Haddad and Haddad estimates remain the only output series for pre-1920 Brazil.

5. For the course of the Brazilian economy from 1822 onward, see Haber and Klein, "The Economic Consequences of Brazilian Independence"; and Leff, "Economic Development in Brazil," 34–60. On the economic costs of colonial trade restrictions, see Sum-

merhill, "Mercantilism in Late Colonial Brazil."

6. Dean, "Latifundia and Land Policy in Nineteenth-Century Brazil"; Carvalho, *Teatro de Sombras*, 84–106; Costa, *The Brazilian Empire*, 78–93.

7. Eisenberg, *The Sugar Industry in Pernambuco*, 63–64.

8. On the accomplishments and setbacks of the *conciliação* cabinet, see Barman, "Brazil at Mid-Empire," 181–204.

9. The GDP series employed here is that of Contador and Haddad, from "Produto Real, Moêda, e Preços." Using AR1 estimation to regress the natural logarithm of per capita GDP on time yields the following parameter estimates for the years 1870–1900:

$$\ln (GDP/POP) = 26.4 - 0.11 \, YEAR$$
$$\qquad\qquad\quad (2.7) \qquad (-2.3)$$

$$R^2 = 0.97 \qquad\qquad D - W = 0.84 \qquad\qquad F = 841$$

and for the years 1901–1913:

$$\ln (GDP/POP) = -131.3 + 0.072 \, YEAR$$
$$\qquad\qquad\quad (-11.7) \qquad (12.1)$$

$$R^2 = 0.99 \qquad\qquad D - W = 1.4 \qquad\qquad F = 918$$

These results give a rough idea of the fin-de-siècle shift detectable in the output estimates. For reasons noted in footnote 4, not too much can be made of either the precise timing or the degree of the shift, given the derivation of the underlying data series.

10. Life expectancy, one indicator of the standard of living, increased appreciably between the late Empire and the early twentieth century. See the discussions in Merrick and Graham, *Population and Economic Development in Brazil*.

11. Fogel, *Railroads and American Economic Growth*; Fishlow, *American Railroads and the Transformation of the Antebellum Economy*; Hawke, *Railways and Economic Growth in England and Wales*; Metzer, *Some Economic Aspects of Railroad Development in Tsarist Russia*; Mc-Greevey, *Economic History of Colombia*; de Vries, "Barges and Capitalism," 237–44; Coatsworth, *Growth Against Development*; Gomez Mendoza, *Ferrocarriles y Cambio Económico en España*; Hurd, "Railways"; Huenemann, *The Dragon and the Iron Horse*; Ramírez, "Railroads and the Colombian Economy"; Feeny, *Political Economy of Productivity*; and the collection of essays in O'Brien, *Railways and the Economic Development of Western Europe*.

12. Lapa, "Um Tema Negligenciado," 601–3.

13. Matos, *Café e Ferrovias*; Mattoon, "The Companhia Paulista de Estradas de Ferro"; Saes, *As Ferrovias de São Paulo*; El-Kareh, *Filha Branca de Mãe Preta*; and Lewis, *Public Policy and Private Initiative*.

14. Zalduendo, *Libras y Rieles*, 228; Matos, *Café e Ferrovias*, 77–142; and Graham, *Britain and the Onset of Modernization in Brazil*, 51–72.

15. Saes, *As Ferrovias de São Paulo*, 99–120.

16. Dean, *Rio Claro*, 42–44; and Costa, *The Brazilian Empire*, 152, 192.

17. Furtado noted that railroads were one possible agent of productivity change, but

he did not believe such productivity improvements were present in Brazil's late-nineteenth-century economy (*Economic Growth of Brazil*, 169). Leff noted that railroads lowered transport costs and conjectured that their impact was large, but he did not undertake an analysis of the transport sector to establish the point (*Underdevelopment and Development in Brazil*, 144–53).

18. Burns, *A History of Brazil*, 160–61, 169, 270–71; Evans, "Continuities and Contradictions in the Evolution of Brazilian Dependence"; Sunkel, *Processo Desenvolvimento–Subdesenvolvimento*, 25; Graham, "Sepoys and Imperialists," 35–36; Coatsworth, *Growth Against Development*, 145, 176; Ridings, *Business Interest Groups in Nineteenth-Century Brazil*, 262; Blasenheim, "Railroads in Nineteenth-Century Minas Gerais"; and Cechin, "A Construção e Operação das Ferrovias no Brasil," 31, 54.

19. Saes's study distinguishes itself by documenting carefully the role of railroads in São Paulo in carrying an increasingly large share of freight for the internal market; at the same time, he explicitly rejects the approaches that have come to be known as "cliometric" as tools for gauging the railroad's overall impact (see *As Ferrovias de São Paulo*, 40).

20. Maddison, *The World Economy in the Twentieth Century*.

21. McClelland, *Causal Explanation and Model Building*, 176.

22. The classic statement in this regard is Fogel, "The Specification Problem in Economic History," 283–308; and Fogel, "Scientific History and Traditional History," 23–40.

23. Gerschenkron, "Some Methodological Problems," (*Continuity in History*) 50–56, presents a masterful discussion of the importance of reasonable counterfactuals in historical research, including their strengths and limitations. For an introduction to many of the philosophical and logical issues involved, see McClelland, *Causal Explanation and Model Building*, 146–68.

24. Indeed, such qualitative characterizations can be made reliably only after using the quantitative evidence to answer Clapham's central questions for economic historians: how large? how long? how often? how representative? (see Clapham, "Economic History as a Discipline," 327).

25. Burns, *The Poverty of Progress*, 141.

26. This view gained currency with the invention of notions of "development of underdevelopment" and later, "associated dependent development," as putative explanations for the Latin American economies' ability to grow despite persistent underdevelopment. See the well-known studies by Frank, *Capitalism and Underdevelopment in Latin America*; and Cardoso and Faletto, *Dependency and Development in Latin America*. For examples of applications of these interpretive frameworks by historians, albeit at starkly different levels of sophistication, see Burns, *The Poverty of Progress*; and Coatsworth, *Growth Against Development*.

27. Imprecise notions of the implicit connection between "development" and income distribution becloud studies juxtaposing "poverty" and "progress," or "growth" and "underdevelopment." One implication of the First Welfare Theorem of microeconomics is that an efficient allocation is also a particular distribution of income. That, however, is not a line of investigation followed by scholars of Latin American underdevelopment. It would certainly be a fruitful one to pursue, however.

28. For a recent exposition of this very point, see Coatsworth, "Welfare." A compelling and thorough survey of the close relationship between levels of GDP per capita and the major indicators of human development is found in Ray, *Development Economics*, 25–33. For the connection between GDP per capita and life expectancy in Latin Amer-

ica, see Sánchez-Albornoz, *The Population of Latin America*, 194–96.

29. For a different reason, Gootenberg has aptly noted that the idea of a poverty of progress in Latin America is underpinned by a remarkable poverty of research (Gootenberg, *Imagining Development*, 16).

30. Inefficiency is used here in its technical sense. A technology is inefficient when there exists a substitute technology that can perform the same function with fewer resources.

31. Burns, *The Poverty of Progress*, 135–41.

32. See the essays in Lewis, *Tropical Development*.

33. Many studies combined aspects of the two branches of dependency. For the classic statement of the development of underdevelopment, see Frank, *Capitalism and Underdevelopment in Latin America*.

34. Stein and Stein, *The Colonial Heritage of Latin America*, 134–35, 155.

35. Cardoso and Faletto, *Dependency and Development in Latin America*, xvi; Santos, "Structure of Dependence," 231–36.

36. Gerschenkron's original insights in this regard hold up well in light of subsequent empirical research (see his *Economic Backwardness in Historical Perspective*).

37. Cardoso and Faletto, *Dependency and Development in Latin America*.

38. Rippy, *British Investments in Latin America*; Platt, *Business Imperialism*.

39. On the growing concentration of slaves in the provinces of the greatest railroad development, see Slenes, "The Demography and Economics of Brazilian Slavery."

40. Topik, *The Political Economy of the Brazilian State*.

CHAPTER 2

1. U.K., House of Commons, "Report by Mr. Consul Lennon Hunt on the Trade and Commerce of Rio de Janeiro during the Year 1869," *Sessional Papers*, 1870, Commercial Reports Received at the Foreign Offices of Her Majesty's Consuls, 1869–1870, vol. 64, no. 3, p. 231.

2. Benévolo, *Introdução a História Ferroviária do Brasil*, 517–24; Gumiero, "Os Tropeiros na História de Goiás," 34.

3. Momsen, *Routes Over the Serra do Mar*, 25–28.

4. Barickman, "'Tame Indians,' 'Wild Heathens,' and Settlers," 353–55.

5. Momsen, *Routes Over the Serra do Mar*, 31–45; Magalhães, "Os Caminhos Antigos," 228–36; and Ribas, "Tropeirismo e Escravidão," 79–93.

6. Pinto, *História da Viação Pública de S. Paulo*, 18–20.

7. The best guide to these early-nineteenth-century roads between Santos and Rio de Janeiro remains Momsen, *Routes Over the Serra do Mar*, 45–76. On the major roads there and elsewhere, see also Silva, *Geografia dos Transportes no Brasil*, 73–87.

8. Felisberto Ignácio Januário Cordeiro to José Bonifácio da Andrada e Silva, Inhauma, 1822, "Memória sobre a segurança das estradas infestadas de salteadores e ciganos," Códice 807, vol. 7, folhas 124–30, AN.

9. *O Agricultor Brazileiro*, June 1854, 1–3.

10. MACOP, *Relatório . . . 1869*, 5.

11. Cechin, "A Construção e Operação das Ferrovias no Brasil," 20; *O Agricultor Brazileiro*, June 1854, 1–3; Bulhões, *Estrada de Ferro da Bahia*, 40.

12. U.K., House of Commons, "Report from Mr. Consul Lennon Hunt of the Trade

of Pernambuco of the Year 1860," *Sessional Papers,* 1865, Commercial Reports Received at the Foreign Office from Her Majesty's Consuls between July 1st and December 31st, 1864, vol. 53, p. 40.

13. Ibid., p. 53.

14. Província de Pernambuco, *Relatório Apresentado ao Exm. Sr. Presidente,* 8–9.

15. U.K., House of Commons, "Report from Consul Doyle on the Trade, Commerce, and Navigation on the Port of Pernambuco of the Year 1871," *Sessional Papers,* 1872, Reports from Her Majesty's Consuls on the Manufactures, Commerce, etc., of their Consular Districts, vol. 58, p. 635.

16. *Times* (London), 16 October 1872, 16.

17. Província de Pernambuco, *Relatório Apresentado á Assembléa Legislativa,* 33.

18. U.K., House of Commons, "Report of Mr. Hill, British Consul at Maranham on the Trade, etc. or the District During the Year 1859," *Sessional Papers,* 1862, Abstract of Reports of the Trade, etc., of Various Countries and Places, for the Years 1859, 1860: Received by the Board of Trade (through the foreign office) from Her Majesty's Consuls, No. 11, vol. 58, p. 9.

19. U.K., House of Commons, "General Report of Mr. Vrendenburg, British Consul at Pará, on the Trade, Commerce, Navigation, etc. within the District of his Consulate," *Sessional Papers,* 1857–1858, Abstract of Reports of the Trade of Various Countries and Places, for the Years 1857-1858-1859: Received by the Board of Trade (through the foreign office) from Her Majesty's Ministries and Consuls, No. 7, vol. 30, p. 20.

20. U.K., House of Commons, "Report of Mr. Wetherell, British Vice-Consul at Paraiba, on the Trade of the Port for the Year 1857," *Sessional Papers, 1857–1858,* Abstract of Reports of the Trade of Various Countries and Places, for the Years 1857-1858-1859 Received by the Board of Trade (through the foreign office) from Her Majesty's Ministries and Consuls, No. 7, vol. 30, p. 22.

21. U.K., House of Commons, "Report by Mr. Consul Morgan on the Trade of Bahia for the Year 1864," *Sessional Papers,* 1862, Commercial Reports Received at the Foreign Offices of Her Majesty's Consuls, vol. 65, p. 4.

22. Província do Espírito Santo, *Relatório,* 22.

23. Bovet, "A Indústria Mineral na Província de Minas Gerais," 33–35. On *mineiro* roads in the nineteenth century, see Pimenta, *Caminhos de Minas Gerais,* 9–73.

24. Gorceix, "Escola de Minas," *Monitor Sul Mineiro* (Campanha), 19 November 1876. On Gorceix's role in the development of mining, see Carvalho, *A Escola de Minas de Ouro Preto,* 25–70.

25. "Retrospecto Commércial de 1874," *JC* (1875), 10.

26. *Correio Paulistano,* 15 August 1865, Parte Official, Supplemento.

27. U.K., House of Commons, "Report by the Honorable H. P. Vereker, British Consul at Rio Grande do Sul, on the Commerce, etc., of That Port, etc., for 1860," *Sessional Papers,* 1862, Abstract of Reports of the Trade, etc., of Various Countries and Places, for the Years 1859, 1860: Received by the Board of Trade (through the foreign office) from Her Majesty's Consuls, No. 11, vol. 58, p. 230.

28. Souza, "Estrada da Serra de Estrela e os Colonos Alemães," 88–102; Esteves, "Mariano Procópio"; Giroletti, "A Companhia e a Rodovia União e Indústria," 41–61.

29. Moreira, *Caminhos das Comarcas de Curitiba e Paranaguá,* 1:314–52; *Cincoentenario da Estrada de Ferro do Paraná,* 25–35; Tourinho, "Bosquejo Histórico da Estrada da Graciosa."

30. *O Agricultor Brasileiro*, 1 October 1854, 13.

31. For descriptions of the use of mules and road conditions in the nineteenth century, see Goulart, *Tropas e Tropeiros na Formação do Brasil*, 165–80; Momsen, *Routes Over the Serra do Mar*, 45–70; Agassiz, *A Journey in Brazil*, 114; Hadfield, *Brazil and the River Plate in 1868*, 62; and Burton, *The Highlands of Brazil*, 57–58.

32. "Plano para o estabelecimento de fazendas de criar cavalhos e bestas muares na Província de São Paulo," Códice 807, vol. 13, folhas 47–49, AN.

33. On the mule trade and its merchants in this period, see Petrone, *O Barão de Iguape*; and Lenharo, *As Tropas da Moderação*.

34. For a detailed assessment of the mule market in central Brazil, see Klein, "A Oferta de Muares no Brasil Central."

35. Pestana, *A Expansão Econômica do Estado de S. Paulo*, 7.

36. *O Agricultor Brazileiro*, 1 October 1854, 13–15.

37. U.K., House of Commons, "Report by the Honorable H. P. Vereker, British Consul at Rio Grande do Sul, on the Commerce, etc., of That Port, etc., for 1860," *Sessional Papers*, 1862, Abstract of Reports of the Trade, etc., of Various Countries and Places, for the Years 1859, 1860: Received by the Board of Trade (through the foreign office) from Her Majesty's Consuls, No. 11, vol. 58, p. 230.

38. U.K., House of Commons, "Report by Mr. Consul Morgan on the Trade of Bahia for the Year 1864," *Sessional Papers*, 1862, Commercial Reports Received at the Foreign Offices of Her Majesty's Consuls, vol. 65, p. 6.

39. U.K., House of Commons, "Report by Mr. Consul Morgan on the Trade of Bahia for the Year 1864," *Sessional Papers*, 1865, Commercial Reports Received at the Foreign Offices of Her Majesty's Consuls, vol. 54, pp. 183–84.

40. Bovet, "A Indústria Mineral na Província de Minas Gerais," 39.

41. EFDPII, *Relatório*, 1888.

42. Bovet, "A Indústria Mineral na Província de Minas Gerais," 52.

43. Ibid.

44. U.K., House of Commons, "Report by the Honorable H. P. Vereker, British Consul at Rio Grande do Sul, on the Commerce, etc., of That Port, etc., for 1860," *Sessional Papers*, 1862, Abstract of Reports of the Trade, etc., of Various Countries and Places, for the Years 1859, 1860: Received by the Board of Trade (through the foreign office) from Her Majesty's Consuls, No. 11, vol. 58, p. 230.

45. Alexandre José do Passos Herculano, Porto do Estrella, 16 de junho 1834, "Sobre as Vantagens Que uma Nação nova tira da abertura, conservação e reparo das Estradas. Acompanhada com demonstração do estado lastimoso em que estão as Estradas Públicas, logo desde as immediações da Côrte e outros lugares," Códice 807, vol. 13, folhas 2–9, AN.

46. U.K., House of Commons, "Report of Mr. Consul Lennon Hunt on the Trade and Commerce of Rio de Janeiro during the Year 1869," *Sessional Papers*, 1870, Commercial Reports Received at the Foreign Office of her Majesty's Consuls 1869–1870, vol. 64, no. 3, p. 230. On road damage from flooding, see also Magalhães, *Relatório dos Trabalhos na Estrada*, 8.

47. Senado Federal, *Constituições do Brasil*, 1:49–53.

48. The leading example of the latter is the case of the Companhia União e Indústria, which constructed and operated Brazil's model macadam road in the 1850s. The opening of the Dom Pedro II railroad, which served the same region, clearly spelled the end for the road company, but later its president and shareholders were able to arrange for

themselves years of subsidized dividend payments and ultimately a buyout by the government. For the government's involvement in this and other road projects, with participation ranging from mere passing interest to outright ownership, see MI, *Relatório* . . . *1847*, 53–58; MACOP, *Relatório* . . . *1866*, 89–97; MACOP, *Relatório* . . . *1877*, 46–54; MACOP, *Relatório* . . . *1878*, 220–27; MACOP, *Relatório* . . . *1880*, 191–97; and MACOP, *Relatório* . . . *1882*, 126–28.

49. MACOP, *Relatório* . . . *1878*, 220.

50. No compendia of information on provincial expenditures on highway construction projects and maintenance have been located; the relevant figures, when available, remain scattered across literally hundreds of provincial reports, and a systematic compilation and assessment of them lies beyond what is possible here. On the limited provincial outlays on roads in São Paulo, see Pinto, *História da Viação Pública de S. Paulo*, 263. For the halting nature of provincial projects, see Província da Bahia, *Falla Regitada*, 98–106. The tapering of interest in funding road maintenance on the part of the central government is readily detectable in the annual reports of the Minister of Agriculture through the 1880s.

51. See Table 4.7.

52. Ibid.

53. The company received subsidized dividend payments from the government (see Companhia União e Indústria, *Relatório* [1860]).

54. Baril, *L'Empire du Brésil*, 85–108.

55. Locomotives were a poor substitute for coastwise shipping, and as a result most rail lines extended from the coast to the interior in an attempt to establish links to rivers and create large internal transport networks.

56. The accounts of numerous travelers to Brazil note the relative dearth of opportunities for internal navigation and the poor navigability of many of Brazil's rivers; a representative assessment is Hartt, *Geology and Physical Geography of Brazil*, 292. For a survey of the navigable portions of inland waterways in Brazil, see Lima, "Rios Navegáveis do Brasil," 710–23; and Lyra, *Cifras e Notas*, 66–71.

57. Bastos, *O Valle do Amazonas*, 175–95.

58. CIB, *O Brasil*, 116.

59. Hartt, *Geology and Physical Geography of Brazil*, 292.

60. Agassiz, *A Journey in Brazil*, 172; Branner, *Cotton in the Empire of Brazil*, 24–26; Przewodowski, "Communicação entre a Cidade de Bahia e a Vila de Juazeiro ," 375–77.

61. CIB, *O Brasil*, 118.

62. Agassiz, *A Journey in Brazil*, 121.

63. Whately, *O Café em Resende no Século XIX*, 23.

64. CIB, *O Brasil*, 127.

65. Ibid., 128.

66. Hartt, *Geology and Physical Geography of Brazil*, 506.

67. CIB, *O Brasil*, 130. For a discussion of the poor navigability of rivers in Paraná, also see Francisco Keller, "Noções geográphicas e estatísticas sobre a Província do Paraná," 1867, Códice 807, vol. 7, AN.

68. CIB, *O Brasil*, 137; Leverger, *Vias de Communicação de Matto-Grosso*, 20–23; Gumiero, "Os Tropeiros na História de Goiás," 33; and Jardim, "Synthese Histórica," 428–30.

69. MACOP, *Relatório* . . . *1865*, Annexo P: "Exploração do Rio Hyapurá e do Rio Araguaya," 30–31; and Doles, *As Comunicações Fluviais*, 81–97.

70. For an example, and what may likely be the most visionary of these, see the ex-

tended study by Moraes, *Navegação Interior do Brasil.*

71. See MACOP, "Relatório sobre a Exploração dos Valles do Parahyba e Pomba," in *Relatório* . . . *1865*; MACOP, Annexo M: "Relatório dos Engenheiros Kellers sobre as explorações do rio Ivahy," and Annexo N: "Relatório dos Engenheiros Kellers sobre as explorações dos rios Tibagy e Paranapanema," in *Relatório* . . . *1866*; MACOP, *Relatório* . . . *1880*, 190; MACOP, *Relatório* . . . *1886*, 173–88; MACOP, *Relatório* . . . *1887*, 157–65.

72. MACOP, *Relatório* . . . *1882*, 106–19.

73. MVOP, *Relatório* . . . *1909*, 309–13.

74. Derived from MVOP, *Relatório* . . . *1914*, 231–44, under the assumption that the average length of haul for each ton of freight equaled one-half the average one-way journey for the company. Any increase in the assumed length of haul simply reduces the estimated freight charge. The subsidy paid to the company for all classes of service in 1913 equaled 874 contos.

75. Denis, *Brazil*, 96.

CHAPTER 3

1. Marichal, *A Century of Debt Crises in Latin America*, 43–67.

2. Palhano de Jesus, "Rápida Notícia da Viação Ferrea do Brasil," 1:723. On this problem, see also Benévolo, *Introdução a História Ferroviária do Brasil*, 20.

3. Sá, *Brazilian Railways*, tables following p. 40. For active concessions as of 1884, see *Revista de Engenharia* 66 (1884).

4. For detailed discussion of each article of the typical railroad concession and guarantee in the nineteenth century, see Benévolo, *Introdução a História Ferroviária do Brasil*, 104–654. For details on concessions, contract modifications, and guarantee arrangements on a line-by-line basis, see Paiva, *Synopse da Legislação da Viação Ferrea Federal*; and Sá, *Código da Viação Ferrea do Brasil.*

5. For the value of capital in the cotton textile industry, see Branner, *Cotton in the Empire of Brazil*, 42–43.

6. This example, from 1883, is taken from the Arêas *fazenda* in Cantagallo, which is discussed in Laërne, *Brazil and Java*, 328–29, 332. The value of the *fazenda*, in excess of 600,000 milréis (p. 331), is just equal to that of the smallest Brazilian railroad in operation in 1887 for which construction costs exist, the Campos a São Sebastião.

7. The value of Brazilian slave stock was calculated by multiplying adjusted figures for Brazil's total slave population in 1887 (see Slenes, "The Demography and Economics of Brazilian Slavery," 617) by the average price of slaves in Rio de Janeiro (see Mello, *A Economia da Escravidão nas Fazendas de Café*, 104).

8. Lei no. 641, 26 June 1852, reprinted in Pessôa, *Estudo Descriptivo das Estradas de Ferro do Brasil*, 3. The discussion of the overall evolution of Brazil's railroad sector is derived from this source; see also Galvão, *Notícia Sobre as Estradas de Ferro do Brasil*; Costa, *Viação Ferrea do Brasil*; Lyon, *Notes sur les Chemins de Fer du Brésil*; Branner, *The Railways of Brazil*; Pinheiro, "Chemins de Fer"; Castro, *Treatise on the South American Railways*, 344–52; Sá, *Brazilian Railways*; U.S. Department of State, "Railways in Brazil"; State of São Paulo, Department of Agriculture, Commerce, and Public Works, *Railroads in the State of São Paulo*; U.K. Foreign Office, Department of Overseas Trade, "Report on the Railway Systems of Brazil"; Pessôa, *Guia da Estrada de Ferro Central do Brasil*; Silva, *Política e Legislação de*

Estradas de Ferro; Cunha, *Estudo Descriptivo da Viação Ferrea do Brazil*; Wiener, "The Railways of Brazil"; and Duncan, *Public and Private Operation of Railways in Brazil.*

9. For the main national transport and communications plans before 1914, see Ministério dos Transportes, *Planos de Viação*, 31–97.

10. By 1874, 122 railroad concessions were in operation, under construction, or under study (see Rebouças, *Garantia de Juros*, 284).

11. For evidence on the price of iron and iron rails, see Mitchell, *British Historical Statistics*, 763; and U.S. Bureau of the Census, *Historical Statistics of the United States*, 208–9.

12. On this process generally, see Edelstein, *Overseas Investment in the Age of High Imperialism*; Stone, *The Composition and Distribution of British Investment in Latin America*; Ice, "British Direct Investments in Brazil up to 1901"; and St. Angel, "British Investment in Brazilian Railroads."

13. Major railroad decrees through 1880 are reproduced in Pessôa, *Estudo Descriptivo das Estradas de Ferro do Brazil.* The principal guides to Brazilian national railroad law are Coruja, *Repertório*; Sá, *Código da Viação Ferrea do Brasil*; and, importantly, the sixteen-volume set by Paiva, *Legislação Ferroviária Federal do Brasil.* None of these provide complete texts of the frequent and lengthy acts and decrees related to the regulation of service and rates, which may be found in the published *Leis do Brasil* for the respective year, or in the *Diário Oficial.* Valuable railroad legal compendia for the larger states include Campista, *Compilação*; Silva, *A Reforma das Tarifas*; and, to a lesser degree, Mesquita, *Viação Ferrea da Bahia.*

14. For the era's most sophisticated normative analysis of the need for dividend guarantees, by one of Brazil's most prominent engineers and publicists, see Rebouças, *Garantia de Juros.*

15. "Retrospecto Commércial de 1874," *JC* (1875), 16–17.

16. Garner, "In Pursuit of Order," 352–436.

17. Ministério da Fazenda, *Consultas*, 5:35–72, 485–87, 509–11, 617–19; Senado Federal, *Atas do Conselho de Estado*, 5:176–99, 6:384–434, 9:5–56.

18. Fishlow, *American Railroads and the Transformation of the Antebellum Economy*, 192–93.

19. Such obligations fell on the central government in cases like the Recife and San Francisco Railway, and the Bahia and San Francisco Railway, where operating deficits were chronic.

20. The most prominent example of subvention was the original line of the Leopoldina, in Minas Gerais; see Pessôa, *Estudo Descriptivo das Estradas de Ferro do Brazil*, 313.

21. Galvão, *Notícia Sobre as Estradas de Ferro do Brasil*, 20–21.

22. *SAJ*, 1 April 1880; 31 March 1881; 4 August 1881; 24 November 1881; 1 February 1883.

23. Fishlow, "Lessons from the Past"; Stone, "British Long-Term Investment in Latin America," 329; Stone, *British Investment in Latin America*; Edelstein, *Overseas Investment in the Age of High Imperialism*; Davis and Huttenback, *Mammon and the Pursuit of Empire*, 30–57.

24. Graham, *Britain and the Onset of Modernization in Brazil*, 51–72.

25. Wilkins, "The Free-Standing Company," 265–77.

26. Adler, *British Investment in American Railways*; Davis and Cull, *International Capital Markets and American Economic Growth.*

27. *SAJ* (6 February 1886, 72) put the value of British investments in Brazil at almost 47 million pounds sterling, with Argentina close behind at 45.6 million pounds.

28. Rippy, *British Investments in Latin America*, 151.

29. Ribenboim, "Uma Análise da Rentabilidade," 12; see also Ferguson, *The House of Rothschild*, 345.

30. El-Kareh, *Filha Branca de Mãe Preta*, 51. In addition to holding railroad securities among their assets, banks also extended short-term credit to railroads (see Hanley, "Capital Markets in the Coffee Economy," 238–45).

31. El-Kareh, *Filha Branca de Mãe Preta*, 50–51.

32. Mattoon, "The Companhia Paulista de Estradas de Ferro," 62–65, appendix D.

33. Ibid., 62–65.

34. Shareholders are listed in *Histórico da Companhia Mogyana de Estradas de Ferro e Navegação*, 13; occupations are derived from *Almanak da Província de São Paulo*, 481–92.

35. *SAJ*, 9 June 1881, 12.

36. The sample includes all the directors for each of those years, drawn from *Bradshaw's Railway Manual*.

37. On "ornamental" and other varieties of directors in British overseas companies, see Wilkins, "The Free-Standing Company," 265–69.

38. See the entries for these companies in *Bradshaw's Railway Manual* for 1867.

39. These other lines included Britain's South Eastern Railway, urban lines in London that later became part of the present-day tube system, the Zafra and Huelva Railway in Spain, the Buenos Aires Great Southern Railway, the Central Argentine, and the Central Uruguay; see *Bradshaw's Railway Manual* for 1900.

40. On Farquhar's various business activities in Latin America, see Gauld, *The Last Titan*. On his Brazilian railroad interests, see Saes, "Os Investimentos Franceses no Brasil," 26–33.

41. Not only did the project require Brazil's highest court to rule on whether central government held authority over pre-Republican railroad concessions, but the resulting expulsion of farmers from the lands transferred to the company under the court's ruling was a precipitating factor in the outbreak of violent conflict in Brazil's south. On the railroad and the violence following the revocation of land titles, see Thomé, *Trem de Ferro*; Queiroz, *Messianismo e Conflito Social*; Diacon, *Millenarian Vision, Capitalist Reality*.

42. On Mauá's banking activities, see Barman, "Business and Government in Imperial Brazil"; Caldeira, *Mauá*, 365–66, 443–46; Mauá, *Autobiografía*, 116–18, 211–78; and Joslin, *A Century of Banking in Latin America*, 69–79.

43. Marchant, *Viscount of Mauá*, 18–22; 31–46; Mauá, *Autobiografía*, 19–23; Caldeira, *Mauá*, 54–70.

44. Mauá, *Autobiografía*, 100–104; Marchant, *Viscount of Mauá*, 49–61.

45. See the operating returns in *Relatório da Imperial Companhia*, 1857, 5–6.

46. See Mauá, *Autobiografía*, 93–278, for Mauá's own description of his myriad business activities up to his bankruptcy in 1875. Mauá himself avoided taking a position in financing the Recife line, but invested a considerable amount in constructing the São Paulo line, much of which he failed to recover (see Caldeira, *Mauá*, 335–36; Mauá, *Autobiografía*, 60–64, 150–62).

47. *Almanak Administrativo, Mercantil e Industrial*, 1252, 1307.

48. Ibid., 1213.

49. Moura, *Governos e Congressos*, 338.

50. Colson, "The Destruction of a Revolution," appendix 1, entry 369.

51. On the Prados, see ibid., entries 517 and 518; see also Levi, *The Prados of São Paulo, Brazil*, 138–58.

52. On the immigrant industrialists, see Dean, *The Industrialization of São Paulo*; on Mexico's early industrialists, see Haber, *Industry and Underdevelopment*.

53. Duncan, *Public and Private Operation of Railways in Brazil*, 28–30.

54. *SAJ*, 19 September 1884; *SAJ*, 1 November 1884; *SAJ*, 2 October 1886.

55. Duncan, *Public and Private Operation of Railways in Brazil*, 50–57; Topik, *The Political Economy of the Brazilian State*, 93–99.

56. Duncan, *Public and Private Operation of Railways in Brazil*, 36–40, details these instances.

57. Ferreira, "A Estrada de Ferro de Baturité," 12–16.

58. Duncan, *Public and Private Operation of Railways in Brazil*, 66.

59. This is treated extensively in Wileman, *Brazilian Exchange*; Calógeras, *A Política Monetária do Brasil*, 216–319; Franco, *Reforma Monetária e Instabilidada Durante a Transição Republicana*, 115–42; and Franco, *Década Republicana*, 33–60.

60. Rodrigues, *Resgate das Estradas de Ferro do Recife a S. Francisco*; Calógeras, *A Política Monetária do Brasil*, 351–65.

61. Duncan, *Public and Private Operation of Railways in Brazil*, 66.

62. Topik, "The Evolution of the Economic Role of the Brazilian State," 330–31.

63. Rodrigues, *Resgate das Estradas de Ferro do Recife a S. Francisco*, 8–96; Ribeiro, "As Garantias Ferroviárias no Brasil," 38–52.

64. The latter point is the chief conclusion in Fendt, "Investimentos Inglêses no Brasil," 535–36; and Ribeiro, "As Garantias Ferroviárias no Brasil," 67."

65. Chapter 6, below, documents the components and magnitude of income leakages resulting from railroads.

66. This percentage varies slightly depending on which estimate of national income is employed; here, it is based on the "domestic income" measure (effectively, the GDP) from Haddad, "Crescimento Econômico do Brasil," 27. The various estimates of Brazilian national income available for this year are discussed further in Chapter 1, n. 4.

CHAPTER 4

1. The savings on transport costs that railroads created serve as an index of the aggregate productivity increase, or efficiency gains, the railroad provided the economy as a whole (see Fishlow, *American Railroads and the Transformation of the Antebellum Economy*, 223; and Metzer, "Railroads and the Efficiency of Internal Markets," 62).

2. Metzer, "Railroads and the Efficiency of Internal Markets."

3. The simple model of the economy that underpins this analysis is that used, implicitly or explicitly, in the various studies of railroad social savings. A thorough derivation of it in axiomatic terms is found in Metzer, *Some Economic Aspects of Railroad Development in Tsarist Russia*, 3–26. For a discussion of the theory, estimating techniques, and main assumptions of the concept of the social savings, see Appendix A.

4. See *O Agricultor Brasileiro* 1 (December 1854).

5. Bovet, "A Indústria Mineral na Província de Minas Gerais," 39.

6. Alden, "Price Movements in Brazil," 358.

7. Quoted in Argollo, *Memória Descriptiva*, 73–74.

8. Local prices in 1854 and 1906 are derived from *município*-level estimates of physical output and crop value; see "Quadro Estatístico de Alguns Estabelecimentos Ruraes da Província de S. Paulo," in *Discurso com que . . . Senhor Dr. José Antonio Saraiva . . . Abrio A Assemblea Legislativa Provincial*; and State of São Paulo, Repartição Estatística e do Archivo, *Annuário Estatístico*, 4–9.

9. McAlpin, *Subject to Famine*, 148–51; McAlpin, "Railroads, Prices, and Peasant Rationality"; Hurd, "Railways and the Expansion of Markets in India"; and Metzer, "Railroad Development and Market Integration."

10. This is certainly what the data in Chapter 6 on the shifting composition of both rail freight and the economy's output mix suggest.

11. Values reported in *SAJ*, 8 January 1879. Real rates of appreciation were derived by adjusting the reported values by the extended wholesale price index for Rio de Janeiro, discussed below.

12. Assembling the desired time series on railroad operations in Brazil is rendered difficult by three major obstacles. For a detailed discussion of these, see Appendix B.

13. See Appendix B for detail on the output estimates and their sources.

14. The techniques employed in estimating the average haul are detailed in Appendix B.

15. Fogel, "Notes on the Social Saving Controversy."

16. Fogel, *Railroads and American Economic Growth*, 26–29.

17. The reported average water charge for 1870 was $046 per ton-kilometer; in 1913 prices, this was $064 (rate is derived from *Anais da Câmara dos Deputados*, 11 September 1882, 407).

18. The data on arrivals in Recife may be found in Eisenberg, *The Sugar Industry in Pernambuco*, 54–55, as well as in the annual reports of the directors of the Great Western of Brazil Railway Company.

19. "Retrospecto Commércial de 1879," *JC* (1880), 55; "Retrospecto Commércial de 1892," *JC* (1893), tabela 7; "Retrospecto Commércial de 1909," *JC* (1910), tabela 17.

20. Brazil's largest mule market virtually collapsed in the years following the introduction of railroads in São Paulo; see Klein, "A Oferta de Muares no Brasil Central," 347–69.

21. Holmstrom, *Railways and Roads in Pioneer Development Overseas*, 34–36, 56.

22. Brazil had 3.2 million mules in 1912, plus an additional 7.3 million horses (*Annuario Estadístico do Brazil*, 1908–1912, 2:3) With more than 10 million horses and mules in 1912, by all appearances Brazil could have supplied the animals required to carry freight. Yet a very large share of these were draft animals used in farming, and their diversion to transport would have still left a large gap in animal supplies.

23. Rates were higher in the wet season when travel was more difficult, road conditions worse, and the risk of loss of animals and goods was greater.

24. On the improvements and construction of a relatively more direct route (the "Estrada do Vergueiro"), see Momsen, *Routes Over the Serra do Mar*, 60.

25. Indeed, labor was sufficiently scarce to sustain the institution of slavery until 1888, and to lead landowners and politicians to foster European immigration—precisely from

the European economies with high unemployment—from the 1880s on.

26. The present analysis assumes that railways played no role in increasing the stock of productive factors.

27. *O Agricultor Brasileiro* 1 (December 1854): 13–15. Further evidence of the high costs to farmers posed by providing their own transport services is provided by Diniz, "Ferrovia e Expansão Cafeeira," 829–30.

28. MACOP, *Relatório . . . 1864*, 4.

29. Província de Pernambuco, *Relatório Apresentado ao Exm. Sr. Presidente*, 16.

30. In the case of the United States, for example, Rothenberg has called into question the use of market freight rates as the basis for imputing the cost of transport to farmers who carried their own goods to market. However, the estimated charges for self-haul by farmers in the United States are actually quite close to the more plausible contemporary commercial rates. This is unsurprising, given that Rothenberg imputes the cost of all but one of the transport inputs (oxen, wagons, and the like) at market rental rates. The labor component of her estimate values labor time at on-farm rates, rather than at the value of teamster labor. This may well be the reason her nineteenth-century rates are $0.18 per ton-mile rather than the commercial rate of $0.20 per ton-mile. The 5 percent difference between the two is small, as one would expect in a reasonably efficient market for transport services; see Rothenberg, *From Market-Places to a Market Economy*, 89–95.

31. The indices are based on a mix of wholesale and retail prices for nine commodities: sugar, rice, codfish, coffee, jerked beef, wheat flour, manioc flour, beans, and butter (see Lobo, *História do Rio de Janeiro*, 748–51). Three different weighting schemes exist for the index, drawn from Brazilian consumer budgets for 1856, 1919, and 1946. The 1856 index, in particular, possesses a certain intuitive appeal. Neither pre-rail overland-transport services, nor its main inputs, were internationally traded. The 1856 weighting assigns greater importance to those Brazilian agricultural products that were less traded internationally, such as jerked beef, manioc flour, and black beans.

32. Indeed, the variant using 1856 weights figures nicely as a Laspeyres index, while the version using 1919 weights can be appropriately taken as a Paasche index. Laspeyres weighting schemes, using early-period budget shares, overstate the rise in consumer prices, whereas Paasche indices, based on terminal period budget shares, understate that increase. While a compromise solution between the two indices exists—a geometric average of them along the lines of a Fisher "ideal" index—here the index with 1919 weights alone is used as the pre-rail deflator for the first estimate of the direct social savings.

33. There were three options available. The first was to use the extended wholesale price index described in the text. Another possibility was to deflate pre-rail charges by the price of one of its inputs, labor. The wages of unskilled labor in Rio de Janeiro rose almost threefold between 1864 and 1913, while the wages of bricklayers more than doubled over the same interval, and wages for carpenters more than tripled (see Lobo, *História do Rio de Janeiro*, 804–5). Those indices are relevant since unskilled and moderately skilled labor was a major input into pre-rail freight transport. Given that muleteers carried goods from the hinterland to the city, they would have been regularly updated on urban wages, and thus on the opportunity cost of their own time and work (see Gumiero, "Os Tropeiros na História de Goiás," 59). Alternately, given the presumed importance of Brazil's export sector in the economy's output mix, and the predominance of export freight among transportables in the pre-rail era, the use of an export price index was a third option. A

Divisia index of the prices of Brazil's eight leading export commodities exhibits an even more modest rise from 1864 to 1913 than the wage series, slightly more than doubling (for the Divisia index, see Summerhill, "The Brazilian Export Sector"). Since it is based on port-of-exit prices, which were declining relative to interior prices, thanks to the actual reduction in transport costs brought about by railroads, it likely understates the rise in the cost of non-rail transport.

34. Catão, "A New Wholesale Price Index for Brazil."

35. Using AR1 regression to control for autocorrelation:

$$\ln\text{(wholesale)} = -.0845 + 0.579 \ln\text{(CPI)}$$
$$\phantom{\ln\text{(wholesale)} = } (-1.6) \quad (8.81)$$
$$R_2 = .64$$

36. The price level for Salvador similarly doubled over the interval 1864–1913. To obtain the index, price indices for individual commodities were weighted by their output shares derived from the 1919–1920 economic census for all of Brazil. The raw prices are from Mattoso, "Au Nouveau Monde."

37. MVOP, Inspectoria Federal das Estradas, *EEF*, 1913.

38. On the São Paulo routes, these distances were indeed virtually identical, as a comparison of length of track and pre-rail road distances reveals. Elsewhere, the haul by rail might well differ from the distances merchandise was carried before the railroad. One conjectures that the railroad, on average, shortened the length of haul in Brazil.

39. Of course, a large, expanded road system in the absence of railroads would have probably been subsidized in response to the same kinds of political and regulatory pressures. Only if the unit subsidy to road shipment in the counterfactual economy were less than the subsidy actually paid on railroad freight would any reduction to the estimated social savings be justified.

40. The lesser of the two estimates of guarantee payments in Brazil and London is taken from Ministério de Fazenda, *Balanço da Receita e Despeza da República no Exercício de 1913*, table 135; the higher estimate is from MVOP, *Relatório . . . 1913*, 21.

41. MVOP, *Relatório . . . 1913*, 21.

42. Note, however, that if the freight rate was subsidized, failing to reflect the true resource costs, and the demand for that service was anything other than perfectly inelastic, then the level of freight service produced would be too "high" at the 1913 railroad charges. In that case, the reduction in the quantity of output required to pull unit charges in line with resource costs would serve to reduce the subsidy required by the railroad.

43. This is based on the GDP estimate for 1913 reported in Contador and Haddad, "Produto Real, Moêda, e Preços." Other estimates exist, but are roughly the same. See Haddad, *Crescimento do Produto Real no Brasil*.

44. More precisely, they would approach a "least-upper-bound" measure. This is due to the attempts made to bias the unit-transport cost savings downward, and because the measure here excludes resource savings on insurance and inventory charges that would have existed without the railroad.

45. A diagrammatic exposition of the lower-bound savings may be found in the methodological appendix in Coatsworth, *Growth Against Development*. A cautionary note is in order, however, because Coatsworth's treatment of the lower-bound social saving ig-

nores a potentially thorny issue. More formally, because the adjusted, or "lower-bound," measure of direct social saving departs from the use of actual 1913 levels of freight service, the social saving can no longer be modeled purely in terms of production in the transport and non-transport sectors. Additional assumptions permit the measurement of the lower-bound social savings as either the consumers' surplus in the market for freight-transport services, the compensating variation, or the equivalent variation. Only in the case where the social welfare function is quasi-linear are the three of those measures the same. See Appendix A, below.

46. Calculated from Milet, *A Lavoura da Cana de Açucar*, 47–61.

47. There is, of course, no one true elasticity. The goal here is to bound the range of likely values of the price elasticity of demand for freight services that prevailed in Brazil in the late nineteenth and early twentieth centuries.

48. The price of coal is taken from the annual reports of the Companhia Paulista; GDP and population are from Contador and Haddad, "Produto Real, Moêda, e Preços"; track, output, and the freight charge are from the series discussed in Appendix B.

49. These two are likely among the most important organizational changes of the era. Control over the privatization of land in the public domain devolved to state governments under the Constitution of 1891, accelerating the modernization of rural property rights. In São Paulo, for example, the ability to gain clear title to property was no doubt an important factor in attracting immigrants. At the same time, the emergence of that institutional feature may well have been an outcome induced by railroads in the state, which, by raising land values, created incentives to establish mechanisms by which rural property could be securely owned and transferred. Capital market reforms in the early 1890s reduced capital costs to industry and promoted the startup of joint-stock companies, helping to pull resources into high value-added manufacturing activities (see Haber, "The Efficiency Consequences of Institutional Change"). This raised GDP, but the magnitude of that increase was likely much less than that afforded by lower transport costs. Extreme upper-bound measures of the gains from (1) declining industrial concentration, and (2) higher total factor productivity arising from access to the capital market, sum to less than 3 percent of GDP in 1915 (see Summerhill, "Notes on Institutional Change").

50. This is because the various studies specify different counterfactual modes of shipment. It is difficult to compare social savings estimates internationally without extensive adjustments, given the wildly different specifications of what social savings comprise in each case. For an attempt to make such comparisons, see O'Brien, "Transport and Economic Growth in Western Europe," 347. For the present analysis, the freight that Brazilian railroads actually hauled in 1913 is assumed to have been carried by the mode of transport that prevailed at the time that railroads were first being constructed, namely, mules and carts.

51. Fishlow, *American Railroads and the Transformation of the Antebellum Economy*, 37, 52.

52. Fogel, *Railroads and American Economic Growth*, chapters 2 and 3.

53. Metzer, *Some Economic Aspects of Railroad Development in Tsarist Russia*, 50–51. Metzer put direct social savings on freight services in Russia at a little less than 900 million rubles, or 4.57 percent of a rough estimate of Russian GNP in 1907. Using Gregory's more recent estimates of Russian net national product (see his *Russian National Income*), that same measure rises to some 6.6 percent of NNP. If the demand for freight transport services in Tsarist Russia was as inelastic as Metzer suggests, and if his upper-bound estimate

is in fact close to the "true" magnitude of the gains resulting from the construction of rail-roads (meaning that it warrants no downward adjustment to reflect a reduction in the quan-tity of freight services, given an increase in the relative price of transport), then the savings estimates appear a good deal more impressive in light of Gregory's NNP figure.

54. Hawke, *Railways and Economic Growth in England and Wales*, 196.

55. Gomez Mendoza, *Ferrocarriles y Cambio Económico en España*, 95–96.

56. Coatsworth, *Growth Against Development*, 102–4. Coatsworth later reworked the 1800–1910 GDP figures, implying a reduction in the share of the Mexican economy ac-counted for the social savings. The revised estimate of GDP in 1910 was 1.6 billion pesos (in 1900 pesos). This means that the upper-bound "A" estimate of the social saving is only 28.5 percent of GDP, not the 38.5 percent reported. And the upper-bound "B" estimate is 18.4 percent of GDP, not the 35 percent reported. Leaving all of Coatsworth's other as-sumptions unchanged and revising only GDP means that the upper-bound "A" estimate is too high by fully one-third, overstating DSS by 10 percent of GDP, and that the "B" es-timate is too high by fully 90 percent, overstating DSS by 16.6 percent of GDP. Of course, loosening Coatsworth's various other restrictive assumptions, which serve to push down the estimate, would then work to raise it back up.

57. See Coatsworth, *Growth Against Development*, 126, in which more than half of the benefits generated by railroad are assigned to Mexico's export sector, the bulk of which was comprised of freight shipped to the United States. Given the direct connection of the United States and Mexico by rail in an area deprived of cheap alternative modes of ship-ment, a joint social saving exercise leaves Mexico bereft of the market for much of what its railroads hauled.

58. The construction costs are derived on a line-by-line basis from information in the *EEF* volumes, and in cases where the capital accounts for large lines are available, from their respective company reports. For the Central, Paulista, Mogiana, and Sorocabana lines, the data come from the outlays on road, rolling stock, and structures as presented in their respective balance sheets for 1913. One large line of 1,300 kilometers, and one small line of 35 kilometers, did not present information on the cost of construction, and per-kilometer construction costs were imputed for these lines using the average for all other lines.

59. McClelland, "Social Rates of Return on American Railroads." St. Angel argued that Brazil overinvested in railroads (see "British Investment in Brazilian Railroads," 13), as did Villela and Suzigan (*Política do Governo e Crescimento da Economia Brasileira*, 389–90). Until the present study, empirical analyses of Brazilian railroads have considered private rates of return but not social rates of return, providing only a partial picture of the return on railroad capital (see Fendt, "Investimentos Inglêses no Brasil"; Ribeiro, "As Garantias Ferroviárias no Brasil"; and Rippy, *British Investments in Latin America*).

60. David, *Technical Choice, Innovation, and Economic Growth*, 307–14.

61. Constant returns to scale exist when a 10 percent increase in all inputs leads to a 10 percent increase in output.

62. Taken from Table 7.5, this volume.

63. Haber, "The Efficiency Consequences of Institutional Change," table 4.

64. Ribenboim, "Uma Análise da Rentabilidade," 32.

65. A more detailed discussion of this problem is found in Chapter 7.

66. Although no estimates of the return to human capital or investments in school-ing in Brazil exist for this period, education is one activity that not only exhibits strong

social returns, but also allows the individual in whom the investment is made to capture a large share of those returns. For an elaboration, see Becker, *Human Capital*. For an historical application in this spirit to the impact of schooling in the early-twentieth-century U.S. south, see Margo, *Race and Schooling in the South*.

CHAPTER 5

1. Boyd and Walton, "The Social Saving."

2. Coatsworth, *Growth Against Development*, 2, 65; and Metzer, *Some Economic Aspects of Railroad Development in Tsarist Russia*, 52.

3. U.S. figures derived from information in Boyd and Walton, "The Social Saving," 244–45. Figures on England and Wales are from Hawke, *Railways and Economic Growth in England and Wales*, 33.

4. LRC, *Report of the Proceedings*, 1905, 5, noted that most of the Leopoldina's passenger services were for commuters. One implication of this is that the travel-time savings estimated below may well be too low. Around the larger cities, manufacturing workers likely comprised a far greater proportion of rail travelers than their share of the overall population would suggest. By precisely how much more may be revealed through further research.

5. Estrada de Ferro Recife ao São Francisco, *Relatório*.

6. Boyd and Walton, "The Social Saving"; and Hawke, "Railway Passenger Traffic in 1865."

7. See the railway notices in the *Anglo-Brazilian Times* (24 January 1880).

8. Boyd and Walton, "The Social Saving"; Winston, "Conceptual Developments in the Economics of Transportation," 74; and Owen and Phillips, "The Characteristics of Railway Passenger Demand," 241, 252.

9. Brazilian passenger trains typically included an animal car, not for livestock, but for the mounts of passengers who needed to travel locally upon their arrival.

10. This assumes that mount ownership was for local travel, or purposes other than long-distance passenger travel. If people bought and maintained these animals solely for travel over distances equal to the typical length of journey by rail, then traveling by mount was not a "free" service at all; such an inconsistency makes the estimate of direct social saving here too high.

11. Winston, "Conceptual Developments in the Economics of Transportation," 77; Gronau, *The Value of Time in Passenger Transportation*; De Vany, "The Revealed Value of Time in Air Travel," 81; and Beesley, "The Value of Time Spent in Travelling," 182.

12. For the various assumptions applied to valuing travel time, see Boyd and Walton, "The Social Saving," 251–53; Coatsworth, *Growth Against Development*, 71–72; de Vries, "Barges and Capitalism," 227–30, 237–44; and Metzer, *Some Economic Aspects of Railroad Development in Tsarist Russia*, 56–63.

13. The identity employed for computing total passenger social savings in the Brazilian case is:

$$DSS_{PAX} = \left[(\alpha w_A + \eta w_N) \left[\frac{2Q_1}{t_D} - \frac{2Q_1}{t_R} + \frac{Q_2}{t_F} - \frac{Q_2}{t_R} \right] \right] + \int_{P_{R1}}^{P_D} DP^\epsilon dp - (Q_2 P_{R2})$$

where:

α is the share of agricultural workers in the population;

η is the share of non-agricultural workers in the population;

w_A is the hourly wage equivalent in agriculture;

w_N is the hourly wage equivalent in the "non-agricultural" sector;

Q_1 is the quantity of first-class passenger-kilometers of service produced by rail, with Q_1

   $= DP^\varepsilon$ and ε being the price elasticity of demand;

Q_2 is the quantity of second-class passenger-kilometers of service produced by rail;

PD is the passenger-kilometer charge by diligence;

PR_1 is the first-class rail charge per passenger-kilometer;

PR_2 is the second-class rail charge per passenger-kilometer;

t_R is the average speed by rail in kilometers per hour;

t_D is the average speed by diligence; and

t_F is the average speed by foot.

The first term (in brackets) is the value of the time saved by the higher speed of the railroad. The identity encompasses the assumptions made in the text, namely that the savings on time was only for those travelers who were in the labor force; that the share of workers among all travelers was equal to the labor force participation rate; that "working" first-class passengers valued their time at twice the wage of their assigned sector of employment; and that "working" second-class passengers valued their time at the wage of their assigned sector. The constituent parts of this expression are elaborated in Tables 5.3, 5.4, and 5.5.

   14. MVOP, Inspectoria Federal das Estradas, *EEF*, 1913, and annual and semester company reports for the San Paulo Railway, Great Western of Brazil Railway, Leopoldina Railway, Central do Brasil, Companhia Paulista, Companhia Mogiana, and Companhia Sorocabana.

   15. The seven lines accounted for 85 percent of all rail passenger service in 1913.

   16. This rate appeared in advertisements in the *Correio Paulistano* in the early months of 1865. Because it was the only advertised rate, and because it was that of a new stagecoach line seeking passengers and a niche in a market that already had several suppliers, one suspects that it may be a bit low.

   17. Drawn from the censuses of 1900 and 1920, as summarized in IBGE, *Estatísticas Históricas do Brasil*. Improved labor-force estimates await revision of the labor-force data in both censuses, each of which suffers from omissions.

   18. This share may be compared to similar computations for Russia and Mexico. In the latter case, half of all travelers were assumed to be nonproductive, while in the former 50 percent of the total travel time for adult travelers is taken as productive time; see Coatsworth, *Growth Against Development*, 69; and Metzer, *Some Economic Aspects of Railroad Development in Tsarist Russia*, 62.

   19. Drawn from MACOP, Directoria do Serviço de Inspecção e Fomento Agrícola, *Aspectos da Economia Rural Brasileira*.

   20. Oakenfull, *Brazil* (1913), 564–67.

   21. Holloway, *Immigrants on the Land*, 83.

   22. See *Correio Paulistano*, 20 June 1865; *Correio Paulistano*, 15 January 1865; Silva, *Geographia dos Transportes no Brasil*, 90; and *Sul de Minas*, 30 August 1861, 1.

23. Speeds in earlier decades were considerably slower, with railroads moving as slow as 20 kilometers per hour (*Correio Paulistano*, 27 December 1865, 2).

24. Contador and Haddad, "Produto Real, Moêda, e Preços."

25. Coatsworth, *Growth Against Development*, 71–72.

26. Metzer, *Some Economic Aspects of Railroad Development in Tsarist Russia*, 75–76.

27. Boyd and Walton, "The Social Saving," 249–50.

28. Hawke, *Railways and Economic Growth in England and Wales*, 49.

29. In this case, the economy's gains from railroad passenger services rival the benefits conferred by institutional changes that improved dramatically the nation's industrial capital markets.

30. Appreciable inter-regional movements of the population, in response to shifting regional economic prospects, transpired between 1890 and 1930. The principal exception was the northeast, which experienced relatively little net migration (see Merrick and Graham, "População e Desenvolvimento no Brasil," 57–58).

31. Laerne, *Brazil and Java*, 191.

CHAPTER 6

1. Burns, *The Poverty of Progress*, 136; Burns, *History of Brazil*, 161. Assessments of the consequences of railroad development in Brazil that indict, in varying degrees, foreign investment or the railroad's role in promoting exports include: Evans, *Dependent Development*, which claims that railroad "concessions and interest guarantees were services to foreign capital" (85), and that "the predilections of British capital" locked Brazil into the classic pattern of dependence (61); Frank, *Capitalism and Underdevelopment in Latin America*, in which railroads were part and parcel of the overall process of underdevelopment and the export of surplus value (145–74); and Graham, "Sepoys and Imperialists," where British railroads manifested imperialistic control in Brazil (35–36).

2. Those connections are further explored in the next chapter, which reconsiders the role of foreign-owned railroads in particular, with special attention to government policies on subsidy and regulation.

3. Fogel, "Notes on the Social Saving Controversy," 5, 45.

4. The pioneering study of Mexico makes a compelling case for considering the impact of railroads in Latin America in the first two of these areas; see Coatsworth, *Growth Against Development*, 140–45.

5. Burns, *The Poverty of Progress*, 138; Zalduendo, *Libras y Rieles*, 102, 222–24; Rabello, "Os Caminhos de Ferro da Província do Rio de Janeiro," 35–36.

6. Examples of classic statements on the presumed vulnerability of the economy to the "excessive" dependence on exports are found in Furtado, *Economic Growth of Brazil*, 184–85, 193–203; and Frank, *Capitalism and Underdevelopment in Latin America*, 164–71.

7. The canonical case is Porfirian Mexico; see Coatsworth, *Growth Against Development*, 122–31. For recent findings disputing the export intensity of Mexico's railroads, see Kuntz Ficker, *Empresa Extranjera y Mercado Interno*, 211–348.

8. Matos, *Café e Ferrovias*, 77–143; Camargo, *Crescimento da População no Estado de São Paulo*, 157–85.

9. Railroads probably dominated total investment in physical capital before 1914. A rough estimate of gross annual railroad construction outlays, derived from company reports and the government's statistical volumes, swamped the value of machinery imports

in every year but one between 1857 and 1913. Railroad investment may also have been mildly countercyclical with respect to the economy's business cycle. The correlation between estimated gross railroad outlays and real export earnings was only .58 from 1857 through 1913.

10. Less-direct backward linkages in Brazil are discussed in Lewis, "Railways and Industrialization"; and Lamounier, "The 'Labour Question' in Nineteenth-Century Brazil."

11. For an illuminating discussion of these concerns in Brazil, see Cechin, "A Construção e Operação de Ferrovia no Brasil," 14, 47.

12. Burns, *The Poverty of Progress*, 138.

13. LRC, *Report of the Directors*, 1906, 8; Costa, *Diccionário de Estradas de Ferro*, 2:85–86.

14. The notion of leakage derives from the elementary "circular-flow-of-income" model of the economy, in which expenditures on imported goods and services escape from the annual stream of national income, whereas revenues from exports create "injections" into that same stream; see Lipsey, *Introduction to Positive Economics*, 485–92. Importantly, this view of the economy differs from the resource-savings model employed in the previous chapter. The latter aims to identify a mechanism of growth, while the former merely traces the flow of some components of GDP in any one year. Only with certain leaps of faith can "leakage" be taken as either an overt loss, or opportunity cost, to the economy, as detailed further below.

15. The Report of the Great Western Railway in 1895 discusses a "general" strike among its workers; that the strike was general suggests that those workers were Brazilians being pressed by the rising prices of the period (see GW, *Report of the Directors*, 1895, 4).

16. While proof solely by analogy is never compelling, it is worth noting that in Mexico, a roughly analogous case to Brazil where there was substantial foreign investment in the rail sector, the estimated remittances and consumption of imports on the part of railroad workers came to less than 4 percent of the total leakage (see Coatsworth, *Growth Against Development*, 143–44).

17. *IMM*, November 1913, 637–39.

18. See Brown, *The South American Year Book*, 66–69; MVOP, *Relatório . . . 1913*, and MVOP, Inspectoria Federal das Estradas, *EEF*, 1913.

19. Wileman, *The Brazilian Year Book, 1909*, 807–8; Brown, *The South American Year Book*, 112–15.

20. Rodrigues, *Resgate das Estradas de Ferro do Recife a S. Francisco*; Duncan, *Public and Private Operation of Railways in Brazil*, 44–66; Topik, *The Political Economy of the Brazilian State*, 94–98; Fendt, "Investimentos Inglêses no Brasil," 525–26; Ribeiro, "As Garantias Ferroviárias no Brasil," 38–53.

21. Imports taken from Ministério da Fazenda, *Commércio Exterior do Brasil*, 15–27.

22. Cechin, "A Construção e Operação de Ferrovia no Brasil," 51.

23. Scattered figures from the Central do Brazil, Leopoldina, and the Companhia Paulista, found in their company reports, show that wood was used as fuel through 1913. The Leopoldina quite consciously selected its mix of wood and coal in light of changes in the exchange rate (LRC, *Report of the Proceedings*, 1907, 18).

24. Zumblick, *Teresa Cristina*, 136–37; Waters, *The Donna Thereza Christina Railway*, 10–13.

25. MVOP, Inspectoria Federal das Estradas, *EEF*, 1913. The estimated relationship, constraining the intercept to be zero, is:

Tons of Coal = .00061 (ton-kilometers of freight)
(15.6)
$R_2 = 0.84$

26. Of course, given the dearth of coal suitable for railroad use in Brazil, this strategy might well have led to an even more rapid deforestation of the Mata Atlantica, creating through environmental degradation an additional social cost of unknown magnitude.

27. Gomez Mendoza, *Ferrocarriles y Cambio Económico en España*, 143–54.

28. Atack and Passell, *A New Economic View of American History*, 454.

29. The rise of the railroad sector in the context of an early-developing industrial sector may well have had strong spillovers later on, despite the weak linkages in the early period. Railroads in the late-nineteenth-century United States were important users of a variety of inputs that likely had important implications for the course of industry. On the importance of resource exploitation in the uniquely American scheme of development, see Wright, "American Industrial Success."

30. Cardoso and Brignoli, *História Econômica da América Latina*, 236–37; Donghi, *The Contemporary History of Latin America*, 122–23; Bulmer-Thomas, *The Economic History of Latin America since Independence*, 106; Stein and Stein, *The Colonial Heritage of Latin America*, 149–50; Frank, *Capitalism and Underdevelopment in Latin America*, 168–69; Matos, *Café e Ferrovias*, 77–143; Burns, *A History of Brazil*, 160–61, 169; Evans, "Continuities and Contradictions in the Evolution of Brazilian Dependence," 33–35. Only Leff has detected the relative dynamism of the non-export sector in the Brazilian economy as a whole; see Leff, *Underdevelopment and Development in Brazil*, 146–49.

31. Burns, *The Poverty of Progress*, 136.

32. Kravis, "The Role of Exports in Nineteenth-Century United States Economic Growth."

33. Export shares by commodity may be found in IBGE, *Repertório Estatístico do Brasil*, 89–90.

34. Ocampo, "El Mercado Mundial de Café," 136–38.

35. Castro, *As Empresas Estrangeiras no Brasil*, 28–56; Matos, *Café e Ferrovias*, 77–143.

36. Holloway, "Migration and Mobility," 165–258; Vangelista, *Os Braços da Lavoura*, 79–154.

37. This point is made in various ways in the methodological literature; see Foreman-Peck, "Railways and Late Victorian Economic Growth," 83–90.

38. The regression results, based on an AR1 procedure to control for autocorrelation are:

ln (coffee/total freight) = 17.9 – .01 Year
(1.43)   (–1.53)

where R_2 is 0.27, and the autocorrelation coefficient is .79 with a t-statistic of 8.6.

39. Coatsworth, *Growth Against Development*, 124–26.

40. All rates are for carrying 1 ton a distance of 200 kilometers, except again in the case of the San Paulo Railway, where the rates are twice those reported for a 100-kilometer haul.

41. If the demand for Brazil's exports was inelastic relative to supply, the burden of high freight rates on export goods would fall disproportionately on foreign consumers. The effect would push the terms of trade in *favor* of Brazil. For a discussion of export taxes and terms of trade effects in the U.S. case, see Harley, "The Antebellum American Tariff." For an estimate of Brazil's terms of trade, see Gonçalves, *Evolução das Relações Comerciais do Brasil com a Inglaterra.*

42. Similar gaps in export and non-export freight rates can be found in 1898. Cateysson, *Indicador Geral da Viação do Brasil,* provides rates for the major Brazilian railroads.

43. The results of regressing the export share of GDP on time, using ordinary least squares, for the two different income series for the period 1861–1913 are:

(A) ln (exports/GDP) = 12.1 − .0072 Year

               (5.2)   (−5.8)

R_2 = .39   d = 1.44

(B) ln (exports/GDP) = 27.8 − .015 Year

              (13.0) (−13.5)

R_2 = .78   d = 2.03

44. David, "Transport Innovation and Economic Growth"; Fogel, "Notes on the Social Saving Controversy," 39–44.

45. A diagrammatic representation of how railroads could enable factories to take advantage of increasing returns to scale inherent in the factory's technology is found in Atack, "Economies of Scale and Efficiency Gains," 322–26. However, that differs from railroad-induced scale economies. The former would be captured by the social savings estimate, and the latter would not because it arises at the level of the industry as a whole rather than at the level of the firm.

46. Denslow, "As Exportações e a Origem do Padrão de Industrialização Regional do Brasil," 23–24.

47. The parameters used are available in unpublished work by Stephen Haber. These results are robust with respect to the form of the production function. Both Cobb-Douglas and translog specifications result in the same elasticity of scale.

48. EFCB, *Relatório,* 1913, 110.

49. Ibid.

50. Textile output in 1913 is reported in the unpaginated production figures in CIB, *Relatório da Directoria.*

51. Haddad, *Crescimento do Produto Real no Brasil,* 130.

52. Let the value-added equal V, and V = $K^\alpha L^\beta$, where $\alpha + \beta = 1.042$. Then the diversion of the capital and labor required to produce the needed transport services in a constant-returns transport sector would reduce textile value-added by $1-(.867)^{1.042}$, or 13.8 percent.

53. Haddad, *Crescimento do Produto Real no Brasil,* 7.

54. Castro, "Relatório do Segundo Grupo," 3–73.

55. Jacob, *Minas Gerais no XXo Século,* 269–70.

56. Suzigan, *Indústria Brasileira,* 76–84; Versiani, *Industrial Investment in an "Export"*

Economy, 14–15.

57. Output is expressed as value of production, capital is the value of machinery and structures reported by the firm, and labor equals the number of workers. Data, by firm, is reported in CIB, *O Brasil*. The locations of the 172 textile firms for which complete data are available were plotted on contemporaneous maps found in Mello and Mello, *Atlas do Brazil*, to determine whether the firm was on the coast or inland. Any firm that did not locate within a locality on the coast, or on a waterway with obvious access to the sea, was recorded as "inland."

58. For the rising share of exports in Mexican GDP from 1877 to 1910, see Coatsworth, "The Decline of the Mexican Economy." For the increase in the share of U.S. GDP accounted for by exports, as well as other international comparisons, see Maddison, *Phases of Capitalist Development*, 44–60.

59. Burns, *The Poverty of Progress*, 134.

CHAPTER 7

1. North, *Structure and Change in Economic History*, 16.

2. Graham, *Patronage and Politics in Nineteenth-Century Brazil*.

3. Duncan, *Public and Private Operation of Railways in Brazil*, 19–66; and Graham, *Britain and the Onset of Modernization in Brazil*, 51–66.

4. Villela and Suzigan, *Política de Governo e Crescimento da Economia Brasileira*, 321. Contemporaries made similar assessments of the wastefulness of guarantees. There was no doubt some truth to these claims with respect to smaller lines (see Table 4.15, this volume; see also *Economista Brasileiro*, 8 February 1878, 40; ibid., 23 February 1878, 50–51; and *Jornal do Agricultor*, 10 March 1888, 167–68).

5. Fendt, "Investimentos Inglêses no Brasil."

6. The same is true of the analysis in Ribeiro, "As Garantias Ferroviárias no Brasil."

7. Burns, *The Poverty of Progress*, 135; Cechin, "A Construção e Operação das Ferrovias no Brasil," 31.

8. In this case, what is being redistributed would be income from the pre-rail transport sector to the consumers of transport services in the economy once it had railroads.

9. See, for example, Burns, *A History of Brazil*, 160–61, 169; Evans, "Continuities and Contradictions in the Evolution of Brazilian Dependence," 33–35.

10. Engerman, "Some Economic Issues Relating to Railroad Subsidies."

11. Atack and Passell, *A New Economic View of American History*, 435–44.

12. Mercer, *Railroads and Land Grant Policy*, 19–26.

13. Paiva, *Synopse da Legislação da Viação Ferrea Federal*, vii. Most investors realized at the time that "the immediate return on capital" was a secondary consideration in railroad subsidy ("A Viação Ferrea e os Engenhos Centraes," *Revista de Estradas de Ferro*, 31 January 1885).

14. The Railroad Law of 1852 maintained the prescribed rates; the major difference between it and the earlier concession was the guarantee of a minimum dividend (see Pessôa, *Estudo Descriptivo das Estradas de Ferro do Brasil*, 3–4).

15. While these companies were required by law to submit their operating and financial reports to the Brazilian government, such reports have not survived in an accessible form within Brazil. The copies consulted are archived in the Guildhall Library, Corporation of London, as detailed in Appendix B.

16. These reports are distributed among several collections in Rio de Janeiro São

Paulo; see Appendix B.

17. These include State of São Paulo, Secretaria da Agricultura, Commércio e Obras Públicas, *Quadros Estatísticos*; MVOP, *Relatórios* . . . , *1893–1913*; and MVOP, Inspectoria Federal das Estradas, *EEF.*These sources are discussed in Appendix B.

18. El-Kareh, *Filha Branca de Mãe Preta*, 117–28; Figueira, *Memória Histórica da Estrada de Ferro Central do Brazil*, 45–50; Pessôa, *Guia da Estrada de Ferro Central do Brasil*.

19. Figueira, *Memória Histórica da Estrada de Ferro Central do Brasil*, 889–911; *Statist* 38 (1896): 986–87.

20. Camara, *Chemins de Fer*, 5–23; Lewis, *Public Policy and Private Initiative*, 12; Pinto, *História da Viação Pública de S. Paulo*, 182–83; and SPR, *Report of the Board of Directors*, 2/1889.

21. Lewis, *Public Policy and Private Initiative*, 12; Pinto, *História da Viação Pública de S. Paulo*, 182–83.

22. See SPR, *Report of the Board of Directors*, 1904.

23. The director of the firm knew all too well the importance of traffic acquired by the SPR from feeder lines (see SPR, *Report of the Board of Directors*, 2/1906, 3–4). On the presumed monopoly power of the SPR, see Miller, *Britain and Latin America in the Nineteenth and Twentieth Centuries*, 160; and Platt, "Economic Imperialism and the Businessman," 300. On the claims for SPR's unusually high profits, see Rippy, *British Investments in Latin America*, 154.

24. Costa, *Viação Ferrea do Brazil*, 287–88; Debes, *A Caminho do Oeste*; Camara, *Chemins de Fer*, 27–28; Mattoon, "The Companhia Paulista de Estradas de Ferro," 43–72; Pinto, *História da Viação Pública de S. Paulo*, 36–46; Saes, *As Ferrovias de São Paulo*, 54–67.

25. CP, *Relatório*, *1894*.

26. Costa, *Viação Ferrea do Brazil*, 79–81; Pessôa, *Estudo Descriptivo das Estradas de Ferro do Brasil*, 158–60; GW, *Reports of the Directors and Statements of Accounts*, 1881–1900.

27. Pinto, *História da Viação Pública de S. Paulo*, 185.

28. Costa, *Viação Ferrea do Brazil*, 79–81; Pessôa, *Estudo Descriptivo das Estradas de Ferro do Brasil*, 158–60; GW, *Reports of the Directors and Statements of Accounts*, 1881; Fonseca, "Os Investimentos Ingleses no Nordeste do Brasil."

29. Rodrigues, *Resgate das Estradas de Ferro do Recife a S. Francisco*.

30. Queiros, *O Resgate da Estrada de Ferro do Recife ao São Francisco*.

31. On the government-owned lines in the northeast, see Rego, *Inquérito sobre as Estradas de Ferro da União*.

32. GW, *Report of the Directors*, 1901.

33. Pinto, *História da Viação Pública de S. Paulo*, 111–41; MVOP, *Relatório* . . . *1909*, 2:107–20.

34. Costa, *Viação Ferrea do Brazil*, 325.

35. Jacob, *Minas Gerais no XXo Século*, 487–97.

36. *Statist* 29 (1892): 438–39.

37. Siqueira, *Resumo Histórico de The Leopoldina Railway Company*, 12–18.

38. *Statist* 39 (1897): 531.

39. Brown, *The South American Year Book*, 71–78.

40. LRC, *Report of the Proceedings*, 1910, 7–8; LRC, *Report of the Proceedings*, 1909, 8–9; LRC, *Report of the Directors*, 1911, 7; LRC, *Report of the Directors*, 1913, 28.

41. Perhaps no other issue in Brazilian history has occasioned so much econometric analysis as has the determinants of the exchange rate (see Fishlow, "Conditionality and

Willingness to Pay," 69; Cardoso, "The Exchange Rate in Nineteenth-Century Brazil," 170–78; Leff, *Underdevelopment and Development in Brazil*, 111–13; and Catão, "The International Transmission of Long Cycles"). For an alternative view (that of the "Campinas school") on the working of the exchange rate in Brazil, see Mello and Tavares, "The Capitalist Export Economy in Brazil," 100–102.

42. For examples of complaints about the poor exchange rate, see SPR, *Report of the Board of Directors*, 2/1891, 1; GW, *Report of the Proceedings, 1896*, 4–5; GW, *Report of the Proceedings*, 1898, 4–4; and RSF, *Report of the Directors*, 2/1894, 2.

43. Mattoon, "The Companhia Paulista de Estradas de Ferro," 149; SPR, *Report of the Board of Directors*, 2/1893, 1; CP, *Relatório*, 1893, 10; RSF *Report of the Directors*, 1/1896, 3.

44. Both the accounting rate of return, and the market rate of return are variants of net income divided by net assets. Neither equals the economic rate of return. Accounting rates of return equal the true economic rate of return only if the depreciation schedule is the time-rate-of-change of the present value of the cash-flow stream. To the extent that the stream is not constant, then the accounting return can depart dramatically from the true return. In the case of railroads, cash-flow streams are rarely constant. See Stauffer, "The Measurement of Corporate Rates of Return," 466–67.

45. Mercer, *Railroads and Land Grant Policy*, 68–70.

46. Since there is no closed-form solution for r, it is calculated in Equation (7.1) using numeric techniques. Because the expression is a polynomial, it has multiple positive real roots, or more than one real positive r for which PV is zero. In practice, the minimum positive real value for r is obtained here by finding the value of r for which slightly increasing and decreasing r causes PV to change sign.

47. This is the extension of the wholesale price index developed in Chapter 4.

48. Note that profits here follow an economic concept of profit rather than a financial one. Economic profits are the real returns to the economy on the physically reproducible capital employed in the railroad. Financial profits would be the sum of dividends and interest payments plus changes in the firm's asset prices in financial markets. These prices, in turn, depend on changes in expectations and overall market conditions. As such, economic profits need not equal financial profits over any particular interval. Since the concern here is with real benefits and resource costs, rather than investor profits, economic profitability is the preferred concept.

49. Mello, "Rates of Return on Slave Capital in Brazilian Coffee Plantations," 75.

50. These are end-of-year quotations from the *Jornal do Commércio* and *Investor's Monthly Manual*.

51. McClelland, "Social Rates of Return on American Railroads."

52. Carlos and Lewis, "The Profitability of Early Canadian Railroads"; Coatsworth, "The Impact of Railroads on the Economic Development of Mexico," 140–42; Davidson, "A Benefit Cost Analysis of the New South Wales Railway System"; Fishlow, *American Railroads and the Transformation of the Antebellum Economy*; Fogel, *The Union Pacific Railroad*; Mercer, *Railroads and Land Grant Policy*; and Ransom, "Social Returns from Public Transport Investment."

53. Computing the social rate of return here is done with numeric techniques in the same manner as for the internal rate of return.

54. Layard and Glaister, *Cost-Benefit Analysis*, 25–44; Rosenthal, *The Fruits of Revolution*, 103–10.

55. Fogel, *The Union Pacific Railroad*, 101–3; and Mercer, *Railroads and Land Grant Policy*, 227–32.

56. This approach uses the change in the consumers' surplus in the market for freight-transport services as a measure of the sum of the increases in consumers' and producers' surpluses in the markets for transportable goods that result from the decline in the cost of shipment.

57. Passenger benefits are ignored, which biases downward the measured social benefits from the railroad. Excluding them does not alter the qualitative findings below.

58. Historians who calculated social benefits for other transport projects by using freight shipments (as opposed to changes in land values) handled this issue in various ways. For example, in the United States, Mercer assumed that the 1870 level of rail shipments was the level that would obtain every year in the absence of the Central Pacific line (see Mercer, *Railroads and Land Grant Policy*, 237). For the New South Wales Railway, Davidson took the freight shipped in the first year that each section opened as the amount that would have been carried absent the railway (summing over time as each increment of track opened), and then added to that one-half of the freight carried by rail beyond that level (see Davidson, "A Benefit Cost Analysis of the New South Wales Railway System," 131). On the Grand Trunk and Great Western Railway in Canada, Carlos and Lewis implicitly set the non-rail freight shipments at zero without regard to what the level pre-rail rates actually were, an assumption that may build their results into their test because it ignores the actual non-rail charge (see Carlos and Lewis, "The Profitability of Early Canadian Railroads," 415–16). In the case of the Mexican Central Railroad, Coatsworth also took freight shipments to be entirely nonexistent without railroads, but at the prevailing pre-rail freight charge (see Coatsworth, "The Impact of Railroads on the Economic Development of Mexico," 140). For the Ohio Canal, Ransom imposed precisely the opposite condition, assuming that, absent the canal, all of the freight that it carried would have still been shipped to market by other means, thereby likely overstating his measure of the "rent" created by the canal. This assumption, of course, biases the results upward, rhetorically weakening the argument (see Ransom, "Social Returns from Public Transport Investment," 1046).

59. Coutinho, *Estradas de Ferro do Norte*, 13.

60. *Economist* 47 (1889): 6, 1495–96; *Statist* 34 (1894): 327–28.

61. *Statist* 21 (1888): 566–67.

62. *Economist* 57 (1899): 609; *Statist* 34 (1894): 327–28.

63. *Economist* 57 (1899): 756–57.

64. The basic model of the legislator's choice in a setting of distributive politics is adapted from Weingast, Shepsle, and Johnson, "The Political Economy of Benefits and Costs."

65. Monetary policy in the 1890s depreciated the currency, increasing dramatically the total cost of railroad dividend guarantees. Setting aside the tax argument in the maximand may thus appear misguided. Rate regulation, however, was under way well before the 1890s, whereas the rapid increase in the cost of guarantees was transitory.

66. Burns, *The Poverty of Progress*, 135.

67. Quotation is from Platt, "Economic Imperialism and the Businessman," 300.

68. The assertions of high profits are widely repeated in the historiography, especially for the SPR (see Love, *São Paulo in the Brazilian Federation*, 65; and Rippy, *British Investments in Latin America*).

69. Fremdling, "Freight Rates and the State Budget."

CHAPTER 8

1. Leff, *Underdevelopment and Development in Brazil*, 117–20.
2. Catão, "A New Wholesale Price Index for Brazil."
3. Gonçalves, *Evolução das Relações Comerciais do Brasil com a Inglaterra*.
4. Fully 78 percent of common manufactures consumed in Brazil in 1913 were supplied by domestic producers (see CIB, *Relatório da Directoria*).
5. Holloway, *Immigrants on the Land*, 147–53.
6. Diacon, *Millenarian Vision, Capitalist Reality*. Large landowners seem to have been just as likely to be expropriated when lands were granted to the railroad. No broader measure of the degree to which concentration or dispossession occurred is presented.
7. This assumes that the labor force participation rates remain constant, an assumption supported by Brazilian population figures.
8. For discussions of the taxing of imports by provinces and states under the Empire and Republic, see Congresso Nacional, Câmara dos Deputados, *Livro do Centenário*, 281–87; Bezerra, "Política Tributária Estadual"; Melo, *O Norte Agrário e o Império*, 247–85; Ridings, *Business Interest Groups in Nineteenth-Century Brazil*, 183–91; Deveza, "Política Tributária no Período Imperial," 72–73; Correia, *O Problema Econômico no Brasil*, 31–34, 297–317; and Chavantes, *Congresso das Vias de Transporte no Brasil*, 143–44.
9. Love, *Rio Grande do Sul and Brazilian Regionalism*, 113–14.
10. Haber, "The Efficiency Consequences of Institutional Change," table 1.
11. On the poor record and high costs of many state-owned activities, see Trebat, *Brazil's State-Owned Enterprises*, 164–74.

APPENDIX A

1. See, especially, McClelland, *Causal Explanation and Model Building*, 146–68; and White, "Railroads and Rigour."
2. Examples include Fishlow, *American Railroads and the Transformation of the Antebellum Economy*, 23–32; White, "The Concept of Social Saving"; O'Brien, *The New Economic History of the Railways*; Fogel, "Notes on the Social Saving Controversy"; Metzer, *Some Economic Aspects of Railroad Development in Tsarist Russia*, 3–26; Coatsworth, *Growth Against Development*, 193–204.
3. For a discussion of possible configurations of linkages suitable for investigation, beyond simply "forward" and "backward," and reference to some specific applications, see Hirschman, "A Generalized Linkage Approach to Development."
4. Galvão, *Notícia Sobre as Estradas de Ferro do Brasil*, 52.
5. Quoted in the *Times* of London, 11 October 1888, 11.
6. This explicit formulation bases itself on Fogel, "Notes on the Social Saving Controversy," 3.
7. None of these assumptions are specific to the social savings approach but rather are general assumptions in textbook discussions of the income and substitution effects, and welfare consequences, of a relative price change.
8. A detailed discussion of the derivation of the data on freight service and the price of that service is found in Appendix B.
9. Coatsworth, *Growth Against Development*, 114–15; Ramírez, "Railroads and the Colombian Economy," 100; Fogel, "Notes on the Social Saving Controversy," 32.
10. Fishlow, *American Railroads and the Transformation of the Antebellum Economy*, 63–95.

11. Gomez Mendoza, *Ferrocarriles y Cambio Económico en España*, 56.

12. Fogel, "Notes on the Social Saving Controversy."

13. See, especially, the criticisms made by McClelland ("Social Rates of Return on American Railroads," 471–88). Mercer offers rebuttal to some of these criticisms at various points in *Railroads and Land Grant Policy*.

14. Both Coatsworth and O'Brien assert that market integration resulting from lower transport costs is actually a linkage effect not captured by the social saving (see Coatsworth, "Indispensable Railroads in a Backward Economy," 953; and O'Brien, *The New Economic History of the Railways*, 72–77). Metzer demonstrated that such a claim is erroneous ("Railroads and the Efficiency of Internal Markets," 66–69).

15. Fogel, "Notes on the Social Saving Controversy," 5.

16. For applications in the cases of the United States and Great Britain, see Williamson, *Late-Nineteenth-Century American Development*, chapter 9; Kahn, "The Use of Complicated Models as Explanations," 185–216; Foreman-Peck, "Railways and Late Victorian Economic Growth," 83–89.

17. Gomez Mendoza, *Ferrocarriles y Cambio Económico en España*, 142–52.

APPENDIX B

1. Reis, *Primeiro Congresso das Estradas de Ferro do Brazil*, 91–94, 369–70.

2. *Revista do Club de Engenharia*, February 1887, 59–61, discussed the need for uniform railroad statistics and noted the Ministry of Agriculture decree prescribing the format and data to be submitted.

3. MVOP, Commissão de Estatistica de Estradas de Ferro, *Questionário*, prescribed the data to be reported by lines under federal guarantee or concession. The responses to the questionnaire were used for the *Estatísticas* volumes that first appeared in 1898.

4. State of São Paulo, Secretaria da Agricultura, Commércio e Obras Públicas, *Quadros Estatísticos*; and State of São Paulo, Inspectoria de Estradas de Ferro e Navegação, *Reforma das Tarifas*.

Bibliography

BRAZILIAN GOVERNMENT DOCUMENTS AND PUBLICATIONS

Ministério da Agricultura, Indústria e Commércio. *Annuario Estatístico do Brazil*.Vol. 2. 1908/1912. Rio de Janeiro, 1916.

Coleção das Leis do Brasil. Various vols. Rio de Janeiro, 1854–1913.

Commissão Central de Estatística. *Relatório Apresentado ao Exm. Sr. Presidente da Província de S. Paulo*. São Paulo, 1888.

Congresso Nacional. Câmara dos Deputados. *Livro do Centenário*.Vol. 2. Rio de Janeiro, 1926.

Directoria do Serviço de Inspecção e Fomento Agrícola. *Aspectos da Economia Rural Brasileira*. Rio de Janeiro, 1922.

Estado de São Paulo. Inspectoria de Estradas de Ferro e Navegação. *A Reforma das Tarifas*. São Paulo, 1901.

———. Repartição Estatística e do Archivo de São Paulo. *Annuário Estatístico de São Paulo (Brasil), 1906*.Vol. 2. São Paulo, 1909.

———. Secretaria da Agricultura, Commércio e Obras Públicas. *Quadros Estatísticos das Estradas de Ferro do Estado de São Paulo*. São Paulo, 1900.

Instituto Brasileiro de Geografia e Estatística. *Repertório Estatístico do Brasil, Quadros Retrospectivos*.Vol. 1. Rio de Janeiro, 1941.

———. *Estatísticas Históricas do Brasil*. 2d ed. Rio de Janeiro, 1990.

———. "Transportes e Comunicações." In *Estatísticas Históricas do Brasil* (1990), 1:445–78.

Ministério da Agricultura, Commércio, e Obras Públicas. *Relatórios Apresentado A Assemblea Geral . . . Pelo Ministro Secretário de Estado dos Negócios da Agricultura, Commércio e Obras Públicas*. Rio de Janeiro, 1861–1892.

Ministério da Fazenda. *Consultas da Secção de Fazenda do Conselho de Estado*. Rio de Janeiro, 1871.

———. *Commércio Exterior do Brasil.* Rio de Janeiro, 1914.

———. *Balanço da Receita e Despeza da República no Exercício de 1913.* Rio de Janeiro, 1924.

Ministério do Império. *Relatórios do Ministério do Império.* Rio de Janeiro, 1847–1855.

Ministério dos Transportes. *Planos de Viação—Evolução Histórica (1808–1973).* Rio de Janeiro, 1973.

Ministério da Viação e Obras Públicas. *Relatórios do Ministério da Viação e Obras Públicas.* Rio de Janeiro, 1893–1913.

———. Commissão de Estatística de Estradas de Ferro. *Questionário.* Rio de Janeiro, 1898.

———. Inspectoria Federal das Estradas. *Estatísticas das Estradas de Ferro da União e das Fiscalizadas pela União.* Rio de Janeiro, 1898–1913.

Província de Bahia. *Falla Regitada na Abertura D'Assemblea Legislativa da Bahia pelo Presidente da Província . . . 10 de março de 1861.* Bahia [Salvador], 1861.

Província de Espírito Santo. *Relatório do Presidente da Província do Espírito Santo, 1859.* Victória, 1859.

Província de Pernambuco. *Relatório Apresentado a Assemblea Legislativa Provincial em o 10 de março de 1866 pelo Presidente de Pernambuco.* Recife, 1866.

———. *Relatório apresentado ao Exm. Sr. Presidente da Província pelo Engenheiro Chefe, Jose Tiburão Pereira de Magalhães, Director das Obras Públicas de Pernambuco em 29 de Janeiro de 1872.* Recife, 1872.

———. *Relatório do Director das Obras Públicas de Pernambuco em 29 de Janeiro de 1872.* Recife, 1872.

Província de São Paulo. *Discurso com que o Illustríssimo e Excellentísimo Senhor Dr. José Antonio Saraiva Presidente da Provínicia de S. Paulo Abrio A Assemblea Legislativa Provincial no Dia 15 Fevereiro de 1855.* São Paulo, 1855.

Senado Federal. *Atas do Conselho de Estado.* 13 vols. Brasília, 1973–1978.

———. *O Governo Presidencial do Brasil, 1889–1930: Guia Administrativo da Primeira República, Poder Executivo.* Brasilia, 1985.

———. *Constituições do Brasil.* Vol. 1. Brasília, 1986.

State of São Paulo. Department of Agriculture, Commerce, and Public Works, *Railroads in the State of São Paulo.* São Paulo, 1903.

COMPANY REPORTS

Bahia and San Francisco Railway Company, Ltd. *Reports of the Directors.* London, 1879–1901.

Brazil Great Southern Railway. *Reports of the Directors and Statement of Accounts.* London, 1887–1905.

Companhia Leopoldina de Estradas de Ferro. *Relatórios.* Rio de Janeiro, 1874–1896.

Companhia Mogiana de Estradas de Ferro. *Relatórios.* São Paulo, 1873–1913.

Companhia Paulista de Estradas de Ferro. *Relatórios da Diretoria.* São Paulo, 1869–1913.

Companhia Sorocabana. *Relatórios.* São Paulo, 1872–1891.

Companhia União e Indústria. *Relatórios.* Rio de Janeiro, 1855–1865.

Companhia União Sorocabana e Ituana. *Relatórios.* São Paulo, 1892–1901.

Estrada de Ferro Central do Brazil. *Relatórios.* Rio de Janeiro, 1890–1913.

Estrada de Ferro Dom Pedro II. *Relatórios.* Rio de Janeiro, 1855–1889.

Estrada de Ferro Recife ao São Francisco. *Relatório da Estrada de Ferro Recife ao São Francisco*. N.p., 1874.

Great Western of Brazil Railway Company, Ltd. *Reports of the Directors and Statement of Accounts*. London, 1881–1900.

————. *Reports of the Proceedings at the Annual General Meetings of Shareholders*. London, 1881–1913.

Leopoldina Railway Company, Ltd. *Proposed Agreement Between The Leopoldina Railway Company, Limited, and the Leopoldina Railway Company, The Macahe and Campos Railway, and the Rio de Janeiro and Northern Railway*. N.p., 1896.

————. *Reports of the Directors*. London, 1898–1913.

————. *Reports of the Proceedings at the Ordinary General Meetings*. London, 1898–1913.

————. *Prospectus*. N.p., n.d.

Recife and San Francisco Railway Company, Ltd. *Reports of the Directors*. London, 1879–1901.

Relatório da Companhia da Estrada de Magé a Sapucaia do Anno de 1867. Rio de Janeiro, 1867.

Relatório da Companhia da Estrada de Mangaratiba. Rio de Janeiro, 1856.

Relatório da Imperial Companhia de Navegação a Vapor e Estrada de Ferro de Petrópolis. Rio de Janeiro, 1857.

San Paulo (Brazilian) Railway Company, Ltd. *Reports of the Board of Directors*. London, 1879–1913.

Sorocabana Railway. *Relatórios*. São Paulo, 1907–1913.

Southern Brazil Rio Grande do Sul Railway. *Reports of the Directors and Statement of Accounts*. London, 1885–1905.

NEWSPAPERS AND MAGAZINES

O Agricultor Brazileiro, 1854
Anais da Câmara dos Deputados, 1882
Anglo-Brazilian Times, 1880
Annex au Moniteur Belge, 1914
Correio Paulistano, 1865
Diário Oficial do Império do Brasil, 1864
Economist, 1889, 1899
Economista Brasileiro, 1878
Investor's Monthly Manual, 1913
Jornal do Agricultor, 1887–1888
Jornal do Commércio, 1875–1910, 1913
Monitor Sul Mineiro (Campanha), 1876
Revista de Estradas de Ferro, 1885
Revista do Club de Engenharia, 1887
South American Journal, 1880–1883, 1884, 1886
Statist, 1888, 1892, 1894, 1896–1897
Sul de Minas, 1861
Times (London), 1854, 1888

272

Bibliography

OTHER WORKS

Adler, Dorothy R. *British Investment in American Railways, 1834–1898.* Charlottesville, 1970.

Agassiz, Louis. *A Journey in Brazil.* Boston, 1868.

Alagôas Railway Company, Ltd. *Petição e Memória Justificativa Apresentada ao Exmo. Sr. Conselheiro Dr. Antonio da Silva Prado.* Rio de Janeiro, 1888.

Alden, Dauril. "Price Movements in Brazil Before, During, and After the Gold Boom, with Special Reference to the Salvador Market, 1670–1769." In *Essays on the Price History of Eighteenth-Century Latin America,* ed. Lyman L. Johnson and Enrique Tandeter. Albuquerque, N.M., 1990.

Almanak da Província de São Paulo. São Paulo, 1873.

Almanak Administrativo, Mercantil e Industrial do Império do Brazil para 1886. Rio de Janeiro, 1886.

Argollo, M. de Teive e. *Memória Descriptiva sobre a Estrada de Ferro Bahia e Minas.* Rio de Janeiro, 1883.

Atack, Jeremy. "Economies of Scale and Efficiency Gains in the Rise of the Factory in America, 1820–1900." In *Quantity and Quiddity,* ed. Peter Kilby. Middletown, Ohio, 1987.

Atack, Jeremy, and Peter Passell. *A New Economic View of American History.* 2d ed. New York, 1994.

Barickman, Bert. J. "'Tame Indians,' 'Wild Heathens,' and Settlers in Southern Bahia in the Late Eighteenth and Early Nineteenth Centuries." *The Americas* 51, no. 3 (1995): 325–68.

Baril, V. L. *L'Empire du Brésil.* Paris, 1862.

Barman, Roderick J. "Brazil at Mid-Empire: Political Accommodation and the Pursuit of Progress under the Conciliação Ministry, 1853–1857." Ph.D. diss., University of California at Berkeley, 1970.

———. "Business and Government in Imperial Brazil: The Experience of Viscount Mauá." *Journal of Latin American Studies* 13, pt. 2 (November 1981): 239–64.

———. *Brazil: The Forging of a Nation, 1798–1852.* Stanford, Calif., 1988.

Bastos, Aureliano C. Tavares. *O Valle do Amazonas.* Rio de Janeiro, 1866.

Becker, Gary. *Human Capital: A Theoretical and Empirical Analysis.* 3d ed. Chicago, 1993.

Beesley, M. E. "The Value of Time Spent in Travelling: Some New Evidence." *Economica* 32, no. 126 (1965): 174–85.

Benévolo, Ademar. *Introdução a História Ferroviária do Brasil.* Recife, 1953.

Bethell, Leslie, and José Murilo de Carvalho. "Empire, 1822–1850." In *Brazil: Empire and Republic, 1822–1930,* ed. Leslie Bethell. Cambridge, 1989.

Bezerra, Agostinho Fernandes. "Política Tributária Estadual: A Questão das Tarifas Internas na Primeira Republica (1889–1930)" M.A. thesis, Universidade de São Paulo, 1984.

Blasenheim, Peter L. "Railroads in Nineteenth-Century Minas Gerais." *Journal of Latin American Studies* 26 (May 1994): 347–74.

Bovet, A. de. "A Indústria Mineral na Província de Minas Gerais." *Annaes da Escola de Minas* 2 (1883): 23–102.

Boyd, J. Hayden, and Gary M. Walton. "The Social Saving from Nineteenth-Century Rail Passenger Services." *Explorations in Economic History* 9 (spring 1972): 233–54.

Bradshaw's Railway Manual, Shareholders Guide, and Official Directory. London, 1867–1900.

Branner, John C. *Cotton in the Empire of Brazil*. Washington, D.C., 1885.

————. *The Railways of Brazil, A Statistical Article*. Chicago, 1887.

Brown, C. S. Vesey, ed. *The South American Year Book*. London, 1913.

Bulhões, A. M. de Oliveira. *Estrada de Ferro da Bahia ao S. Francisco: Estudos Definitivos de Alagoinhas ao Joazeiro e Casa Nova*. Rio de Janeiro, 1874.

Bulmer-Thomas, Victor. *The Economic History of Latin America since Independence*. Cambridge, 1994.

Burns, E. Bradford. *The Poverty of Progress*. Berkeley, 1980.

————. *A History of Brazil*. 3d ed. New York, 1993.

Burton, Richard F. *The Highlands of Brazil*. Vol. 1. London, 1869.

Caldeira, Jorge. *Mauá: Empresário do Império*. São Paulo, 1995.

Calógeras, João Pandiá. *A Política Monetária do Brasil*. São Paulo, 1960.

Camara, José Ewbank da. *Caminhos de Ferro do Rio Grande do Sul: Competência com as vias de communicação existentes n'essa Provincia e na Republicas do Prata*. Rio de Janeiro, 1875.

————. *Chemins de Fer de la Province de St. Paul (Brésil)*. Rio de Janeiro, 1875.

Camargo, José Francisco de. *Crescimento da População no Estado de São Paulo e Seus Aspectos Econômicos*. São Paulo, 1981.

Campista, Davi. *Compilação de Leis, Decretos, Regulamentos, e Contratos Relativos ás Estradas de Ferro do Estado de Minas Gerais*. Belo Horizonte, 1902.

Cardoso, Ciro Flamarion, and Héctor Pérez Brignoli. *História Econômica da América Latina*. 2d ed. Rio de Janeiro, 1988.

Cardoso, Eliana. "The Exchange Rate in Nineteenth-Century Brazil: An Econometric Model." *Journal of Development Studies* 19 (January 1983): 170–78.

Cardoso, Fernando Henrique, and Enzo Faletto. *Dependency and Development in Latin America*. Berkeley, 1979.

Carlos, Ann M., and Frank Lewis. "The Profitability of Early Canadian Railroads: Evidence from the Grand Trunk and Great Western Railway Companies." In *Strategic Factors in Nineteenth Century American Economic History*, ed. Claudia Goldin and Hugh Rockoff. Chicago, 1992.

Carone, Edgard. *O Centro Industrial do Rio de Janeiro e Sua Importante Participação na Economia Nacional (1827–1977)*. Rio de Janeiro, 1978.

Carvalho, José Murilo de. *A Escola de Minas de Ouro Preto: O Peso da Glória*. São Paulo, 1978.

————. *A Construção da Ordem: A Elite Política Imperial*. Rio de Janeiro, 1980.

————. *Teatro de Sombras: A Política Imperial*. São Paulo, 1988.

Castro, Agostinho Vioto de. "Relatório do Segundo Grupo," in Antonio José de Souza Rangel, ed. *Relatório da Segunda Exposião Nacional de 1866*. Rio de Janeiro, 1869.

Castro, Ana Célia. *As Empresas Estrangeiras no Brasil, 1860–1913*. Rio de Janeiro, 1978.

Castro, Juan José. *Treatise on the South American Railways*. Montevideo, 1893.

Catão, Luis A. V. "The International Transmission of Long Cycles Between 'Core' and 'Periphery' Economies: A Case Study of Brazil and Mexico, c. 1870–1940." Ph.D. diss., University of Cambridge, 1991.

————. "A New Wholesale Price Index for Brazil during the Period 1870–1913." *Revista Brasileira de Economia* 46, no. 4 (1992): 519–33.

Cateysson, J. *Indicador Geral da Viação do Brazil*. Paris, 1898.

Cechin, José. "A Construção e Operação das Ferrovias no Brasil do Século XIX." M.A. thesis, Universidade Estadual de Campinas, 1978.

Centro Industrial do Brasil. *O Brasil: Suas Riquezas Naturaes, Suas Indústrias.* Vol. 3: *Indústria de Transportes, Indústria Fabril.* Rio de Janeiro, 1909.

———. *Relatório da Directoria.* Rio de Janeiro, 1915.

Chavantes, Alcino José. *Congresso das Vias de Transporte no Brazil em Dezembro 1909. Archivo dos Trabalhos.* Rio de Janeiro, 1910.

Cincoentenario da Estrada de Ferro do Paraná, 1885—5 de fevereiro—1935. Publicacão Comemorativa da Rede de Viacão Paraná–Santa Catarina. Curitiba, 1935.

Clapham, J. H. "Economic History as a Discipline." *Encyclopaedia of the Social Sciences.* Vol. 5. New York, 1931.

Coatsworth, John H. "The Impact of Railroads on the Economic Development of Mexico, 1877–1910." Ph.D. diss., University of Wisconsin, 1972.

———. "Obstacles to Economic Growth in Nineteenth-Century Mexico." *American Historical Review* 83, no. 1 (February 1978): 80–100.

———. "Indispensable Railroads in a Backward Economy: The Case of Mexico." *Journal of Economic History* 39 (December 1979): 939–60.

———. *Growth Against Development: The Economic Impact of Railroads in Porfirian Mexico.* DeKalb, Ill., 1981.

———. "The Decline of the Mexican Economy, 1800–1860." In *America Latina en la Epoca de Simon Bolivar: La Formacion de las Economias Nacionales y los Intereses Economicos Europeos, 1800–1850*, ed. Reinhard Liehr. Berlin, 1989.

———. "Welfare." *American Historical Review* 101, no. 1 (February 1996): 1–17.

———. "Economic and Institutional Trajectories in Nineteenth-Century Latin America." In *Latin America and the World Economy Since 1800*, ed. John H. Coatsworth and Alan M. Taylor. Cambridge, Mass., 1998.

Colson, Roger F. "The Destruction of a Revolution: Polity, Economy, and Society in Brazil, 1750–1895." Ph.D. diss., Princeton, 1979.

Conrado, Jacobo de Niemeyer. *Relatório dos Trabalhos Concluidos na Estrada do Commercio entre os Rios Iguassú e Parahiba.* Rio de Janeiro, 1844.

Contador, Cláudio. "Crescimento, Ciclos Econômicos e Inflação: Uma Descrieão do Caso Brasileiro." *Revista Brasileira de Mercados de Capitais* 4, no. 12 (1978): 379–401.

Contador, Cláudio, and Cláudio Haddad. "Produto Real, Moêda, e Preços: A Experiência Brasileira no Período 1861–1979." *Revista Brasileira de Estatística* 36 (July/September 1975): 407–40.

Correia, Serzedelo. *O Problema Econômico no Brasil.* 1903. Reprint, Brasilia, 1980.

Coruja, Jr., Antônio Alvares Pereira. *Repertório das Leis, Decretos, Consultas, Instruções, Portarias, Avisos, e Circulares Relativos á Concessão, Administração e Fiscalização das Estradas de Ferro.* Rio de Janeiro, 1886.

Costa, Emilia Viotti da. *The Brazilian Empire: Myths and Histories.* Chicago, 1985.

———. "Empire, 1870–1889." In *Brazil: Empire and Republic, 1822–1930*, ed. Leslie Bethell. Cambridge, 1989.

Costa, Francisco Barreto Picanço. *Viação Ferrea do Brazil.* Rio de Janeiro, 1884.

———. *Diccionário de Estradas de Ferro.* 2 vols. Rio de Janeiro, 1892.

Costa, Hernani Maia. "As Barreiras de São Paulo." M.A. thesis, Universidade de São Paulo, 1984.

Coutinho, João M. da Silva. *Estradas de Ferro do Norte*. Rio de Janeiro, 1888.

Cunha, Ernesto Antonio Lassance. *Estudo Descriptivo da Viação Ferrea do Brazil*. Rio de Janeiro, 1909.

David, Paul A. "Transport Innovation and Economic Growth: Professor Fogel On and Off the Rails." *Economic History Review* 22 (December 1969): 506–25.

———. *Technical Choice, Innovation, and Economic Growth*. Cambridge, 1975.

Davidson, B. R. "A Benefit Cost Analysis of the New South Wales Railway System." *Australian Economic History Review* 22, no. 2 (1982): 127–50.

Davis, Lance E., and Robert J. Cull. *International Capital Markets and American Economic Growth, 1820–1914*. Cambridge, Mass., 1994.

Davis, Lance E., and Robert A. Huttenback. *Mammon and the Pursuit of Empire*. Cambridge, 1988.

Dean, Warren. *The Industrialization of São Paulo, 1880–1945*. Austin, 1969.

———. "Latifundia and Land Policy in Nineteenth-Century Brazil." *HAHR* 51 (November 1971): 606–25.

———. *Rio Claro: A Brazilian Plantation System*. Stanford, Calif., 1976.

———. "Economy." In *Brazil: Empire and Republic, 1822–1930*, ed. Leslie Bethell. Cambridge, 1989.

Debes, Célio. *A Caminho do Oeste (História da Companhia Paulista de Estradas de Ferro)*. São Paulo, 1968.

Denis, Pierre. *Brazil*. London, 1911.

Denslow, David. "As Origens da Desigualdade Regional no Brasil." *Estudos Econômicos* 3, no. 1 (April 1973): 65–88.

———. "Sugar Production in Northeastern Brazil and Cuba, 1858–1908." Ph.D. diss., Yale University, 1974.

———. "As Exportações e a Origem do Padrão de Industrializaçaõ Regional do Brasil." In *Dimensões do Desenvolvimento Brasileiro*, ed. Werner Baer, Pedro Pinchas Geiger, and Paolo Roberto Haddad. Rio de Janeiro, 1978.

De Vany, Arthur. "The Revealed Value of Time in Air Travel." *Review of Economics and Statistics* 56, no. 1 (1974): 77–82.

Deveza, Guilherme. "Política Tributária no Período Imperial." In *História Geral da Civilização Brasileira*, vol. 2: *Declínio e Queda do Império*, ed. Sérgio Buarque de Holanda and Pedro Moacyr Campos. São Paulo, 1971.

de Vries, Jan. "Barges and Capitalism: Passenger Transportation in the Dutch Economy." *A.A.G. Bijdragen* 21 (1978): 33–398.

Diacon, Todd A. *Millenarian Vision, Capitalist Reality: Brazil's Contestado Rebellion, 1912–1916*. Durham, 1991.

Dias, José Roberto de Souza. "A Primeira Ferrovia do Rio Grande do Sul." M.A. thesis, Universidade de São Paulo, 1978.

———. "A E.F. Porto Alegre á Uruguaiana e a Formação da Rede Viação Ferrea do Rio Grande do Sul: Uma Contribuição a Estudo dos Transportes no Brasil Meridional, 1866–1920." Ph.D. diss., Universidade de São Paulo, 1981.

Diniz, Diana Maria de Faro Leal. "Ferrovia e Expansão Cafeeira: Um Estudo da Modernização dos Meios de Transporte." *Revista de História* 52, no. 2 (1975): 825–52.

Doles, Dalísia Elizabeth Martins. *As Comunicações Fluviais pelo Tocantins e Araguaia no Século XIX*. Goiânia, 1973.

Donghi, Túlio Halperin. *The Contemporary History of Latin America*. Durham, 1993.

Duncan, Julian Smith. *Public and Private Operation of Railways in Brazil*. New York, 1932.

Edelstein, Michael. *Overseas Investment in the Age of High Imperialism: The United Kingdom, 1850–1914*. New York, 1982.

Eisenberg, Peter. *The Sugar Industry in Pernambuco, 1840–1910*. Berkeley, 1974.

El-Kareh, Almir Chaiban. *Filha Branca de Mãe Preta: A Companhia da Estrada de Ferro D. Pedro II, 1855–1865*. Petrópolis, 1982.

Engerman, Stanley. "Some Economic Issues Relating to Railroad Subsidies and the Evaluation of Land Grants." *Journal of Economic History* 32, no. 2 (1972): 443–63.

Esteves, Albino de Oliveira. "Mariano Procópio." *Revista do Instituto Histórico e Geográfico Brasileiro* 230 (January–March 1956): 3–398.

Estrada de Ferro Leopoldina: Histórico da Companhia até 1886. Rio de Janeiro, 1887.

Estudo Sobre a Estrada de Ferro do Norte. Pernambuco [Recife], 1881.

Evans, Peter. "Continuities and Contradictions in the Evolution of Brazilian Dependence." *Latin American Perspectives* 3, no. 2 (1976): 30–54.

———. *Dependent Development: The Alliance of Multinational, State, and Local Capital in Brazil*. Princeton, 1979.

Feeny, David. *The Political Economy of Productivity: Thai Agricultural Development, 1880–1975*. Vancouver, 1982.

Fendt, Roberto, Jr. "Investimentos Inglêses no Brasil, 1870–1913: Uma Avaliação da Política Brasileira." *Revista Brasileira de Economia* 31, no. 3 (1977): 521–39.

Ferguson, Niall. *The House of Rothschild: The World's Banker, 1849–1998*. Vol. 2. New York, 1998.

Fernández, Jesús Sanz. *Historia de los Ferrocarriles de Iberoamérica (1837–1995)*. N.p. [Spain], 1998.

Ferreira, A. de S. Pires. *Esbanjamentos Comprovados do Engenheiro Aristides Galvão de Queiroz na Direcção das Estradas de Ferro do Governo em Pernambuco*. Recife, 1889.

Ferreira, Benedito Genésio. "A Estrada de Ferro de Baturité, 1870–1930." M.A. thesis, Universidade Federal do Ceará, 1984.

Figueira, Manuel Fernandes. *Memória Histórica da Estrada de Ferro Central do Brazil*. Rio de Janeiro, 1908.

Fishlow, Albert. *American Railroads and the Transformation of the Antebellum Economy*. Cambridge, Mass., 1965.

———. "Lessons from the Past: Capital Markets during the Nineteenth Century and the Interwar Period." *International Organization* 39, no. 3 (1985): 382–439.

———. "Conditionality and Willingness to Pay: Some Parallels from the 1890s." In *The International Debt Crisis in Historical Perspective*, ed. Barry Eichengreen and Peter Lindert. Cambridge, Mass., 1989.

Fogel, Robert William. *The Union Pacific Railroad: A Case in Premature Enterprise*. Baltimore, 1960.

———. *Railroads and American Economic Growth: Essays in Econometric History*. Baltimore, 1964.

———. "The Specification Problem in Economic History." *Journal of Economic History* 27, no. 3 (September 1967): 283–308.

———. "Notes on the Social Saving Controversy." *Journal of Economic History* 39, no. 1 (1979): 1–54.

———. "Scientific History and Traditional History." In *Which Road to the Past?: Two Views of History*, ed. Robert William Fogel and G. R. Elton. New Haven, 1983.

Fonseca, Celia Freire A. "Os Investimentos Ingleses no Nordeste do Brasil e a Ferrovia 'The Great Western of Brazil Railway Company Limited' (1872–1920)." In *Capitales, Empresarios y Obreros Europeos en America Latina*. Stockholm, 1983.

Foreman-Peck, James. "Railways and Late Victorian Economic Growth." In *New Perspectives on the Late Victorian Economy: Essays in Quantitative Economic History, 1860–1914*, ed. James Foreman-Peck. Cambridge, 1991.

Franco, Gustavo Henrique Barroso. *Reforma Monetária e Instabilidade Durante a Transição Republicana*. Rio de Janeiro, 1983.

———. *A Década Republicana: o Brasil e a Economia Internacional, 1888/1900*. Rio de Janeiro, 1991.

Frank, Andre Gunder. *Capitalism and Underdevelopment in Latin America: Historical Studies of Chile and Brazil*. New York, 1969.

Fremdling, Rainer. "Freight Rates and the State Budget: The Role of the National Prussian Railways, 1880–1913." *Journal of European Economic History* 9, no. 1 (1980): 21–40.

Galvão, Manoel da Cunha. *Notícia Sobre as Estradas de Ferro do Brasil*. Rio de Janeiro, 1869.

Garner, Lydia Magalhães. "In Pursuit of Order: A Study in Brazilian Centralization, The Section of Empire of the Council of State, 1842–1889." Ph.D. diss., Johns Hopkins, 1987.

Gauld, Charles A. *The Last Titan: Percival Farquhar, American Entrepreneur in Latin America*. Stanford, Calif., 1964.

Gerschenkron, Alexander. *Economic Backwardness in Historical Perspective*. Cambridge, Mass., 1966.

———. *Continuity in History and Other Essays*. Cambridge, Mass., 1968.

Giroletti, Domingos Antonio. "A Companhia e a Rodovia União e Indústria e o Desenvolvimento de Juiz de Fora, 1850 a 1900." Belo Horizonte (mimeograph), 1980.

Goldsmith, Raymond W. *Brasil, 1850–1914: Desenvolvimento Financeiro Sob Um Século de Inflação*. São Paulo, 1986.

Gomez Mendoza, Antonio. *Ferrocarriles y Cambio Económico en España, 1855–1913*. Madrid, 1982.

Gonçalves, Reinaldo. *Evolução das Relações Comerciais do Brasil com a Inglaterra: 1850–1913*. Instituto de Economia Industrial, Textos de Discussão, no. 1. Rio de Janeiro, 1982.

Gootenberg, Paul. *Imagining Development: Economic Ideas in Peru's "Fictitious" Prosperity of Guano, 1840–1880*. Berkeley, 1993.

Goulart, José Alípio. *Tropas e Tropeiros na Formação do Brasil*. Rio de Janeiro, 1961.

Graham, Richard. *Britain and the Onset of Modernization in Brazil, 1850–1914*. Cambridge, 1969.

———. "Sepoys and Imperialists: Techniques of British Power in Nineteenth-Century Brazil." *Inter-American Economic Affairs* 23, no. 2 (1969): 22–37.

———. "Empire, 1850–1870." In *Brazil: Empire and Republic, 1822–1930*, ed. Leslie Bethell. Cambridge, 1989.

———. *Patronage and Politics in Nineteenth-Century Brazil*. Stanford, Calif., 1990.

Gregory, Paul R. *Russian National Income*. Cambridge, 1980.

Gronau, Reuben. *The Value of Time in Passenger Transportation: The Demand for Air Travel.*
New York, 1970.

Gumiero, Marisela Porfirio da Paz. "Os Tropeiros na História de Goiás, Séculos XVIII e
XIX." M.A. thesis, Universidade Federal de Goiás, Goiânia, 1991.

Haber, Stephen. *Industry and Underdevelopment: The Industrialization of Mexico, 1890–1940.*
Stanford, Calif., 1989.

———. "The Efficiency Consequences of Institutional Change: Financial Market Regulation and Industrial Productivity Growth in Brazil, 1866–1934." Stanford, Calif.
(mimeograph), 1996.

Haber, Stephen, and Herbert S. Klein. "The Economic Consequences of Brazilian Independence." In *How Latin America Fell Behind: Essays on the Economic Histories of
Brazil and Mexico,* ed. Stephen Haber. Stanford, Calif., 1997.

Haddad, Cláudio L. S. *Crescimento do Produto Real no Brasil, 1900–1947.* Rio de Janeiro,
1978.

———. "Crescimento Econômico do Brasil, 1900–1976." In *Economia Brasileira: Uma
Visão Histórica,* ed. Paulo Neuhaus. Rio de Janeiro, 1980.

Hadfield, William. *Brazil and the River Plate in 1868.* London, 1869.

Hanley, Anne Gerard. "Capital Markets in the Coffee Economy: Financial Institutions
and Economic Change in São Paulo, Brazil, 1850–1905." Ph.D. diss., Stanford
University, 1995.

Harley, C. Knick. "The Antebellum American Tariff: Food Exports and Manufacturing."
Explorations in Economic History 29 (October 1992): 375–400.

Hartt, Charles Fredrick. *Geology and Physical Geography of Brazil.* Boston, 1870.

Hawke, Gary. *Railways and Economic Growth in England and Wales, 1840–1870.* London,
1970.

———. "Railway Passenger Traffic in 1865." In *Essays on a Mature Economy: Britain after
1840,* ed. D. N. McCloskey. London, 1971.

Hirschman, Albert O. "A Generalized Linkage Approach to Development with Special
Reference to Staples." *Economic Development and Cultural Change* 25, Supplement
(1977): 67–98.

Histórico da Companhia Mogyana de Estradas de Ferro e Navegação. N.p., n.d.

Holloway, Thomas Halsey. "Migration and Mobility: Immigrants as Laborers and
Landowners in the Coffee Zone of São Paulo, Brazil, 1886–1934." Ph.D. diss.,
University of Wisconsin, 1974.

———. *Immigrants on the Land: Coffee and Society in São Paulo, 1886–1934.* Chapel Hill,
1980.

Holmstrom, J. Edwin. *Railways and Roads in Pioneer Development Overseas.* London, 1934.

Huenemann, Ralph William. *The Dragon and the Iron Horse: The Economics of Railroads in
China, 1876–1937.* Cambridge, Mass., 1984.

Hurd, John M., II. "Railways and the Expansion of Markets in India, 1861–1921." *Explorations in Economic History* 12, no. 3 (1975): 263–88.

———. "Railways." In *Cambridge Economic History of India,* vol. 2., ed. Dharma Kumar.
Cambridge, 1983.

Ice, Orva Lee, Jr. "British Direct Investments in Brazil up to 1901." M.A. thesis, University of Chicago, 1948.

Jacob, Rodolpho. *Minas Gerais no XXo Século.* Rio de Janeiro, 1911.

Jardim, Marechal Jeronimo Rodrigues de Moraes. "Synthese Histórica das Tentativas

Feitas para a Utilização, como Vias Navegaveis, dos Grandes Rios que Banham o Estado de Goyaz." *Revista do Instituto Histórico e Geográfico Brasileiro*, pt. 2 (1915): 411–32.

Joslin, David. *A Century of Banking in Latin America: Bank of London and South America Limited, 1862–1962*. Oxford, 1963.

Kahn, Charles. "The Use of Complicated Models as Explanations: A Re-examination of Williamson's Late-Nineteenth-Century America." *Research in Economic History* 11 (1986): 185–216.

Klein, Herbert S. "A Oferta de Muares no Brasil Central: O Mercado de Sorocaba, 1825–1880." *Estudos Econômicos* 19, no. 2 (1989): 347–69.

————. "The Supply of Mules to Central Brazil: The Sorocaba Market, 1825–1880." *Agricultural History* 64, no. 4 (1990): 1–25.

Kravis, Irving. "The Role of Exports in Nineteenth-Century United States Economic Growth." *Economic Development and Cultural Change* 20 (April 1972): 387–405.

Kroetz, Lando Rogério. "As Estradas de Ferro de Santa Catarina, 1910–1960." M.A. thesis, Universidade Federal de Paraná, 1975.

————. "As Estradas de Ferro do Paraná, 1880–1940." Ph.D. diss., Universidade de São Paulo, 1985.

Kuntz Ficker, Sandra. *Empresa Extranjera y Mercado Interno: El Ferrocarril Central Mexicano, 1880–1907*. Mexico City, 1995.

Laërne, C. F. Van Delden. *Brazil and Java. Report on the Coffee-Culture in America, Asia and Africa*. London, 1885.

Lamounier, Maria Lúcia. "The 'Labour Question' in Nineteenth-Century Brazil: Railways, Export Agriculture, and Labour Scarcity." Araraquara (mimeograph), 2000.

Lapa, José Roberto do Amaral. "Um Tema Negligenciado." *Revista de História* (São Paulo) 55 (April–June 1977): 601–3.

Layard, Richard, and Stephen Glaister, ed. *Cost-Benefit Analysis*. 2d ed. Cambridge, 1994.

Leff, Nathaniel. *Underdevelopment and Development in Brazil*. Vol. 1. London, 1982.

————. "Economic Development in Brazil, 1822–1913." In *How Latin America Fell Behind: Essays on the Economic History of Brazil and Mexico, 1800–1914*, ed. Stephen Haber. Stanford, Calif., 1997.

Lenharo, Alcir. *As Tropas de Moderação*. São Paulo, 1979.

Leverger, Augusto. *Vias de Communicação de Matto-Grosso*. Cuyabá, 1905.

Levi, Darell E. *The Prados of São Paulo, Brazil: An Elite Family and Social Change, 1840–1930*. Athens, Ga., 1987.

Lewis, Colin M. "Railways and Industrialization: Argentina and Brazil, 1870–1929." In *Latin America, Economic Imperialism, and the State*, ed. Colin M. Lewis and Chistopher Abel. London, 1985.

————. *Public Policy and Private Initiative: Railway Building in São Paulo, 1860–1889*. London, 1991.

Lewis, W. Arthur, ed. *Tropical Development, 1880–1913: Studies in Economic Progress*. London, 1970.

Lima, Armando de Miranda. "Rios navegáveis do Brasil." In *Diccionário Histórico, Geográphico e Ethnográphico do Brasil*, ed. Instituto Histórico e Geográphico Brasileiro. Rio de Janeiro, 1922.

Lima, José Porfirio de. *Memorias sobre as Vias de Communicação por Canaes Navegaveis,*

Acompanhadas de um Projecto para Sua Realização na Provincia de S. Paulo. São Paulo, 1849.

Lipsey, Richard. *Introduction to Positive Economics*. London, 1963.

Lobo, Eulália Maria Lehmeyer. *História do Rio de Janeiro (Do Capital Comercial ao Capital Industrial Financeiro)*. Vol. 2. Rio de Janeiro, 1978.

London Stock Exchange. *Railway Intelligence*. Vol. 20. London, 1879.

Love, Joseph. *Rio Grande do Sul and Brazilian Regionalism, 1882–1930*. Stanford, Calif., 1971.

————. *São Paulo in the Brazilian Federation, 1889–1937*. Stanford, Calif., 1980.

Lyon, Max. *Note sur les Chemins de Fer du Brésil*. Paris, 1885.

Lyra, João. *Cifras e Notas*. Rio de Janeiro, 1924.

Maddison, Angus. *Phases of Capitalist Development*. Oxford, 1982.

————. *The World Economy in the Twentieth Century*. Paris, 1989.

Magalhães, Basílio de. "Os Caminhos Antigos pelos Quaes Foi o Café Transportado do Interior para o Rio de Janeiro e para Outros Pontos do Littoral Fluminense." In *Minas e o Bicentenário do Cafeeiro no Brazil, 1727–1927*. Bello Horizonte, 1929.

Magalhães, Guilherme Pinto de. *Relatório dos Trabalhos na Estrada que Conduz de Magé a Sapucaia*. Rio de Janeiro, 1847.

Marchant, Anyda. *Viscount of Mauá and the Empire of Brazil*. Berkeley, 1965.

Margo, Robert A. *Race and Schooling in the South, 1880–1950*. Chicago, 1990.

Marichal, Carlos. *A Century of Debt Crises in Latin America*. Princeton, 1989.

Matos, Odilon Nogueira de. *Café e Ferrovias: A Evolução Ferroviária e o Desenvolvimento da Cultura Cafeeira*. São Paulo, 1974.

Mattoon, Robert Howard, Jr. "The Companhia Paulista de Estradas de Ferro, 1868–1900: A Local Railway Enterprise in São Paulo, Brazil." Ph.D. diss., Yale University, 1971.

Mattoso, Katia M. de Queirós. "Au Nouveau Monde: Une Province d'un Nouvel Empire: Bahia au XIXe Siècle." Ph.D. diss., Sorbonne, 1986.

Mauá, Visconde de. *Autobiografía. ("Exposição aos Credores e ao Público"). Seguida de "O Meio Circulante no Brasil."* Edição Prefaciada e Anotada por Cláudio Ganns. 3d ed. Rio de Janeiro, 1978.

McAlpin, Michelle. "Railroads, Prices, and Peasant Rationality: India 1860–1900." *Journal of Economic History* 34, no. 3 (1974): 662–84.

————. "The Effects of Expansion of Markets on Rural Income Distribution in Nineteenth Century India." *Explorations in Economic History* 12 (July 1975): 289–302.

————. *Subject to Famine: Food Crises and Economic Change in Western India, 1860–1920*. Princeton, 1983.

McClelland, Peter D. "Social Rates of Return on American Railroads in the Nineteenth Century." *Economic History Review* 25, no. 3 (1972): 471–88.

————. *Causal Explanation and Model Building in History, Economics, and Economic History*. Ithaca, N.Y., 1975.

McCloskey, D. N. *Applied Theory of Price*. New York, 1982.

McGreevey, William Paul. *Economic History of Colombia*. Cambridge, 1971.

Medrano, Lilia Ines Zanotti de. "A Livre Navegação dos Rios Paraná e Uruguay: Uma Analise do Comércio entre o Império Brasileiro e a Argentina, 1852–1889." Ph.D. diss., Universidade de São Paulo, 1989.

Melo, Evaldo Cabral de. *O Norte Agrário e o Império, 1871–1889*. Rio de Janeiro, 1984.

Mello, Barão Homem de, and Francisco Homem de Mello. *Atlas do Brazil.* Rio de Janeiro, 1909.

Mello, João Cardoso de, and Maria da Conceição Tavares. "The Capitalist Export Economy in Brazil, 1884–1930." In *The Latin American Export Economies: Growth and the Export Sector, 1880–1930,* ed. Roberto Cortes Conde and Shane J. Hunt. New York, 1985.

Mello, Pedro Carvalho de. *A Economia da Escravidão nas Fazendas de Café: 1850–1888.* Rio de Janeiro, 1984.

————. "Rates of Return on Slave Capital in Brazilian Coffee Plantations, 1871–1881." In *Without Consent or Contract: Markets and Production,* Technical Papers, vol. 1, ed. Robert William Fogel and Stanley Engerman. New York, 1992.

Memória Justificativo dos Planos Apresentados ao Governo Imperio para a Construcção da Estrada de Ferro de Porto Alegra á Uruguayana. Rio de Janeiro, 1875.

Mercer, Lloyd J. *Railroads and Land Grant Policy: A Study in Government Intervention.* New York, 1982.

Merrick, Thomas W., and Douglas H. Graham. *Population and Economic Development in Brazil, 1800–Present.* Baltimore, 1979.

————. "População e Desenvolvimento no Brasil: Uma Perspectiva Histórica." In *Economia Brasileira: Uma Visão Histórica,* ed. Paulo Neuhaus. Rio de Janeiro, 1980.

Mesquita, Elpidio de. *Viação Ferrea da Bahia.* Rio de Janeiro, 1910.

Metzer, Jacob. "Railroad Development and Market Integration: The Case of Tsarist Russia." *Journal of Economic History* 34, no. 3 (1974): 529–49.

————. *Some Economic Aspects of Railroad Development in Tsarist Russia.* New York, 1977.

————. "Railroads and the Efficiency of Internal Markets: Some Conceptual and Practical Considerations." *Economic Development and Cultural Change* 33, no. 1 (1984): 61–70.

Milet, Henrique Augusto. *A Lavoura da Cana de Açucar.* Recife, 1881.

Miller, Rory. *Britain and Latin America in the Nineteenth and Twentieth Centuries.* New York, 1993.

Mitchell, B. R. *British Historical Statistics.* Cambridge, 1988.

Momsen, Richard P., Jr. *Routes Over the Serra do Mar.* Rio de Janeiro, 1964.

Moraes, Eduardo José de. *Navegação Interior do Brasil.* Rio de Janeiro, 1894.

Moreira, Júlio Estrela. *Caminhos das Comarcas de Curitiba e Paranaguá (Até a Emancipação da Província do Paraná).* Vol. 1. Curitiba, 1975.

Mornay, Edward de. *Report on the Proposed Railway in the Province of Pernambuco, Brazil.* London, 1855.

Moura, Carlos Dunshee de Abranches. *Governos e Congressos da República dos Estados Unidos do Brasil.* Vol. 1. Rio de Janeiro, 1918.

Müller, Marechal D. P. *Ensaio d'um Quadro Estatístico da Província de S. Paulo.* São Paulo, 1838.

North, Douglass C. *Structure and Change in Economic History.* New York, 1981.

Oakenfull, J. C. *Brazil (1913).* Frome, n.d.

O'Brien, Patrick Karl. *The New Economic History of the Railways.* New York, 1977.

————. "Transport and Economic Growth in Western Europe, 1830–1914." *Journal of European Economic History* 11 (fall 1982): 269–334.

————, ed. *Railways and the Economic Development of Western Europe, 1830–1914.* New York, 1983.

Ocampo, José António. "El Mercado Mundial de Café y el Surgimiento de Colombia como un Pais Cafetero." *Desarrollo y Sociedad* 5 (January 1981): 125–56.

Owen, A. D., and G. D. A. Phillips. "The Characteristics of Railway Passenger Demand." *Journal of Transport Economics and Policy* 21 (September 1987): 231–53.

Paiva, Alberto Randolpho. *Synopse da Legislação da Viação Ferrea Federal.* Rio de Janeiro, 1918.

————. *Legislação Ferroviária Federal do Brasil.* 16 vols. Rio de Janeiro, 1922.

Palhano de Jesus, J. "Rápida notícia da viação ferrea do Brasil." In *Diccionário Histórico, Geográphico, e Estatístico do Brasil,* vol. 1, ed. Instituto Histórico e Geográphico Brasileiro. Rio de Janeiro, 1922.

Pessôa, Junior, Cyro Diocleciano Ribeiro. *Estudo Descriptivo das Estradas de Ferro do Brazil.* Rio de Janeiro, 1886.

Pessôa, V. A. de Paulo. *Guia da Estrada de Ferro Central do Brasil.* Vol. 1. Rio de Janeiro, 1902.

Pestana, Paulo R. *A Expansão Econômica do Estado de S. Paulo num Século (1822–1922).* São Paulo, 1923.

Petrone, Maria Thereza Schorer. *O Barão de Iguape.* São Paulo, 1976.

Pimenta, Dermeval José. *Caminhos de Minas Gerais.* Belo Horizonte, 1971.

Pinheiro, Fernandes. "Chemins de Fer." In *Le Brésil en 1889,* ed. F. J. de Santa-Anna Nery. Paris, 1889.

Pinto, Adolpho Augusto. *História da Viação Pública de S. Paulo (Brasil).* São Paulo, 1903.

Platt, D. C. M. "Economic Imperialism and the Businessman: Britain and Latin America Before 1914." In *Studies in the Theory of Imperialism,* ed. Roger Owen and Bob Sutcliffe. London, 1972.

————, ed. *Business Imperialism, 1840–1930: An Inquiry Based on the British Experience in Latin America.* Oxford, 1977.

Przewodowski, André. "Communicação entre a Cidade da Bahia e a Vila de Juazeiro." *Revista do Instituto Histórico e Geográfico Brasileiro* 10 (1848): 374–86.

Queiros, Aristedes Galvão de. *O Resgate da Estrada de Ferro do Recife ao São Francisco.* Rio de Janeiro, 1884.

Queiroz, Maurício Vinhas de. *Messianismo e Conflito Social (A Guerra Sertaneja do Contestado: 1912–1916).* 2d ed. São Paulo, 1977.

Questão da Estrada Mangaratiba. Exposição á Assembléa Provincial do Rio de Janeiro pela Directoria do Banco Rural e Hypothecário. Rio de Janeiro, 1872.

Rabello, Andréa Fernandes Considera Campagnac. "Os Caminhos de Ferro da Província do Rio de Janeiro: Ferrovia e Café na Segunda Metade do Século XIX." M.A. thesis, Universidade Federal Fluminense, 1996.

Ramírez, María Teresa. "Railroads and the Colombian Economy." Bogotá (mimeograph), n.d.

Ransom, Roger L. "Social Returns from Public Transport Investment: A Case Study of the Ohio Canal." *Journal of Political Economy* 78, no. 5 (September/October 1970): 1041–60.

Ray, Debraj. *Development Economics.* Princeton, 1998.

Rebouças, André. *Tramway de Antonina a Curityba: Memória Justificativa.* Rio de Janeiro, 1859.

————. *Garantia de Juros: Estudos para Sua Applicação ás Emprezas de Utilidade Pública no Brazil.* Rio de Janeiro, 1874.

Rego, General F. Raphael de Mello. *Inquérito sobre as Estradas de Ferro da União, Relatório.* Rio de Janeiro, 1893.

Reis, Aarão Leal de Carvalho. *Primeiro Congresso das Estradas de Ferro do Brazil, Archivo dos Trabalhos.* Rio de Janeiro [1884].

Ribas, Rogério de Oliveira. "Tropeirismo e Escravidão: Um Estudo das Tropas de Café das Lavouras de Vassouras, 1840–1888." M.A. thesis, Universidade Federal do Paraná, 1989.

Ribeiro, Ruy Monteiro. "As Garantias Ferroviárias no Brasil: Uma Análise dos Recission Bonds e do Resgate das Estradas de Ferro." Monografia de Final de Curso, Pontifícia Universidade Católica do Rio de Janeiro, 1993.

Ribenboim, Guilherme. "Uma Análise da Rentabilidade dos Empréstimos Externos ao Governo Central do Brasil (1865–1931)." Monografia de Final de Curso, Pontifícia Universidade Católica do Rio de Janeiro, 1993.

Ridings, Eugene. *Business Interest Groups in Nineteenth-Century Brazil.* Cambridge, 1994.

Rippy, J. Fred. *British Investments in Latin America, 1822–1949.* Minneapolis, 1959.

Rodrigues, J. C. *Resgate das Estradas de Ferro do Recife a S. Francisco e de Outras que Gozavam da Garantia de Juros.* Rio de Janeiro, 1902.

Rosenbloom, Joshua L. "One Market or Many? Labor Market Integration in the Late-Nineteenth-Century United States." *Journal of Economic History* 50, no. 1 (1990): 85–108.

Rosenthal, Jean-Laurent. *The Fruits of Revolution.* Cambridge, 1992.

Rothenberg, Winifred. *From Market-Places to a Market Economy.* Chicago, 1992.

Sá [Pereira de Castro], [João] Chrockatt de. *Brazilian Railways, Their History, Legislation, and Development.* Rio de Janeiro, 1893.

———. *Código da Viação Ferrea do Brasil.* 6 vols. Rio de Janeiro, 1898–1901.

Saes, Flávio Azevedo Marques de. *As Ferrovias de São Paulo, 1870–1940.* São Paulo, 1981.

———. "Os Investimentos Franceses no Brasil: O Caso da Brazil Railway Company (1900–1930)." *Revista de História*, no. 119 (1985–1988, July–December): 23–42.

———. *Crédito e Bancos no Desenvolvimento da Economia Paulista: 1850–1930.* São Paulo, 1986.

Sánchez-Albornoz, Nicolás. *The Population of Latin America: A History.* Berkeley, 1974.

Santos, Theotonio dos. "Structure of Dependence." *American Economic Review* 60 (May 1970): 231–36.

Schmidt, Carlos Borges. "Tropas e Tropeiros." *Boletim Paulista de Geografia* 32 (July 1959): 31–53.

Schulz, John. *A Crise Financeira da Abolição.* São Paulo, 1996.

Silva, Clodomiro Pereira da. *A Reforma das Tarifas: Desenvolvimento, Regimen Legal, e Tarifas das Ferrovias de São Paulo.* São Paulo, 1901.

———. *Política e Legislação de Estradas de Ferro.* São Paulo, 1904.

Silva, Francisco Alves da. "Abastecimento em São Paulo (1835–1877): Estudo Histórico do Aprovisionamento da Província via Barreira de Cubatão." M.A. thesis, Universidade de São Paulo, 1985.

Silva, Moacir M. F. *Geografia dos Transportes dos Brasil.* Rio de Janeiro, 1949.

Siqueira, Edmundo. *Resumo Histórico de The Leopoldina Railway Company.* Rio de Janeiro, 1938.

Slenes, Robert W. "The Demography and Economics of Brazilian Slavery: 1850–1888." Ph.D. diss., Stanford University, 1976.

Souza, José Antônio Soares de. "Estrada da Serra de Estrela e os Colonos Alemães." *Revista do Instituto Histórico e Geográfico Brasileiro* 322 (January–March 1979): 5–180.

St. Angel, Frank. "British Investment in Brazilian Railroads, 1880–1913." M.A. thesis, University of Chicago, 1948.

Stauffer, Thomas R. "The Measurement of Corporate Rates of Return: A Generalized Formulation." *Bell Journal of Economics and Management Science* 2, no. 2 (1971): 434–69.

Stein, Stanley. *The Brazilian Cotton Manufacture: Textile Enterprise in an Underdeveloped Area.* Cambridge, Mass., 1957.

Stein, Stanley J., and Barbara H. Stein. *The Colonial Heritage of Latin America.* Oxford, 1970.

Stone, Irving. "British Long-Term Investment in Latin America, 1865–1913." *Business History Review* 42, no. 3 (1968): 311–39.

———. *The Composition and Distribution of British Investment in Latin America, 1865 to 1913.* New York, 1987.

Summerhill, William. "The Brazilian Export Sector: Price and Quantity Estimates, 1850–1913." Los Angeles (mimeograph), 1994.

———. "Mercantilism in Late Colonial Brazil." Los Angeles (mimeograph), 1996.

———. "Notes on Institutional Change: Capital Markets and Manufacturing Productivity in Fin-de-Siècle Brazil." Los Angeles (mimeograph), 1996.

———. "Transport Improvements and Economic Growth in Brazil and Mexico." In *How Latin America Fell Behind,* ed. Stephen Haber. Stanford, Calif., 1997.

———. "Profit and Productivity on Argentine Railroads, 1857–1913." Los Angeles (mimeograph), 2000.

Sunkel, Osvaldo. *O Marco Histórico do Processo Desenvolvimento—Subdesenvolvimento.* Rio de Janeiro, 1973.

Suzigan, Wilson. *Indústria Brasileira: Origem e desenvolvimento.* São Paulo, 1986.

Thomé, Neilson. *Trem de Ferro: História da Ferrovia no Contestado.* Florianópolis, 1983.

Topik, Steven. "The Evolution of the Economic Role of the Brazilian State, 1889–1930." *Journal of Latin American Studies* 11, no. 2 (1979): 325–42.

———. *The Political Economy of the Brazilian State, 1889–1930.* Austin, 1987.

———. "The Economic Role of the State in Liberal Regimes: Brazil and Mexico Compared, 1888–1910." In *Guiding the Invisible Hand,* ed. Joseph L. Love and Nils Jacobsen. New York, 1988.

Tourinho, Francisco Antonio Monteiro. "Bosquejo Histórico da Estrada da Graciosa." Curitiba (mimeograph), 1882.

Trabalho da Commissão da Junta de Lavoura Sobre os Meios de se Fazer a Estrada de Ferro da Bahia ao Joazeiro. Bahia [Salvador], 1852.

Trebat, Thomas J. *Brazil's State-Owned Enterprises: A Case Study of the State as Entrepreneur.* Cambridge, 1983.

Triner, Gail D. *Banking and Economic Development: Brazil, 1889–1930.* New York, 2000.

United Kingdom. Department of Overseas Trade. "Report on the Railway Systems of Brazil," by H. C. Lowther. *British Foreign and State Papers, Diplomatic and Consular Reports,* 1904.

———. "A Report on the General Economic and Financial Conditions of Brazil for the Year 1919." *British Foreign and State Papers, Diplomatic and Consular Reports,* 1920.

United Kingdom. House of Commons. "General Report of Mr.Vrendenburg, British Consul at Pará, on the Trade, Commerce, Navigation, etc. within the District of his Consulate." *Sessional Papers,* 1857–1858, Abstract of Reports of the Trade of Various Countries and Places, for the Years 1857-1858-1859 Received by the Board of Trade (through the foreign office) from Her Majesty's Ministries and Consuls, No. 7. 1857–1858.Vol. 30.

———. "Report of Mr.Wetherell, British Vice-Consul at Paraiba, on the Trade of that Port for the Year 1857." *Sessional Papers,* 1857–1858, Abstract of Reports of the Trade of Various Countries and Places, for the Years 1857-1858-1859 Received by the Board of Trade (through the foreign office) from Her Majesty's Ministries and Consuls, No. 7. 1857–1858.Vol. 30.

———. "Report from Mr. Consul Lennon Hunt of the Trade of Pernambuco of the Year 1860." *Sessional Papers,* 1865, Commercial Reports Received at the Foreign Office from Her Majesty's Consuls between July 1st and December 31st, 1864. 1865.Vol. 53.

———. "Report by Mr. Consul Morgan on the Trade of Bahia for the Year 1864." *Sessional Papers,* 1865, Commercial Reports Received at the Foreign Offices of Her Majesty's Consuls. 1865.Vol. 54.

———. "Report from Consul Doyle on the Trade, Commerce, and Navigation on the Port of Pernambuco of the Year 1871." *Sessional Papers,* 1872, Reports from Her Majesty's Consuls on the Manufactures, Commerce, etc., of their Consular Districts. 1872.Vol. 58.

———. "Report of Mr. Hill, British Consul at Maranham on the Trade, etc. of the District During the Year 1859." *Sessional Papers,* 1862, Abstract of Reports of the Trade, etc., of Various Countries and Places, for the Years 1859, 1860: Received by the Board of Trade (through the foreign office) from Her Majesty's Consuls, No. 11. 1862.Vol. 58.

———. "Report by the Honorable H. P. Vereker, British Consul at Rio Grande do Sul, on the Commerce, etc., of That Port, etc., for 1860." *Sessional Papers,* 1862, Abstract of Reports of the Trade, etc., of Various Countries and Places, for the Years 1859, 1860: Received by the Board of Trade (through the foreign office) from Her Majesty's Consuls, No. 11. 1862.Vol. 58.

———. "Report of Mr. Consul Lennon Hunt on the Trade and Commerce of Rio de Janeiro during the Year 1869." *Sessional Papers,* 1870, Commercial Reports Received at the Foreign Office of her Majesty's Consuls 1869–1870. 1870.Vol. 64.

U.S. Bureau of the Census. *Historical Statistics of the United States: Colonial Times to 1970.* New York, 1976.

———. Department of State. "Railways in Brazil." In *Consular Reports,* vol. 63, no. 239 (August). Washington, D.C., 1900.

Vangelista, Chiara. *Os Braços da Lavoura: Imigrantes e "Caipiras" na Formação do Mercado de Trabalho Paulista (1850–1930).* São Paulo, 1991.

Veiga, Luiz Francisco da. *Repertório Jurídico da Companhia Estrada de Ferro Leopoldina.* Rio de Janeiro, 1893.

Versiani, Flávio Rabelo. *Industrial Investment in an "Export" Economy: The Brazilian Experience before 1914.* London, n.d.

Villela, Annibal, and Wilson Suzigan. *Política do Governo e Crescimento da Economia Brasileira, 1889–1945.* 2d ed. Rio de Janeiro, 1975.

Waters, Paul E. *The Donna Thereza Christina Railway*. Bromley, 1985.

Weingast, Barry, Kenneth A. Shepsle, and Christopher Johnson. "The Political Economy of Benefits and Costs: A Neoclassical Approach to Distributive Politics." *Journal of Political Economy* 89, no. 4 (1981): 642–64.

Whately, Maria Celina. *O Café em Resende no Século XIX*. Rio de Janeiro, 1987.

White, Colin M. "Railroads and Rigour." *Journal of European Economic History* 4, no. 1 (1975): 187–96.

———. "The Concept of Social Saving in Theory and Practice." *Economic History Review* 29, no. 1 (1976): 82–100.

Wiener, Lionel. "The Railways of Brazil." In *The South American Year Book*, ed. C. S. Vesey Brown. London, 1913.

Wileman, J. P. *Brazilian Exchange: The Study of an Inconvertible Currency*. Buenos Aires, 1896.

———. *The Brazilian Year Book*, 1909. Rio de Janeiro, 1909.

Wilkins, Mira. "The Free-Standing Company, 1870–1914: An Important Type of British Foreign Direct Investment." *Economic History Review* 41, no. 2 (1988): 259–82.

Williamson, Jeffrey. *Late-Nineteenth-Century American Development: A General Equilibrium History*. New York, 1974.

Winston, Clifford. "Conceptual Developments in the Economics of Transportation: An Interpretive Survey." *Journal of Economic Literature* 23 (March 1985): 57–94.

Wright, Gavin. "American Industrial Success, 1879–1914." *American Economic Review* 80, no. 4 (1990): 651–68.

Zalduendo, Eduardo A. *Libras y Rieles: Las Inversiones Británicas para el Desarrollo de los Ferrocarriles en Argentina, Brasil, Canadá, e India durante el Siglo XIX*. Buenos Aires, 1974.

Zumblick, Walter. *Teresa Cristina: A Ferrovia do Carvão*. Tubarão, 1967.

Index